CONFLICT
IN
INDO-CHINA

W9-AMW-081

CONFLICT IN INDO-CHINA

A Reader on the Widening War in Laos and Cambodia

Edited by
MARVIN AND SUSAN GETTLEMAN
AND
LAWRENCE AND CAROL KAPLAN

VINTAGE BOOKS A Division of Random House, New York

Library of Congress Catalog Card Number:
72–139571

Acknowledgment is gratefully extended to the following for permission
to reprint from their works:

Cornell University Press: For two maps and excerpts from "Laos" and
"Cambodia" by Roger M. Smith in George McTurnan Kahin (editor):
GOVERNMENTS AND POLITICS OF SOUTHEAST ASIA. Copyright
© 1959, 1964 by Cornell University.

Current History, Inc.: "Cambodian Neutrality," by W. E. Willmott, January, 1967 issue of Current History.

Far Eastern Economic Review: "Sealing Their Own Doom," by T. D.
Allman, April 2, 1970. Copyright © 1970 by Far Eastern Economic Review.

Foreign Affairs: "Cambodia Neutral: The Dictate of Necessity," by
Prince Norodom Sihanouk, July, 1958 issue of Foreign Affairs. Copyright
© 1958 by the Council on Foreign Relations, Inc., New York.

Monthly Review, Inc.: "The War Spreads," by Paul Sweezy and Harry
Magdoff, May, 1970, Monthly Review. Copyright © 1970 by Monthly
Review, Inc.

The New Republic: "Laotian Tragedy: The Long March," by Carl Strock,
May 9, 1970. Copyright © 1970 by Harrison-Blaine of New Jersey, Inc.

The New York Review of Books: "Laos: The Story Nixon Won't Tell,"
and "Cambodia: Why the Generals Won," by Peter Dale Scott. Copyright
© 1970 by The New York Review.

The New York Times: "Better Dead Cambodians Than Red," by Anthony Lewis, June 27, 1970. Copyright © 1970 by The New York Times
Company.

Praeger Publishers, Inc.: Map from END OF A WAR: Indochina 1954,
by Philippe Devillers and Jean Lacouture, 1969.

Georges Borchardt, Inc.: "Cambodia Joins the Free World," by Jean
Daniel, Le Nouvel Observateur.

*For the people of Indochina
in their heroic
struggle for liberation*

Contents

PART I   Early Heritage and Colonialism

PART II   Independence and the Geneva Accords of 1954

PART III The Struggle for Neutrality in Laos

PART IV The Struggle for Neutrality in Cambodia

PART V   The Furtive War in Laos

PART VI   The War Spreads to Cambodia

Introduction

In offering this collection of documents, sources, and essays on Indochina we hope to further scholarly interest in Southeast Asia, and, more importantly, to help bring peace to that strife-torn region. Our approach has been to explore the roots of contemporary struggles so that it will be more difficult for brutal policies to be justified by reference to one-sided, partisan versions of history. An historical perspective also fosters a humane regard for the values and traditions of other people, and inspires respect for the way in which their unique histories unfold. We arrive, by this route, at a vivid consciousness of the Indochinese people as actors in their own destiny. The deployment of American power there since World War II has placed a great obstacle athwart the history of Southeast Asia. Our book must therefore examine the origins of United States policy, consider the rationale for United States intervention, and expose the official justifications for such action. We have no illusions that we have done more than preliminary work and made available some useful materials. We hope that serious thought, further scholarship, and political action will effect the long-delayed liberation of Indochina from foreign domination.

We have included many types of material in this anthology: official documents, speeches, texts of international agreements, monitored radio broadcasts,[1] congressional hearings, scholarly articles and journalistic analyses. We have used, in translation, a number of items from the French press,[2] which in its coverage of Indochinese affairs is far

---

[1] We wish to call to the attention of researchers the Foreign Broadcast Information Service, *Daily Reports* of monitored radio broadcasts (1947—), an invaluable source for contemporary history.

[2] Selections 25, 26, and 34, this volume.

superior to even the most distinguished American newspapers.[3] Generous amounts of space are given to the presentation of the views of those Indochinese insurgents who for decades have struggled against foreign domination. Now that these dedicated revolutionaries are contending against massive American military power, it is even more important that their position be set forth fairly in the United States. Our aim throughout has been to view the current crisis in Southeast Asia as a struggle waged by actual people defending their way of life and the right to control their own destiny, and not as a competing set of abstract forces and interests.

In preparing this book, we have had the advice and help of many friends and colleagues. We wish to acknowledge and thank Cyrilly Abels of New York City, Mr. Otto Bauer of the Library for Political Studies in New York, Bruce and Kathy Brown of New York City, Frank Collins, Louis Menashe, David Mermelstein and Murray Rothbard of the Polytechnic Institute of Brooklyn, Noam Chomsky of the Massachusetts Institute of Technology, George McT. Kahin of Cornell University, Gabriel Kolko of York University, Saburo Kugai of the Institute of American Studies, Tokyo, John J. Simon, Jane Clark Seitz, Susanne Conley, Hilary Maddux, Helen and Jerome Goodman of Random House, Morris Pasternak of New York City, Conrad Shirokauer of the City College of New York, Arthur H. Westing of the Harvard Botanical Museum, and Janice Wolf of the Library of the Polytechnic Institute of Brooklyn.

Finally, this is a genuinely collaborative effort among the four of us whose names appear on the title page. We have shared the tasks of editing and writing this volume and

---

[3] The *New York Times* coverage of Cambodia has been adequate. However, their coverage of Laos is little short of scandalous, especially in light of the occasionally high-level reportage on Vietnam during the early 1960's. For a good, critical examination of journalistic delusions in Indochina, see I. F. Stone, *In a Time of Torment* (New York, 1967), pp. 307–315.—eds

we share its viewpoint. We take joint responsibility for the book's shortcomings, but hope that they are outweighed by its positive contributions as a work of committed, radical scholarship.

Marvin Gettleman
Susan Gettleman
Lawrence Kaplan
Carol Kaplan
New York City and
Englewood, New Jersey
July 1970

PART I

EARLY
HERITAGE
AND
COLONIALISM

Introduction

As the eighth decade of the twentieth century opens, all Indo-china is aflame with war. The struggle there has not been a momentary creation; it has deep roots in the history of many nations, some of them, like France, no longer parties to the conflict. Even American involvement in Southeast Asia is not the accident of a particular President, but is the latest stage of a policy that goes back at least half a century.[1] It is therefore necessary to adopt an historical approach in order fully to understand the current crisis in Indochina. Such an approach is doubly important as an antidote to that "crackpot existentialism" which urges us to forget the past and deal only with the exigencies of the present. This argument has frequently been heard from supporters of US intervention in Indochina who fear public scrutiny of the historical record.

We affirm the relevance of historical understanding; indeed, this has been our orientation throughout the book. In the section that follows we offer readings and documents on the early history of Laos[2] and Cambodia.[3] These materials clearly show that the present situation has its antecedents in earlier decades, and that there has been an essential continuity in struggles of the indigenous people in both countries for freedom from foreign domination.[4]

For the almost two decades of intense American involvement in Indochina, US government spokesmen have minimized native elements in insurgent movements. They have preferred a push-

[1] William A. Williams, *The Tragedy of American Diplomacy* (New York: Delta Books, 1962), Ch. II.

[2] See Selections 1 and 2, this volume.

[3] See Selections 3–5, this volume.

[4] Few writers have first-hand knowledge of the countryside of Indochina, and their understanding of insurrectionary movements suffers correspondingly. The reportage of Wilfred G. Burchett is thus of great importance, since he almost alone among journalists has travelled in the rural regions, where, after all, the majority of Laotians and Cambodians live. See Selections 25, and 9, this volume.

button theory of insurrection. According to this "official" interpretation, the existence of rebellion is evidence that outside influence is at work, that a button is pushed in some distant place and guerrillas spring out of the earth. Applied to Indochina this theory brands Vietnamese revolutionaries as creatures of Moscow or Peking. Guerrilla fighters of the National Liberation Front of South Vietnam become "infiltrators from the north," the Pathet Lao are "revealed" as "Viet Cong," and all Cambodian insurgents battling invaders of their country are transformed into North Vietnamese. It is only by denying the long history of liberation struggles in these countries that this distortion can be maintained.

Laos: Social and Historical Background

ROGER M. SMITH *

Laos is a landlocked country of about 91,000 square miles situated in the middle of the Indochina Peninsula. It averages about 150 to 200 miles in width and from north to south extends nearly 700 miles. The jungled mountains and narrow river valleys which form its northern terrain give way in the south to sparsely forested tablelands. From the long mountain chain separating Laos and Vietnam many rivers flow westward toward the Mekong River, which serves as the major communications link between north and south and forms the greater length of the Laos-Thailand border. Laos is also bordered by China and Burma in the north and northwest and by Cambodia in the south.

Approximately one-half of Laos' population belongs to the Lao branch of the Thai[1] peoples who today also inhabit Thailand, northeastern Burma, southern Yunnan, northern Vietnam, and Hainan. Most of the Lao are settled along the upper Mekong, and the majority of them live not in Laos but in northeastern Thailand. In Laos, they are plains and river-valley dwellers and practice wet rice cultivation. Two other principal ethnic groups compose most of the remaining population of Laos: (1) the Méo and Yao, who migrated from southwestern China in

[1] According to current usage, Tai is the generic term used to refer to those peoples who, originating in South China, are today scattered throughout northern portions of Southeast Asia. Thai refers in particular to Tai who live in Thailand. To be consistent with usage in other units of this book, however, the term Thai is used in both the generic and the specific sense.

* Roger M. Smith, "Laos," in George McT. Kahin, ed., Governments and Politics of Southeast Asia (2nd ed., Ithaca, N.Y.: Cornell University Press, 1964), pp. 527–38, 564–71. By permission.

the nineteenth century, and (2) the aboriginal Kha, a people believed to be of Indonesian stock, who dwell for the most part in the upland areas of the south. Other groups include the Black Thai, whose settlements are concentrated in the northern river valleys, and the small communities of Chinese, Vietnamese, and Indians in the towns.

EARLY HISTORY

The history of Laos probably begins in the twelfth century, when the kingdom of Muong Swa was established in northern Laos with its capital located in what is now Luang Prabang province.[2] To the south lay the Khmer empire, whose seat was in Angkor. During the twelfth and thirteenth centuries there was a steady movement of Lao southward into Khmer territory, which culminated in the establishment of the principalities of Xieng Khouang, Vientiane, and Champassak. Lao encroachment upon Khmer territory met little resistance, for by that time the strength of the Khmer empire was already waning before the growing power of the Thai kingdom of Sukhothai.

Around 1340 Phaya Fa Ngum, with the aid of a Khmer army, deposed his grandfather from the throne of Muong Swa and succeeded also in subjugating the three Lao principalities of the south.[3] With these conquests he founded the kingdom of Lan

[2] Modern scholarship suggests that the Thai peoples had probably resided in the northern part of the Indochina Peninsula since early in the first millennium A.D. See Georges Coedès, "L'Année du Lièvre, 1219 A.D.," *India Antiqua* (Leyden: E. J. Brill, 1947), pp. 83–88, and "Une période critique dans l'Asie du Sud Est: Le XIII siècle," *Bulletin de la Société des Etudes Indochinoises* (Saigon), n.s. XXXIII, no. 4 (1958), pp. 387–400, and also Kachorn Sukhabanij, "The Thai Beach-Head States in the Eleventh and Twelfth Centuries," *Silapakon Journal* (Bangkok), vol. I, nos. 3 and 4 (1957). On the founding of Muong Swa, see "Annals of Lan Xang," in René de Berval, *et al., Kingdom of Laos,* Saigon: France-Asie, 1959, pp. 375–410.

[3] See Katay D. Sasorith, "Historical Aspects of Laos," in Berval, *Kingdom of Laos,* p. 26. In this same volume, Coedès states that Fa Ngum's success was facilitated by the decline of Sukhothai, which in the thirteenth century exercised sovereignty over the Mekong Valley but later became a vassal of the kingdom of Ayutthaya, which was founded in 1350 on the lower Menam (Chao Phraya). See *ibid.,* p. 20.

Xang, which during the reign of his son was extended from China to the northeastern parts of present day Cambodia and from the Annamese mountain chain as far beyond the Mekong as Korat in Thailand.

The glory of Lan Xang was short lived. The kingdom was soon demoralized by unceasing strife over succession to the throne, a situation which rendered it vulnerable to the covetousness of its neighbors. During the fifteenth and sixteenth centuries Lan Xang was subjected to Annamese attempts to seize portions of its eastern territory, Burmese invasions and occupations, and intrigues on the part of the Siamese kingdom of Ayutthaya. With the death of Souligna Vongsa in 1694, and the resulting wrangle over succession, which rival aspirants tried to resolve by enlisting the assistance of Annam and Siam, the disintegration of Lan Xang was completed, and the separate kingdoms of Luang Prabang, Vientiane, and Champassak were established.[4]

From the early eighteenth century until 1830, Lao history was marked by five interfamilial quarrels which contributed to widespread instability and made the people an easy prey for political and military conquests by Siam, Burma, and Annam. By the end of the eighteenth century Siam had emerged as the sole suzerain of the territory formerly comprising the kingdom of Lan Xang.[5] In 1804, Chao Anou, a member of the junior branch of the Vientiane royal family, was placed on the throne of that kingdom by Siam. Later, because of his assistance in quelling a revolt by the Khas in Champassak, he was able to obtain the Champassak crown for his son. In 1826, receiving word that Bangkok was being invaded by Great Britain, he proceeded to recruit an army with which he hoped to remove the three Lao

[4] According to its annals, Champassak developed independently during the seventeenth century from a mere town situated on the Mekong River into a quasi-principality whose jurisdiction was confined to a small area and whose control over the populace was limited. That it remained outside of the mainstream of events in the north was probably due to its relative isolation and the weakness and disinterest of its neighbors. See "History of Champassak," *Collected Chronicles,* LXX, Thailand, Department of Fine Arts, Bangkok, 1941, pp. 1–23 (in Thai), and Thao Nhouy Abhay, "En marge de l'histoire du Laos," *France-Asie,* III, no. 25 (Saigon), April, 1948, pp. 460–63.

[5] See David K. Wyatt, "Siam and Laos, 1767–1827," *Journal of Southeast Asian History,* IV, no. 2, September, 1963, pp. 13–21.

kingdoms from the tutelage of Siam while that country's attention was being diverted. The rumor of British invasion proved to be groundless, however, and his rebellion was easily crushed by the Siamese. Chao Anou fled to Annam, where he gained the sympathy of the court of Hue. In 1828, he again attempted to free the three kingdoms from Siamese influence, this time with the support of an Annamese army. Siam retaliated by ravaging Vientiane and deporting thousands of its inhabitants to Siam.[6] While Siamese efforts were turned to halting Chao Anou's attack, the Annamese exploited the opportunity to seize eastern Lao regions, including Xieng Khouang, which had up to that time acknowledged the suzerainty of Luang Prabang. Until the French takeover late in the century the kingdoms of Luang Prabang and Champassak continued to recognize Siamese suzerainty, while Vientiane was ruled directly by Siam.[7]

FRENCH INTERVENTION
AND COLONIAL RULE

There was little significant European contact with Laos until the mid-nineteenth century, when French influence was being established in Southeast Asia. Between 1858, when Napoleon III first sent a military expedition to Annam, and the 1880's, France colonized Cochinchina and undertook the protectorates of Cambodia, Annam, and Tonkin. France's subsequent intervention in Laos was pressed on grounds of upholding an alleged Annamese right of suzerainty,[8] but it was motivated by two

[6] In the course of the first of these attacks, Chao Anou penetrated Siam as far as Saraburi, within three days' march of Bangkok. See *ibid.*, pp. 30–31, and Walter F. Vella, *Siam under Rama III,* Locust Valley, N.Y.: J. J. Augustin, Inc., 1957, pp. 80–86.

[7] For further details of Laotian history prior to the French period, see Paul Le Boulanger, *Histoire du Laos français: Essai d'une étude chronologique des principautés laotiennes,* Paris: Plon, 1931; Katay D. Sasorith, *Le Laos: Son évolution politique, sa place dans l'Union française,* Paris: Editions Berger-Levrault, 1953; D. G. E. Hall, *A History of Southeast Asia* (London: Macmillan, 1955), pp. 207–10, 217, 376–85, 591–612.

[8] Annam's "rights" in Laos were, historically, more virtual than real and were grossly exaggerated to serve France's cause. For a discussion of some aspects of suzerainty in Southeast Asia, see François Iché,

more practical matters: (1) the security of France's new possession was being threatened by an increase of Siamese control in regions where the interests of Bangkok and the court of Hue had been in competition for over a century,[9] and (2) it was stimulated by rivalry with Great Britain over what were thought to be important trade routes to the Yangtze River valley in China.

With the encouragement of Great Britain, which regarded the Thais as a potential barrier against French expansion into its own recently acquired territory in the Shan States, Siam sought to strengthen its position on the east bank of the Mekong. Upon the request of the king of Luang Prabang, Siam in the 1880's dispatched troops to repel marauding Hos, Chinese bandits recently descended from Yunnan who were threatening Luang Prabang. Having successfully forced the Hos to retreat into northwest Tonkin, Siam then occupied the whole of Laos north of Luang Prabang and established military outposts in the valleys of the Black River as far east as Lao Chau in Tonkin.

To constrain this encroachment, France obtained an agreement with Siam by which both recognized the *status quo* and which sanctioned the creation of a French consulate at Luang Prabang. The Siamese received the French consul, Auguste Pavie, coldly, but he soon maneuvered himself into a position where he was able to persuade the king of Luang Prabang that a French protectorate was a preferable alternative to Siamese occupation. Thenceforth, in the course of two more missions to Laos, 1889–1895, and without the benefit of any formal treaty or agreement with a Laotian ruler,[10] Pavie extended French tutelage over the entire east bank of the Mekong.

Le statut politique et internationale du Laos français—Sa condition juridique dans la communauté du Droit des Gens, Paris: Rousseau et Cie, 1935.

[9] See the argument of Francis Garnier in his *Voyage d'exploration en Indo-Chine, 1866–1868,* (Paris: Hachette et Cie, 1873), I, pp. 322, 488, 548–49.

[10] On his first mission to Laos, 1887–1888, Pavie rescued the king from his palace during a Siamese-Ho battle. The grateful king was reported to have told him: "Our country is not a Siamese conquest. Luang Prabang, desiring protection, voluntarily offered tribute. Now, by its interference, our ruin is complete. If my son consents, we will offer ourselves as a gift to France, sure that it will guard us from future unhappiness." See Auguste Pavie, "Géographie et voyages: Pas-

In defiance of the convention by which it had agreed on the *status quo,* Siam, in 1889, thrust forward its military outposts into the Annamese cordillera near Hue. France countered with its own troop movements along the Mekong, but Siam's efforts to retain its physical presence in Laos were not ended until a French naval blockade of Bangkok and an approaching Anglo-French *rapprochement* in Europe convinced Siam that its only course was to accept France's terms. These were embodied in a treaty of October 3, 1893, and included Siam's renunciation of all its rights to territory on the east bank of the Mekong—an arbitrary demarcation line in view of the fact that most Laotians lived along the west bank[11]—and its acquiescence to the demilitarization of a fifteen-mile zone along the west bank of the river.

Great Britain reluctantly accepted the principle of a common frontier in the Shan states, fixed in the *thalweg* of the upper Mekong, and by a common declaration with France in 1896 agreed that the Menam Valley constituted a north-south neutral zone in which they would refrain from seeking a predominant position.[12]

The territory which the French were to call Laos came within the administrative framework of the Indochinese Union, a federation which included the colony of Cochinchina and the protectorates of Cambodia Annam, and Tonkin. The federal administration was conducted from Hanoi, capital of Tonkin, and was headed by a Governor General; it had exclusive or wide powers in foreign affairs, defense, finance, justice, customs, and public

---

sage du Mé-Khong au Tonkin, 1887–1888, in Auguste Pavie, *et al., Mission Pavie: Indochine, 1879–1895,* VI, Paris: E. Leroux, 1911, pp. 113–14. (This translation and others from the French were made by the author.)

[11] This mistake was partially corrected by France in treaties with Siam in 1902 and 1907 which returned the west bank regions of Sayaboury and Champassak to Laos.

[12] For further details of the French intervention, see Auguste Pavie, "Geographie et voyages," in Pavie, *Mission,* II (1906), 214–376, and Thao Katay [Katay D. Sasorith], *Contribution a l'histoire du mouvement d'indépendance nationale lao* (Bangkok: Phanich Suphaphon Press, 1948). The Anglo-French agreement of 1896 and the fourteen-power Declaration on Laotian Neutrality of 1962 bear a remarkable similarity. See the text of the 1962 agreement in the *New York Times,* July 22, 1962. On the Anglo-French rivalry generally, see Hall, *History of Southeast Asia,* pp. 591 ff.

works and in the appointment of officials. In Laos, however, the Laotian administrative organization was left fairly intact. In this, the French were inspired by their Siamese predecessors, who had respected Laotian institutions.

Because of Pavie's relationship with King Oun Kham, the kingdom of Luang Prabang, comprising the provinces of Luang Prabang, Houa Phan, Phong Saly, and Sayaboury, retained a separate identity throughout the French period. There, the king ruled jointly with a viceroy, called *maha oupahat.* The latter, usually a member of the junior branch of the royal family, was the king's alter ego in matters of routine administration, his commanding general, and his chief diplomat. Prior to the French arrival, the *maha oupahat* very often succeeded to the throne in dynastic struggles. In addition to the viceroy, the king was assisted by a consultative body of princely ministers. They were the king's advisers, planners, and executives, who presided over a simple hierarchy of civil servants. The provinces of the kingdom were administered locally. Although the governor was usually a royal appointee, the lack of adequate communications and the remoteness of many areas dictated that the king's absolute rule should be limited as long as the proper taxes were regularly paid.[13]

The rest of Laos, including what is now known as Houa Khong province north of Luang Prabang, Xieng Khouang, the former kingdom of Vientiane, and the kingdom of Champassak,[14] was divided into eight provinces, each presided over by a French *résident,* who wielded almost complete power over all public services. Under the *résidents* there functioned smaller administrative units governed by Laotian officials. Over all of Laos there presided a *résident supérieur,* who maintained his headquarters in Vientiane.[15] The legal status of Laos—protectorate or colony or both—was not explicitly defined until 1941.

Just prior to the occupation of Indochina by Japan in 1941, France at last officially defined the Luang Prabang king's attri-

[13] Le Boulanger, *Histoire du Laos,* pp. 323–24.
[14] A small area around Bassac, on the west bank of the Mekong River, was claimed by Thailand but was ceded to Laos. The western and southern limits of Laos were fixed by the Franco–Siam treaty of 1907. See *ibid.,* pp. 342, 349–51.
[15] *Ibid.,* pp. 338–339.

butes and the character of the colonial administration of the rest of Laos.[16] The protectorate treaty of August 29, 1941, annexed Vientiane, Xieng Khouang, and Houa Khong provinces to Luang Prabang and established a royal cabinet composed of a premier and ministries of interior, defense, finance, education, general economy, public works, justice, and religious affairs. The ministers, like their counterparts in the other protectorates, enjoyed few if any powers. In fact, they were simply high ranking civil servants charged with coordination, in the king's name, of affairs at an intermediary level between the Laotian provincial authorities and the *résident supérieur*. The rest of Laos, meanwhile, continued to be ruled as a colony. This administrative reorganization was brought about by a Japanese-mediated Franco-Siamese conflict in early 1941, which resulted in the cession to Siam of that part of the kingdom of Luang Prabang on the west bank of the Mekong (Sayaboury) and a similar part of Champassak. Had the conflict not occurred, it is likely that France would have continued to pay only scant attention to its possession along the Mekong.[17]

PROGRESS TOWARD INDEPENDENCE

After over half a century of French rule, Laos emerged from the Second World War still very much an underdeveloped country. Only one percent of the population, estimated at just over 1.1 million persons, was receiving an elementary education (in Lao), while secondary education (in French) was being provided for only 200 students. Commerce, dominated by privileged French and Chinese merchants, was restricted in the prov-

[16] An agreement of Dec. 3, 1895, had been negotiated with the king to settle matters of internal administration but never received French ratification. A second convention, to determine the king's authority, was signed in February 1914 but was suspended while modifications to it were discussed. Still a third was completed in 1917, but only between the Governor-General and King Sisavang Vong and thus had only the effect of an internal administrative act of the Governor's office. See *ibid.*, pp. 316–17, and Iché, *Le Statut Politique*, p. 70.

[17] See Luang Vichitr Vadakarn, *Thailand's Case* (Bangkok: Thai Commercial Press, 1941), chs. iii–iv, and *Contemporary Japan*, Tokyo, June 1941, pp. 840–42.

inces by a tendency on the part of the scattered population to cater to its own needs and by the absence of adequate transportation facilities. Perhaps more important was the fact that no curb had been placed on the traditional authority exercised by princely families over centuries-old fiefs (especially in Luang Prabang and Champassak). The neglect of the Lao was in great part due to French preoccupation with more profitable commercial ventures in Cochinchina and Tonkin. This may also have been due to the quixotic bent of certain French administrators who discovered in the Lao the "noble savage" image of Rousseau and were determined to protect them from the corruptive influence of more sophisticated civilization.

Unlike other Southeast Asian colonial countries where passionate nationalistic sentiments blossomed forth during the confusion of the immediate postwar period, in Laos the initial striving for independence received its impetus from the revival of an age old rivalry among aristocratic Lao families for control of the country. This took on nationalistic overtones but was incidental to the personal political ambitions of the elite, as the continuation of the rivalry since expulsion of the French from Laotian soil has revealed.[18]

[18] Wilfred Burchett presents a strikingly different picture of the Laotian struggle for independence. He traces it back to early revolts, especially those of the despised and oppressed mountain people who were never completely subdued by the French. Ong Keo, a Lao Teng chief, led a revolt which began in 1910. When he was killed another tribal chief, Kommadam, took up the fight and began to unite scattered hill tribes throughout Laos. Kommadam developed an anti-colonialist political program—including refusal of taxes, conscription and labor services—and established a written language for his people. The Ong Keo–Kommadam revolt ended when Kommadam was killed in 1937. Kommadam's sons, Sithone and Khampan, became leading Pathet Lao cadres, and his grandson, the son of Sithone, is also a resistance fighter. The Lao Son began their resistance against the French opium tax and *corvée* system in 1918. Faydang, the Pathet Lao leader who is a Lao Son, considers himself in the tradition of Chao Pha Pachay, leader of the 1918–1922 revolt. Burchett, Wilfred, *Mekong Upstream*, Hanoi, 1957, pp. 239–50, *passim*.

Burchett's description of Prince Souphanouvong is also at odds with Smith's conception of the Laotian independence movement as an intra-elite rivalry. "I met Souphanouvong first at his headquarters deep in the jungle just as the battle of Dienbienphu was getting under way . . . . His speech is direct and clear as befits a technician and no time is lost with the superficial courtesies which one often encounters with

The first signs of a renewal of an intra-elite contest for power were manifested in 1941 when, following the protectorate treaty, King Sisavang Vong of Luang Prabang bestowed the title *maha oupahat* on Prince Phetsarath and appointed him premier. The assumption of the viceroyship by Phetsarath reportedly precipitated a rivalry between him and the king's eldest son, Prince Savang Vatthana,[19] who may have seen in this appointment a direct threat to his chances for succeeding his father to the throne.[20]

When on March 9, 1945, Japan demanded that King Sisavang proclaim independence, Savang vacillated between retaining his allegiance to France and cooperating with Japan.[21] Phetsarath, on the other hand, expressed determination to abolish the protectorate. In September, 1945, a small but dynamic part of the elite from both Luang Prabang and the southern areas of Laos joined him in the formation of the Lao Issara, or Free Lao, movement, which had as its stated goals the removal of French rule from Lao territory and the unification of north and south under a single leadership.

Upon the capitulation of Japan in August, the governors of Laos' southern provinces, acting on the orders of Prince Boun

---

even progressive figures from the feudal classes in Asia. Souphanouvong by his contacts with the people had identified himself completely with them and it did not take much time among his troops and cadres, or among the villagers near his headquarters, to feel that he was respected and loved by the people. They saw in him a patriot who had shared their sufferings for many years on end; not a prince of the feudal hierarchy." *Ibid.,* p. 258—eds.

[19] Pierre Gentil, *Sursauts de l'Asie: Remous du Mékong* (Paris: Charles-Lavauzelle, 1950), p. 27.

[20] While accession to the throne was generally based on primogeniture, the French had been known to depart from this practice when it suited their convenience, and the junior branch of the royal family from which Phetsarath was descended appeared to have enjoyed a favored relationship with French administrators since Pavie's time. On the other hand, Phetsarath had an assertive personality, a fact that would argue against his being named king by the French, who traditionally sought to place submissive and cooperative figures on the thrones in their colonies. See Le Boulanger, *Histoire du Laos,* pp. 252, 322.

[21] The king proclaimed this independence for Luang Prabang only, preferring to let the ruling family of Champassak make its own decision. See Katay D. Sasorith, *Le Laos,* p. 59.

Oum of Champassak,[22] invited France to return. But Phetsarath, speaking now as the representative of the national unity movement, announced on September 1 the abrogation of the protectorate, accused King Sisavang of treason for receiving a delegate from General de Gaulle, and declared the independence and unity of all Laos. Sisavang, on October 17, issued counterproclamations and dismissed Phetsarath from both his offices, but the latter, with the assistance of Chinese troops which occupied northern Laos in accordance with the Potsdam Agreement, formed a provisional assembly, nominated a cabinet, and completed the upheaval ten days later by deposing the king.

In the meantime, Phetsarath's half brother, Prince Souphanouvong,[23] with a band of Vietminh trained and armed guerrillas, had gained control of most of central Laos. He was invited to join the Lao Issara and was appointed foreign minister in the new cabinet. He continued, however, to remain in the field directing guerrilla operations against advancing French troops and withdrew from these activities only when he was wounded in a skirmish at Thakhek.[24]

Aware that France would never agree to deal with a government established as his had been, Phetsarath tried to substantiate the Lao Issara's claim to control of the government by negotiat-

[22] Boun Oum is the son of Chao Ratsadanay, who ascended the throne of Champassak in 1900. Following the Franco-Siamese treaty of 1907, Ratsadanay took an oath of loyalty to France and was made Governor of what was then Champassak. It is not certain whether in this post he retained royal prerogatives, nor is it certain whether Boun Oum may rightfully claim them.

[23] Souphanouvong attended the Lycée Albert Sarraut in Hanoi. There, short of money, he was befriended by an innkeeper, whose daughter, a member of the Vietnamese Communist Party, he later married. In 1937, at the age of twenty-five, he graduated from the Ecole des Ponts et Chaussées in Paris. He then returned to Hanoi, where he was employed by the public works department. In 1945, he was contacted by the Vietminh, who sent him south to Vinh; there he was joined by seventy Laotian and Vietnamese guerrillas with whom he attacked Tchépone in east central Laos. See Sisouk na Champassak, *Tempête sur le Laos,* Paris: Table Ronde, 1961, pp. 18–23; Quang Minh, *Au pays du million d'éléphants,* Hanoi: Editions en Langues Etrangères, 1961, p. 17; Wilfred Burchett, *Mekong Upstream* (Hanoi, Red River Publishing House, 1957), pp. 257–58.

[24] To the Laotian people the battle of Thakhek was more than a "skirmish." See Selection 2, this volume—eds.

ing for King Sisavang's return to the throne in the role of a constitutional monarch. Although the king's assent to this arrangement was at last extorted on April 20, 1946, it was by then too
late to prevent the expulsion of the Lao Issara government from
Vientiane by French troops.[25] The king welcomed the French in
Luang Prabang in early May, annulled all acts of the provisional Lao Issara government which he had signed, and reaf-
firmed his declaration of August 30, 1945, to General de Gaulle,
in which he had looked forward to renewed French administration and assistance in regaining the provinces turned over to
Siam by the Japanese at the beginning of the war.[26]

With the advance of French troops to Vientiane, the leaders
of the Lao Issara fled to Bangkok. There bitter quarrels arose
between Souphanouvong, who advocated Vietminh support of
an armed resistance against the French, and Phetsarath, who
wished to exclude the Vietminh from such an undertaking. Subsequently, Souphanouvong appeared in northeastern Burma and
northern Thailand, and from these areas he launched guerrilla
operations against the French. As a result of his collaboration
with the Vietminh at this time he was expelled from the Lao
Issara in May, 1949.[27]

In August, 1946, following the reinstatement of the French
colonial regime, a *modus vivendi* [28] was signed with a government
led by another brother of Phetsarath, Prince Souvannarath,
which implicitly recognized the unity and autonomy of Laos; in
the following March, elections were held for a constituent assembly, which, under French direction, completed its task on
May 11, 1947, when a constitution was promulgated. The pre-

[25] For a detailed account of the Lao Issara, see Sasorith, *Le Laos,*
pp. 59–63; Thao Katay, *Contribution,* pp. 173–204; Gentil, *Sursauts,*
pp. 26–34; Sisouk na Champassak, *Tempête,* pp. 14–17.

[26] The portions of Sayaboury and Champassak on the west bank of
the Mekong were returned to Laos by the Washington Conference,
1946–47. See Thao Katay, *Contribution,* pp. 52–3, 128–131.

[27] An entirely different interpretation of Souphanouvong's break with
the Lao Issara, and an explanation of the ideological basis of his alliance with the Vietminh, is given in Burchett. See Selection 2, this
volume—eds.

[28] Text in Roger Lévy, *L'Indochine et ses traités, 1946,* Centre
d'Etudes de Politique Etrangère, Section d'Information, Pub. no. 19,
(Paris: 1947), pp. 55–60.

amble to this constitution[29] proclaimed the unity of all Laos under King Sisavang Vong and declared the status of the kingdom
to be that of an independent state within the French union. In
a secret protocol annexed to the *modus vivendi* of 1946, Prince
Boun Oum "renounced," for the sake of Lao unity, the sovereign
rights of Champassak.[30] But when the constituent assembly met
in 1947, representatives of Champassak asserted that the real
unity of the country would never be attained until the rights of
the Champassak royal family were assured. A compromise was
finally agreed upon, with French mediation, whereby Boun Oum
was named Inspector General of the Kingdom for life and became president of the King's Council—the upper house of the
Laotian legislature—thus gaining participation in the naming of
the king's successor.

At the conclusion of the Elysée Agreement with Bao Dai's
Vietnam in early 1949, France drew up a similar convention
with Laos,[31] by which France recognized Laos' independence
and the Laotians affirmed their adherence to the French union
as an associated state. This independence was, however, qualified
in several important ways: French citizens were to enjoy extra-
territorial rights under the jurisdiction of newly established
French union courts; Laos was to have its own army, but in war
—a state of affairs then prevailing—it was to be pooled with
other union forces under French command. Foreign policy was
to be exercised within the framework of union policy, thus giving
a power of veto to France. A further convention signed on February 6, 1950, transferred some of the internal functions and
powers of government to Laos. Finally, by agreements reached
with Vietnam, Cambodia, and France in the Pau Conference,
June 28–November 27, 1950, Laos undertook to coordinate its
communications, immigration control, economic planning, customs, foreign trade, and finance—over all of which France exercised exclusive control—with those of its Indochina neighbors,

---

[29] Text in Sasorith, *Le Laos,* pp. 93–4. See also Allan B. Cole, ed.,
Conflict in Indochina and International Repercussions, Ithaca, N.Y.:
Cornell University Press, 1956, p. 56.

[30] Sasorith, *Le Laos,* pp. 81–4.

[31] See *ibid.,* pp. 117–30, for the text of the General Franco–Laotian
Convention, with protocol annexed, July 19, 1949.

and to participate in a number of quadripartite bodies and inter-governmental conferences.

With the signing of the 1949 convention, the Lao Issara, still exiled in Bangkok, voted to dissolve itself. Announcing that the principal aims of the resistance were achieved by the agreement, the exiled government called upon its supporters, who by then represented a large proportion of the Lao political elite, to return to Laos and undertake the task of building an independent nation.[32]

Shortly after the dissolution of the La Issara, Souphanouvong organized, with Vietminh encouragement and support, the Pathet Lao, or Lao National, movement, which had as its aim the removal of the last vestige of French influence from Laos. It also opposed the Royal Lao Government (RLG), which expressed readiness to compromise itself with the French, and this fact and its affiliation with the Vietminh have contributed to the recent dispute between the Pathet Lao and the pro-Western ruling group in Vientiane.

Faced with defeat by the Vietminh, who wished to rid all of Indochina of French influence, France announced in the summer of 1953 that in view of the development of governmental institutions and the army, the time had come "to perfect the independence and sovereignty" of Laos. Negotiations culminated in the October 22, 1953, Franco-Laotian Treaty of Friendship by which Laos was accorded full independence. Annexed to the treaty were conventions which transferred to Laos military, diplomatic, and judicial powers hitherto reserved to France. The system of economic coordination established under the Pau agreements was ended at the Paris Conference of December 1954; henceforth, Laos was to have complete control of its economic affairs.

[32] *Ibid.,* pp. 131–35. Phetsarath, however, remained in Bangkok. Two factors contributed to his decision to remain behind: first, because of his uncompromising attitude toward the French, he had lost his hold on other Lao Issara members; second, King Sisavang Vong had not yet pardoned him for his activities against the throne. It was not until 1957 that the king finally forgave him and permitted his return to Laos. His position as Viceroy was restored, but the fact that he had been out of touch with political developments for eleven years prevented him from regaining an influential position among the elite. He died in 1959.

THE ECONOMY

Laos is an agricultural country in which some ninety percent of its population, estimates of which range from 1,450,000
to 2,500,000 persons, are engaged in subsistence farming. It has
traditionally been self-sufficient, especially in rice, but since the
advent of independence it has been subject to food shortages due
to a combination of the growth of towns, droughts, poor transportation facilities, and the civil war which has limited the
amount of surplus food the villages produce for marketing. But
the Lao villager himself continues to be remarkably self-sufficient: he grows his own food, produces his own fibers, and
spins and weaves his own cloth.[33]

The staple food of Laos is glutenous rice, grown in irrigated
paddies in river valleys. A second type of rice cultivation, *ray*,
or slash-and-burn, is practiced by the nomadic Kha tribes of upland Laos. Corn, tobacco, and sugar cane are also grown in the
valleys, and truck crops along the river banks during the dry
season; cotton, silk worms, and opium poppies are cultivated in
the hill areas. Strangely enough, the richest agricultural area, the
Bolovens Plateau in Champassak and Attopeu provinces, which
has been estimated by American agricultural experts as capable
of producing enough truck crops for all of Southeast Asia, until
recently received little attention from the Lao peasant. This was,
perhaps, because of the problem of transporting the food products to other parts of Laos.

Laos' forests abound with teak and pine, but the growth of a
lumber industry has been restricted by a lack of adequate transportation facilities. Prospecting has revealed deposits of iron,
coal, manganese, lead, and copper, but because of transportation
costs these have not been exploited; the only mineral deposits
being worked in 1961 were a tin mine at Phon Tiou in central

[33] See Howard K. Kaufman, *Village Life in Vientiane Province*
(Vientiane, 1956; mimeographed), and Tsuneo Ayabe, "The Village of
Ban Pha Khao, Vientiane Province—A Preliminary Report," *Japanese
Journal of Ethnology*, vol. XXIII, no. 12, 1959, reproduced by J. M.
Halpern, ed., as paper no. 14 of the Laos Project, Department of
Anthropology, University of California at Los Angeles, n.d. [1960?]).

Laos and a few gold mines scattered throughout the country. Industries are confined to a few small plants—for rice milling, bottling, and the making of brick and tile, cigarettes, matches, soap, and candles—and cottage industries, including basket weaving, silk and cotton weaving, woodworking, and pottery making.

The inadequacy of transportation represents a major obstacle not only in the development of the country's resources and in its foreign trade relations and internal distribution of goods but also in the maintenance of central control by the government. There are no railways, and none of the country's four major roads, leading north, south, and east from Vientiane, are traversable all the year round. Most exports and imports must be carried overland through Thailand by rail or road or through Vietnam or Cambodia by road or water, all at great cost. The Mekong River, which is navigable between Vientiane and Savannakhet, is an important communications medium, although rapids make transshipments necessary north and south of this 312 mile stretch. Improvements in the road system have been planned by the government with United States and French aid.[34] When these are completed, road transportation should be possible between most of the major towns south of Luang Prabang for the greater part of the year.

Laos' total exports for 1959 amounted to less than $1 million, of which tin concentrates shipped to Malaya represented a third; other main items were teak, coffee, cardamom, stick-lac, and benzoin.[35] Another principal source of revenue is opium; it is an illegal export, however, and its contribution to the economy is therefore impossible to assess.[36] Total imports in 1959 amounted

[34] The first improvement, a 130 mile road between Vientiane and Luang Prabang, resulted in the expenditure of $1.6 million for a road which was unusable during the rainy season. See U.S. House of Representatives, *U.S. Aid Operations in Laos* (Washington, D.C.: Government Printing Office, 1959), p. 4. A second project, an $8.6-million all-weather road from Nam Cah Dinh to Thakhek, was suspended because of the fighting; the bridges for it, already built in place by the French, were left to the jungle.

[35] USOM/Laos, *Annual Statistical Report, 1959* (Vientiane, 1960), Table F-6.

[36] See J. M. Halpern, *The Rural and Urban Economies of Laos,* Laos Project Paper no. 18, Dept. of Anthropology, U.C.L.A., 1960, pp. 74–7.

to over $12 million,[37] the gap being filled by United States aid.

A five year plan of economic development, drawn up during Prince Souphanouvong's tenure as Minister of Economic Planning in 1957–1958, was adopted in 1959 by the Phoui Sanani-kone government.[38] It envisaged an annual expenditure of $35 million, of which forty percent would be for social welfare and forty percent for public works, transportation, and communications. Although it states that it will encourage private investment with business loans and appropriate legislation, it is clear that the major source of financing will have to come from foreign aid. At present the plan remains a mere working paper rather than a final statement of intention.

In 1955, at the request of the Lao government, the United States established an operations mission (USOM) in Vientiane whose purpose was to support the royal army and begin the task of strengthening the country's economic base. Until 1962, more than two-thirds of US aid was devoted to the defense support program. Of the remaining one-third, twenty-five percent was directed toward the development of Laos' transportation needs.

A French mission for economic aid and technical assistance was established in Laos in 1955. Through 1960 it had expended over $12 million, mostly for road building and the construction of airfields, including the international airport at Vientiane.[39] In addition to various small expenditures on telecommunications, hospitals, rural irrigation, technical studies, and training programs, France constructed in 1956–1957 Laos' only complete high school, the *Lycée Pavie* in Vientiane, and it provides almost all of the teachers for the school's students (the only exception being a Lao teacher of the Lao language and literature). Japan has undertaken an aid plan for certain specific projects, including a new water supply and drainage system for Vientiane, costing an estimated $2.8 million. In addition to aid given in the form of technical cooperation under the Colombo Plan, Great Britain has agreed to provide some $400,000 for bridges and improve-

[37] USOM/Laos, *Report 1959*, Table F-2.

[38] Royaume du Laos, Ministère du Plan, *Plan de développement économique et social—Périod de 5 ans du 1 juillet 1959 au 30 juin 1964* (Vientiane, 1959).

[39] See Mission Française d'Aide Economique et Technique au Laos, *L'aide française au Laos* (Saigon: 1960).

ment of Laos' radio communications network. Laos is also participating with Cambodia, South Vietnam, and Thailand in a project which involves the surveying of the lower Mekong basin for large-scale development of the area for irrigation, power, and other resources. A five year program of studies was in progress in 1961–1962 with international assistance.

THE SOCIETY

The dominant cultural group in Laos is the Lao. Ethnically and linguistically related to the Thai, they are plains and valley dwelling people who until recently were content to lead a subsistence existence based on wet rice agriculture.[40] Introduction of Western influences has brought about small but perceptible changes in traditional Lao society. The age old pattern of a self-contained village life has come more and more under the influence of urbanization along the Mekong; the importation of cheap, factory-made articles has caused a decline in village handicrafts; and the attraction of relatively large salaries in the army has contributed to a shortage of young men for cultivating the soil and to a decline of traditional values.[41]

Also showing signs of decline is the authoritarian structure which for centuries has placed the peasantry in a subservient position before the local elite. The elite have tended to remove themselves to urban centers and return to the villages only during elections, when they campaign with promises of irrigation works and improved roads, promises which, complain the villagers, are never kept.[42] Because villagers seldom see the elite and even less often receive benefits from them, feelings of loyalty to them are rapidly waning. At the same time many peasants

[40] See Frank M. LeBar and Adrienne Suddard, eds., *Laos: Its People, Its Society, Its Culture,* New Haven: Human Relations Area Files Press, 1960, chs. I, VI and IX. See also Kaufman, *Village Life* and Berval, *Kingdom of Laos,* section V.

[41] See Georges Condominas and C. Gaudillat, eds., *La Plaine de Vientiane*—Rapport d'étude (Paris: Bureau pour la Développement de la Production Agricole for Royaume du Laos, Commissariat au Plan), 1959; (mimeographed), p. 68.

[42] J. M. Halpern, *Aspects of Village Life and Culture Change in Laos* (New York: Council on Economic and Cultural Affairs, 1958), p. 107.

experience feelings of futility which are manifested in the attitude: "We're only farmers, so what's the use?" [43] The Pathet
Lao, by publicizing the ostentatious display in the towns and
calling attention to the gap in the standards of living between
the peasantry and elite have further undermined the authoritarian structure.

Buddhism, often characterized as a unifying force of the countries in which it is predominant, is one of the few features of
Lao culture which the peasants and the elite have in common.
Some of the Lao elite have complained about the decadence
into which the religion has fallen, of the indolence and lack of
dedication on the part of the clergy,[44] but it is likely that the
sangha, or brotherhood, which numbers some 6,000 monks and
8,000 novices, continues to exercise an important influence over
the people as well as to perform important religious and educational functions. The giving of alms to the monks and support
of *that* (temple) projects remain a basic part of the life of
the villager and an effective way to gain merit toward a better
life in the hereafter.

Buddhism in Laos is of the Theravada form, and it is organized on lines parallel with those of the government. The king
is the "protector" of the faith and appoints the *phra sangkharaja,*
the actual religious head of the church, who administers the
affairs of the clergy through a number of advisory and dis-
ciplinary councils. Below him, provincial leaders are appointed
by royal ordinance upon nomination by the religious heads of
districts and with the concurrence of the Ministry of Religious
Affairs. Below this level, the religious leaders are appointed
by their provincial religious superiors upon the recommendation of a conference of religious and political leaders of the
area with the concurrence of the political head at the level of the
appointing authority.[45] All of the clergy must take an oath of
loyalty to the king, and they are prohibited from participation
in political affairs.

In the villages the monk is honored and respected as a re-

[43] Kaufman, *Village Life,* p. 11.
[44] See Thao Nhouy Abhay, "Buddhism in Laos," in Berval, *Kingdom
of Laos,* pp. 253–55.
[45] See Kruong Pathoumxad, "Organization of the Sangha," in Berval,
Kingdom of Laos, pp. 257–67.

ligious figure; his education and moral stature make him a natural leader whose advice may be sought on a variety of subjects. It is precisely because of this fact that the monk has become a target for the conflicting pressures of the royal government and the Pathet Lao. The former seeks to preserve his loyalty to the crown, and the latter tries to sow the seeds of disaffection, and both are fully aware of and seek to control the influence which the saffron-robed monks could wield if they ever took it upon themselves to do so. The importance which the Pathet Lao accords the monks was amply demonstrated by what it sought, and gained, in the 1957 agreement on a coalition government—the Ministry of Religious Affairs. During his tenure as head of that government department, Phoumi Vongvichit made a special effort to cultivate the friendship of the Buddhist monks. Between 1958 and 1962, the government was somewhat heavy-handed in its dealing with the clergy. Its activities included the forced reorganization of the administrative hierarchy and the placing of informants in the *thats*—acts which may very well have caused discontent among the *sangha* and increased its reported susceptibility to Pathet Lao propaganda. At present, the Ministry of Religious Affairs is headed by a member of Souvanna Phouma's entourage. The influence of the clergy is probably less in the towns where other institutions compete with the *that,* particularly in its roles as social and educational center for the youth.

The tribal minorities, in their number and in the extent of territory which they cover, form a grave problem for the future of the country. At the bottom of the social scale, one finds the Khas, or Lao Teng. Living in the upland areas, especially in the south, they are the largest of the minorities, their number having been estimated in 1959 at 346,000. They are split into many subgroups, for example, Khmu, Kha Ko, and so on, and engage in slash-and-burn agriculture. The Khas are regarded as little better than slaves in the Lao social classification, and in Lao communities one finds them most often in the position of coolies on public works projects and as agricultural laborers.[46]

[46] Wilfred Burchett believes that the mountain-dwelling Kha, in the course of their struggles against the French, gave their people a sense of national identity and purpose. See footnote 18 and his *Mekong Upstream,* pp. 239–50—eds.

The attitude toward the tribal Thai, notably the Black Thais, or Lao Thai, is less discriminatory, probably because of their use of the same linguistic forms and methods of rice cultivation as the Lao. They are set apart, however, by the retention of their traditional dress, animistic beliefs, and their strong cohesion as a group.[47] As for the Méos and Yaos, or Lao Som, who number around 70,000 and live on the mountaintops, their more aggressive and "activist" character places them in a peculiar position. A key factor in any estimation of their position is the cash value of their opium crop, which is reported to provide a large percentage of the Lao government's total revenues.[48]

The tribal peoples are reported to feel dissatisfied because they have not received any of the benefits of economic development. They lack access to most government services and are prevented from participation in the government in a way which their size would normally dictate. Educational facilities which would increase their social mobility and assimilation into Lao society have, to a large extent, been denied them. The government has appeared to lack a well-defined policy on the minorities, although thinking members of the ruling group in Vientiane are aware that the dissatisfaction brewing among these groups poses a potential threat to the country's security. Others, however, appear to be ignorant of the problem or deny its importance. The only voice which the tribal peoples have had in the government is through the Lyfoung brothers, Touby and Toulia, Laotianized Méos of a powerful clan in Xieng Khouang province, who for some years have defended the interests of the Méos and other tribal groups in the National Assembly and the government.[49] Two Khas, Sisana Sisane and Sithone Kommadam, ran successfully as NLHS candidates from Savannakhet

[47] See Condominas and Gaudillat, eds., *La Plaine de Vientiane,* pp. 50–51. See also Keiji Iwata, "Ethnic Groups in the Valley of the Nam Song and the Nam Lik: Their Geographical Distribution and Some Aspects of Social Change," *Japanese Journal of Ethnology,* vol. XXIII, nos. 1–2, 1959 (trans. by H. Sakomoto, el. by J. M. Halpern, Laos Project Paper no. 15, Dept. of Anthropology, U.C.L.A., 1960).

[48] See G. L. Barney, "The Meo of Xieng Khouang Province," 1957, and Keiji Iwata "Minority Groups in Northern Laos," *Shilin,* Tokyo, vol. I, 1960 (ed. by J. M. Halpern, Laos Project Papers nos. 13 and 16, Dept. of Anthropology, U.C.L.A., 1961).

[49] See Gentil, *Sursauts,* pp. 125–26.

and Saravane provinces in the 1958 elections. The Pathet Lao has reportedly succeeded in exploiting tribal discontent by promising them their own local governments, schools conducted in their own languages, and adequate representation before the central government. Most of the fighting forces of the Pathet Lao have been recruited from among the Khas.

Another major ethnic minority, the Chinese, whose population was estimated in 1959 at 40,000, makes its home in Laos' urban centers and plays an important role in the commercial life of the country. The Chinese are organized into *Groupements Administratif Chinois Régionaux,* institutions which are based on the old *congrégations* established by the French in Indochina. These units are headed by a chairman, chosen from among the Chinese community with government approval, whose job it is to collect taxes and in general administer the community for the authorities. The Chinese do not seem to be a closely integrated group in Laos, as they are in many parts of Southeast Asia. There are no barriers to their assimilation, and many marry Laotians, especially at the highest levels of society.[50] These alliances are now particularly sought after by the Chinese because of the recent legislation directed against alien-owned businesses.

The best estimates place Laos' Vietnamese population at 15,000 to 20,000, concentrated mainly in Vientiane, Paksé, and Savannakhet. Like the Chinese, the Vietnamese have their own administrative organizations and occupy important positions in commerce and service industries. Vietnamese were brought to Laos before the war in large numbers by the French to staff the middle and lower echelons of the colonial service; in 1943 they constituted as much as sixty percent of the populations of the provincial capitals. With the assumption by Laotians of more autonomy after the Second World War, however, over half of the Vietnamese, including those in government service, left Laos. Those who continue to make Laos their home, including now a few refugees from North Vietnam, find many

[50] See J. M. Halpern, *The Role of the Chinese in Lao Society* (P-2161; Santa Monica, Calif.: Rand, Dec. 15, 1960, rev. March 1, 1961).

obstacles to their assimilation, probably because of a traditional Laotian antipathy toward Vietnamese.

The ruling class, or elite, stems largely from the traditional Lao aristocracy and numbers around 2,000 persons, who hold most of the major political and nonpolitical (civil service and military) offices in the country. They are the descendants of the royal and quasi-royal families of Luang Prabang, Vientiane, Champassak, and Xieng Khouang provinces or commercial leaders in the towns, all of whom the French favored by maintaining the existing administrative structure.[51] Many maintain profitable business alliances with Chinese and Europeans; this is a mutually advantageous arrangement because the government has restrictions on alien-owned (especially Chinese) and operated businesses and because the arrangement gives a substantial economic base outside of the government to the elite, which has no other sources of income, such as extensive landholdings, on which to depend. Some of them have chosen military careers and today occupy the first and second echelons of the staff and line organizations of the royal army.

[51] This group includes the king and his immediate relatives; his cousins, Souvanna Phouma and Souphanouvong; the Somsaniths and Panyas (Luang Prabang); the Sananikones and Souvannavongs (Vientiane); the Nokams (Xieng Khouang); the Abhays, Voravongs, and Chounramanys, Prince Boun Oum and his nephew Sisouk na Champassak, the Phannareths, Visavongs, Insisiengmays, Suryadhays, and Sopsaisanas—all from the southern provinces—and perhaps a dozen others.

2

Dawn of the Laotian National Struggle

WILFRED G. BURCHETT *

A decisive battle was fought on March 21, 1946, at Thakhek on the Mekong, a strategic road junction where the main road leading west from Vietnam meets the main road leading north from Cambodia. The French used their planes to bomb the town, landing their first bombs in the crowded market place, and machine gunning the people as they fled. Thousands were killed within a few hours. After further bombing and shelling French infantry attacked. Souphanouvong personally commanded his troops in this decisive battle and was badly wounded. "The colonial troops behaved like savages," he said, "as our forces had to withdraw block by block, the enemy sacked the town and massacred every person they could find. Even little children were thrown by scores into the Mekong. The town was entirely wiped out, and scarcely a living person escaped. March 21, 1946 will always be remembered by us as a day to symbolise colonial barbarity." [. . .]

Souphanouvong's forces were badly decimated but he was able to withdraw part of them across the Mekong to Thailand—at that time with a government more sympathetic to fellow Asiatics engaged in an anti-colonial struggle. But the fight still continued: Pathet Lao forces elsewhere in the country resisted the French at every step. It was not until five months after

* From Wilfred G. Burchett, *Mekong Upstream* (Hanoi: Red River Publishing House, 1957), pp. 259–73. by permission Wilfred G. Burchett is an Australian journalist with two decades of experience reporting on the liberation movement in Southeast Asia. We have altered the spelling of a number of ethnic terms and names in this piece to conform to current usage—eds.

the Thakhek battle that the French had established control over the main towns and the roads which led to them. The provisional government also withdrew to Thailand and set itself up there as a government-in-exile, still with Phetsarath as Chief of State. . . .

After Souphanouvong had recovered from his wounds, he began with some of his most intimate supporters, summing up their successes and failures. Some members of the provisional government had already started to weaken. Not Souphanouvong, however. By this time the resistance war was already well under way in Vietnam. No attempts had been made to defend towns there except as delaying actions while men and materials were moved to bases in the rear. Ho Chi Minh had already announced plans for a protracted war of resistance based on the country-side. Souphanouvong and his supporters began to analyze the situation in their own country and quickly came to the conclusion that a mistake had been made in basing their revolution solely on the towns. They studied the rich heritage of revolutionary activities by the mountaineers and quickly saw that Laotian mountains and jungle and the redoutable tribespeople offered precious reserves for a long struggle. If one based resistance on the people, success was sure and the people meant all the people. Not just the urban intelligentsia but the peasants too; not just the Lao but the Lao Teng, Lao Som and all the others united in a solid front.

While other members of the provisional government discussed affairs in the teahouses of Bangkok, Souphanouvong began looking over his forces in Thailand educating and encouraging them for the difficult tasks ahead. He slipped back into Laos with all he could persuade to accompany him. Of the original provisional government, he was the only one to return. The others adopted a "wait and see" attitude. Souphanouvong found that the remnants of his armed forces had been carrying on as well as they could on their own. Isolated resistance bases existed. Loosely coordinate commands had even been set up over quite large areas, especially in the mountains along the frontiers with Vietnam. He found there were all sorts of allies only awaiting the chance to be organized.

There was Faydang for instance, the Lao Som leader. Faydang

was chief of a village atop a thousand meter high peak near Nong Et, in Xieng Khouang province, not far from the Vietnamese border. And he was a chief in the truest sense of the word. He was elected to lead his people in war and peace. On one occasion he had left his mountain peak to go to far distant Luang Prabang to demand of the king that he protect the interests of the Lao Som people and punish the agents who ravaged the region.

"It was in our area where the repression was the most severe," Faydang told me when I asked how he had come to join the resistance movement. "When the Japanese came we had hopes of something better, but they were just the same. Villages were destroyed, crops burned on the ground, our people massacred. The French came back and they carried on in the same way. They set up a post only about seven kilometers from our village," he continued. "Soldiers were sent all the time to pillage our people. They took everything, from rice and alcohol even to our buffalo. Our people were very poor but even the little they had was taken by the troops. Once they robbed us of our last grain of rice. I had to go down to the plains to buy rice for our people to eat. On my way back, I was arrested and even the rice I had bought was taken away. It was To Bi and To Jeu [two Lao Som chiefs who had collaborated with the French] who caused my arrest. They knew I hated the French. I escaped and went back to the village. The French sent troups to encircle us. With four of my friends and two boys, I slipped through the encirclement at night, into the jungle. We took our guns and crossbows with us, but did not shoot at the French. They shot at us and two of my friends were killed. We waited for the French to go, but they stayed, so we went off to a mountain close to the border and set up a base there. Soon after we arrived, the enemy sent a patrol of sixty troops commanded by two French officers after us. We set an ambush and waited till they came very close. We were only three adults and two boys, but we killed eight of them with our crossbows and the rest fled. This was our first victory. The French didn't like our poisoned arrows and left us alone for a time."

Faydang sent word back to his village as to where he was and what was happening. The whole village moved over to him and after that two neighboring villages. When the French came next time they ran into a veritable hornet's nest. Faydang himself is a noted hunter, expert with the flintlocks he makes himself, or the crossbow. He prefers the latter. "It is silent and it always kills," he said. "Even a scratch from one of our poisoned arrows always kills within a few minutes." I found his wife always accompanied him when he set his ambushes. A battle might last all day and even longer and often there was not time to have a sufficient stock of arrows on hand. Faydang's wife dug herself into the ground at a respectable distance behind her husband to allow him room for maneuvering. In the heat of the battle, she cut and shaped the bamboo arrows, fitted in the steel tips—and fired them from her own crossbow into the coil of hair which Faydang, as all Lao Som men, wears on the nape of his neck. He thus had a permanent stock of arrows in the natural quiver at the back of his head and only had to pluck them out, dip them into his little pot of poison and fire them into the enemy. He had to be very agile. No good staying behind one tree too long or he would attract the bullets of the enemy. Numerous of the Lao Som warriors were similarly served by their wives in battle. Faydang's private war against the French started as soon as the latter returned to Laos. In his remote mountains Faydang knew little about the Pathet Lao or the provisional government, but he did hear about the terrible battle of Thakhek.

"I heard there had been a great battle and that the towns-people, under a prince, had fought very bravely against the French," Faydang said. "I thought it would be very good if we could fight together against the same enemy. I went down to the plains myself and tried to find this prince. He had already left and was in Thailand. I sent him a message and the reply came back. 'Arouse the people. Create a strong organization. Later we will fight together.' So I returned to the mountains and began to organize all the Lao Som villages from our own base. The French attacked us many times, but each time they suffered bigger defeats. They sent in agents to offer me much money if I would join them. When that failed they sent in others to assassinate me. But those agents never returned.

"I visited village after village throughout our mountains and talked with the chiefs and the people. Everyone hated the French and was glad to know our plans to fight. Every village appointed organizers and formed scouts and defense corps."

All this meant long, patient work. It was the period between 1946–50 . . . when there was little military activity in Cambodia and Laos, the French concentrating on "pacification" and the resistance forces on organization. Faydang created the Lao Som Resistance League which included virtually every Lao Som village in the whole of Xieng Khouang province. They created such strong inter-village organizations and set up such formidable defenses, that the French and their agents—including the tax-collectors—scarcely dared set foot in the Lao Som areas.

Similar activity was going on all over the country. When Souphanouvong returned, he found the resistance bases set up after the Thakhek defeat by Nou Hac in the eastern mountains and by Thao Seum in the western districts were solidly established. From these bases, he set up a network of guerrilla bases and laid the groundwork for a united national struggle which would encompass all elements of the population. . . .

In August 1950, something quite unique in all Laotian history took place. It was possible only by the patient, difficult work of leaders and patriots like Souphanouvong, Faydang, Sithone (who had been organizing the Lao Teng as Faydang had been the Lao Som), Nou Hac, Thao Seum, Chau Suk Vong Sak— who had been organizing the Lao under the very noses of the French in Vientiane province and others. A congress was held attended by delegates from all nationalities and all sections of the population. Nothing of the sort had ever been dreamed of before. Souphanouvong traced the history of previous insurrections and of the 1945 uprising. He presented his ideas for a united movement of all the peoples. Faydang had been chosen by the Lao Som people as their delegate, Sithone by the Lao Teng. All the other leading minorities were represented. It was unanimously agreed to create the Neo Lao Issara, or National United Front, and to set up a new government of national resistance. Souphanouvong was unanimously chosen as President of the front and Prime Minister of the new government. Sithone and Faydang also became ministers. From that moment, the struggle of the Laotian people entered a new phase.

Town and countryside were as one, the Lao Teng "slaves" and the Lao were allies and comrades on a basis of complete equality, "minority" and "majority" peoples were forged into a single, real national entity. The provisional government elected was one which really represented the varied national interests and was of a very different quality to that set up in August 1945.

"When the program of the front was distributed among our Lao Som people," Faydang continued, "they saw it answered their deepest wishes. Equality for all races. Nobody had ever spoken of this before. A united fight against the French. We had never thought it possible. Abolition of unjust taxes. The French had burned and plundered our villages, massacred our people, taken our women in collecting taxes in the past. Of course there were difficulties. We could not immediately improve the lives of the people. But it was not long before the people could see the benefits of our alliance with the Lao and others. They felt the efforts made by the front and government to improve their lives. In place of our poisoned arrows and flintlocks we began to get some modern arms, some automatics and light machine guns. Great efforts were made to get salt to our villages. The opium tax was abolished and other taxes lightened. We formed women's associations and a youth movement. At first membership was slow. Each village is on an isolated mountain top and it was difficult to get people together. But after a few months people saw this was a very good thing and they joined up with great enthusiasm. From the self-defense corps we set up guerrilla bases, first of all in our own province of Xieng Khouang and then in the neighboring ones. We have 40,000 Lao Som in our province alone and later on we were able to form whole Lao Som companies from our guerrilla bases and attach them to the regular Pathet Lao forces formed by Souphanouvong.

"The political level of our people was raised as they got together and talked things over. They could clearly see who were their enemies and who were their friends." And as it was with the Lao Som, so it was with all the minority peoples. Relations between themselves and with the Lao were as between members of one family. Consolidation of forces within the country had its counterpart the following year when Neo Issara front delegates, headed by Souphanouvong, took part with delegates of the Vietminh and Khmer Issarek to form the alliance between the peoples of Vietnam, Cambodia and Laos and coordinate their fight till final victory."

Who were the recruits among the ordinary people and why did they join? They came from very different strata of the population. Vikham, for instance, whom I met on one of the Pathet Lao fronts in the jungles of Sam Neua is a Lao from Vientiane. He was a fairly well-to-do peasant. In Laos, the amount of land one owns is usually calculated on how many kilograms of seed rice are necessary to sow it. He had "240 kilograms of land" as he expressed it. "But it only meant," he said, "that the more land you had, the more buffalo you had, the more you were exploited. I had to pay 300 piastres (about ten dollars) as head tax, taxes for the fields and buffalo and plough. I had to pay two kilograms of opium as tax and twenty four kilograms of cotton. We didn't grow opium in our area, so I had to sell rice to buy the opium. Every year I had to give fifteen days to *corvée* for the French, another eight days as a transport coolie and at least five days for the village chief. I had to give presents to the chief twice a year and if I managed to kill a deer or some other game, the best half had to go to him.

"I had heard of the Issara months before I saw them. Then some cadres came to our village and I secretly helped them to get food. A friend warned me the French knew about me and I would be arrested. I fled and joined a guerrilla group. We had flintlocks and crossbows and carried out some ambushes. Later I went back to a village as a cadre, I was elected to the village committee, and then on to the district committee of Lao Issara.

"In 1952, I was arrested. The French buried me in a hole in the ground with only my head above the soil. They left me there for seven days and eight nights. Then I was taken out and whipped till I lost consciousness. After that they tortured me with electricity. When I fainted, they threw water on my face and started questioning me. They wanted to know about our organization, where the guerrillas were, who were the leaders, where we got our arms and supplies. I told them nothing and they kept torturing me with electricity and I kept fainting. I don't know how many times I was tortured on that first day of questioning."

Later, Vikham, a serious, slow-spoken man of thirty-two years when I met him, a typical peasant from the plains, was flung into jail and put to work on breaking stones. The prisoners were often marched outside the jail to work on roads and fortifications and he began to make contact with the population. They gave him food and he learned from them that there were some other Issara members in prison. He contacted them and they soon built up an organization. Each member was given the task of recruiting two others. Because of his contacts outside the prison, Vikham was allotted himself the job of organizing escapes. On six different occasions, he organized the escape of a total of ninety prisoners. The sixth time a group of fifty killed two guards, wounded a third and grabbed twelve rifles in their break-out.

"The French never suspected me," Vikham said, "I was regarded as a quiet, model prisoner. After the big break-out, I was given the job of burying the dead. I talked with the sentry and said he should join us. He refused, so I killed him with my spade and took his rifle and fled. That was October, 1953, and I've been with the regular Pathet Lao forces ever since."

A very different type was Chan Keo, a Lao Teng and also from Vientiane province, a swarthy mountaineer of forty years, with hollow cheeks but muscular arms and legs and an expression of granite-like determination. "I hated the imperialists ever since I could think," he said. "From childhood, I knew the only way to liberate ourselves is to fight. One day my father told me about Ong Keo and Kommadam. It sounded like a legend. His country was very far from our village but I made up my mind to join Kommadam. But it was just the moment when he was killed. I lost all hope then. In our village we had to go on *corvée*, three times a year, for at least fifteen days each time. We got no pay at all and had to provide our own food. At first I thought when the Japanese came it would be better. But it was the same. Only for the few months after we had our own government in 1945 it was better. Then the French came back and things were worse than ever. I remembered Kommadam's words. 'Don't become soldiers of the enemy! Don't go as labor slaves for the French! Oppose *corvée!*' My father had told me of this. I started talking with the rest of our villagers. Once when the French sent their agents to collect us for *corvée,* we refused. Six hundred of us. They sent puppet troops to the village to take me, because they knew I was the organizer. I was tied up to a post for twenty-four hours and then they started to whip me, in front of everybody. I was whipped till only the ropes stopped me from falling down.

"In those days there was nothing we could do. I lost hope again. But a few years later when Lao Issara cadres came to our village, there were no doubts as to what we should do. Everyone supported it. Many of us asked only for arms and a target. Since then life has changed for me. I've been able to kill the enemy but also to study. I'm treated as an equal by everybody. I've learned a lot and one day will take everything I've learned back to my village and help our people to build a different life." Chan Keo was a natural people's leader.

It was typical that those who had been most oppressed under the colonialist-feudal regime should be the most enthusiastic supporters of Lao Issara. The Lao Teng had suffered most and their women had suffered still more from the triple oppression of the feudal-colonialist regime, the slave status of their people in relation to the Lao and their own inferior backward status within the community as females. It was amazing to see how people leaped centuries forward through even a slight opening in the jungle gloom of feudalism-*cum*-imperialism which had oppressed them for generations.

Nang Phet was a twenty-year-old girl when I met her in a cadres' school in northern Laos in late 1955. She is a lovely girl with coal black eyes, a cherry-brown face and mischievous smile. With her thick, wavy hair and perfect pearls of teeth, she would be considered a beauty in any land. For five years she had been an outstanding veteran fighter.

"I worked in the 'ray' like the other children of our village," she said. "We helped cut the small brushwood and burn it. We carried water and set traps for squirrels and went to the markets to sell fruits and bring back goods from the plains. In 1950, the enemy came to our village because we had not paid some taxes. They burned everything, including our home. From that moment, I knew that unless we smashed the French, we could never have any happiness. I had heard there were Issara guerrillas in our mountains so I set out to find them. At first they didn't want to take me. I was very young—and a girl—they said. But I told them all that had happened in our village and they agreed to accept me. This was the happiest moment of my life," she said with one of her rich smiles.

"I was given the task of finding out everything possible about an enemy post not very far from my own village. I had some relatives there who had been deceived by the enemy into entering the army. They were very ashamed of this when I explained things to them and they agreed to help. One cousin in particular from the very first told me everything about troop movements; where the French intended to carry out 'pacification' operations and when. I got to know every target of their movements and which tracks they intended to take from one village to another, how many buffalo and pigs they intended to grab, how much rice and alcohol. Everything. Our guerrillas were able to set very successful ambushes and the villages were able to hide their buffalo and pigs and rice in the jungle. The French arrived after lots of them had been killed and wounded and found nothing. The people thought the Lao Issara were wonderful."

I asked if she took part in the actions and she explained that the guerrillas never had enough arms, but that she helped lay the traps and fed arrows and bullets to those who fired them.

"After some months," she continued, "I had won over three cousins and they had won over five more of their friends in the fort. I proposed to our guerrillas to set a really big trap. And they agreed.

"My cousins introduced me to the French lieutenant and I pretended to be very friendly with him. One day we arranged a rendezvous with him and some non-commissioned officers with myself and some of my girl friends. We arranged to meet outside the fort, in town. As soon as the lieutenant had left, my cousins locked up the armory inside the post. Then our unit attacked. The troops rushed to get their arms but they were all locked up. In a few minutes the fort was in our hands. Thirty soldiers were killed and ninety-seven captured. My friends and

I captured the lieutenant and the others. About twenty soldiers escaped, but we captured all the arms and six pouches stuffed with money. This was our biggest coup."

Later her guerrilla unit became part of the regular Pathet Lao forces. Nang Phet became a cadre at parish and then at district level. She learned to read and write not only the script of her own people but also that of the Lao. She turned out to be an excellent propagandist and became a member of a mobile educational team. At the age of twenty, Nang Phet is already a veteran cadre who has a splendid future ahead of her in service to the Lao Teng and the Laotian people.

The few examples cited above could be multiplied by thousands and tens of thousands. They illustrate something of the quality of those who joined the Pathet Lao and the background and forces which impelled them into the movement. They illustrate also the perspectives which the Lao Issara movement offered for the first time in history to the most oppressed strata of Laotian society. These were the forces on which the struggle for real independence for the Laotian nation was to be based.

3

Cambodia: Social and Historical Background

ROGER M. SMITH *

The Kingdom of Cambodia is what remains today of the once powerful Khmer empire, which at its height in the twelfth and thirteenth centuries extended throughout a large part of that area of Southeast Asia now occupied by Cambodia, Laos, Thailand, and Vietnam. Situated between the tenth and fifteenth north parallels in the southwest portion of the Indochina Peninsula, Cambodia is about the size of the state of Missouri and is inhabited by nearly six million people. It forms a gigantic, fertile basin for the lower Mekong River and is the site of the largest lake in Southeast Asia, the Tonle Sap. Nearly one-tenth of its 66,000 square miles is water, a proportion which more than doubles during the monsoon rains. Its broad alluvial expanse is surrounded by densely forested hills and mountain chains: the Elephant and Cardamom mountains in the west and the Dangrek chain in the north, which form Cambodia's frontier with Thailand and Laos, and the Annamese cordillera in the east and northeast, beyond which is Vietnam. To its south is the Gulf of Siam.

EARLY HISTORY

The earliest of the states from which the Kingdom of Cambodia evolved and about which historical evidence is available was Funan, the Kingdom of the Mountain, which was probably

* Roger M. Smith, "Laos," George McT. Kahin, ed., *Governments and Politics of Southeast Asia*, 2nd ed. (Ithaca: Cornell University Press, 1964), pp. 595–604, 632–38.

established before the first century A.D.[1] With its capital located
in the modern province of Prey Veng, in southeast Cambodia,
Funan not only exercised dominion over the lower valleys of
the Mekong River, the area around the Tonle Sap, and a part
of the Mekong delta region, but also commanded vassalage from
smaller states in northern Cambodia, southern Thailand and
Laos, and the northern portion of the Malay Peninsula. Asian
merchants and diplomats, whose quest for spices brought them
to the area, discovered there a society which engaged in wet
rice cultivation and which had a fairly well developed system
of authority based on the controlled distribution of water and
a religious mythology involving water spirits and sacred mountains.

The dominion exercised by Funan over its vassals declined
in the early sixth century when frequent civil wars and dynastic
quarrels disrupted its internal stability. By the middle of the
century, it had been replaced as the dominant power on the
Indochina Peninsula by Chenla, a state located in what is now
the southern part of Laos, which in a successful revolt cast off
centuries of Funanese tutelage and in turn came to exercise
suzerainty over Funan. During the next 300 years the people of
Chenla, who like the people of Funan were Khmers, conquered central and upper Laos and brought western Cambodia
and southern Thailand under their direct rule.

Quarrels among members of the monarchy in the eighth century split the Chenla empire into rival northern and southern
centers of power—called by French scholars *T'chen-la de terre*
and *T'chen-la de l'eau*—with capitals in the present-day Cambodian provinces of Kompong Thom and Takeo. During the next
hundred years, while the northern portion seems to have maintained a relatively stable existence, the southern portion was

[1] Much of this section is based upon Georges Coedès, *Les états
hindouisés d'Indochine et d'Indonésie* (Paris: E. de Boccard, 1948).
See also E. Aymonier, *Le Cambodge* (3 vols.; Paris: E. Leroux, 1900-
04); L. Palmer Briggs, *The Ancient Khmer Empire* (Transactions of
the American Philosophical Society, n.s., vol. IV, pt. 1; Philadelphia:
American Philosophical Society, 1951); D. G. E. Hall, *A History of
Southeast Asia* (London: Macmillan, 1955); A. Leclère, *Histoire du
Cambodge* (Paris: P. Geuthner, 1914); G. Maspéro, *L'empire khmèr*
(Phnompenh: Imprimerie du Protectorat, 1904); J. Moura, *Le royaume
du Cambodge* (2 vols.; Paris: Leroux, 1883).

further split asunder as rival dynasties strove for supremacy, a condition which rendered it particularly vulnerable to attacks by pirates and to the establishment of suzerainty over it in the late eighth century by the Sailendra dynasty of Java. It was not until Jayavarman II ascended the throne of *T'chen-la de l'eau* that the Javanese suzerainty was cast off in 802 and the reunification of the Khmers undertaken. Under his reign, the Khmer empire was founded. Jayavarman II eventually moved his capital from southeastern Kompong Cham to the plain of Siem Reap, and from there, during the next 550 years, he and his successors extended the borders of the empire into northern Laos, to the South China Sea in the east and southeast, and to the Bay of Bengal in the west. The empire's history is also a record of the erection of the Angkor complex of magnificent temple-palaces and of the construction of an extensive hydraulic network, which controlled the distribution and conservation of water for the mainstay of the economy, rice.

During the first millennium A.D., Khmer culture was subjected to an almost continuous inflow of Indian ideas and practices relating to royalty, law, and religious mythology. Perhaps the most influential of these among the Khmer kings were notions on the organization of the state and the religious justification of kingly rule. As they were assimilated and modified, they reached their apogee in the politico-religious concept of the devaraja, or god-king, which was adopted by Jayavarman II.

According to the concept of the devaraja, the state was a manifestation of the universe and its capital was the earthly symbol of the city of heaven.[2] As the cult was practiced in the Khmer empire, a divine king served as the intermediary between the gods, especially those controlling water and the fertility of the soil, and the social order. Among members of the monarchy and the aristocracy, the devaraja cult centered on the worship of a royal linga, which embodied the king's sacred personality as transmitted to him by the gods through the medium of Brahman

[2] For details of this symbolism, see Georges Coedès, *Pour mieux comprendre Angkor* (2d ed.; Paris: A. Maisonneuve, 1948), ch. v, and Bernard P. Groslier, with the collaboration of C. R. Boxer, *Angkor et le Cambodge au XVIe siècle d'après les sources portugaises et espagnoles* (Annales du Musée Guimet, Bibliothèque d'Etudes, vol. LXIII; Paris: Presses Universitaires de France, 1958), ch. iv.

priests. The prosperity of the empire was believed to be closely linked with the worship of the linga, and thus the great temples, which were the glory of the empire, were built by each king as sanctuaries for it.

For the peasants, the court was a distant structure with which they could scarcely identify.[3] If the world of the monarchy and the aristocracy had any meaning for the people, it was probably in its role as the ultimate source of authority and as the preserver of peace and order. The kings justified their ability to perform these tasks through the prestige of unbroken dynastic rule and the claim that the political order was an extension and application of the cosmic order. But in terms that were probably more meaningful to the people, authority was justified by the effective management of the extensive hydraulic system,[4] which distributed and conserved water for agriculture, and the maintenance of a standing army to defend the peace of the country. Unfortunately massive temple-building programs and expansionist wars, which necessitated the organization of corvées and the imposition of heavy taxes upon the peasantry, soon became the major preoccupation of the rulers.[5] With the consequent neglect of the hydraulic system and the diversion of manpower from agriculture to construction programs and military campaigns, the economic strength of the nation declined. About the mid-twelfth

[3] Croslier, *Angkor et le Cambodge,* pp. 155–64.

[4] The choice of city sites by the Khmer kings was dictated by the needs of the economy. The plain of Siem Reap, where Angkor is located, is an area of some five million hectares, and it had the two essential ingredients of wet rice culture: rich and flat land and water. The main problem (as it still is in Cambodia) was the disposition of water. It rained heavily four months of the year, but the water quickly ran off to the rivers and lake, leaving the people without adequate supplies for the rest of the year. The solution to this problem was found in the construction of a hydraulic network. Hundreds of large reservoirs and artificial lakes were built, including, for example, the Bari Occidental, which was five miles by 1.5 miles in area and held an estimated thirty million cubic meters of water. Water was distributed by a network of canals and ditches as needed by the system. According to one observer of the twelfth century, as many as four harvests a year were produced as a result. See Paul Pelliot, trans. and ed., *Mémoires sur les coutumes du Cambodge de Tcheou Ta-kouan* (Paris: A. Maisonneuve, 1951), p. 24.

[5] Groslier, *Angkor et le Cambodge,* pp. 118–21; Briggs, *Ancient Khmer Empire,* pp. 258–61.

century, an exploited peasantry began to express its discontent in a prolonged series of revolts.

Under the reign of Suryavarman II (1112–ca.1150), the empire's domain was extended by a series of successful wars against the Kingdom of Champa, which controlled the area now known as South Vietnam, against the Annamese, and against peoples living as far westward as the region between the Salween and Irrawaddy rivers in Burma. Suryavarman II has gone down in history also as the builder of Angkor Wat, which is not only the largest religious building in the world but also the greatest single work of architecture in Southeast Asia. His reign was followed by thirty years of dynastic quarrels and a war with marauding Chams, who in 1177 destroyed the city of Angkor. The invaders were finally pushed back and Champa was again defeated, this time by the armies of Jayavarman VII (1181–ca.1215), under whom the empire's domain reached its greatest expansion. To him is attributed the Angkor Thom complex with its ten miles of walls, the many-towered Bayon, and countless other temples.

With the passing of Jayavarman VII in the early thirteenth century, Khmer power began to wane. At least four factors contributed to the eventual disappearance of the empire. First among these was the rebellion of the people against the demands of the kings for forced labor and military campaigns. Second, as an increasingly heavy labor and military burden was placed upon the people, the hydraulic system was neglected, and thus the empire's economic strength was weakened. Third, the arrival of a new religious doctrine helped to turn the tide against the old regime: Theravada Buddhism, which was introduced into the empire at the end of the twelfth century, preached the salvation of the individual through his own efforts. Thus there was more to recommend it to the people than a Hindu metaphysics fostering an aristocracy whose opulence was based upon the virtual slavery of the masses. Fourth, these changes took place at about the same time as the growth of power and influence of the Thai peoples who, in the twelfth and thirteenth centuries, began to replace Khmer authority in the Menam (Chao Phraya) basin and along the upper Mekong River. It was in the face of these events that the way was laid open to the sack of Angkor by the Thais in 1432 and the subsequent collapse of the empire. Cambodia then entered upon a troubled and unhappy epoch from which it was not to emerge until the French intervention in the mid-nineteenth century.

FRENCH INTERVENTION AND COLONIAL RULE

During the 400 years following the fall of the Khmer empire, Cambodia was beset from within by a long series of dynastic rivalries and subjected from without to encroachments by Siam and Annam. Only by adroit diplomatic maneuvering was Cambodia able to maintain its independence, but at a cost of rendering vassalage to both Siam and Annam and of sacrificing provinces along its northern frontier and in Cochinchina.[6] When, in the mid-nineteenth century, France embarked upon its program of colonial expansion in Asia, King Ang Duong was striving to rehabilitate Cambodia, which had only recently emerged from nearly a decade of Annamese colonial rule and a devastating but inconclusive Siam-Annam war fought on its soil. Fearing that upon his death these neighbors would seek to partition Cambodia between them, Ang Duong appealed to Napoleon III for assistance.[7] His effort, however, was foiled by Siam, which threatened reprisals if negotiations were entered into with Napoleon's ambassador. During 1857–59, France intervened in Annam to protect French Jesuit missionaries and to establish a commercial foothold on the Indochina Peninsula and in the process released Cambodia from Annamese pressures; Ang Duong made another attempt to establish relations with France, but he died before an accord could be concluded.

His efforts bore fruit posthumously in 1863 when, following

[6] Siamese tutelage was imposed upon Cambodia in 1594. In 1673 Ang Non ascended to the Cambodian throne with Annamese support. Thereafter Annam, in competition with Siam, sought to exercise influence over Cambodia and began to colonize the provinces of Prey Kôr (Saigon), Kâmpéâp Srêkatrey (Bien Hoà), and Baria in the Mekong delta. These areas were officially annexed by Annam in the eighteenth century—eds.

[7] See R. Stanley Thomson, "The Establishment of the French Protectorate over Cambodia," *Far Eastern Quarterly,* IV, no. 4 (Aug. 1945), pp. 313–40, and "Siam and France, 1863–70," *ibid.,* V, no. 1 (Nov. 1945), pp. 28–46.

the consolidation of its position in Cochinchina, France offered Ang Duong's son, Norodom, its protection against external attacks and internal strife. This was an attractive offer on both counts, for Norodom's brother, Sivotha, coveted the throne for himself and was preparing to renew the revolutionary activity which had provoked the reentry of Siamese soldiers into Cambodia in 1861–62, and it would enable Norodom to remove Cambodia from under Siamese tutelage. In return, Norodom had only to permit Frenchmen to settle in Cambodia, to grant them rights to exploit the land, to bring in goods free of duty, and to allow the establishment of separate courts for foreigners. Norodom accepted the French offer. While the treaty was undergoing ratification in Paris, however, Siam threatened to invade Cambodia and to retain the royal insignia without which he was not the king in the eyes of the people.[8] He was thus forced to sign a secret agreement with Siam by which he recognized its suzerainty and ceded the northern provinces which Siam then occupied: Siem Reap, Battambang, and parts of Kompong Thom and Stung Treng. But Siam's triumph was short-lived: a clever combination of military bluff and diplomatic persuasion exercised by the French in Bangkok and Cambodia induced the Siamese to return the royal insignia. Norodom's crown was thus obtained for him by France and he was, in fact, crowned by the new French *résident* in 1864. But it was not until 1867 that France succeeded in persuading Siam to renounce its suzerainty over Cambodia. In return, France, acting on Cambodia's behalf, abandoned claims to Battambang and Siem Reap; King Norodom protested this action in vain, for the French at the time considered it a good bargain.[9]

[8] In 1847 Siam and Annam agreed to exercise joint suzerainty over Cambodia, but Siam retained its right to select and crown Cambodia's kings. The royal insignia had been in Bangkok since Norodom's brief exile there in 1861, and Norodom had not yet been crowned when France made its offer.

[9] France wished to consolidate its position on the peninsula and did not want to risk the Siamese government's falling more under British influence. The *faux pas* was rectified forty years later when Siamese violation of other treaties led France to reopen the issue. In return for concessions along the Mekong River, Siam abandoned its claims in Cambodia by conventions signed in 1902, 1904, and 1907. The northern provinces were again annexed by Siam at the beginning of the Second World War but were returned after the war.

The French protectorate was not uncontested within Cambodia. Revolts, led by a self-proclaimed prince named Pukoumbo, broke out in 1866-7, and Prince Sivotha remained a constant threat to Norodom until the late 1870's. Franco-Cambodian troops, some of which were under the command of another of the king's brothers, Prince Sisowath, were able to quell the rebellions. Following Pukoumbo's defeat in 1867, France attempted to introduce much-needed reform in the poorly organized and corrupt Cambodian administration. These attempts further alienated Norodom, who continued to rue the loss of the northern provinces. The French were able to overcome the king's opposition to their modifications only by threatening in 1877 to withdraw and leave Norodom to the mercy of Sivotha, who was then embarking upon still another rebellion. But after Sivotha's defeat, France became preoccupied with events in Tonkin, and the reforms fell into disuse. Norodom began to resume full control over Cambodia. When, in 1884, he refused to participate in a customs union with Cochinchina and Annam, the Governor General of Cochinchina, Charles Thomson, reasserted France's dominance. On June 17, 1884, Thomson arrived in Phnompenh from Saigon with a contingent of French troops and several gunboats. With these placed in strategic positions around the royal palace, Thomson coerced Norodom into signing the convention which made Cambodia a *de facto* colony of France.[10]

France's primary interest in Cambodia was defensive. Once it had gained control over the rich coastal area of the peninsula, which is today Vietnam, it needed to control Cambodia in order to prevent Siam, and possibly England also, from challenging its new acquisition. Its principal activity in Cambodia, therefore, was directed toward the maintenance of law and order;

[10] According to one account of Thomson's meeting with Norodom, Kol de Monteiro, a descendant of a Portuguese adventurer who was the king's interpreter, told the king, "Sire, this is not a convention which is proposed to Your Majesty; it is an abdication." See Paul Collard, *Cambodge et Cambodgiennes* (Paris: Société d'Editions Géographiques, Maritimes et Coloniales, 1925), p. 111. (This translation and others in this section were made by the author.) See also Protectorat du Cambodge, *Recueil des actes du gouvernement cambodgien* (Saigon, 1920), I, 63-5, for the text of the treaty.

only secondarily was it interested in the development of natural or human resources.

The administration of colonial Cambodia was directed by a skeleton hierarchy of French *résidents* and small staffs, which were placed in key positions throughout the country.[11] A centralized and highly bureaucratic Cambodian administration was maintained in existence by the French,[12] but its top officials were merely figureheads. To the French, the Cambodians in general appeared to be incapable of serving in administrative capacities. They were relegated to minor government positions which were under strict supervision by the *résidents;* at the more important operating levels of government, and especially in the police, the French preferred to utilize Hanoi and Saigon trained Vietnamese, in whose competence they expressed more faith.

The French did little to train Cambodians to fill positions of responsibility and trust. A School of Administration, created in 1917, graduated several score of Cambodian administrators, but it was not until after 1936 that they were used at any but the lowest levels of government. This movement to associate Cambodians with direct responsibility, however, barely got under way before the Second World War brought it to an abrupt halt. Education was not otherwise encouraged. It did not suit the French purpose to have an educated elite which might demand government reform or, worse, independence. Thus by 1939 only four students (in a population estimated at slightly over three million) had been graduated from a senior high school established in 1935. Others in search of higher education were usually sent to high schools in Hanoi or Saigon. Only a very few, sons of royal and aristocratic families, managed to go to French universities. Education was left primarily to Buddhist wat and community supported schools, of which there were 256 providing three years of primary instruction to 9,645 children in 1931.[13] State-run primary schools, in which

---

[11] For details of the colonial administration, see René Morizon, *Monographie du Cambodge* (Hanoi: Imprimerie d'Extrême-Orient, 1931), pp. 51–5, and A. Silvestre, *Le Cambodge administratif* (Phnompenh, 1924), pp. 42–54.

[12] Protectorat du Cambodge, *Recueil des actes,* pp. 83–4, 131–5.

[13] Morizon, *Monographie du Cambodge,* pp. 180–2.

French was the language of instruction, numbered 111, with 10,691 students, in the same year.[14] In 1941, there were 192 primary schools, with 22,280 pupils, a total of 845 "modernized" Buddhist wat schools were providing instruction for 35,834 pupils; and Cambodia's only secondary school, the *Lycée* Sisowath, had 537 students.[15]

Cambodians did not enjoy any meaningful participation in the affairs of their country. Coincident with their territorial reorganization of Cambodia during 1919–25, the French set up a system of townships (khums), which included restricted popular elections for ruling councils.[16] However, those who were "elected" were, in fact, designated by the colonial officials.[17] Educated poorly, if at all, they had little conception of their duties. The French innovation served only to increase their social prestige and power among· a gullible people rather than to inculcate ideas of responsibility. Likewise, provincial assemblies and a National Assembly, created as consultative bodies for the French *résidents,* were nothing more than rubber stamps for French action.[18] They were all suspended upon the outbreak of the Second World War.

The institution of the monarchy was supported and encouraged in the eyes of the people, and as a result it continues today to be a key factor in the country's stability and unity. But at that time, the French were exploiting the loyalty which the crown commanded from the people, for as long as the people owed allegiance to the king and he was controlled by the

[14] *L'enseignement au Cambodge* (Phnompenh, 1958), pp. 1–2.
[15] Charles Bilodeau, "Compulsory Education in Cambodia," in Charles Bilodeau, Somlith Pathammavong, and Lê Quang Hông, *Compulsory Education in Cambodia, Laos, and Viet-Nam* (Studies on Compulsory Education, no. xiv; Paris: UNESCO, 1955), p. 67.
[16] See Protectorat du Cambodge, *Organisation de la commune* cambodgienne (Phnompenh, 1919), and André Homont, "La commune cambodgienne," *Annales de la Faculté de Droit et des Sciences Economiques de Phnompenh,* III (1961), 7–123.
[17] See Roger Pinto, *Aspects de l'évolution gouvernementale de l'Indochine française* (Paris: Librairie de Recueil Sirey, 1946), p. 38, and M. de Lens, *Le mékhum dans l'administration cambodgienne* (Pnompenh, 1939).
[18] See Silvestre, *Le Cambodge Administratif,* pp. 42–54, and A. Pannetier, *Notes cambodgiennes: Au coeur du pays khmer* (Paris Payot et C¹ᵉ, 1921).

French, then France could govern with a minimum expenditure of money and effort. As far as the people were concerned, the king exercised his traditional powers of lawmaking, directed Cambodian administration, supervised the Buddhist hierarchy, and was responsible for their well-being. They were not aware that all of his acts were subject to the approval of the *Résident Supérieur,* whose role was facilitated by his control of the Cambodian Council of Ministers and by the fact that the provincial representatives of the king were employees of the *résidents.*

Further control over the monarchy was obtained by manipulating succession to the throne. Under ordinary circumstances, the king would designate his own successor, or, failing in that, a new king would be chosen by the King's High Council. But when Norodom died in 1904, the French forced the passing over of his sons in order to reward the loyalty of his brother, Sisowath, who had helped the French to put down several rebellions. Sisowath was succeeded by his son, Monivong, in 1927. When the latter died in 1941, France was faced with a difficult decision, for Monivong's son, Monireth, appeared to be too independent and independence-minded at a time when France was beset with defeat in Europe and Japanese encroachments upon Indochina. Thus it was that Norodom Sihanouk, a great-grandson of King Norodom then attending high school in Saigon, was elevated to the throne.[19] He was thought to be weak and accommodating, but in this appraisal the French were later to discover that they had been badly mistaken.[20]

In its administration of the Indochinese Union, France revealed that the eastern states, that is, Cochinchina, Annam, and Tonkin, were more important to it than Cambodia. Much

[19] The French justified their decision by pointing to a quarrel between the Norodom and Sisowath branches of the royal family over the throne and noting that Sihanouk, an offspring of both sides, would help to reconcile the dispute. See J. Decoux, *A la barre de l'Indochine: Histoire de mon gouvernement général, 1940–1945* (Paris: Plon, 1949), pp. 285–6. It must have been well known to the French, however, that Monireth was also the offspring of both branches. See Princess Yukanthor, "Personalité de S. M. Norodom Suramarit," *France-Asie* (Saigon), XII, no. 113 (Oct. 1955), pp. 242–7.

[20] For interpretive discussions of Sihanouk's rule see Selection 5, and Part IV, especially Selections 17 and 19, in this volume which continue the historical narrative—eds.

of the revenue from Cambodia was channeled to support public services in Cochinchina. Customs and monetary offices did not exist. All foreign trade was transshipped at Saigon and financed and controlled from there. The extensive road and rail network built by the French in Cambodia was designed to bring the protectorate closer to Cochinchina, especially in order to facilitate the shipment of rice, rubber, and other agricultural goods to Saigon.

THE ECONOMY

Cambodia is dominated by one city, Phnompenh, and one industry, the government. Phnompenh is the center of Cambodia's financial and economic interests. It is on the capital that the country's transportation network converges and, until the recent development of a seaport at Sihanoukville, its position at the confluence of the Mekong and Bassac rivers made it Cambodia's gateway to international trade. A city of nearly 500,000 people, Phnompenh is the seat of Cambodia's oldest and most revered institutions, the monarchy and Buddhism, and it is also the center of higher education and other social and cultural activities. But if Phnompenh is the pivot of Cambodia's political and economic power and of its tradition and modern institutions, the nation depends on the countryside for its livelihood.

Cambodia is essentially an agricultural country whose major products include rice, rubber, fish, and timber. Rice is the mainstay of Cambodian economy and in times of good harvest is the major export commodity. Of some 28,000 square miles of arable land, approximately 7,000 square miles, or 4,480,000 acres, are under regular cultivation; of these, about three million acres are devoted to rice. Although rice yields in Cambodia are among the lowest in the world—about .5 metric ton or less per acre, owing to outmoded cultivation techniques—there has almost always been an exportable surplus. Unmilled rice production for the 1962–63 crop year was estimated at 1,600,000 metric tons, which was an average crop. Because of abnormally heavy rains, however, exports of milled rice and rice products in 1962 were limited to 181,000 metric tons.[21]

About eighty percent of Cambodia's estimated population of 5,800,000 earn their livelihood from the land. The farm population lives in small, nearly self-sufficient villages, which are usually surrounded by rice fields or are located along river banks.[22] Farming is chiefly a family enterprise, with five to six persons per family working an average landholding of about five hectares. The size of the farm is generally limited to the area a family can work with water buffalo or cattle as power and with simple implements. Rice cultivation occupies the farmers' attention for six to eight months of the year. During this period, monsoon rains and floodwaters provide needed moisture and fertilization; irrigation is uncommon, as is the use of other methods of modern agricultural technology. There is almost no land tenure problem as each family owns its land. The main problem for the Cambodian farmer has been the lack of adequate credit to carry on his operations. Excessive interest rates and the inability of the farmers to accumulate their own operating capital have frequently put the control of crop sales into the hands of moneylenders, the greater majority of whom are Chinese. The latter are often also the rice brokers, and thus repayment of loans is usually in produce and at the lowest market price. The creation of the *Office Royal de Coopération* in 1956 was designed to combat this problem, but it has not yet resulted in any major changes in the pattern of Cambodia's farm economy.

Rubber constitutes the second major agricultural crop. Thir-

[21] See *L'œuvre du Sangkum Reastr Niyum: Bilan de décembre 1962 à juin 1963, présenté au XVe Congrès national* (Phnompenh: Imprimerie du Ministère de l'Information, 1963), pp. 35, 63. For information on previous years' production and exports, see Royaume du Cambodge, Ministère du Plan, *Annuaire statistique rétrospectif du Cambodge, 1937–57* (Phnompenh, June 1958), pp. 35, 122, and Royaume du Cambodge, Direction de la Statistique et des Etudes Economiques, Bulletin Mensuel de Statistique (Phnompenh), no. 7 (July 1962), p. 22.

[22] On Cambodia's peasantry generally, see Jean Delvert, *Le payson cambodgien* (Paris: Mouton, 1961). See also G. Monod, *Le Cambodgien* (Paris: Editions Larose: 1931).

teen plantations, most of them under the control of French interests which established the industry in Cambodia in the 1920's, cover an area of nearly 93,000 acres, mainly in the province of Kompong Cham. Soil and climatic conditions have been found suitable for the planting of rubber in other areas, and the government is currently promoting the creation of privately owned Cambodian estates and a small-holder rubber program for individual farmers. Current production is over 40,000 tons annually, most of which is shipped to the United States in the form of smoked, crepe, and latex rubber. Among other crops are corn, soya and green beans, palm sugar, oleaginous plants, pepper, cotton, tobacco, jute, and kapok.[23]

Fish products are another source of considerable wealth. Cambodia's rivers, streams, the Tonle Sap, its coast line, and even the smallest rice paddy abound with fish. The fresh-water catch is estimated at between 130,000 and 150,000 tons annually; the marine catch amounts to some 10,000 tons. Domestic consumption is estimated at 100,000 tons annually, the rest being exported as dried and smoked fish and fish sauces.

Cambodia's natural resources include an abundant supply of timber, all of which is in the public domain and consists mainly of tropical hardwoods. Because of the inaccessibility of much of the more than twenty-one million acres of forested area, only twenty-five percent of this land is currently being exploited. A recently completed survey of Cambodia's natural resources indicates that the possibilities for the exploitation of minerals are extremely limited.

Industrial activity is on a small scale and is confined largely to the processing of agricultural and forest products for local consumption. In addition, a small consumer-goods industry, a small-sized automobile assembly operation, and a pharmaceutical manufacturing and packaging plant have made up the ensemble of Cambodia's industry until very recently. In 1960, with the assistance of Chinese foreign aid, Cambodia established and put into operation manufacturing plants for textiles, plywood, and paper. A cement plant, also made possible by Chi-

[23] See *L'œuvre du Sangkum Reastr Niyum*, pps. 31-5.

nese aid, was near completion in 1963. Additional Chinese aid
and also that of Czechoslovakia will provide, in the near future, tire and tool factories, a palm-sugar refinery, a glass factory, and a tractor assembly plant. Plans are also being made
for a phosphate processing plant and a marine fish cannery.
A loan fund, financed by the United States, for the development of small industries has made possible the creation and
enlargement of twenty-two small private enterprises. In 1962,
the US aid mission in Cambodia announced its plans to encourage the establishment of a development loan bank to provide dollar credits to businessmen who will establish agro-indus-
tries utilizing domestic raw materials. The United States also
tried in 1962 to persuade the Cambodian government to take
advantage of international and bilateral lending institutions for
larger industrial development; a jute bag factory was proposed
as the first project worthy of such an international development
loan.[24]

Commerce is almost totally in the hands of Cambodia's Chinese population, whose trucks and small boats traverse the
entire country. An extensive network of over 2,000 miles of
paved roads connects Phnompenh with almost every provincial
and district center. This network is increased during the dry
season of the year by innumerable miles of dirt roads. A 250-
mile railroad connects Phnompenh with the principal rice-growing area of Battambang, and there is a direct rail connection
with Bangkok via Poipet and Aranyapradet at the Thai-Cam-
bodian frontier. Construction of a new line, from the capital
to Sihanoukville, on the Gulf of Siam, was underway in 1962–
1963, and plans were being considered for a line to Stung
Treng in northeastern Cambodia. River transportation is confined mainly to the Mekong and Bassac rivers. Ships of up to
4,000 tons may use the Phnompenh river port, but increasingly
Cambodia's exports and imports will be carried through its recently completed, French-built seaport, Sihanoukville, which is
connected to Phnompenh by an American-built highway.

[24] See *Aide économique américaine au Cambodge en 1962* (Phnom-
Penh: U.S. Agency for International Development, 1962), pp. 28–30.

THE PEOPLE

Cambodians, who make up approximately eighty-five percent of a population of nearly six million people, are for the most part rice farmers. The few who do not earn their livelihood by farming are, in general, government employees or Buddhist monks. Buddhism, of the Theravada school, is an important factor uniting Cambodians from all walks of life.

The largest ethnic minorities[25] in Cambodia are the Chinese and Vietnamese, who are concentrated primarily in and around Phnompenh. The best estimates of the Chinese population place their number at between 350,000 and 400,000. During the protectorate, the French favored the Chinese, who were already established in influential positions in the economy as commercial agents of the Crown. The French organized the Chinese into five *congrégations,* according to their area of origin in China. Under this system, they enjoyed the privileges of extraterritoriality and were granted the same commercial privileges as French residents. Their advantageous position enabled them to gain virtual monopolies on imports, private banking, rice milling, money lending, bus transportation, and control of almost all of the distribution of consumer and industrial goods. The *congrégations* were abolished by the Cambodian government in 1958 on grounds that they constituted a state within a state and as such offered unlimited opportunities for subversion by Chinese Communists.

Even after several generations of residence in Cambodia, many Chinese have not become assimilated into Cambodian society, and they are not under government pressure to become so. They maintain close contact with China and exercise great effort to preserve their identity as Chinese. . . . On the surface, the Chinese appear to enjoy good relations with the government. Discriminatory practices in other parts of South-

[25] For a discussion of the ethnic groups making up Cambodia's population, see D. J. Steinberg *et al., Cambodia: Its People, Its Society, Its Culture* (New Haven: Human Relations Area Files Press, 1957).

east Asia have made the Chinese in Cambodia circumspect in their public actions, and they have taken advantage of every opportunity to declare their loyalty to the government. Although there is no official policy of discrimination against the Chinese, their precarious position in Cambodian society often makes them easy prey for exploitation by corrupt, lower echelon government officials. The hostility expressed by the average Cambodian against the Chinese is usually tempered with awe of their "cleverness." Chinese who adopt Cambodian citizenship are easily integrated into Cambodia society and many find their way into positions of prominence in the government; this observation would indicate that barriers to assimilation are not so much imposed by Cambodians as they are erected by the Chinese themselves.

The population of Vietnamese in Cambodia is thought to number between 400,000 and 450,000. In the economy they occupy positions of merchants and artisans, and a few farm riceland in southeastern Cambodia. Like the Chinese, they have maintained themselves as a community apart from the Cambodians. It is believed that two-thirds of their number are sympathetic to the views of the North Vietnamese government, and it is believed by Cambodians that many are behind-the-scenes supporters of the small Cambodian Communist Party, the Pracheachon. Probably because of the long history of enmity between the two peoples, the Cambodians fear the Vietnamese, whom they regard as treacherous, even more than they do the Chinese. Their questionable loyalty and the present tension in the relationship between the Cambodian and South Vietnamese governments have provoked the government's harassment of Vietnamese residents in Cambodia, both on an organized basis (such as the mass displacement and deportation of a large number of Vietnamese living along the river bank in Phnompenh's suburbs in 1960 and 1961) and on an individual basis.

A third distinct group in Cambodia is comprised of the Chams. This group, totaling some 100,000 people, is made up of descendants of the people of the former Kingdom of Champa and of more recent immigrants from the Malay Peninsula. Most are Muslims and speak a Malayo-Polynesian language but are regarded as full citizens of Cambodia. In the main they are fishermen, cattle herders, and lumberjacks. They pose no special problem to the government.

The hill tribes in the eastern and western mountains make up a fourth group set apart from the Cambodians. Called collectively Khmer Loeu (Cambodians of the mountains), or sometimes phnong (savages), these people have organized themselves into several more or less nomadic tribes, the total population of which has been estimated at more than 40,000. They practice slash-and-burn rice cultivation and recognize no national boundaries in their wanderings. The social and administrative unit of these people is the village, each one independent and governed by a council of elders. Some subgroups within the tribes recognize an area authority, but generally the chief of the village council is the most important person. Those living in the eastern hills have become a serious problem for Cambodia because of their movements back and forth across its border with South Vietnam and because of reported North Vietnamese subversive activity among them. The Cambodian government has, since 1958, undertaken to integrate them, mainly by persuading them to settle in permanent villages, built and supplied by the government well away from the border, and by providing them with schools, medical facilities, and the means of transporting their goods to market. The several tribes in the east are generally conceded to have originated from the same ethnic stock as Cambodians, but the smaller groups in the western mountains are thought to be Negrito. The government is also pursuing a policy of assimilation among the western tribes, but progress is slow because of the inaccessibility of the area.

4

The Anti-Imperialist Struggle in Cambodia: The Early Years*

The French colonialists are actively carrying on their policy of division, using the Khmers to fight their own compatriots and the Lao and Vietnamese. Their numerous secret agents have been playing off the Khmers against each other, trying to hamper and sabotage the revolutionary rule and destroy the organizations of the Khmer national united front. Their commandos have been kidnapping quite a number of militants.

To undermine the resistance front, they use Khmer riffraff to pillage the population under the usurped name of Khmer people's troops. They continuously undertake raids into the liberated area in an attempt to shatter the morale of the people. Within the first months of 1950 the two regions in the Southeast and Southwest were attacked not less than thirty-five times.

As the increasing successes of the Vietnamese resistance more and more inspire the Khmer people, French spies are doing their utmost to create feud[s] between the two communities, throwing Khmer rascals against the Vietnamese nationals in the Khmer territory, and South Vietnamese traitors against the Khmer border villages and towns.

American interference in Khmer, like that in Pathet Lao and Vietnam, becomes more apparent with every passing day. The US agents are trying to buy off a number of people, maintaining close contact with the Democratic Party, backing up the Huk Tok Lien pirates who are terrorizing the northern part of the country against the Khmer resistance. They have also set up pepper stations in Kampot to rake off Khmer wealth. At the same time they are planning to have the two provinces of Battambang and Siem Reap occupied by Thai troops. They have

---

* From *Khmer Armed Resistance* (n.p.: pamphlet of the Khmer Peace Committee, October, 1952). We wish to thank Mr. Saburo Kugai of Tokyo for bringing this rare document to our attention—eds.

already built up garrisons in Battambang for the future use of Thai troops. More noteworthy is the present construction by the Americans of the two strategic roads between Sourin (Thai) and Sisophon-Battambang, between Oubon (Thai) and Kompongcham, Lower Lao and the Western Tablelands (Vietnam).

It is obvious that the American interventionists are using Thailand as a base from which they can fall upon Vietnam, Khmer, Pathet Lao and China, suppress the national liberation movements in Southeast Asia and destroy world peace.

THE KHMER SEVEN-YEAR-OLD RESISTANCE

To oppose the French colonialists and the American interventionists the Khmer people have been using all means to fight for their national independence. Their capital, Phnompenh, was the theater of the first struggles. Civil servants left their jobs, students quit schools, to go to the countryside and take part in the resistance. The first armed groups started their operations against the French in Battambang, at the same time initiated the Khmer people's long-term resistance.

Under the leadership of Khmer patriots and with the wholehearted support of the Vietnamese people, the resistance of the Khmer people has been making headway in every field, political, military, economic, cultural as well as social.

POLITICAL

The Khmer patriots have done their best to build up a national united front and a people's government, as groundwork of the resistance and national construction.

The close solidarity of the various strata of the Khmer people in the struggle against the common enemy has been materialized in the national united front called the Nekhum Issarak Khmer (Khmer Freedom Front).

In 1948 the Khmer National Liberation Committee, or

Khmer Provisional Government, was founded, which gave a powerful impetus to the people's resistance. Owing to the enemy's ruthless repression, the Committee was dispersed. But thanks to the ardent patriotism of the Khmer people and to the efforts of clearsighted and resolute patriots, the resistance continued to progress. Bases, more and more numerous, have been established. The influence of the resistance in the cities and in the countryside is on the upgrade. More and more puppet troops are won over. Many bourgeois intellectuals, formerly fooled by colonialists' tricks, have been awakened and have come back to the fold.

In early 1950, a People's Congress was convened, attended by 200 representatives of people from all walks of life, and [the] Buddhist clergy. It officially recognized the Nekhum Issarak Khmer Front as the only national united front of the Khmer people, passed its platform and regulations, and elected its Central Executive Committee. Toussamouth, an authoritative priest who had built up the Southwest liberated zone, was unanimously chosen as the Chairman of the Front.

The Congress also elected a new Provisional National Liberation Committee or Provisional Government, with as Chairman Son Ngoc Minh, an influential priest, a revolutionary militant credited with many achievements. As a result the people's rule from village to provincial levels has been further consolidated. . . .

MILITARY

At the beginning of the resistance the Khmer combatants fought heroically to stem the enemy's advance. But in the face of an enemy many times more powerful in strength as well as in equipment, and too well acquainted with the job of invader, they had to withdraw progressively to Battambang and Siem-Reap to preserve their forces and set up guerrilla bases.

In 1946, Issarak troops attacked Siem Reap city, annihilated the entire French garrison and captured its whole stock of arms. In addition, guerrilla activities in other localities enhanced the enthusiasm of the people and made them realise that to win independence armed struggle is necessary. Khmer troops have shown their strength in their actions in the North-west (Pursat, Battambang), in the Southeast (Soirieng), and particularly in the Southwest. They sometimes fought right in Takeo or at six kilometers from Kampot or within the limits of Kompongspeu. These attacks threw the enemy into greater bewilderment, and, [. . .] strengthened the people's confidence in the final victory.

Since late 1948, Issarak troops have been very active, carry-ing out armed propaganda, establishing people's organizations' bases, arming the population, expanding guerrilla warfare. The mobile groups are entrusted with the task of protecting the liberated areas, undertaking operations behind the enemy's line, opposing his repression and raids, harassing and annihilating his troops, and safeguarding the people's crops and properties. In the very heart of big cities, under the aggressors' noses, groups of shock fighters have been busy killing hundreds of French troops and secret agents. Sabotage, harassment, execu-tion of traitors are making headway.

The slogan "Take the enemy's arms to kill the enemy" has been put into practice with handsome results. Local factories turn out a part of arms and ammunitions of the Issarak troops, the rest comes from war booties.

In November, 1951, right in Phnompenh city which the French regarded as their most secured stronghold, a Khmer guerrilla executed De Raymond, French Commissioner in Khmer, which has caused much fear to the French and their puppet Sihanouk clique.

As rearguard of the troops, militia has been created in the liberated villages and hamlets. In many places, the population have carried out the "empty house, empty garden" tactics, and refused to cooperate with the enemy. Khmer guerrilla warfare is expanding, and large guerrilla zones in Siem Reap, Battam-bang, Pursat Kompongthom, Soirieng [have been established] where people's organizations have been also set up. Armed propaganda teams keep infiltrating behind the enemy's line. The resistance has spread to the [region] South of the Tonlesap lake, to built up bases in the wealthy and populated Northwest, [and] to Southwest areas where the enemy's most vital communications lie and the biggest mountains [found]. . . . Guerrillas have been laying ambushes, sabotaging roads, particularly between Go Dau and Bac Nam, Kampot and Phnompenh, Phnompenh and Chau Doc (South Vietnam), causing heavy losses to the French.

Command has been gradually unified in all the provinces. One-third of the total area with more than a million population has been liberated. The Eastern free area comprises High Chilong, Mimot, Laon, Laca, Akran; the Western one almost [all of] the provinces of Battambang and Pursat; the Southern one Kuhdak, Soirieng, Preyveng, Kampot. Since 1949 these free areas have been linked up into a corridor from the South Vietnam border quite to the end of the Khmer-Thai frontier. This is a good springboard for the expansion of guerrilla warfare and the establishment of solid bases for the long-term and hard resistance of the Khmer people.

The Khmer people have been greatly encouraged by the Vietnamese and Lao military successes. With the lessons drawn from the Vietnamese experience of stepping up guerrilla warfare, Khmer troops and people have been doing their best to build up and consolidate their own strength in order to annihilate most possible enemies.

As evidence of its growing strength, some of the Issarak Liberation Army's recent achievements should be mentioned:

On January 18, 1951, an enemy, fully equipped company from Kampot which was being engaged in raid[s] of terrorism met with a strong opposition from Khmer local troops and guerrillas who killed seventy-one French, wounded fourteen, and captured a large booty. The wounded were cared for and released. At the end of February, 1952, engagement after engagement occurred. On the Phnompenh-Battambang railroad, at fifty kilometers from the capital, a fifteen-carriage train loaded with enemy soldiers was completely destroyed, and more than 100 of these [soldiers were] killed and wounded. A huge amount of arms was seized. In the meantime, behind the enemy's line, guerrillas were very active. Young people of both sexes underwent an intensive military training. In spite of the French control the population kept in close touch with guerrillas, supplying them with food and information. Associations of "Combatants' Mothers" have been organized to tend troops and cadres. Late in 1951 and early 1952, Takeo militiamen caused heavy losses to the French colonialist forces. Local troops of Kompongspeu sometimes have succeeded in defending the peoples' lives and properties by repulsing whole enemy battalions engaged in mopping-up operations. Following that the guerrilla activities against enemy mopping-up operations in Dreysardek and other areas have frightened the enemy and checked his arrogance. Much impressed by the Liberation Army's increasing strength, a number of puppet troops have gone over to the resistance's side.

Through the rapid growth of free Khmer in the military as well as in other fields the French colonialists feel the approach of their doom in the country which they had planned to turn into their reserve in their aggressive war against Vietnam and Pathet Lao. For this reason they have brought to Khmer thousands of reinforcement troops from South Vietnam in spite of their successive heavy defeats in Vietnam. At present more than 30,000 are bogged down in Khmer, owing to the increasing activities of the Khmer army and people.

ECONOMIC, CULTURAL AND SOCIAL

For the past seven years of hard resistance, besides military successes the Khmer people have achieved much in the economic and cultural fields. A drive for increasing production has been started with a view to building up a self-sufficient economy, securing enough supplies for the army and frustrating the enemy's economic blockade. In the meantime all the colonialist predatory taxes have been abolished.

Parallel to the movement for increasing production, the Khmer people have been striving to sabotage the enemy's economy. Ambushes of enemy convoys and destruction of enemy vital communication lines have resulted in heavy damages for the enemy's commerce. Workers in rubber plantations have waged ceaseless struggles against the exploitation of the French capitalists and tried by all means to undermine the production of rubber. In the first six months of 1951 alone five big stores of latex and many other materials and machines were destroyed by Khmer workers. These acts of sabotage have been responsible for the great decrease of the enemy rubber output.

At the beginning of 1952 the Khmer National Liberation Committee launched a country-wide movement for increasing production which elicited a warm response from the entire people. Meetings were organized throughout the country at which representatives of the people, army and administration discussed ways and means to fulfill the increased production plan. In Preamchor district, Preyveng province, for example, eighty representatives of the people, army and administration met at the end of 1951 to review the work done in the year, exchange their production experiences and draw up plans for the following year.

In the cultural and social spheres, the schools opened in the liberated areas have taught a great number of people how to read and write Pali. In some places the percentage of literacy among the population amounts to seventy as compared to ten under the French domination.

A healthy life is being developed in the liberated areas. People are competing with each other in producing and learning. Bad customs and habits are gradually waning.

On the contrary, the population in the enemy-occupied areas are suffering from misery and repression, their properties plundered and their lives constantly endangered. The French colonialists and the American interventionists are spreading their corrupt, pornographic and bellicose culture with a view to poisoning the minds of the people and breaking down their patriotism and fighting spirit. But the Khmer people are fully aware of the enemy's criminal designs, and together with the Vietnamese and Lao peoples are fighting with increasing heroism for their national independence and for the defense of world peace.

[The pamphlet from which these excerpts are taken came from the left wing, of the Khmer Issarak, a group which was not only anti-colonialist but also tended to identify Sihanouk with the French. This group apparently disbanded after the Geneva accords. (For explicit agreement on this point, see Selection 8, this volume). But the experience of struggle against the French lingered on in the form of an underground resistance tradition in Cambodia. The events of 1970 suggest that elements of the earlier resistance movement rallied behind Sihanouk after the right wing coup and the American invasion. See Part VI, this volume—eds.]

5

Sihanouk and the Khmer Issarak

WILFRED G. BURCHETT *

The French forces in Indochina were . . . on the strategic defensive. In Cambodia, by March, 1953, they had been reduced to a mere two battalions of "pacification" troops, and five battalions of the Royal Khmer Army under French command. Sihanouk used this situation, plus the mounting activities of the Khmer Issarak movement, to put pressure on the French for more and more concessions. Essentially the main bone of contention between the French and Sihanouk by 1953, was the question of Cambodia's adhesion to the French union and the French demand to continue to use Cambodia as a base for operations in Vietnam and Laos respectively. . . .

In a note to the French President on March 5, 1953, Sihanouk showed that he was aware of French policy to reconquer one colony at a time. He also made greater claims for the success of the Khmer Issarak movement than were ever made by the movement itself. "The present policy of France in Indochina is based," he wrote, "on the idea that the principal aim at the moment is success in the fight against the Vietminh and that once this success has been obtained, all other problems will easily be settled. . . ." He said such a policy may be all right for Vietnam, but not for Cambodia, where the people "above all desire peace and are sincerely attached to the ideas of liberty and independence. The real situation from a military and political viewpoint," he continued, "is the following: three-fifths of our territory are occupied by the Vietminh. . . . (The maximum ever claimed by the Khmer Issarak movement, loosely described here as "Vietminh" was one third of their territory liberated.) Sihanouk however was not using this argument to ask the French to stay on and fight the "Vietminh." On the

* From Wilfred G. Burchette, *Mekong Upstream* (Hanoi: Red River Publishing House, 1957), pp. 115–27, 141–46.

contrary. The only solution, he said, was complete independence for Cambodia so as to deprive the Khmer Issarak and the "Vietminh" of their popular support.

He pointed out that the Khmer Issarak had deep roots among the people—"native sons, peasants and even townspeople . . . their patriotic proclamations find a favorable response among the population, and also among the clergy whose influence is enormous throughout the kingdom, and they are assured of faithful followers among the masses as well as amongst the elite of our nations. . . . The Issarak danger is real in itself . . . these rebels frequently mount ambushes against our patrols of provincial guards, police and soldiers and recently—alone or together with the Vietminh—have obtained results which have greatly affected public opinion by the assassination of a governor, a chief of province and districts chiefs . . ." (Among those killed was the French high commissioner for Cambodia, de Raymond, executed in Phnompenh by a Khmer Issarak guerrilla in November 1951). . . .

The main grounds on which the Khmer Issarak found such support among the population, Sihanouk points out in his note, is the fact that Cambodia is not really independent. "What can I reply," he asked, "when the Issarak propaganda proves to the people and the clergy that Cambodia is not really independent . . . ?"

In an interview with the *New York Times*, Sihanouk repeated that only independence would satisfy the Cambodian people. In reply to questions as to whether he was not aware of the "communist menace" he replied: "Among intellectual circles of the Cambodian people, there has been created a growing conviction during the past years in the theory that the Vietminh communists fight for the independence of their country." He added that such circles "did not want to die for the French and help them to remain in Cambodia." He stressed that real powers were still in French hands. "One of the greatest difficulties," he said, "is the French insistence on having the majority of Cambodian troops under their command, with their restrictions of legal and economic sovereignty. Cambodian justice does not apply to the French. Our police cannot touch them. In economic affairs we are tied hand and foot. We can not import and export freely and we do not even have the liberty to control taxation. . . ."

On June 14, 1953, Sihanouk left Phnompenh abruptly for Bangkok, as he expressed it, to alert world opinion and give a final warning to the French. When Sihanouk returned from Bangkok he did not go to Phnompenh but set up his headquarters at Battambang. At that time, the royal army consisted of eight battalions. The French had withdrawn eleven of the country's fourteen provinces and five of the eight battalions from the Cambodian military command. Siem Reap, Sisophon and Battambang remained under the Cambodian command which is why Sihanouk removed his residence there. The French reply to Sihanouk's message to the nation was to concentrate troops in Phnompenh and set up artillery pieces on Phnompenh airport, their barrels pointing towards the royal palace. French civilians in Phnompenh were issued arms, the capital was encircled. Vietnamese and North African troops were brought in to reinforce the French garrison. . . .

By early July, 1953, the situation was approaching "flash point." Sihanouk told the French he was restraining with great difficulty a nationwide uprising. He still hoped, it seems, to gain independence by the non-violent diplomatic way, taking advantage of Navarre's[1] preoccupations with Vietnam and Laos. One of the elements which the French counted on to maintain their position was that although the Khmer Issarak forces were strongly entrenched in just those provinces to which Sihanouk had transferred his headquarters, there was no cooperation between the two. The Khmer Issarak had not appreciated, and there was no way of them even knowing, the efforts made by Sihanouk. Sihanouk, in his internal policies at least, did not recognize the genuine patriotism of the Khmer Issarak forces and the Vietnamese volunteers in Cambodia, and the VPA [Vietnamese Peoples' Army] over the borders in Vietnam.

The struggle on the diplomatic and on the military-political fronts was a parallel one without conscious coordination. Often it was the opposite. Both had fallen into the imperialist trap of fighting each other. Khmer Issarak patriots were slaughtered

[1] Henri Navarre was then French military commander in Indochina —eds.

by royal army troops, the latter were ambushed by the Khmer Issarak. In any case, the outcome for Cambodian independence could not be decided on Cambodian soil alone. Cambodia stood or fell with the sister states. The Khmer Issarak saw this clearly. It is not as certain if this was equally clear to Sihanouk at that time. . . .

*   *   *

If France really wanted to have a military showdown with Sihanouk, then Navarre would have to concentrate far more troops than had ever been employed until then against Cambodia. Either he would have to fight on two fronts, against the Khmer Issarak and Sihanouk's troops, or even worse from the French point of view, he might push the two forces together. At least this would delay the Washington-imposed grand strategy, but it would almost certainly hasten the loss of Cambodia. Toughness and bluster against Sihanouk had failed. The French bluff had been called. Washington was pressing for a speed-up in starting the Navarre Plan. The French government again decided to play for time by a pretended retreat.

The Laniel-Bidault government offered to transfer "complete" independence in all spheres, including military and police powers. But when it came down to negotiations, it was seen that "complete independence" included a formula which meant that the French High Command would retain Cambodia as an operational base until the end of the war. Textually the French demanded "temporary facilities for the necessary means of assuring operational command of units stationed east of the Mekong. This operational command, the extent of which depends on the evolution of the military situation, will be ended as soon as an improvement in the situation permits." The modest term "east of the Mekong" covered the whole of Vietnam, the whole of Laos and about one third of Cambodia. It included also the "strategic routes indispensable for the threatened areas in Laos and East and Northeast Cambodia." [2]

One could have no clearer proof that for the French the war in Indochina was fought as a whole. Cambodia was an essen-

[2] These demands were formulated in a note to the Cambodian government on July 24, 1953.

tial base for continuing the "dirty war" in Vietnam and Laos. What Sihanouk must have realized also, was that if the French succeeded in crushing the resistance forces in Vietnam and Laos, they would then concentrate their entire military effort on Cambodia. It is important to understand the interdependence of the various fronts and rear areas. A glance at the map of Vietnam shows the very narrow waist along the whole of central Vietnam. A large part of this waist was in the hands of the Vietnam Peoples Army, and all French communications through this area were subject to day and night attack. The war would have ended much sooner had the French not been able to use alternative communication routes and bases in Cambodia. As the war developed, these bases and routes were also subject to attack by the Khmer Issarak forces and the Vietnamese volunteers. The main French north-south line of communications became strategic route 13, which ran from Saigon through Kratie and Stung Treng in Cambodia up to Pakse and Savannakhet in Laos and on to Vientiane and Luang Prabang. The French also used Cambodia, with its rich food reserves, to feed their forces elsewhere in Indochina. In the note which Sihanouk sent the French government on November 19, 1953, he referred to "the continuous convoys of trucks and ships laden with fish, cattle, poultry and rice to feed the French and Vietnamese troops fighting on Vietnamese soil. . . ." and pointed out that sixty-five percent of all French exports from Indochina were taken out of Cambodia.

It was against the supply lines along which these convoys traveled that the Khmer Issarak waged a ceaseless struggle. US propagandists in Cambodia later pointed to the destroyed roads and bridges as evidence of "Issarak-Vietminh" atrocities, But the people know that without this sabotage and the military struggle which complemented Sihanouk's activities on the diplomatic front, the war would have dragged on much longer. It would have been very convenient for the French to have had bases in Cambodia and Laos into which they could retreat without fear of punishment whenever they were hard pressed in Vietnam. It would have been convenient also to have had communication lines not subject to attack in Cambodia and Laos, along which they could maneuver and concentrate for outflanking attacks against the VPA in South and North Vietnam; to have attack-free bases in Cambodia from which to attack Laos, and attack-free bases in Laos from which to attack Cambodia. This is precisely what the French were demanding of Sihanouk and by Sihanouk's reactions, he understood perfectly. His reply was terse and to the point.

In a brief reply sent on July 27, Sihanouk referred to the "explicit contradictions" in the French government's promise to transfer all powers to Cambodia and the demands that the French High Command have facilities "for assuring operational command of units east of the Mekong." Sihanouk bluntly demanded an end to such nonsense and the transfer of all powers including police and military commands by September 1, 1953. He repeated, however, an earlier offer that certain "sub-sectors," jointly to be determined by the two governments, could be reserved for French troops. Faced with the first reverses for the Navarre Plan in Vietnam, where Operation Atlanta had ground down to a halt after heavy losses, the French beat another retreat. Four days after Sihanouk's note, the French ambassador in Phnompenh informed Prime Minister Penn Nouth that France was now ready to transfer all powers including the military command to Cambodia and to negotiate on the question of "sub-sectors." Negotiations for the transfer started on August 27. Agreement was quickly reached on the transfer of police and judicial powers, but bogged down again on the question of the military command. The transfer of police powers suited the French because Navarre wanted to get his hands on French troops doing police duty in Cambodia.

A curious incident occurred at this time which caused a howl of anger against Sihanouk in the French and US press and earned him for the first time the label "neutralist." The prime minister under Sihanouk's instructions had issued an appeal to "Issarak, Khmer Vietminh and Vietminh," as he termed them, informing them of the transfer of police and judicial powers and assuring them that Cambodia was on the threshold of real independence. The question of the transfer of military powers also would soon be settled. The proclamation recalled that "the ideal which you have never ceased to proclaim to the Khmer people is the fight for the independence of the country" and as independence had been gained there was "no longer any reason to remain outside the national community."

Resistance fighters were told they would be "welcomed with open arms by the government" and an amnesty was promised. In a special passage addressed to "Vietminh" (the Vietnamese volunteers) the appeal stated: "Although we are not communists, we do not oppose communism as long as the latter is not to be imposed on our people by force from outside. . . . what happens in Vietnam is none of our business. . . ." In Washington and Paris this appeal, for all its harsh phrases against "communism," was correctly interpreted as meaning Sihanouk had no intention of using independence to take part in an anti-communist or anti-Vietminh crusade. *Le Monde* commented: "Washington does not hide the fact that its whole policy in Southeast Asia is in danger from a wave of 'neutralism' which the example of Cambodia has just launched. . . ."

Sihanouk's position was clear. He was an honest nationalist. He wanted real independence. He did not like communists, or Khmer Issarak or Vietminh. But he knew that the Khmer Issarak did not menace the country's independence and he had no intention of joining hand in hand with the French in their "dirty war." If the Vietminh managed to beat French colonialism in Vietnam—it was their affair. But the French promise to transfer police and military powers was based on the Paris and Washington concept of a common front against communism. The appeal of September, 1953, was the first sign that an independent Cambodia would have an independent policy—one that was later to stick like a thorn in the sides of Washington policy makers. And in the face of the howls which went up after the appeal, including threats of both France and the US to cut aid to Cambodia, the Cambodian government issued a declaration which said among other things ". . . Cambodia demands its independence more than any aid. The fact that we are threatened that economic aid will be cut if we refuse to fight against communists outside the borders of Cambodia; the fact that our rights in principle to consider communism and communist governments as other than our mortal enemies. . . . the fact that small countries only have the right to carry out the orders of their great 'allies or friends' who reserve for themselves the right to start or end wars with these small countries without consulting them—all these facts worry us. . . ."

PART II

INDEPENDENCE AND THE GENEVA ACCORDS OF 1954

Introduction

The Geneva Conference on Indochina of 1954 marked an early attempt to achieve "peaceful coexistence" in the post World War II period. Not only was peaceful coexistence the announced aim of British, French and Soviet foreign policy, but the People's Republic of China also gave support to the pacific policies of compromise and conciliation between east and west. The most authoritative account of this period is the book *End of a War* (1969) by Philippe Devillers and Jean Lacouture (first published in French in 1960). These authors, and others,[1] point out that despite the overwhelming victory won by the Vietminh revolutionaries over the French in Indochina, the communists at Geneva made many concessions. In Vietnam, they accepted a temporarily divided country.[2] In Cambodia, they withdrew their demand of recognition for the Khmer Issarak insurgents. And in Laos, the Pathet Lao agreed to join in a coalition government.[3] As British Foreign Secretary Anthony Eden put it: the Geneva accords were "about the best bargain France and the associated states could have made." [4]

It is not necessary to assume that the motivations of the communist delegations at Geneva were pure and free from considerations of national interest. The general threat of global

[1] See also Donald Lancaster, *The Emancipation of French Indochina* (London, 1961), chap. XVII. A recent book by Robert F. Randle (*Geneva, 1954* [Princeton, 1969]) is a lame attempt to reinterpret the Geneva Conference in such a way as to enhance the tarnished reputation of John Foster Dulles.

[2] See Selection 6, this volume, Articles 6 and 7. The refusal of the United States and its client government in South Vietnam to allow elections prevented the reunification of Vietnam by the scheduled time in 1956. See Philippe Devillers, "The Struggle for the Unification of Vietnam," in Marvin E. Gettleman, ed., *Vietnam: History, Documents and Opinions* (2d ed., New York, 1970), selection 49.

[3] See Selections 11, 13, in Part III, this volume.

[4] Anthony Eden, *Full Circle* (Boston, 1960), p. 160. Cf. Devillers and Lacouture, *End of a War*, chap. 23; Lancaster, *Emancipation of French Indochina*, Chap. XVII.

confrontation and war doubtless influenced the Russians and probably the Chinese as well.[5] The Soviets were anxious to enlist French support for a scaling down of cold war tensions in Europe, and were willing to urge the Vietminh to make concessions to that end.[6] The Chinese delegation, headed by Chou En-lai, wished to protect China's southern borders; that could be accomplished by a friendly government in Hanoi, and a neutral Laos and Cambodia free of hostile (i.e., American) military bases.

The renewal of conflict in South Vietnam undermined the edifice of international conciliation constructed at Geneva. American actions, as we will show,[6] were mainly responsible for this, and American intransigence was already evident at the Conference in 1954. Dismayed at the French defeat in Indochina, Dulles wished the war against communist insurgents there to continue. Unable to bring that about, he did the next best thing from his point of view, which was to show the displeasure of his government with the peace settlement. The US delegation played no constructive role at Geneva, and indicated that it would not sign any declaration that the Chinese endorsed.[7] When the Conference went so far as to assuage American anti-communist sensibilities by arranging to produce an agreement (The Final Declaration of the Geneva Conference, July 21, 1954)[8] that nobody signed, the head of the US delegation made a separate statement dissassociating his country from the text.[9]

But so pervasive was the sentiment in behalf of peaceful coexistence at Geneva that American hostility to the accords was muted. Walter Bedell Smith promised that the United States would respect the agreements and "refrain from the threat or the use of force to disturb them." [10] Soon, however, America

---

[5] Eden, *Full Circle*, p. 139.

[6] See the Introduction to Part V, this volume.

[7] Dulles, according to one observer, ostentatiously refused the outstretched hand of Chou En-lai. Edgar Snow, *The Other Side of the River: Red China Today* (New York, 1962), p. 695.

[8] See Selection 6, this volume.

[9] *Ibid.*

[10] *Ibid.*

would break this promise, and in throwing its power against the policy of peaceful coexistence in Indochina in the 1950's it helped bring on the escalated conflicts of the 1960's and 1970's.

Final Declaration of the Geneva Conference on Indochina, July 21, 1954*

Participants: Cambodia, The Democratic Republic of Vietnam, France, Laos, The People's Republic of China, The State of Vietnam, The Union of Soviet Socialist Republics, The United Kingdom and The United States of America.

1. The Conference takes note of the agreements[1] ending hostilities in Cambodia, Laos, and Vietnam and organizing international control and the supervision of the execution of the provisions of these agreements.

2. The Conference expresses satisfaction at the ending of hostilities in Cambodia, Laos, and Vietnam; the Conference expresses its conviction that the execution of the provisions set out in the present declaration and in the agreements on the cessation of hostilities will permit Cambodia, Laos, and Vietnam henceforth to play their part in full independence and sovereignty, in the peaceful community of nations.

3. The Conference takes note of the declarations made by the Governments of Cambodia and of Laos of their intention to adopt measures permitting all citizens to take their place in the national community, in particular by participating in the next general elections, which in conformity with the constitutions of each of these countries, shall take place in the course of the

* From *Further Documents Relating to the Discussion of Indochina at the Geneva Conference* (Miscellaneous, no. 20 [1954], Command Paper, 9239). London: Great Britain Parliamentary Sessional Papers, XXXI (1953/1954), pp. 9–11.

[1] See Selections 7 and 8, this volume. The ceasefire agreement for Vietnam, not reprinted in this volume, may be found in Marvin E. Gettleman, ed., *Vietnam: History, Documents and Opinions* (2d. ed., New York, 1970), selection 27—eds.

year 1955 by secret ballot and in conditions of respect for fundamental freedoms.[2]

4. The Conference takes note of the clauses in the agreement on the cessation of hostilities in Vietnam prohibiting the introduction into Vietnam of foreign troops and military personnel as well as of all kinds of arms and munitions. The Conference also takes note of the declarations made by the Governments of Cambodia and Laos of their resolution not to request foreign aid, whether in war materiel, in personnel, or in instructors except for the purpose of the effective defense of their territory and, in the case of Laos, to the extent defined by the agreements on the cessation of hostilities in Laos.

5. The Conference takes note of the clauses in the agreement on the cessation of hostilities in Vietnam to the effect that no military base at the disposition of a foreign State may be established in the regrouping zones of the two parties, the latter having the obligation to see that the zones allotted to them shall not constitute part of any military alliance and shall not be utilized for the resumption of hostilities or in the service of an aggressive policy. The Conference also takes note of the declarations of the Governments of Cambodia and Laos

---

[2] Cambodia offered the following declaration in reference to this article:

> "The Royal Government of Cambodia,
> In the desire to ensure harmony and agreement among the peoples of the Kingdom,
> Declares itself resolved to take the necessary measures to integrate all citizens, without discrimination, into the national community and to guarantee them the enjoyment of the rights and freedoms for which the Constitution of the Kingdom provides;
> Affirms that all Cambodian citizens may freely participate as electors or candidates in general elections by secret ballot."

The Laotian government offered an identical Declaration, with the addition of one paragraph, announcing ". . . furthermore, that it will promulgate measures to provide for special representation in the Royal Administration of the provinces of Phong Saly and Sam Neua during the interval between the cessation of hostilities and the general elections of the interests of Laotian nationals who did not support the Royal forces during hostilities" [i.e., the Pathet Lao insurgents who fought against the French and against the Royal Laotian Forces associated with the French]—eds.

to the effect that they will not join in any agreement with other States if this agreement includes the obligation to participate in a military alliance not in conformity with the principles of the charter of the United Nations, or, in the case of Laos, with the principles of the agreement on the cessation of hostilities in Laos or, so long as their security is not threatened, the obligation to establish bases on Cambodian or Laotian territory for the military forces of foreign powers.[3]

[3] In reference to articles four and five of the Final Declaration of the Geneva Conference, Cambodia offered the following Declaration:

"The Royal Government of Cambodia is resolved never to take part in an aggressive policy and never to permit the territory of Cambodia to be utilized in the service of such a policy.

"The Royal Government of Cambodia will not join in any agreement with other States, if this agreement carries for Cambodia the obligation to enter into a military alliance not in conformity with the principles of the Charter of the United Nations, or, as long as its security is not threatened, the obligation to establish bases on Cambodian territory for the military forces of foreign Powers.

"The Royal Government of Cambodia is resolved to settle its international disputes by peaceful means, in such a manner as not to endanger peace, international security and justice.

"During the period which will elapse between the date of the cessation of hostilities in Vietnam and that of the final settlement of political problems in this country, the Royal Government of Cambodia will not solicit foreign aid in war materiel, personnel or instructors except for the purpose of the effective defence of the territory."

Laos offered an almost identical Declaration:

"The Royal Government of Laos will never join in any agreement with other States if this agreement includes the obligation for the Royal Government of Laos to participate in a military alliance not in conformity with the principles of the Charter of the United Nations or with the principles of the agreement on the cessation of hostilities or, unless its security is threatened, the obligation to establish bases on Laotian territory for military forces of foreign Powers.

"The Royal Government of Laos is resolved to settle its international disputes by peaceful means so that international peace and security and justice are not endangered.

"During the period between the cessation of hostilities in Vietnam and the final settlement of that country's political problems, the Royal Government of Laos will not request foreign aid, whether in war materiel, in personnel or in instructors, except for the purpose of its effective territorial defence and to the extent defined by the agreement on the cessation of hostilities."—eds.

6. The Conference recognizes that the essential purpose of the agreement relating to Vietnam is to settle military questions with a view to ending hostilities and that the military demarcation line should not in any way be interpreted as constituting a political or territorial boundary. The Conference expresses its conviction that the execution of the provisions set out in the present declaration and in the agreement on the cessation of hostilities creates the necessary basis for the achievement in the near future of a political settlement in Vietnam.

7. The Conference declares that, so far as Vietnam is concerned, the settlement of political problems, effected on the basis of respect for the principles of independence, unity, and territorial integrity, shall permit the Vietnamese people to enjoy the fundamental freedoms, guaranteed by democratic institutions established as a result of free general elections by secret ballot.

In order to ensure that sufficient progress in the restoration of peace has been made, and that all the necessary conditions obtain for free expression of the national will, general elections shall be held in July, 1956, under the supervision of an International Commission composed of representatives of the member States of the international supervisory commission referred to in the agreements on the cessation of hostilities. Consultations will be held on this subject between the competent representative authorities of the two zones from July, 1955, onwards.

8. The provisions of the agreements on the cessation of hostilities intended to ensure the protection of individuals and of property must be most strictly applied and must, in particular, allow everyone in Vietnam to decide freely in which zone he wishes to live.

9. The competent representative authorities of the northern and southern zones of Vietnam, as well as the authorities of Laos and Cambodia, must not permit any individual or collective reprisals against persons who have collaborated in any way with one of the parties during the war, or against members of such a person's family.

10. The Conference takes note of the declaration of the French Government to the effect that it is ready to withdraw its troops from the territory of Cambodia, Laos, and Vietnam, at the request of the Governments concerned and within a

period which shall be fixed by agreement between the parties except in the cases where, by agreement between the two parties, a certain number of French troops shall remain at specified points and for a specified time.

11. The Conference takes note of the declarations of the French Government to the effect that for the settlement of all the problems connected with the reestablishment and consolidation of peace in Cambodia, Laos, and Vietnam the French Government will proceed from the principle of respect for the independence and sovereignty, unity, and territorial integrity of Cambodia, Laos, and Vietnam.

12. In their relations with Cambodia, Laos, and Vietnam each member of the Geneva Conference undertakes to respect the sovereignty, the independence, the unity, and the territorial integrity of the above mentioned States, and to refrain from any interference in their internal affairs.

13. The members of the Conference agree to consult one another on any questions which may be referred to them by the international supervisory commission in order to study such measures as may prove necessary to ensure that the agreements on the cessation of hostilities in Cambodia, Laos and Vietnam are respected.

[After the agreement on this declaration (which was not signed by any of the participating nations), the United States delegate, Walter Bedell Smith, rose to make his government's "unilateral declaration of its position in these matters":

"The Government of the United States being resolved to devote its efforts to the strengthening of peace in accordance with the principles and purposes of the United Nations takes note of the agreements concluded at Geneva on July 20 and 21, 1954, between (a) the Franco-Laotian command and the command of the People's Army of Vietnam; (b) the Royal Khmer Army Command and the Command of the People's Army of Vietnam; (c) the Franco-Vietnamese Command and the Command of the People's Army of Vietnam, and of paragraphs one to twelve of the declaration presented to the Geneva Conference on July 21, 1954.

"The Government of the United States of America declares

with regard to the aforesaid agreements and paragraphs that (1) it will refrain from the threat or the use of force to disturb them, in accordance with article two (section four) of the Charter of the United Nations dealing with the obligation of members to refrain in their international relations from the threat or use of force; and (2) it would view any renewal of the aggression in violation of the aforesaid agreements with grave concern and as seriously threatening international peace and security. . . .

"We share the hope that the agreement will permit Cambodia, Laos and Vietnam to play their part in full independence and sovereignty, in the peaceful community of nations, and will enable the peoples of that area to determine their own future."
—eds.]

7

Agreement on the Cessation of Hostilities in Laos, July 20, 1954*

CHAPTER I—CEASEFIRE AND EVACUATION OF FOREIGN ARMED FORCES AND FOREIGN MILITARY PERSONNEL

Article 1

The commanders of the armed forces of the parties in Laos shall order and enforce the complete cessation of all hostilities in Laos by all armed forces under their control, including all units and personnel of the ground, naval and air forces.

Article 2

In accordance with the principle of a simultaneous ceasefire throughout Indochina the cessation of hostilities shall be simultaneous throughout the territory of Laos in all combat areas and for all forces of the two parties.

In order to prevent any mistake or misunderstanding and to ensure that both the cessation of hostilities and the disengagement and movements of the opposing forces are in fact simultaneous.

> (a) Taking into account the time effectively required to transmit the ceasefire order down to the lowest echelons of the combatant forces on both sides, the two parties are agreed that the complete

* *Further Documents Relating to the Discussion of Indochina at the Geneva Conference* (Miscellaneous, no. 20 [1954], Command Paper, 9239). London: Great Britain Parliamentary Sessional Papers, XXXI (1953/1954), pp. 39–48.

and simultaneous ceasefire throughout the territory
of Laos shall become effective at [o]8[oo] hours
(local time) on August 6, 1954. It is agreed that
Peking mean time shall be taken as local time.

(b) The Joint Commission for Laos shall draw
up a schedule for the other operations resulting
from the cessation of hostilities.

> *Note:* The ceasefire shall become effec-
> tive fifteen days after the entry into force
> of the present agreement.

Article 3

All operations and movements entailed by the cessation of
hostilities and regrouping must proceed in a safe and orderly
fashion:

(a) Within a number of days to be determined
on the spot by the Joint Commission in Laos each
party shall be responsible for removing and neutralizing mines, booby traps, explosives and any
other dangerous substance placed by it. In the
event of its being impossible to complete the work
of removal and neutralization in time, the party
concerned shall mark the spot by placing visible
signs there.

(b) As regards the security of troops on the
move following the lines of communication in accordance with the schedule previously drawn up
by the Joint Armistice Commission in Laos, and
the safety of the assembly areas, detailed measures
shall be adopted in each case by the Joint Armistice
Commission in Laos. In particular, while the forces
of one party are withdrawing by a line of communication passing through the territory of the
other party (road or waterways) the forces of the
latter party shall provisionally withdraw two kilometers on either side of such line of communica-

tion, but in such a manner as to avoid interfering with the movement of the civil population.

Article 4

The withdrawals and transfers of military forces, supplies and equipment shall be effected in accordance with the following principles:

(a) The withdrawals and transfers of the military forces, supplies and equipment of the two parties shall be completed within a period of 120 days from the day on which the armistice agreement enters into force.

The two parties undertake to communicate their transfer plans to each other, for information, within twenty-five days of the entry into force of the present agreement.

(b) The withdrawals of the Vietnamese People's Volunteers from Laos to Vietnam shall be effected by provinces. The position of those volunteers who were settled in Laos before the hostilities shall form the subject of a special convention.

(c) The routes for the withdrawal of the forces of the French union and Vietnamese People's Volunteers in Laos from Laotian territory shall be fixed on the spot by the Joint Commission.

(d) The two parties shall guarantee that the withdrawals and transfers of all forces will be effected in accordance with the purposes of this agreement, and that they will not permit any hostile action or take action of any kind whatever which might hinder such withdrawals or transfers. The parties shall assist each other as far as possible.

(e) While the withdrawals and transfers of the forces are proceeding, the two parties shall not permit any destruction or sabotage of any public property or any attack on the life or property of the local civilian population. They shall not permit any interference with the local civil administration.

(f) The Joint Commission and the International Commission shall supervise the implementation of measures to ensure the safety of the forces during withdrawal and transfer.

(g) The Joint Commission in Laos shall determine the detailed procedures for the withdrawals and transfers of the forces in accordance with the above-mentioned principles.

Article 5

During the days immediately preceding the ceasefire each party undertakes not to engage in any large scale operation between the time when the agreement on the cessation of hostilities is signed at Geneva and the time when the ceasefire comes into effect.

CHAPTER II—PROHIBITION OF MILITARY PERSONNEL, ARMAMENTS AND MUNITIONS

Article 6

With effect from the proclamation of the ceasefire the introduction into Laos of any reinforcements of troops or military personnel from outside Laotian territory is prohibited.

Nevertheless, the French High Command may leave a specified number of French military personnel required for the training of the Laotian National Army in the territory of Laos; the strength of such personnel shall not exceed one thousand five hundred (1,500) officers and non-commissioned officers.

Article 7

Upon the entry into force of the present agreement, the establishment of new military bases is prohibited throughout the territory of Laos.

Article 8

The High Command of the French forces shall maintain in the territory of Laos the personnel required for the maintenance of two French military establishments, the first at Seno and the second in the Mekong valley, either in the province of Vientiane or downstream from Vientiane.

The effectives maintained in these military establishments shall not exceed a total of three thousand five hundred (3,500) men.

Article 9

Upon the entry into force of the present agreement and in accordance with the declaration made at the Geneva Conference by the Royal Government of Laos on July 20, 1954, the introduction into Laos of armaments, munitions and military equipment of all kinds is prohibited, with the exception of a specified quantity of armaments in categories specified as necessary for the defense of Laos.

Article 10

The new armaments and military personnel permitted to enter Laos in accordance with the terms of article nine above shall enter Laos at the following points only: Luang Prabang, Xieng Khouang, Vientiane, Seno, Pakse, Savannakhet and Tchépone.

CHAPTER III—DISENGAGEMENT OF THE FORCES—ASSEMBLY AREAS— CONCENTRATION AREAS

Article 11

The disengagement of the armed forces of both sides, including concentration of the armed forces, movements to rejoin the provisional assembly areas allotted to one party and provisional withdrawal movements by the other party, shall be completed within a period not exceeding fifteen (15) days after the ceasefire.

Article 12

The Joint Commission in Laos shall fix the site and boundaries:

—of the five (5) provisional assembly areas for the reception of the Vietnamese People's Volunteer Forces,

—of the five (5) provisional assembly areas for the reception of the French forces in Laos,

—of the twelve (12) provisional assembly areas, one to each province, for the reception of the fighting units of "Pathet Lao."

—The forces of the Laotian National Army shall remain *in situ* during the entire duration of the operations of disengagement and transfer of foreign forces and fighting units of "Pathet Lao."

Article 13

The foreign forces shall be transferred outside Laotian territory as follows:

(1) *French Forces:* The French forces will be moved out of Laos by road (along routes laid down by the Joint Commission in Laos) and also by air and inland waterway:

(2) *Vietnamese People's Volunteer Forces:* These forces will be moved out of Laos by land, along routes and in accordance with a schedule to be determined by the Joint Commission in Laos in accordance with principle of simultaneous withdrawal of foreign forces.

Article 14

Pending a political settlement, the fighting units of "Pathet Lao," concentrated in the provisional assembly areas, shall move into the provinces of Phong Saly and Sam Neua, except for any military personnel who wish to be demobilized where they are. They will be free to move between these two provinces in a corridor along the frontier between Laos and Vietnam bounded on the south by the Line Sop Kin, Na Mi-Sop Sang, Muong Son.

Concentration shall be completed within one-hundred-and-twenty (120) days from the date of entry into force of the present agreement.

Article 15

Each party undertakes to refrain from any reprisals or discrimination against persons or organizations for their activities during the hostilities and also undertakes to guarantee their democratic freedoms.

CHAPTER IV—PRISONERS OF WAR AND CIVILIAN INTERNEES

Article 16

The liberation and repatriation of all prisoners of war and civilian internees detained by each of the two parties at the coming into force of the present agreement shall be carried out under the following conditions:

> (a) All prisoners of war and civilian internees of Laotian and other nationalities captured since the beginning of hostilities in Laos, during military operations or in any other circumstances of war and in any part of the territory of Laos, shall be liberated within a period of thirty (30) days after the date when the ceasefire comes into effect.
>
> (b) The term "civilian internees" is understood to mean all persons who, having in any way contributed to the political and armed strife between the two parties, have been arrested for that reason

or kept in detention by either party during the period of hostilities.

(c) All foreign prisoners of war captured by either party shall be surrendered to the appropriate authorities of the other party, who shall give them all possible assistance in proceeding to the destination of their choice.

CHAPTER V—MISCELLANEOUS

Article 17

The commanders of the forces of the two parties shall ensure that persons under their respective commands who violate any of the provisions of the present agreement are suitably punished.

Article 18

In cases in which the place of burial is known and the existence of graves has been established, the commander of the forces of either party shall, within a specified period after the entry into force of the present agreement, permit the graves service of the other party to enter that part of Laotian territory under his military control for the purpose of finding and removing the bodies of deceased military personnel of that party, including the bodies of deceased prisoners of war.

The Joint Commission shall fix the procedures by which this task is carried out and the time limits within which it must be completed. The commanders of the forces of each party shall communicate to the other all information in his possession as to the place of burial of military personnel of the other party.

Article 19

The present agreement shall apply to all the armed forces of either party. The armed forces of each party shall respect the territory under the military control of the other party, and engage in no hostile act against the other party.

For the purpose of the present article the word "territory" includes territorial waters and air space.

Article 20

The commander of the forces of the two parties shall afford full protection and all possible assistance and cooperation to the Joint Commission and its joint organs and to the International Commission and its inspection teams in the performance of the functions and tasks assigned to them by the present agreement.

Article 21

The costs involved in the operation of the Joint Commission and its joint groups and of the International Commission and its inspection teams shall be shared equally between the two parties.

Article 22

The signatories of the present agreement and their successors in their functions shall be responsible for the observance and enforcement of the terms and provisions thereof. The commanders of the forces of the two parties shall, within their respective commands, take all steps and make all arrangements necessary to ensure full compliance with all the provisions of the present agreement by all military personnel under their command.

Article 23

The procedures laid down in the present agreement shall, whenever necessary, be examined by the commanders of the two parties and, if necessary, defined more specifically by the Joint Commission.

CHAPTER VI—JOINT COMMISSION AND INTERNATIONAL COMMISSON FOR SUPERVISION AND CONTROL IN LAOS

Article 24

Responsibility for the execution of the agreement on the cessation of hostilities shall rest with the parties.

Article 25

An International Commission shall be entrusted with control and supervision over the application of the provisions of the agreement on the cessation of hostilities in Laos. It shall be composed of representatives of the following States: Canada, India and Poland. It shall be presided over by the representative of India. Its headquarters shall be at Vientiane.

Article 26

The International Commission shall set up fixed and mobile inspection teams, composed of an equal number of officers appointed by each of the above-mentioned States.

The fixed teams shall be located at the following points: Pakse, Seno, Tchepone, Vientiane, Xieng Khonang, Phong Saly, Sophao (province of Sam Neua). These points of location may, at a later date, be altered by agreement between the Government of Laos and the International Commission.

The zones of action of the mobile teams shall be regions bordering the land frontiers of Laos. Within the limits of their zones of action, they shall have the right to move freely and shall receive from the local civil and military authorities all facilities they may require for the fulfilment of their tasks (provisions of personnel, access to documents needed for supervision, summoning of witnesses needed for holding enquiries, the security and freedom of movement of the inspection teams etc. . . .). They shall have at their disposal such modern means of transport, observation and communication as they may require.

Outside the zones of action defined above, the mobile teams may, with the agreement of the command of the party concerned, move about as required by the tasks assigned to them by the present agreement.

Article 27

The International Commission shall be responsible for supervising the execution by the parties of the provisions of the present agreement. For this purpose it shall fulfill the functions of control, observation, inspection and investigation connected with the implementation of the provisions of the agreement on the cessation of hostilities, and shall in particular:

> (a) Control the withdrawal of foreign forces in accordance with the provisions of the agreement on the cessation of hostilities and see that frontiers are respected:
>
> (b) Control the release of prisoners of war and civilian internees:
>
> (c) Supervise, at ports and airfields and along all the frontiers of Laos, the implementation of the provisions regulating the introduction into Laos of military personnel and war materiel;
>
> (d) Supervise the implementation of the clauses of the agreement on the cessation of hostilities relating to rotation of personnel and to supplies for French union security forces maintained in Laos.

Article 28

A Joint Commission shall be set up to facilitate the implementation of the clauses relating to the withdrawal of foreign forces.

The Joint Commission shall form joint groups, the number of which shall be decided by mutual agreement between the parties.

The Joint Commission shall facilitate the implementation of the clauses of the agreement on the cessation of hostilities re-

lating to the simultaneous and general ceasefire in Laos for all
regular and irregular armed forces of the two parties.

It shall assist the parties in the implementation of the said
clauses; it shall ensure liaison between them for the purpose of
preparing and carrying out plans for the implementation of the
said clauses; it shall endeavor to settle any disputes between the
parties arising out of the implementation of these clauses. The
joint groups shall follow the forces in their movements and shall
be disbanded once the withdrawal plans have been carried out.

Article 29

The Joint Commission and the joint groups shall be composed of an equal number of representatives of the commands
of the parties concerned.

Article 30

The International Commission shall, through the medium
of the inspection teams mentioned above, and as soon as possible, either on its own initiative, or at the request of the Joint
Commission, or of one of the parties, undertake the necessary
investigations both documentary and on the ground.

Article 31

The inspection teams shall submit to the International Commission the results of their supervision, investigation and observations; furthermore, they shall draw up such special reports
as they may consider necessary or as may be requested from
them by the Commission. In the case of a disagreement within
the teams, the findings of each member shall be transmitted to
the Commission.

Article 32

If an inspection team is unable to settle an incident or considers that there is a violation or a threat of a serious violation,
the International Commission shall be informed; the latter shall

examine the reports and findings of the inspection teams and shall inform the parties of the measures which should be taken for the settlement of the incident, ending of the violation or removal of the threat of violation.

Article 33

When the Joint Commission is unable to reach an agreement on the interpretation of a provision or on the appraisal of a fact, the International Commission shall be informed of the disputed question. Its recommendations shall be sent directly to the parties and shall be notified to the Joint Commission.

Article 34

The recommendations of the International Commission shall be adopted by majority vote, subject to the provisions contained in article thirty-five. If the votes are equally divided, the chairman's vote shall be decisive.

The International Commission may make recommendations concerning amendments and additions which should be made to the provisions of the agreement on the cessation of hostilities in Laos, in order to ensure more effective execution of the said agreement. These recommendations shall be adopted unanimously.

Article 35

On questions concerning violations, or threats of violations, which might lead to a resumption of hostilities, and in particular,

> (a) refusal by foreign armed forces to effect the movements provided for in the withdrawal plan;
> (b) violation or threat of violation of the country's integrity by foreign armed forces,

the decisions of the International Commission must be unanimous.

Article 36

If one of the parties refuses to put a recommendation of the International Commission into effect, the parties concerned or the Commission itself shall inform the members of the Geneva Conference.

If the International Commission does not reach unanimity in the cases provided for in article thirty-five, it shall transmit a majority report and one or more minority reports to the members of the Conference.

The International Commission shall inform the members of the Conference of all cases in which its work is being hindered.

Article 37

The International Commission shall be set up at the time of the cessation of hostilities in Indochina in order that it may be able to fulfill the tasks prescribed in article twenty-seven.

Article 38

The International Commission for Supervision and Control in Laos shall act in close cooperation with the International Commissions in Vietnam and Cambodia.

The Secretaries General of these three Commissions shall be responsible for coordinating their work and for relations between them.

Article 39

The International Commission for Supervision and Control in Laos may, after consultation with the International Commissions in Cambodia and Vietnam, having regard to the development of the situation in Cambodia and Vietnam, progressively reduce its activities. Such a decision must be reduced unanimously. These recommendations shall be adopted unanimously.

CHAPTER VII

Article 40

All the provisions of the present agreement, save paragraph (a) of article two, shall enter into force at 24[00] hours (Geneva time) on July 22, 1954.

Article 41

Done in Geneva (Switzerland) on July 20, 1954, at 24[00] hours, in the French language.

For the Commander-in-Chief of the Fighting Units of the "Pathet Lao" and for the Commander-in-Chief of the People's Army of Vietnam

[signed] TA-QUANG-BUU

Vice-Minister of National Defense of the Democratic Republic of Vietnam

For the Commander-in-Chief of the Forces of the French Union in Indochina

[signed] [HENRI] DELTEIL

Général de Brigade

8

Agreement of the Cessation of Hostilities in Cambodia, July 20, 1954*

CHAPTER I—PRINCIPLES AND CONDITIONS GOVERNING EXECUTION OF THE CEASEFIRE

Article 1

As from July 23, 1954, at 0800 hours (Peking mean time) complete cessation of all hostilities throughout Cambodia shall be ordered and enforced by the commanders of the armed forces of the two parties for all troops and personnel of the land, naval and air forces under their control.

Article 2

In conformity with the principle of a simultaneous ceasefire throughout Indochina, there shall be a simultaneous cessation of hostilities throughout Cambodia, in all the combat areas and for all the forces of the two parties.

To obviate any mistake or misunderstanding and to ensure that both the ending of hostilities and all other operations arising from cessation of hostilities are in fact simultaneous.

> (a) due allowance being made for the time actually required for transmission of the ceasefire order down to the lowest echelons of the combatant forces of both sides, the two parties are agreed that the

* *Further Documents Relating to the Discussion of Indochina at the Geneva Conference* (Miscellaneous, no. 20 [1954], Command Paper, 9239). London: Great Britain Parliamentary Sessional Papers, XXXI (1953/1954), pp. 49–58.

complete and simultaneous ceasefire throughout the territory of Cambodia shall became effective at [o]8[oo] hours (local time) on August 7, 1954. It is agreed that Peking mean time shall be taken as local time.

(b) Each side shall comply strictly with the timetable jointly agreed upon between the parties for the execution of all operations connected with the cessation of hostilities.

Article 3

All operations and movements connected with the execution of the cessation of hostilities must be carried out in a safe and orderly fashion.

(a) Within a number of days to be determined by the commanders of both sides, after the ceasefire has been achieved, each party shall be responsible for removing and neutralizing mines, booby traps, explosives and any other dangerous devices placed by it. Should it be impossible to complete removal and neutralization before departure, the party concerned will mark the spot by placing visible signs. Sites thus cleared of mines and any other obstacles to the free movement of the personnel of the International Commission and the Joint Commission shall be notified to the latter by local military commanders.

(b) Any incidents that may arise between the forces of the two sides and may result from mistakes or misunderstandings shall be settled on the spot so as to restrict their scope.

(c) During the days immediately preceding the ceasefire each party undertakes not to engage in any large scale operation between the time when the agreement on the cessation of hostilities is signed at Geneva and the time when the ceasefire comes into effect.

CHAPTER II—PROCEDURE FOR THE WITHDRAWAL OF FOREIGN MILITARY PERSONNEL FROM CAMBODIA

Article 4

1. The withdrawal outside the territory of Cambodia shall apply to:

(a) the armed forces and military combatant personnel of the French union;

(b) the combatant formations of all types which have entered the territory of Cambodia from other countries or regions of the peninsula;

(c) all the foreign elements (or Cambodians not natives of Cambodia) in the military formations of any kind or holding supervisory functions in all political or military, administrative, economic, financial or social bodies, having worked in liaison with the Vietnam military units.

2. The withdrawals of the forces and elements referred to in the foregoing paragraphs and their military supplies and materials must be completed within ninety days reckoning from the entry into force of the present agreement.

3. The two parties shall guarantee that the withdrawals of all the forces will be effected in accordance with the purposes of the agreement, and that they will not permit any hostile action or take any action likely to create difficulties for such withdrawals. They shall assist one another as far as possible.

4. While the withdrawals are proceeding, the two parties shall not permit any destruction or sabotage of public property or any attack on the life or property of the civilian population. They shall not

permit any interference with the local civil administration.

5. The Joint Commission and the International Supervisory Commission shall supervise the execution of measures to ensure the safety of the forces during withdrawal.

6. The Joint Commission in Cambodia shall determine the detailed procedures for the withdrawals of the forces on the basis of the above-mentioned principles.

CHAPTER III—OTHER QUESTIONS

A. THE KHMER ARMED FORCES, NATIVES OF CAMBODIA

Article 5

The two parties shall undertake that within thirty days after the ceasefire order has been proclaimed, the Khmer resistance forces shall be demobilized on the spot; simultaneously, the troops of the royal Khmer army shall abstain from taking any hostile action against the Khmer resistance forces.

Article 6

The situation of these nationals shall be decided in the light of the declaration made by the Delegation of Cambodia at the Geneva Conference, reading as follows:

"The Royal Government of Cambodia,

In the desire to ensure harmony and agreement among the peoples of the Kingdom,

Declares itself resolved to take the necessary measures to integrate all citizens, without discrimination, into the national community and to guarantee them the enjoyment of the rights and

freedoms for which the Constitution of the Kingdom provides;

Affirms that all Cambodian citizens may freely
participate as electors or candidates in general elections by secret ballot."

No reprisals shall be taken against the said nationals or their
families, each national being entitled to the enjoyment, without
any discrimination as compared with other nationals, of all constitutional guarantees concerning the protection of person and
property and democratic freedoms.

Applicants therefore may be accepted for service in the regular
army or local police formations if they satisfy the conditions
required for current recruitment of the army and police corps.

The same procedure shall apply to those persons who have
returned to civilian life and who may apply for civilian employment on the same terms as other nationals.

B. BAN ON THE INTRODUCTION OF
MILITARY PERSONNEL, ARMAMENTS
AND MUNITIONS, MILITARY BASES

Article 7

In accordance with the declaration made by the Delegation
of Cambodia at 2400 hours on July 20, 1954 at the Geneva
Conference of Foreign Ministers:

"The Royal Government of Cambodia will not
join in any agreement with other States, if this
agreement carries for Cambodia the obligation to
enter into a military alliance not in conformity with
the principles of the Charter of the United Nations,
or, as long as its security is not threatened, the
obligation to establish bases on Cambodian territory
for the military forces of foreign powers.

"During the period which will elapse between the
date of the cessation of hostilities in Vietnam and

that of the final settlement of political problems in
this country, the Royal Government of Cambodia
will not solicit foreign aid in war materiel, personnel
or instructors except for the purpose of the effective
defense of the territory."

C. CIVILIAN INTERNEES AND PRISONERS OF WAR—BURIAL

Article 8

The liberation and repatriation of all civilian internees and
prisoners of war detained by each of the two parties at the coming into force of the present agreement shall be carried out
under the following conditions:

(a) All prisoners of war and civilian internees of
whatever nationality, captured since the beginning
of hostilities in Cambodia during military operations
or in any other circumstances of war and in any
part of the territory of Cambodia, shall be liberated
after the entry into force of the present armistice
agreement.

(b) The terms "civilian internees" is understood
to mean all persons who, having in any way contributed to the political and armed struggle between
the two parties, have been arrested for that reason
or kept in detention by either party during the
period of hostilities.

(c) All foreign prisoners of war captured by
either party shall be surrendered to the appropriate
authorities of the other party, who shall give them
all possible assistance in proceeding to the destination of their choice.

Article 9

After the entry into force of the present agreement, if the
place of burial is known and the existence of graves has been

established, the Cambodian commander shall, within a specified period, authorize the exhumation and removal of the bodies of deceased military personnel of the other party, including the bodies of prisoners of war or personnel deceased and buried on Cambodian territory.

The Joint Commission shall fix the procedures by which this task is to be carried out and the time limit within which it must be completed.

CHAPTER IV—JOINT COMMISSION AND INTERNATIONAL COMMISSION FOR SUPERVISION AND CONTROL IN CAMBODIA

Article 10

Responsibility for the execution of the agreement on the cessation of hostilities shall rest with the parties.

Article 11

An International Commission shall be responsible for control and supervision of the application of the provisions of the agreement on the cessation of hostilities in Cambodia. It shall be composed of representatives of the following States: Canada, India and Poland. It shall be presided over by the representative of India. Its headquarters shall be at Phnompenh.

Article 12

The International Commission shall set up fixed and mobile inspection teams, composed of an equal number of officers appointed by each of the above mentioned States.

The fixed teams shall be located at the following points: Phnompenh, Kompong Cham, Kratié, Svay Rieng, Kampot. These points of location may be altered at a later date by agreement between the Government of Cambodia and the International Commission.

The zones of action of the mobile teams shall be the regions bordering on the land and sea frontiers of Cambodia. The mobile teams shall have the right to move freely within the limits of their zones of action, and they shall receive from the local civil and military authorities all facilities they may require for the fulfillment of their tasks (provision of personnel, access to documents needed for supervision, summoning of witnesses needed for inquiries, security and freedom of movement of the inspection teams, etc.). They shall have at their disposal such modern means of transport, observation and communication as they may require.

Outside the zones of action defined above, the mobile teams may, with the agreement of the Cambodian command, move about as required by the tasks assigned to them under the present agreement.

Article 13

The International Commission shall be responsible for supervising the execution by the parties of the provisions of the present agreement. For this purpose it shall fulfill the functions of control, observation, inspection and investigation connected with the implementation of the provisions of the agreement on the cessation of hostilities, and shall in particular:

> (a) control the withdrawal of foreign forces in accordance with the provisions of the agreement on the cessation of hostilities and see that frontiers are respected;
> (b) control the release of prisoners of war, and civilian internees;
> (c) supervise, at ports and airfields and along all the frontiers of Cambodia, the application of the Cambodian declaration concerning the introduction into Cambodia of military personnel and war materiel on grounds of foreign assistance.

Article 14

A Joint Commission shall be set up to facilitate the implementation of the clauses relating to the withdrawal of foreign forces.

The Joint Commission may form joint groups the number of which shall be decided by mutual agreement between the parties.

The Joint Commission shall facilitate the implementation of the clauses of the agreement on the cessation of hostilities relating to the simultaneous and general ceasefire in Cambodia for all regular and irregular armed forces of the two parties.

It shall assist the parties in the implementation of the said clauses; it shall ensure liaison between them for the purpose of preparing and carrying out plans for the implementation of the said clauses; it shall endeavor to settle any disputes between the parties arising out of the implementation of these clauses. The Joint Commission may send joint groups to follow the forces in their movements; such groups shall be disbanded once the withdrawal plans have been carried out.

Article 15

The Joint Commission shall be composed of an equal number of representatives of the commands of the parties concerned.

Article 16

The International Commission shall, through the medium of the inspection teams mentioned above and as soon as possible, either on its own initiative or at the request of the Joint Commission or of one of the parties, undertake the necessary investigations both documentary and on the ground.

Article 17

The inspection teams shall transmit to the International Commission the results of their supervision, investigations and observations; furthermore, they shall draw up such special reports as they may consider necessary or as may be requested from them by the Commission. In the case of a disagreement within the teams, the findings of each member shall be transmitted to the Commission.

Article 18

If an inspection team is unable to settle an incident or considers that there is a violation or threat of a serious violation, the International Commission shall be informed; the Commission shall examine the reports and findings of the inspection teams and shall inform the parties of the measures to be taken for the settlement of the incident, ending of the violation or removal of the threat of violation.

Article 19

When the Joint Commission is unable to reach agreement on the interpretation of a provision or on the appraisal of a fact, the International Commission shall be informed of the disputed question. Its recommendations shall be sent directly to the parties and shall be notified to the Joint Commission.

Article 20

The recommendations of the International Commission shall be adopted by a majority vote, subject to the provisions of article twenty-one. If the votes are equally divided, the Chairman's vote shall be decisive.

The International Commission may make recommendations concerning amendments and additions which should be made to the provisions of the Agreement on the cessation of hostilities in Cambodia, in order to ensure more effective execution of the said agreement. These recommendations shall be adopted unanimously.

Article 21

On questions concerning violations, or threats of violations, which might lead to a resumption of hostilities, and in particular,

> (a) refusal by foreign armed forces to effect the movements provided for in the withdrawal plan,

(b) violation or threats of violation of the country's integrity by foreign armed forces,

the decisions of the International Commission must be unanimous.

Article 22

If one of the parties refuses to put a recommendation of the International Commission into effect, the parties concerned or the Commission itself shall inform the members of the Geneva Conference.

If the International Commission does not reach unanimity in the cases provided for in article twenty-one, it shall transmit a majority report and one or more minority reports to members of the Conference.

The International Commission shall inform the members of the Conference of all cases in which its work is being hindered.

Article 23

The International Commission shall be set up at the time of the cessation of hostilities in Indochina in order that it may be able to perform the tasks prescribed in article thirteen.

Article 24

The International Commission for Supervision and Control in Cambodia shall act in close cooperation with the International Commissions in Vietnam and Laos.

The Secretaries General of those three Commissions shall be responsible for coordinating their work and for relations between them.

Article 25

The International Commission for Supervision and Control in Cambodia may, after consultation with the International Commissions in Vietnam and in Laos, and having regard to the development of the situation in Vietnam and in Laos, progressively reduce its activities. Such a decision must be adopted unanimously.

CHAPTER V—IMPLEMENTATION

Article 26

The commanders of the forces of the two parties shall ensure that persons under their respective commands who violate any of the provisions of the present agreement are suitably punished.

Article 27

The present agreement on the cessation of hostilities shall apply to all the armed forces of either party.

Article 28

The commanders of the forces of the two parties shall afford full protection and all possible assistance and cooperation to the Joint Commission and to the International Commission and its inspection teams in the performance of their functions.

Article 29

The Joint Commission, composed of an equal number of representatives of the commands of the two parties, shall assist the parties in the implementation of all the clauses of the agreement on the cessation of hostilities, ensure liaison between the two parties, draw up plans for the implementation of the agreement, and endeavor to settle any dispute arising out of the implementation of the said clauses and plans.

Article 30

The costs involved in the operation of the Joint Commission shall be shared equally between the two parties.

Article 31

The signatories of the present agreement on the cessation of hostilities and their successors in their functions shall be responsible for the observance and enforcement of the terms and provisions thereof. The commanders of the forces of the two parties shall, within their respective commands, take all steps and make all arrangements necessary to ensure full compliance with all the provisions of the present Agreement by all personnel under their command.

Article 32

The procedures laid down in the present agreement shall, whenever necessary, be examined by the commands of the two parties and, if necessary, defined more specifically by the Joint Commission.

Article 33

All the provisions of the present agreement shall enter into force at 00 hours (Geneva time) on July 23, 1954.

Done at Geneva on July 20, 1954.

For the Commander-in-Chief of the Units of the Khmer Resistance Forces and for the Commander-in-Chief of the Vietnamese Military Units

[signed]   TA-QUANG-BUU

Vice-Minister of National Defense of the Democratic Republic of Vietnam

For the Commander-in-Chief of the Khmer National Armed Forces

[signed] GENERAL NHIEK TIOULONG

PART III

THE STRUGGLE
FOR NEUTRALITY
IN LAOS

Introduction

British scholar Hugh Toye, in his important study on Laos,[1] shows how, before the arrival of colonialism, Laos played the role of buffer between the "indianized" countries west of the Mekong, and "sinicized" Annam (Vietnam) to the west. With the onset of European imperialism in Indochina the situation became more complicated; British influence spread to nearby Burma, and Siam (Thailand) emerged as a semi-independent state. Toye shows in fascinating detail how colonialism, and French policy in particular, tended to reinforce Laos' role as a buffer among these forces, imparting to it a "neutralist" orientation.

When the United States became the successor to French power in Indochina,[2] Laos was no longer permitted to remain a buffer; it became instead a full-scale battleground in the struggle between indigenous revolutionary forces and American armed might. The recent aspects of this struggle have taken on the character of genocide, as the vast arsenal of American (non-nuclear, for the time being) firepower is unleashed against rebel territories.

American policymakers have justified the subversion of Laotian neutrality on two grounds. For many Americans the ideology of anti-communism was sufficient. During the congressional committee hearings of 1959 on Laos, the State Department officially vied with congressmen for the loudest denunciation of the "evil communist revolutionaries" of Indochina.[3]

[1] We have been unable to reprint from Mr. Toye's book *Laos: Buffer State or Battleground* (London: Oxford University Press, 1968)—eds.

[2] The succession which took place after the Geneva accords of 1954 was no mere mechanical substitution of one traditional colonial regime for another. American neocolonialism was a qualitatively different phenomenon, even if the difference was minimal to the indigenous population. For a discussion of these changing modern styles of colonialism, see the introduction to Part I, this volume.

[3] See Selection 12, this volume. On the general theme of anti-communism, see Michael Parenti, *The Anti-Communist Impulse* (New York: Random House, 1969).

A persistent theme of the anti-communist is the notion of "outside agitators." Indigenous revolutionaries are never seen as operating in their own interest, but are characterized as the "pawns" of outside manipulators. This has been particularly true of American views on Laos. Despite overwhelming evidence of the historical and ethnic roots of Pathet Lao rebellion, the Laotian revolutionaries are invariably seen by US policymakers as "agents" of North Vietnam, who in turn get their orders from the masterminds of the world communist conspiracy in Peking and/or Moscow. This comic strip version of modern history allows Americans conveniently to overlook the fact that the United States has been the most spectacular outside agitator in Laos. As the US ambassador himself admitted, about the period when all Laotian parties were drawing together in a coalition government,[4] "I struggled for sixteen months to prevent a coalition." [5]

If simple anti-communism was sufficient for some, a more sophisticated doctrine was needed to sell US intervention in Laos to others. American "aid" was the answer. The benevolent concept of aid, the generous efforts of affluent America to share some of its surplus wealth with primitive Laos, was hard to challenge. Who could criticize such a policy? American aid could be the answer to communist subversion, policymakers urged, combining altruism with self-interest. But it was only a matter of time before questions like "What kind of aid?," "For which sectors of the population?," "What is its impact on an underdeveloped society?" would be asked. Arthur J. Dommen's account[6] of the American role in Laos shows how the pouring of American money into Laos, however much it may have enriched an elite of merchants and military officers, brought little blessing to the average Laotian. In fact, it proved disastrous to the entire economy.

[4] See the documents on the post-Geneva conciliation that seemed to be breaking out in Laos in the mid-1950's, until the United States, through its support of right wing elements undermined the hopeful efforts. Selections 9–12 this volume.

[5] See James G. Parson's statement at the conclusion of Selection 12, this volume.

[6] Arthur J. Dommen, *Conflict in Laos: The Politics of Neutralization* (New York: Praeger, 1964).

In sum, the American impact on Laos has been totally negative. Aid programs are primarily military, and the Royal Laotian Army has the dubious distinction of being the only foreign army anywhere in the world *wholly* supported by US taxpayers.[7] The American attempt to eradicate the Pathet Lao, a movement with deep historic roots in the country, has, by the 1970's led to a hideous *reductio ad absurdum*: wholesale destruction of the Laotian people and their society.[8]

[7] See Noam Chomsky, "Destroying Laos," *New York Review of Books,* XV (July 23, 1970), p. 24.

[8] See Part V, this volume. See also Introduction to Part I, this volume.

9

Pathet Lao Fights:
A Front-Line Village

WILFRED G. BURCHETT *

Beginning in late November, 1955, the biggest offensives were launched against the Pathet Lao positions, and in December Katay held elections from which the Pathet Lao were excluded. About this time, I visited the Pathet Lao area and was able to meet the leaders, cadres, rank and file soldiers and the people who lived in the regions administered by the Pathet Lao.

I found everyone from Souphanouvong down to the front-line soldiers superbly confident that they could hold out indefinitely. They were conscious also that the densely timbered mountains they were defending were the front-lines of the peace camp. In the front-line areas, by the time I got there, there was a sort of Dienbienphu situation. But upside down. And the same American boy scout tactics and blind refusal to accept political realities were responsible. At Dienbienphu the French were in a valley surrounded by mountains. They could not get out. In Sam Neua and Phong Saly, the royal army troops were sitting on tops of mountain peaks where they had been dropped by US planes, and they could not come down. Because it was a people's war. In the valley and around the flanks of the mountains were people whose lives had been changed radically for the better by the Pathet Lao. They had their self-defense corps, their hunter-partisans whose traps and poisoned arrows kept the royal troops at bay until the regular Pathet Lao troops could come along.

According to prisoners captured, US military "advisers" were directing operations from a base just south of Sam Neua prov-

* From Wilfred J. Burchett, *Mekong Upstream* (Hanoi: Red River Publishing House, 1957), pp. 285–304.

ince, in Xieng Khouang. They had tried to send troops in by land routes, but these had been blocked by the guerrillas. So planes were used to parachute them in. American strategy was to form a line running southwest-northeast and hinged on a point about thirty miles from the provincial capital. As soon as the line was formed, it would swing around on its southern axis to encompass the town of Sam Neua. With another swing or two, it would clear the province up to the Vietnamese frontier.

Like the Dienbienphu operation, it must have looked good on the war maps the Americans are such experts in preparing. At first a platoon was dropped on a mountain peak and was promptly wiped out. Next time two platoons were dropped and eventually a company for each peak. Peaks were occupied in triangle fashion, and each corner of the triangle absorbed one company. A battalion per triangle. And there are nothing but mountain peaks in Sam Neua and Phong Saly provinces. Worst of all from the US-Katay viewpoint, the companies could not establish contact. They could not get down into the valleys to link up their positions. They tried, but were cut to pieces by either guerrillas or regular Pathet Lao troops.

By mid-December, a large proportion of the best troops of the royal army were like the unfortunate hunter "up a tree and couldn't get down" because of the tiger at the bottom. Six infantry battalions, one company of parachutists and fifteen companies of commandos were sitting on top of a total of thirty-five peaks in Sam Neua and there were thousands more to cover. They could not move and they could not link up. Attempts to join up and form a definite line cost them heavy casualties. Pathet Lao fire sent them scuttling back to their trenches on the mountain tops again. They could not move even to requisition food. They had to be supplied by parachute.

If all this sounds as if things were easy for the Pathet Lao, it was not so. It was an exceedingly bitter and difficult struggle. The enemy could choose its mountain peaks and land troops on them within half-an-hour's flight or less from its forward air bases. Pathet Lao troops had to move up by jungle paths, often mere animal tracks. From the air, one sees nothing but the closely packed ridges. From the ground, one moves by crossing these ridges into successions of ascending and descending valleys. Along the rims of the valleys the going is easy enough. There are paths connecting the various bamboo and thatch Lao villages which enclose the bowl of the valleys. After that it is often a good half-day's climb up steep tracks which are little more than tunnels in the steamy undergrowth, through bamboo thickets and an endless variety of creepers, undergrowth and tall timber through which comes hardly a glimmer of sunshine. There are nimble-footed mountain ponies which pick their way up the steep tracks with the delicacy of cats, but the rider must lie flat with his head along the pony's neck—and even risk having his backbone bared by a hanging sliver of razor-sharp bamboo. It is very beautiful, very picturesque when one clears the top of the ridge and can look back at the green speck of valley from which one has come or ahead to the other green speck which must be the staging point for the night.

Along these steep rocky trails in November and December, 1955, convoys of porters were moving in endless lines, baskets of rice and bags of salt, grenades and mines from the jungle arsenals, uniforms and blankets from "soldiers' aid" cooperatives swinging from their carrying poles, or packed around bicycles. . . . Empty convoys passed the laden ones; gay figures racing along the downward paths on bicycles, jog-trotting along with carrying poles shouldered like rifles; hurrying back for more munitions, rice and salt for the front; calling out cheery greetings as they passed; stopping to exchange news from the front for that of the rear. The atmosphere was cheerful and the morale high. Occasionally there were halts to cook rice and to brew tea. But they were not for long during the daytime. The need at the front was too urgent and the porters knew it. It was their own brothers, husbands, kinsmen and tribesmen who suffered if they were late. Ahead of the convoys, the troops were toiling along according to where the latest enemy troops had been parachuted. And ahead of the regular troops were the local guerrillas usually taking the first shock of a new invasion, but with limited stocks of arms. Troops marched and fought for days without any food at all to relieve the guerrillas and to prevent the enemy from linking up and consolidating their positions.

Floating over those blue and purple ridges in a plane, it was impossible to imagine the ferment below. If a pilot caught a momentary glimpse through a break in the undergrowth, he would have seen what looked like lines of ants moving past each other, occasionally pausing an instant to exchange greetings and then hurrying along on their urgent tasks.

Katay's November–December offensives were a failure. A line of mountain tops in Sam Neua was occupied. But the flanks of the mountains remained in Pathet Lao hands. Behind the ridges, the whole area was in guerrilla hands. Ahead of them were the regular Pathet Lao forces. When orders were given for the great sweep, a few disjointed parts creaked forward only to run into a hail of fire. The sweep ground down to a halt before it really started. US planes zoomed over and dropped bags of rice marked with clasped hands and the US-Laotian flags with a portrait of King Sisavangvong inside. A good proportion of them fell into Pathet Lao hands and cold, weary and starving royal conscripts stumbled down from the mountains with white flags, cursing Katay, cursing the Americans and asking to surrender. They were welcomed as brothers. The leader of one group of twenty complained as they threw down their arms "Where were you? We have been looking for you for days past."

US technique was once again breaking down before the will of the people. There was no lack of planes, no lack of modern weapons or ammunition. Only one thing was lacking and that was morale. And morale cannot be built into a machine. In the Pathet Lao areas, there were few machines but morale in the front and at the rear was magnificently high.

Our ponies had daintily picked their way up a razor-edged, flinty track for a good six hours till midday. Most of the way there was a sheer drop of thirty or forty meters into a ravine, along which dashed an ever narrowing foamy stream. Every two hours we stopped and unsaddled the sweating ponies and a guide cut them armfuls of lush grass or feathery bamboo tips. On pony back in mid-December it had been icy when we started out, and even at noon it was cool enough in the shadows. But in the occasional clear patches, it was burning hot. Along the valley which we had followed for an hour or two after daybreak, the cut grain lay in terraced fields. Here and there, rough shelters had been set up. Troops and peasants were working together, thrashing out the rice grains on to a reed mat by whacking the heads of the sheaves on a log. Others were throwing the results into the air from a woven scoop, catching the grain after the wind had blown away the chaff.

Steep mountains hemmed in the valley and formed what looked like an impenetrable barrier ahead. We had been up well before dawn, but even before we dressed we could hear the rhythmic thudding of the primitive rice-pounders which exist under every Laotian house, as the womenfolk husked the daily ration. Children stood around yawning under the floor of the houses, bamboo torches in one hand, the other pushing the rice back into the mortars in between the rise and fall of the wooden pestles. Heads of babies still fast asleep hung listlessly from swathes on their mothers' backs, swaying from side to side with the rhythmic tread of their mothers' feet on the long pestle arms. Eyes of buffalo and pigs glowed greenly in the light of the bamboo torches and cooking fires. . . .

It was a day similar to many others. Often we managed in a dawn to dusk march to clamber up and down only one of the ridges which separated the valleys. Sometimes we managed two, or even three. On this day, as our guide had planned, by half an hour before sunset we had slithered down from the jungle on an abrupt rocky path into a broad valley. Our destination for the night lay ahead of us. A bamboo and thatch village, houses high up on piles and surrounded by banana and area palms. The stream, which had been a leaping, foaming fury a few hours before, now lay in placid, sunfilled pools, into which naked children were leaping and splashing about in front of the houses. A few score paces upstream, fishermen were standing on rocks intently regarding the water and now and again throwing a weighted net and leaping in after it to secure the fish. On platforms flooded with sunlight at the end of the thatched homes, women were twirling their spinning wheels and men sucking at their bubble pipes in the last minutes of sunlight. They abandoned spinning wheels and pipes to gather around as our little convoy crossed the swaying bamboo bridge which spanned the stream to bring us among their houses.

Houses of the Lao are usually oval shaped, with projecting

eaves at each end to shelter the platforms on which most of the housework is done. The walls are of flattened out bamboo arranged in a tight trellis fashion. Leaves from a special type of palm form the base of the thatched roofs, but they are usually finished off with rice straw. The floors are bamboo of giant caliber which, when slit and flattened out, form solid slabs at least twelve inches wide. The framework of the house is of solid bamboo poles lashed together with jungle creepers. No nails are used at all.

At the end of each home is the guest room with its own fireplace, always available for the passing traveller. The rest of the hut is a single large room in which the whole family lives. A central feature is the fireplace of clay, packed down on to the bamboo floor in about the center of the common room and around which the family, including dogs and cats, gather in the evening while the rice cooks and the teapot boils. Fuel is usually dried bamboo which burns almost without smoke—so there are no chimneys. The bamboo poles above the fire, however, are stained a smooth polished ebony from generations of smoke. Ranged along one of the walls are the sleeping-mats and home-woven mosquito nets, each with wide swathes of beautifully embroidered cloth at top and bottom. In addition to the parents, the home will contain married daughters and their husbands—or suitors if they are not yet married. The clothes they wear will all have been woven at the weaving frames under the house from homespun threads.

At the village where we had arrived there was the usual competition to house the foreigner, once the villagers knew he was a friend. I was quickly allotted a guest room in a house overlooking the stream. Fishing nets drooped down from the roof, crossbows and quivers of arrows hung from pegs driven into the smoke-stained bamboo posts. Like the pipes of a pipe organ, bamboo tubes of varying calibers leaned against the walls, filled with water, salt and rice. Alongside them were spinning wheels, a plough, a set of harrows with bamboo spikes and a fearsome looking steel-toothed tiger trap. In a hammock of pleated jungle vines a baby was being swung back and forth by an elder sister. Silk worms were scattered on wild mulberry leaves in a many-tiered bamboo cage.

By the time the sun had gone down, the members of our little party were all installed in various guest rooms. While we were disposing of a supper of chopped raw meat and green leaves, fish soup and glutenous rice, villagers slipped in by twos and threes until the guest room and then the whole house was quite filled. Our host produced a huge earthenware jar, around which some of the older men gathered. Women and children kept well in the background, the latter peering through the legs of their elders. A clay seal was chipped off the neck of the jar and one of the old men began pouring in water from a buffalo horn while our host poked half a dozen flexible canes, each a good six feet long and no thicker than a little finger, deep into the jar. The canes were bent over towards half-a-dozen mouths. As we sucked, squatting on the floor around the jar, a very pleasant and potent liquid trickled down our throats.

The jars were in fact portable "breweries." They had been filled months previously with grains of glutenous rice and some other ingredients, sealed up with clay and stored away under the house. Within a month or two the rice was transformed into malt. After the "guests of honor" had drunk with the host and the old men of the village, as is obligatory for any visitors from afar, more water was added and the cane "straws" passed from mouth to mouth. Tobacco was laid out on banana leaves near the alcohol jar and the bamboo water pipe produced. We began to discuss conditions in the village, and as we talked, each smoker took the pipe in turn, poking a small pellet of tobacco leaf into the tiny bowl and after two or three powerful sucks accompanied by the gurgling sound of water in the stem, passed it on to his neighbor.

When I asked about living conditions, the villagers were silent at first, then nudged one of their number into speaking. He was Phai Sik, a small, round-headed man with deep furrows across his forehead and a back rounded with hard work. He looked much older than his thirty years.

"Before I tell you about our life now," he said, "I will tell you how it was before. In this part of the country, each village had a *nai ban* (chief). Under him were two *thao khoun*. One of the *thao khoun* neither paid taxes nor did he go on *corvée*. The

other paid taxes but did not go on *corvée*. They were nominated
by the *tasseng* (sub-district chief) who was appointed by the
French. The *nai ban* had three times as much land as the rest
of us. The *thao khoun* had twice as much. We had to work the
land for the *nai ban*. He did nothing at all, except collect taxes
and round us up for *corvée*. We paid 120 piastres . . . for
every member of the family as head tax, seventy piastres for the
paddy-field, thirty for the jungle patch, five piastres for each alcohol jar and three for each of the children who did not drink.

"Any time the *nai ban* wanted to give a feast, he would im-
pose a levy of forty or fifty piastres. We had to sell our pigs
and buffalo and the cloth our women wove to pay the taxes. But
worst of all was the *corvée*." He paused to take a turn at the
bubble pipe. Our fire had burned down to a glow of red ashes.
The portable brewery still functioned and the rice beer seemed
to lose none of its flavor or strength even after a dozen or so
horns of water had been emptied into the malt. Night had well
settled in. There were occasional grunts from buffalo and pigs
stalled under the house, a whinny from our ponies, a shriek from
a night bird or the harsh cough of some wild animal in the surrounding jungle, but otherwise complete calm.

I asked how many days *corvée* they had to give in a year.
Faces grew bitter at the question. Pham Sik said: "They took
us whenever they wanted. They would take us for ten or fifteen
days. We would come home again and after four or five days
be rounded up again. You never knew when or for how long.
No matter what you were doing, you had to drop it, pack up
some food and go. We were paid nothing and had to provide
our own food. When we had to go as porter coolies, they
marched us from before dawn till after dark with hardly a stop.
The French were always on horseback, and they changed their
guards at the different posts. They marched us with guns at our
backs. Plenty died on the road. Even in the rainy seasons, if
they were going to fight the Pathet Lao, they made us carry their
food and equipment. Once when the French were attacking
Muong Sai we came to a river too high and the current too
strong for any but the strongest to cross. We refused. They
shot six of us on the spot and forced the rest to cross. The

youngest and weakest were swept away and drowned." How many days? He turned to the villagers and there was an animated discussion between the men.

"From the time the French came back, it was at least a hundred days a year," he replied. (This was another explanation why labor power was so precious, especially the labor of women who were generally exempt from *corvée*.) "This was in addition to what we had to do for the *nai ban* and *tasseng*," Pham Sik continued. "The *tasseng* could force people to work for him for nothing for all their lives and take as many as he wanted to work his fields or reap the harvest. He took our women as he wanted. We were slaves and draft animals."

As for life now, this was another matter. "First of all, the system of *tassengs, nai ban* and *thao khouns* is finished. Instead we have a committee elected by all the villagers. *Corvée* is finished. We pay a single tax based on our actual production." There was a long discussion at this point to establish just what they did pay. The tax varied according to the quality of the rice-field and the area. There were three categories. The first paid six, the second five, the third paid three kilograms of rice for every kilogram of seed sown. This applied only to the valley rice-fields. Pham Sik for instance had "twelve kilograms" of first quality rice-fields—that is, an area on which he sowed twelve kilograms of seed. He had reaped just short of 1,000 kilograms of which he must pay seventy-two kilograms in taxes. First quality land yielded eighty fold for every kilogram of seed sown. As for the jungle patches, nothing was paid if they harvested less than sixty baskets of rice, but if they sowed over twenty kilograms of seed, they paid twice that amount in tax.

"This is very reasonable," Pham Sik said in his serious, deliberate way. "Before, the more we produced, the more we were plundered. Now we have good reason to produce more. We have become human beings again. We have something to live and work for. Everybody pays their taxes willingly and often give up more than they need, because they know it goes to the army and the cadres who brought us our new life. The same with labor. The *corvée* system is gone for ever, but we know the needs at the front. The imperialists and feudalists are attacking us. They want to put the *tassengs* and *nai ban* back in power. Some of us fight at the front, others who stay in the rear give fifteen days labor a year to the administration. These are things we have discussed among ourselves and agreed on. Many volunteer to give more days on transport and other work. Nowadays we provide the first two days' food ourselves and the administration looks after the rest. It's regulated how many hours a day we march and how many pounds we carry. If a team decides to march more, it can, but no one may increase the loads."

One old man, with a deeply wrinkled face, who had been listening intently and nodding his head in approval at the various points Pham Sik had made said "It's all much fairer than it was. No one comes worrying us any more. We are our own masters. Everybody can work his fields. Pham Sik there couldn't work any land before. Now everybody in our village can work their land." This required more explanations. Every one of the forty families in the village had the same amount of land, except the *nai ban* and *thao khoun,* but seven families, including that of Pham Sik, could not work it because years previously they or their parents had been forced to sell their last buffalo and even farm implements to pay taxes. If they had not paid the taxes, they would have been imprisoned, their houses burned. "Now we have mutual aid," the old man continued. "Everybody's land is worked properly, with all the village buffalo and everybody reaps what grows on his own land." Pham Sik, it appeared, had been the poorest peasant in the village but had been elected chairman of the people's committee because he was very honest and hard-working and had always stood up to the colonialists.

When I asked for other changes, a young woman in the background spoke up: "We never had schools before." Blushing furiously, she was then pushed forward to the square of smouldering ashes around which the men were sitting. Little more than a girl, her sturdy bare feet showing from under the embroidered skirts that are the pride of Laotian women, she was the village schoolteacher.

"We never had any schools at all before," she said. "But I went to an Itsala cadres' school. Now we have a little school and I teach twelve children to read and write so they will later be able to go to a sub-district school. It will open before the rainy season."

Pham Sik interrupted to say: "She teaches at night, too. All our village is now divided up into ten mutual-aid teams. The same teams that work the land together in the daytime study together at night, and she keeps an eye on them all. She's a very clever girl." Covered with still deeper blushes, the schoolteacher wriggled her way to the back of the crowd again.

Public health? The local health officer was away having a three weeks' course learning how to give injections. "We haven't got very much yet," Pham Sik said apologetically, "but we had nothing but sorcerers before. Now we have a little dispensary. The health officer collects roots, herbs and leaves from the forest and makes medicines from them. If anyone is badly ill, he can send to the district office for a nurse. He gives us talks about the importance of cleanliness and that we can drink cold water in the village but if we move anywhere else we should boil water before drinking it. People can get advice and treatment free from the health officer. Before you had to give a chicken or a pig to the sorcerer according to the sickness. He would burn some paper or make some colored smoke and no-one got any better from it."

It was already quite late. Ours was the only house showing as much as a pin point of light. The visitors began to glide out like shadows to be swallowed up by the jet black night. One stocky middle-aged man, with his head wrapped in a scarf, turned before he left to say:

"We have a new life now. It's what our fathers and grandfathers dreamed about. But if we don't defend this village and the others; if we don't organize our defenses and hold these provinces in the North, everything we have built up will be destroyed. We'll have the *tassengs* and *nai bans* on our necks again." He was the head of the local self-defense corps. Mention of the *nai bans* prompted me to ask what had happened to the *nai ban* and *thao khouns* of the village. "They are still here," the sturdy guerrilla replied. "But they behave themselves now. They still have their land. But they work it themselves like everyone else. If they need extra labor, they have to pay for it," he added with evident satisfaction.

The last of our guests left at that; some more bamboo was piled on the fire; mosquito nets were lowered and we turned in for what was left of the night with the stertorous breathing and frequent belchings of the buffalo as a lullaby. It seemed after a wearying day that we had scarcely closed our eyes when we could hear what sounded very much like mortar fire, and as my eyes opened there were suspicious looking flashes between the slits in the bamboo. Investigation showed that the noise came from a group of a dozen women of a mutual aid team, standing half on each side of a long wooden trough, pounding at rice with long wooden clubs. The flashes were from bamboo torches in the hands of sleepy-eyed, yawning children watching their mothers. It was only four a.m. and work had started especially early that morning because the whole village was going to the sub-district center to elect a new committee.

The village and evening discussion there were typical of many in the weeks I spent traveling in the Pathet Lao areas.

In the front line, I found a battalion almost entirely composed of Lao Teng guarding two of Katay's battalions "treed" on six mountain peaks. A sturdy lad with cheeks of burnished copper, who was squatting in a clump of bamboo cleaning a machine gun when we met him, replied that "it was much too cold," when asked how he felt. Nheua Noi was only sixteen years old and had been a guerrilla for two years. Only recently he had been transferred to the regular forces. He was a Lao Teng from the Kommadom country and joined the guerrillas in late 1953 because: "Six French and sixty other troops came and burned down our village. They killed all the buffalo and pigs. My father was beaten up and my brothers arrested. We had an old hunting rifle that the French never found, so I took it and joined the guerrillas."

A few days before our arrival his squad of four, well entrenched in a mountain side, had held up an enemy company which was probing around and trying to join up with another holding a neighboring hill. "A platoon came first," he said, "and we opened up with machine gun fire. Several were killed and the rest rushed back. From both hills, they poured mortar fire for over an hour on where they thought we were. But we had moved up closer to them. Another platoon came swinging down the track and we took them completely by surprise. They must have thought we were wiped out or at least had moved further away. They pulled back very quickly after we opened up with the machine gun.

"The area was shelled again for a couple of hours. But we had moved again and changed our tactics too. We split up into four different positions, further away this time. Three of us divided up all the hand grenades and I took the machine gun to the rear. They attacked with two platoons. This time they moved very cautiously until they had passed our first two positions, probing into the jungle each side of the track. Then they became more confident and marched straight ahead. We allowed their forward elements to pass and then the others hurled their grenades as fast as they could throw them right in the midst of the enemy lines. I opened up on the forward elements and swung my machine gun back and forth along the track, sending bursts into their forward and following elements. They thought they were surrounded by a big force and pulled back again.

"They shelled the whole area very heavily—but shells don't do much in this sort of country," and he waved his hand to the clumps of giant bamboo and its almost impenetrable cover of tightly interlaced trees and creepers. "Towards evening," continued this bright young hunter-tactician, "they attacked with their full company. And then they were really surrounded, because our company had moved up in the meantime. They lost heavily and haven't tried to move since.

"They have no morale," he said. "They don't want to fight, and whenever they get a chance they come over to us." As to how he felt far from his native province, he repeated: "We find it very cold here after the south. But it must be colder still on the mountain tops. The main thing is that ever since I've been here, apart from the cold, I've felt as if I were in my native village. The people treat us just like their own sons. If we don't hang on and defend our bases, here," and he pointed round to the somber encircling mountains, which extended in every di-

rection as far as the eye could see, "then we can never return to
our own villages."

Many of the troops from the south felt the cold; they con-
tracted malaria and bronchial troubles. In November–December
1955, the period of Katay's greatest efforts to wipe them out,
they went cold and hungry for days on end. But they never complained. They knew why they were fighting. And the people
throughout all the regions administered by the Pathet Lao knew
why they were fighting. On the mountain summits, Katay's
troops did not know why they were fighting. They had been
told they were being sent to deal with "invaders" from Vietnam
or China. But they found they were called on to kill their own
brothers and own tribespeople.

As the press gangs scoured the royal provinces for new recruits, young men in the south fled to the mountains. There were
demonstrations in Vientiane demanding an end to the civil war
and, as a first step, real negotiations to end it. The defeat of
Katay's November–December operations could be concealed for
a time but not forever. Vientiane hospitals were full of armless
and legless victims of the policies Katay was carrying out on
behalf of the Americans. And buried in the jungles of distant
mountain tops, cursing Katay as they went into battle, cursing
him as they died, were many more. Katay tried to disperse the
wounded as far as possible in the provinces, and during the
campaign for the December 1955 elections he presented his defeat as a great "victory."

Katay and Dulles and everything they stood for had been
defeated in one more round of US efforts to put the chains back
around the necks of Asian peoples. The US government had
spent $50,000,000 a year on smashing the Pathet Lao forces.
But they reckoned without the people, without the Lao, the Lao
Teng and Lao Som warriors defending their own mountains and
villages, or fighting for the right to go back to their own villages with full citizen rights as promised by the Geneva agreements. With their superior technique of planes and parachutes,
Katay and Dulles overlooked the volunteer porters toiling up
and down endless steep slopes to feed munitions and rice to
their warrior sons and brothers. They could not imagine the

peasants in the rear villages planting extra kilograms of seed in their paddy-fields and jungle patches to send food to their compatriots at the front. Nor could they imagine the unity of front and rear, unity of racial groups, the hospitable reception that those of the north accorded to those that had come from the deep south. The fall of Katay was a sign that a settlement with the Pathet Lao could not be achieved by military means. There could be no "liquidation" of the Pathet Lao forces and no military "occupation" of the two northern provinces.

10

The Laos Tangle: Undermining Neutrality

BERNARD B. FALL *

The Laos crisis of 1960–1961 is almost a schoolbook example of what C. L. Sulzberger, the European editorialist of the *New York Times,* has aptly defined as "brushfire peace"—an uneasy combination of internal political crises and external military pressures. If one couples to such a situation a large measure of pure and simple ignorance abroad of the geographical, ethnic, and political factors involved, the result is likely to be bafflement (at best) or (at worst) policy decisions made on largely erroneous premises. In the words of a recent American traveler to Laos, ". . . indeed, if you want to get a sense of the universe unraveling, come to Laos. Complexity such as this has to be respected." [1]

Basically, the Laotian problem has not changed one iota since 1953, when the small kingdom for the first time faced countrywide insecurity based upon native rebels backed by North Vietnamese troops (with the difference that in 1953 an actual Vietminh invasion *had* taken place and that there still were about 20,000 French troops in the country to face it). What has changed since 1953—and that, of course, is a key element in the equation—is that Laos has become a pawn in the Cold War, with every small change on the Laotian scene

* From *International Journal: A Canadian Quarterly* [Toronto], XVI (Spring, 1961), pp. 138–156. By permission. Bernard Fall (1926–1967) until his death was Professor of Government at Howard University in Washington, D.C. He was the author of many books and articles in Indochina, including *The Two Vietnams* (New York, 1963) and *Anatomy of a Crisis: The Laos Crisis of 1961* (Garden City, N.Y., 1969).

[1] Norman Cousins, "Report from Laos," The *Saturday Review,* February 18, 1961.

being immediately projected on the front pages of the world's newspapers and being gravely discussed in the world powers' chanceries. The hard fact remains that since the early 1950's not one single *internal* factor of the Laotian problem has materially changed: then as now, the native pro-communist forces numbered about 4,000 men under the command of Prince Souphanouvong; then as now, the party of moderation was led by his half-brother Prince Souvanna Phouma; then as now, the government in Vientiane controlled little of the land beyond the garrison towns in the valleys. And whether under French or American aegis, an attempt at solving Laos' problems by force of arms has proven largely futile.

It is this feeling of utter helplessness in the face of over-whelming force which accounts in large part for the apparent lethargy of the average Laotian. He has seen all these events before—in 1953, 1954, 1957, 1959 and now—and has sur-vived them, largely without outside aid and without effective guidance from his own authorities. To anyone who has visited Laos for longer than a few days, this feeling is well known; a European resident explained it to a visiting American scholar in the following words:

> It's true—there's nothing for them to worry about. You Americans will go on taking care of the poli-ticians, and the people will go on taking care of themselves, and crises will go on blowing up and then blowing over.[2]

This, then, is the general context within which the whole Laotian problem must be considered—a context which nearly all the journalists and most of the diplomats fail to understand as they seek to judge the local situation by Western standards and in the light of Western values.

[2] Hanna, Willard A., "State of the States of Indochina" Part II, American Universities Field Staff Report VIII/2, New York, March 13, 1960, p. 11.

I

To understand the present situation, it is necessary to evoke briefly the history of Laos since the Geneva ceasefire of July 20, 1954.[3] The end of hostilities found regular communist Vietnamese forces deeply implanted in Laotian territory, particularly in the north of the country, where the two border provinces of Phong Saly and Houa Phans (the latter better known by the name of its capital, Sam Neua) had been solidly held by them for over a year. Those areas were administered locally by members of the Pathet Lao (State of Laos) movement, composed of Laotians loyal to the Vietminh.

Originally, the members of the Pathet Lao had simply been the left wing of the Lao Issara (Free Lao) nationalist movement seeking to gain independence from France. When Laos gained its formal independence from France in 1949, the non-communist members of the Lao Issara (including Prince Souvannaphouma) returned to Vientiane and took over the reins of government. Prince Souphanouvong and his followers disappeared from their exile in Bangkok to reappear a few months later at Ho Chi Minh's mountain hideout in Tuyên Quang, North Vietnam, where they proclaimed the Pathet Lao on August 13, 1950. The Pathet Lao was supplemented in November, 1950, by a "front" organization, the Néo Lao Issara (Free Lao Front), designed to attract non-communist "progressive" elements. A full-fledged Laotian Communist Party was created in 1952, called Phak Khon Ngan Lao (PKNL, the "Laotian Workers' Party"), entirely patterned on the Vietnamese Lao-Dong (Workers) Party. The PKNL is a secret "cadre party," which, according to best intelligence estimates, probably has not more than seventy-five members and whose top leadership is unknown. It is asserted that Prince Souphanouvong, though a member, is not the leader of the party. Lastly, in an attempt

[3] For an excellent study of the 1954 Geneva agreements, see Lacouture, J., and Devillers, P., *La Fin d'un Guerre—Indochine 1954*, Paris 1960: Les Editions du Seuil. An English translation of this book was published in 1969—eds.

at broadening the popular base of the movement, a "legal" party was created in January, 1956, the Néo Lao Hak Sat (NLHX, or "Lao Patriotic Front") which began an intensive recruitment drive throughout the country and soon succeeded in setting up a well-working network of cells in all the provinces of the kingdom.

According to the provisions of the Geneva ceasefire agreement, the two provinces temporarily administered by the Pathet Lao as "regroupment zones" were eventually to be transferred to the royal administration and the Pathet Lao armed groups —better known by their French initials of UCPL (*Unités Combattantes Pathet Lao*) were to be integrated into the Royal Lao Army. It was the problem of the terms on which the Pathet Lao was to enter the national community which became the subject of lengthy negotiations finally culminating in an agreement between Princes Souvanna Phouma and Souphanouvong, signed in Vientiane in November, 1957. According to that agreement, the administration of the two northern provinces was to be transferred to the royal administration; two UCPL battalions were to be integrated into the Royal Lao Armed Forces; and supplementary elections were to be held in which the NLHS could compete as a legal political party.[4]

The first and the last points were implemented without great difficulty. Royal governors were installed at Phong Saly and Sam Neua, and in the complementary elections held on May 4, 1958 fourteen out of the twenty-one seats at stake went to the NLHS or its allies of the neutralist *Santiphab* (Neutrality) Party. Two cabinet posts, that of planning (i.e., dealing largely with foreign aid) and religion and cults, were occupied by NLHS members. In fact, Souphanouvong—who has a public works engineering degree from the famous *Ecole des Ponts et Chausées* in Paris—personally took over the portfolio of the ministry of Planning.[5] This placed American aid officials in the

[4] For a more detailed study of Laotian diplomacy during that period, see Fall, B., "The International Position of Laos," in *Kingdom of Laos* (René de Berval, ed.), Editions France-Asie, Saigon, 1959, pp. 471–486. See Selections 11 this volume—eds.

[5] Both Souvanna Phouma and Souphanouvong are among the best educated people in their country. Souphanouvong gained practical experience as a senior engineer in the French colonial public works

somewhat awkward position of having to discuss their programs with a Communist—a situation thus far not repeated elsewhere except in Yugoslavia—and perhaps contributed much to the negative American response to the arrangement.

The question of how to integrate the UCPL became the major stumbling block. The Pathet Lao insisted on two major points: (a) that the two battalions remain together as constituted units; and (b) that they be given a higher complement of officers than other royal army units. The royal government insisted that integration was to take place on an individual basis, i.e., that the approximately 1,300 men involved take an oath of allegiance to the king and enlist individually in the royal army, where they would be assigned to various units according to the needs and desires of the army. This the UCPL refused to do and the two battalions remained in their respective cantonments, UCPL Battalion No. 1 at Xieng Ngeun near the royal residence city of Luang Prabang, UCPL No. 2 at Xieng Khouang on the Plain of Jars plateau 150 miles northeast of Vientiane.

Prime Minister Souvanna Phouma felt his position sufficiently consolidated to be able to dispense with the presence of the International Supervisory and Control Commission (ISCC), composed of Indian, Canadian and Polish members, which still operated in Laos under the terms of the 1954 ceasefire agreement. The royal government felt that with the acceptance of the NLHS as a legal party, its participation in the government, and the reunification of the territory, the mission of the ISCC had ended, as far as Laos was concerned.[6] Informally, it was also asserted that the ISCC's activities were (whether by intention or not) more beneficial to the Pathet Lao than to the royal government. Neither Britain nor France had particularly strong feelings in the matter, while the United States welcomed the step as a sign of the pro-Western leanings of the Lao government. The Soviet Union, with Britain a co-chairman of the Geneva Conference, at first made the usual references to "SEATO aggressors" but then acquiesced in the indefinite ad-

---

service in his own country, while his half-brother obtained three engineering degrees: marine, electrical and construction engineering.
[6] *L'Indépendent* (weekly), Vientiane, May 27, 1958.

journment of the ISCC in a joint Soviet-British statement issued on February 4, 1959.[7] Thus far, then, Prime Minister Souvanna Phouma's policy had been an unqualified success: the country was at peace for the first time since 1945; it was reunified; and the communists and their allies held a total of fourteen seats out of fifty-nine in the legislative assembly. Given a modicum of intelligent economic aid and political support from the outside, Laos had a fighting chance—*toutes proportions gardées* —of becoming an Asian Finland or Austria.

II

The parting of the ways, however, between Laotian government policy and the Pathet Lao was not long in coming. In August, 1958, a new cabinet under Phoui Sananikone, centered around the "young Turk" *Comité pour la Défense des Intérêts Nationaux* (CDIN), had taken over the reins in Vientiane and immediately proceeded to embark upon a solidly pro-Western course. In presenting his new cabinet for approval to the National Assembly, Sananikone spelled out the foreign policy of his government in the following terms:

> As far as peaceful coexistence is concerned, we shall clearly inform neighbouring countries and the world that we shall coexist with the Free World only. We trust only those countries that really and sincerely support us.

Official sources are not yet available on what ensued next; but the available evidence shows that the Sananikone government rightfully or erroneously expected all out United States support in a stand that was bound to bring it into serious conflict with its two communist neighbours, Red China and North Vietnam, with whom it shares almost 1,000 miles of uncontrollable jungle border. In a report recently issued by social scien-

[7] The *New York Times*, February 5, 1959. The ISCC had held its last meeting on July 19, 1958, at which both the Canadian and Indian members had voted for indefinite adjournment over the negative vote of the Polish representative.

tists of the Rand Corporation, in which the 1959 Laos crisis was examined for the benefit of US Government agencies, the assessment of blame is very clearly made:

> It is now apparent that the government in Vientiane brought on the friction that occurred in the fall of 1958 by undertaking the program of reform and suppression [of the NLHS] it had promised the National Assembly when it took office . . .[8]

As to the role of the United States in the matter, recent press statements, ranging from the liberal to the conservative, appear to agree that Washington feared that "a coalition cabinet containing Pathet Lao . . . would be creating another Czechoslovakia,"[9] and that the United States therefore "discouraged efforts to bring about unification in 1957 and 1958 through Pathet Lao participation in the government."[10] The phrase "Laos a Key to Southeast Asia" became a *leitmotiv* along the lines of the 1954 slogan of "If Vietnam goes, all of Southeast Asia falls like a set of dominoes." The argument runs roughly as follows, with only a few variations in the wording:

> . . . Its location at the heart of Southeast Asia made the small and backward land of utmost strategic importance. Its loss to the communists would open up long borders of friendly powers such as Thailand and South Vietnam to infiltration by the communists. It was also felt here [in Washington] that the loss of Laos to the communists would prove an irreparable blow to United States and Western prestige throughout Asia.[11]

[8] Halpern, A. M., and Fredman, H. B., *Communist Strategy in Laos.* Santa Monica, Calif.: The Rand Corporation, June 1960, p. 23. Perhaps unavailable to Fall was information on the extensive CIA involvement in Laotian affairs at the time. See on this, David Wise and Thomas B. Ross, *The Invisible Government* (New York: Random House, 1964), Chap. 9—eds.

[9] The *Washington Post,* January 5, 1961.

[10] *Ibid.,* December 27, 1960. (Editorial).

[11] The *New York Times,* December 18, 1960. Both that article and another of October 23 bore the catchword title "Laos a Key to Southeast Asia."

The columnist Joseph Alsop stated on January 6, 1961, that the loss of Laos would put South Vietnam in the position of Czechoslovakia after the Munich pact of 1938 deprived it of the Sudetenland: "What threatens in Laos, in short, is a major disaster." [12]

The Royal Lao Government apparently assumed (wrongly, as it turned out) that the West was willing to back it militarily to the hilt. In the words of the Rand Corporation report, Laos began "to view the trickle of military aid as the prelude to a huge flood of equipment and an adequate training mission" which would enable it to respond with confidence to all internal and external pressures.[13] This led to a very serious miscalculation in the Lao government's attitude towards its internal opposition: instead of pursuing a course tending to consolidate its internal position throughout the country by a series of long-overdue socio-economic reforms—an indispensable point of departure for any sound anti-communist operation, as Western successes in the Philippines and Malaya have shown—the Sananikone Administration concentrated on outright repression. The latter sooner or later had to bring about an open reaction on the part of Laos' communist neighbors which, until 1959, had been remarkably subdued.

For Red China and North Vietnam, Laos is *not* a major invasion route to anywhere. With its non-existent road net and chaotic geography, Laos is an excellent buffer or barrier, rather than an avenue of approach for an invasion of Southeast Asia. As the situation stands at the beginning of 1961, South Vietnam is as badly infiltrated by communist guerrillas as Laos is— and by guerrillas who had no need for bases in Laos to perpetrate their depredations. Nor had the situation in Laos ever influenced terrorism in Malaya, and infiltrations into Thailand are far more likely to come from the short northern corridor of the Shan states. In fact, the supply of large communist forces operating in Laos from either Red China or North Vietnam across the jungle-covered Annamite cordillera would be a great deal more difficult than it would be for SEATO to supply

[12] Alsop, J., "The Yawning Drain," the *Washington Post,* January 6, 1961.

[13] Halpern and Fredman, *Communist Strategy in Laos,* p. 45.

Laotian forces from Thai depots on the other side of the Mekong. There can be little doubt today that the initial round of fighting which broke out in July, 1959, was at first little else but an attempt on the part of the Pathet Lao to escape total destruction:

> . . . while the Sananikone government knew, at the time, that it was running a serious risk of open conflict with the NLHS and its mentors in Hanoi, the pattern of communist behavior up through mid-May [1959] had not been sufficiently belligerent to deter it.[14]

The policies of France and Britain towards Laos ran largely parallel, and still do. With their considerable experience in jungle warfare in that part of the world, both countries realize full well the implications of getting bogged down in a protracted guerrilla war.[15] Both countries feel that Laos was doing quite well up to mid-1958 with its policy of prudently pro-Western neutralism and that with a chance at consolidating its internal position it could keep its own communists from taking over in the same way as other small countries have managed to survive on the edge of the Iron or Bamboo Curtain. It should also not be forgotten here that Red China, in the Souvanna Phouma–Mao Tse-tung joint declaration of 1956, explicitly recognized Laos' right to maintain within its boundaries "such foreign bases as authorized by the Geneva agreements"—thus Red China in a way guarantees France's right to maintain troops in Laos. France, it will be remembered, is of course a member of SEATO, and Laos, as the only Indochinese state, has a valid bilateral mutual assistance treaty with France.

Hence, both Britain and France feel that there are sufficient

---

[14] *Ibid.*, p. 51.

[15] US Army guerrilla warfare studies have shown that one well-trained guerrilla may tie down as many as fifteen regular soldiers. For example, more than 220,000 troops were tied up in Malaya for close to twelve years fighting 8,000 terrorists. In a more recent case, less than 25,000 Algerian rebels tied up 500,000 French troops. This explains why 4,000 Laotian rebels easily tie up the whole 29,000 man Laotian Army without any proven "invasion" by North Vietnamese troops. More will be said on this later.

safeguards in existence today to keep Laos from becoming another Czechoslovakia without actually going to war over it. Small wonder that the two Laos crises gave the world the spectacle of widely divergent views between the United States and her two major European allies on how to cope with the problem.

Allied relations were further complicated on the American side—and still are, as of this moment—by even more extreme positions taken by the governments of the small pro-Western states most directly touched by events in Laos: Thailand and South Vietnam. Here, beyond a doubt, the psychological impact of a communist takeover in Laos would be absolutely disastrous and thus cannot be condoned. Both Marshal Sarit Thanarat and President Ngo Dinh Diem, and—for somewhat different reasons, the Philippines—are in favour of a strong Western stand in Laos, up to and including direct military support if the situation were to warrant it. They, along with official American opinion up to a point, feel that Laotian "neutralism" would soon turn into outright communism. The British and French argument is that a sound Western policy in Laos could turn "neutralism" into effective neutrality along Austrian lines—including, if possible (as in the Austrian case), a joint big power declaration or treaty guaranteeing Loatian neutrality.

Events were soon to put those various theories to the test.

III

On May 11, 1959, the Sananikone government felt ready to challenge the recalcitrant rebel UCPL battalions which thus far had failed to comply with the terms of the 1957 agreement. UCPL No. 2 was surrounded by five royal army battalions on the Plain of Jars and ordered to present itself to the army chief of staff for the integration ceremony. The unit remained in its cantonments. Drawing out the negotiations for a week, the unit finally slipped through the encirclement during the night of May 18, taking with it all its light weapons and equipment, as well as the women and children who had lived with it in camp. In spite of immediate pursuit by the royal units, UCPL No.

2 disappeared across the border in North Vietnam. UCPL No. 1 was not as lucky—or the Laotians had learned a lesson. It was cornered in its camp and forced to lay down its arms and take the oath to the king. The bulk of the battalion re-deserted to the Pathet Lao on August 8, 1959.

In Vientiane, however, the royal government succeeded in arresting Prince Souphanouvong and most of his lieutenants as soon as the escape of UCPL No. 2 had become known. To all appearances, therefore, the first round of the fight had gone to a certain extent in favor of the royal administration: the opposition was leaderless and had lost one-half of its fighting potential. An almost total calm reigned throughout the kingdom until July 16. On that day, Sop-Nao, a Laotian outpost close to the Vietnamese border due west of Dienbienphu, was overrun and captured by Thai tribesmen. Within the next three weeks, fighting erupted throughout the whole northeast of the country, with Laotian army posts being attacked in some cases by green-clad regulars supported by mortars.

In a matter of days, press headlines throughout the world spoke of a "North Vietnamese invasion," and the world's great journalists converged on the meager hotel facilities of Vientiane, eagerly looking for "the war." Fantastic stories began to circulate, citing Vietnamese unit numbers, hundreds of Vietnamese prisoners, non-existent artillery calibres[16] and other "proofs" of a Vietnamese communist invasion. The Department of State issued a White Book on Laos and UN Secretary General Hammarskjold sent an investigation commission composed of such largely pro-Western countries as Argentina, Italy, Japan and Tunisia. The commission arrived in Vientiane in September 15, 1959. There were no Vietnamese prisoners to be seen; the bulk of the captured equipment was as American as that of the Royal Laotian Army, with the exception of some Red Chinese hand grenades and ammunition. The best the UN commission could do was to state that "certain of these hostile operations must have had centralized coordination," without,

---

[16] For example, Joseph Alsop, who then visited Laos, spoke of "125-millimeter cannon" allegedly firing from North Vietnam on Laotian posts seventeen miles away.

however, asserting that such centralized coordination had necessarily come from elements outside the Pathet Lao.[17]

Here also, allied differences had been sharp. The French who, by virtue of fifty years' presence, have by far the best intelligence system in Laos and North Vietnam, soon had identified the green-clad regulars as members of UCPL No. 2, who, after their narrow escape through the jungle, had indeed been refitted and equipped in North Vietnam. At no time throughout the 1959 crisis did the French accept as genuine the "foreign invasion" theory. Britain, after a few days' hesitation, had obtained a similar view through her own sources. The United States, on the other hand, professed belief in the invasion story until it was too late to make a graceful exit.

The Pathet Lao had fulfilled all the limited objectives it apparently had set itself. It had completely destroyed the moral standing of the Sananikone Administration by showing that a few guerrilla units could play cat and mouse with the government's regular troops; it had also shown Vientiane that reliance on automatic Western support for a "hard" policy was an assumption based either on wishful thinking or on an erroneous interpretation of Western intentions; and, lastly, it had breached the thinly-patched wall of allied solidarity by making the United States "cry wolf."

It would at least be small consolation to be able to report that the 1959 fiasco had taught anyone a lesson. This, unfortunately, was not to be the case. When a new crisis broke out late in 1960, much of the world press,[18] Washington and the Laotians promptly headed down the same garden path as before.

[17] United Nations Security Council, *Report S/4236* of November 5, 1959, p. 31.

[18] It should be stated here in all fairness that, aside from most French and British newspapers, among the American publications refusing to accept the "invasion" story both in 1959 and in 1961 were *Life, Time,* and the *Wall Street Journal.* Such usually well-informed sources as The *New York Times* and The *Washington Post* uncritically printed every canard circulated in Laos.

IV

The 1960 crisis started under circumstances which were almost a carbon copy of the previous events. The one positive element left behind from the events of 1959 was what was called the "United Nations presence"—a small observer group in Vientiane, headed at first by a former Finnish premier, Tuomioja, later replaced by a Swiss citizen, Zellweger. Little use, unfortunately, was made of that UN presence to come to grips with the *real* problem facing Laos: to use the UN induced lull to consolidate the internal position of the royal government; or to resume the attempt at settling the Pathet Lao problem by force, regardless of the international consequence.

As it turned out, neither of those courses—or, for that matter, any other clear-cut course—was adopted in Vientiane. Premier Phoui Sananikone, seriously shaken by what he considered a lack of American support against the Pathet Lao, now suddenly advocated a policy of neutrality hardly different from that of Souvanna Phouma. This deprived him of the political support of the extreme right wing of the "Young Turks" now headed by a politician who had chosen an army career, General Phoumi Nosavan (who also happens to be a nephew of Thailand's strong man Marshal Sarit Thanarat). Laos embarked upon a series of cabinet crisis under the guidance of ephemeral coalition and caretaker cabinets. The erosion of government authority became fully manifest when on May 24, 1960, all the Pathet Lao leaders, held in Laos' maximum-security central prison, escaped completely unscathed and proceeded to join the two UCPL battalions still holding the field in the northeast, while smaller communist units in the south of Laos began to reduce the government's area of control to little else but the Mekong valley.

The showdown came from an entirely unexpected quarter and in an entirely "un-Laotian" form. Until then, Laotian politics had been a matter of "musical chairs" played by a small group of the élite; and most foreign observers, particularly the anthropologists among them, had devised elaborate theories on what combinations were likely to come to power under particular sets of circumstances. No one—neither the anthropologists nor the diplomats nor the intelligence experts—would have picked a twenty-six-year-old paratroop captain of mixed Laotian and tribal parentage as the likely leader for a revolution that was to topple from power the traditional Laotian leaders and upset all the nice and safe theories about Laotian politics built up over the past decade. Yet Captain Kong-Lê (also spelled Khong-Lae or Cong-Lé) did exactly that. Since August 9, 1960 —when his paratroops occupied the public buildings of Vientiane and shooed out the Somsanith government—Western specialists have searched in vain his brief curriculum vitae for clues to his political behavior. All agree that Kong-Lê was, if anything, pro-American, a feeling that was apparently further enhanced by a brief training course at an American base either in the Philippines or Okinawa. It was thus with stunned disbelief that the Western chanceries listened to the young captain's program: he wished to end the "killing of Lao by Lao"; the graft and corruption reigning in his country; the alleged control of American advisers over the royal army; and, above all, he proposed the return of his country to a policy of "true neutrality" as advocated by Prince Souvanna Phouma. The latter, in semi-exile as Ambassador to France, now returned to Vientiane and was duly invested as Prime Minister by the ever-responsive National Assembly.[19]

Souvanna Phouma simply resumed where he had left off two years earlier in his negotiations with the Pathet Lao. That, in all probability, proved to be his major mistake, for he had lost sight of the changes in the internal and external position of Laos: internally, the situation had so deteriorated that Vientiane no longer negotiated from a position of relative strength; externally, Western support had proved unreliable while at the

[19] Much has been said in the world press about the respective "legality" of the various Laotian factions. In actual point of fact, none of them really is at present truly "legal," for the present legislature was elected on April 24, 1960, under conditions of blatant vote fraud considered unheard of even in Laos. Not a single opposition member was seated—yet the same assembly voted both for Souvanna Phouma's neutrality policy in August, 1960, and for General Phoumi's pro-Western policy on January 4, 1961.

same time communist pressure had shown its brutal effectiveness. Within the Laotian power élite also, a fatal cleavage had
appeared: the extreme right wing no longer saw its interests
bound to those of the more moderate elements but hoped, with
American help, to be able to play the power game on a winner-
take-all basis. General Phoumi Nosavan broke with Souvanna
Phouma in October, 1960, and withdrew to his southern stronghold of Savannakhet with a sizeable part of the Laotian armed
forces. From that moment onward, events in Laos took on
the ominous shape of a three-cornered fight: the Souvanna
Phouma-Kong-Lê combination nominally controlling northwest-
ern Laos; the Pathet Lao controlling much of the northeast and
the southern hinterland; and the Phoumi Nosavan group (controlling the large arms depots in the south and thus militarily
the strongest of the three) holding much of southern Laos.
To further compound the confusion, the king had adopted a policy of neutrality between the contending factions (explicable in
part by what appears to be a personal animosity towards Souvannaphouma), thus depriving the Vientiane government of
what would have been its most important prop under the circumstances—royal approval.

At the same time, Allied relations hit a new low. Britain and
France had openly welcomed the return of Souvanna Phouma's
neutrality policy, while the Eisenhower Administration made the
hard choice of siding with the right wing elements in Savannakhet. The American decision not to back Souvanna Phouma

> ". . . was a calculated decision, on the basis that
> the coalition with the communists which Souvanna
> was seeking would result in communist domination
> and would panic Laos' nervous neighbors. It may
> have been wrong." [20]

That decision was in all probability made during the first part
of October, 1960. In a series of see-saw press declarations and
denials which have become the hallmark of a policy interregnum
in Washington, General Williston Palmer, head of the Military
Assistance Program, stated on October 1, 1960, in Manila, that

[20] The *Washington Post,* December 16, 1960.

military aid to Laos had been suspended "until there is sta-
bilization." [21] That report was immediately denied by the United
States Embassy in Laos, although it conceded "that delivery
of supplies had nearly ceased" since the August 9 coup.[22] On
October 7, on the other hand, Premier Souvannaphouma officially announced that US military aid had been suspended,
and this time the fact was no longer denied in Washington.[23]
This suspension of aid—coupled by an almost total land blockade of supplies exerted by Thailand upon Vientiane which
created a scarcity of essential goods as of mid-October—was
coupled by an emergency mission of the American Assistant Secretary of State for Far Eastern Affairs, J. Graham Parsons, to
Laos. Parsons had been United States Ambassador to Laos during the earlier tenure of Souvanna Phouma. Rightly or wrongly,
Souvanna Phouma credited him with a large share of his difficulties in 1958. In any case, it is safe to say that no love
was lost between the two men. Parsons arrived in Vientiane
on October 12, 1960. Three days later, the talks ended in an
obvious failure to come to an agreement. Phouma refused to
abandon his policy of neutrality and the United States refused
to drop its support of the Phoumi forces in the south (the rebel
forces, for example, still continued to draw their pay from the
coffers of the government's treasury in Vientiane), overruling,
apparently, the recommendations to the contrary made by US
Ambassador Winthrop G. Brown in Vientiane. From that
moment on, the Laotian crisis took on the foredoomed aspects of
a Greek tragedy: beset by two internal rebellions, on the verge
of economic and financial collapse, the Souvanna Phouma government groped for straws. The handiest of them proved a Soviet
offer of immediate economic aid, along with diplomatic recognition of the Soviet Union as a counterpoise to the pressure on
Vientiane. On October 27, 1960, the USSR's ambassador to
Cambodia, Aleksandr N. Abramov, presented his credentials to
King Savang Vatthana in Luang Prabang. A Russian airlift,
at first of badly-needed gasoline and later extended to military

[21] *Ibid.,* October 2, 1960.
[22] The *New York Times,* October 4, 1960.
[23] *Ibid.,* October 8, 1960.

equipment, began as of November 23. The die was cast: the United States gave up Souvanna Phouma as a communist tool and actively promoted the anti-communist forces of General Phoumi, now also backed by Prince Boun Oum, an influential southern Laotian politician.[24]

Among the United States' allies, France particularly was caught in a quandary. Fully persuaded that salvation lay in a policy of effective neutrality, France remained aloof from the Phoumi forces. Yet at the same time, France's only base in Laos, Séno, was located at the outskirts of Savannakhet, Phoumi's stronghold. Incidents broke out between Phoumi and the French, which explain at least in part the subsequent anti-French policies of the Boun Oum administration.[25] Those policies later resulted in the withdrawal of many of the French aid technicians, a request by the Boun Oum régime that all French troops leave immediately, the partial occupation of Séno Air Force Base in violation of the Geneva accords, and on February 13, 1961, in a siege of the French embassy in Vientiane by Laotian troops seeking to arrest a French newspaper reporter.[26]

But time ran out for Souvanna Phouma. With right wing troops beating at the doors of Vientiane, he fled to Cambodia on December 9 after handing over the reins of government to the military commanders who, in turn handed them to Quinim Pholsema, Souvanna's pro-Pathet Lao information minister. The USSR, after a strong protest over "imperialist intervention," began to deliver artillery and heavy mortars to Kong-Lê. In the ensuing artillery duel fought in the capital between December 14 and 16, 1960, much of the center of the town was destroyed and close to 400 victims (mostly civilian) were counted before it was over.

---

[24] Unna, Warren, "U.S. Switches its policy in Laos; Casts about for anti-Red regime." The *Washington Post*, November 30, 1960.

[25] *Le Monde*, Paris, November 27, 1960.

[26] The anger of the Boun Oum government is also explained by the fact that the French journalists, more able than their Anglo-Saxon colleagues to converse with Laotians, proved largely skeptical to some reports provided by the official information services: and that the forces of Kong-Lê let French Army advisory personnel go unscathed —a seeming indication of mutual sympathy.

V

The battle for Vientiane had at least one advantage: by destroying the middle-of-the-road Souvanna Phouma group, it now left face to face the pro-American wing of Prince Boun Oum and General Phoumi, and the pro-communist Pathet Lao forces with whom Captain Kong-Lê now made common cause. In fact, Kong-Lê became, on January 30, 1961, the President of the "Laotian National Military Committee," grouping all the anti Phoumi forces, including presumably the UCPL.[27] Militarily, the loss of Vientiane had not weakened the Pathet Lao or Kong-Lê. By a lightning stroke on the vital airfield complex of the Tran Ninh plateau, the Kong-Lê forces occupied Xieng Khouang and the Plain of Jars, thus creating a vast bulge in the center of northern Laos. (As of February 20, government forces have been unable to reconquer the area.) Until the end of December, 1960, both sides sought to take stock of their position and to consolidate what they had.

On December 30, the Boun Oum government apparently had decided that the best policy would be one which would compel the Western powers, particularly the United States, to come out openly and strongly in its support; and it used exactly the same methods which already had worked so well under the premiership of Phoui Sananikone: it simply announced to the world that it was the subject of a foreign invasion.

On that day, the Kingdom's UN delegate informed Mr. Hammarskjold that 2,000 "foreign troops" had entered Laotian territory via Nong Het, on the North Vietnamese border. This declaration was followed on the following day by the declaration issued in Vientiane that the total number of invaders had increased to seven battalions (i.e., about 5,000 men). A second Laotian communication was presented to the UN on January 2, 1961—*but no request was made for a meeting of the Security Council*.[28] That alone should have indicated that once more the Laotian government had insufficient proof to back up its

---

[27] *Le Monde,* January 31, 1961.
[28] The *New York Times,* January 4, 1961. [Author's italics—eds.]

assertion. But the American press, in Pavlov-like reaction, took up the "invasion" cry.[29] On January 3, the US Department of State announced that "substantial numbers of North Vietnamese personnel were parachuted and landed in [Lao rebel] areas," [30] and the London reporter of The *Washington Post* hopefully announced that Britain might now change its stand in view of the State Department's presentation of "positive proof" of communist invasion in Laos.[31]

The simultaneous alerting of American forces in the Pacific and of airborne forces in the continental United States for possible deployment in Southeast Asia added to the sense of crisis. Allied attempts at a more sober appraisal were rejected as almost defeatist, and an Indian attempt to revive the control commission (ISCC) was termed "unrealistic." What amounted almost to an anti-French press campaign began, referring to the "embittered, dog-in-the-manger attitude" of the French and their refusal to see the situation in as dark a light as it was seen in Washington.[32]

The attitude of SEATO, contrary to expectation, was commendable in its realism and restraint and should give the lie to those who accuse that organization of "imperialistic interference" in Laotian affairs. A first meeting of the SEATO Council was held on January 2 at the request of the United States; at the conclusion of the meeting, the council limited itself to stating that evidence tending to show that an invasion of Laos had taken place was "circumstantial." At the conclusion of the

[29] The *Washington Post* (editorial), January 3, 1961.
[30] The *New York Times*, January 4, 1961.
[31] The *Washington Post*, January 4, 1961.
[32] For example, The *Washington Post*'s Pentagon reporter stated on January 5 that the "continuing dominant French military position in Laos also means that the US is not allowed to have military ground observers in the field. The French apparently have not sent any to the areas where the fighting is under way." That paragraph alone contains several misstatements of facts. First of all, French forces in Laos do not exceed 500 men (instead of the 3,500 permitted under the 1954 Geneva agreements); their existence has no bearing on the US sending observers anywhere. And secondly, the very fact that the French were present in combat areas—sometimes much to their own surprise, as in the case of Xieng Khouang, where seven French officers and men were overrun along with the Royal forces holding the area—provided one of the major sources of French-Laotian irritation.

second meeting on January 3, SEATO Secretary General Pote Sarrasin stated that the "SEATO members now feel that a political settlement was preferable" to military action. Finally, on January 5, with the Western embassies in Vientiane already reporting that there had been no proof of any foreign invasion, SEATO definitely abandoned all thought of military support of Laos, recommending instead that "every effort should be made to arrive at a peaceful solution." Needless to say, such moderation did not sit too well with all the members concerned; Thailand and particularly the Philippines reproached the United States for having let itself be influenced by the British and French and having ridden roughshod over the feelings of the smaller Asian powers.[33] The fact remains that SEATO did act as a moderating influence on everyone concerned rather than as an irritant.

In Washington itself, the fact that apparently no direct invasion of Laos had taken place—the Soviets' airlifting of equipment to the rebels being a matter of public record—was slow in being accepted. Or rather, it was hard to accept that one could have fallen victim to the same type of misinformation two years in a row. Once the fact was accepted, however, changes were made relatively swiftly to adapt American policies to the new circumstances. A White Paper was issued by the Department of State on January 7, 1961, which attempted to justify the American record in Laos since 1959. It spoke of a "course of internal progress" in Laos until the Kong-Lê coup plunged the country into chaos, and justified the Boun Oum takeover by the flight of the Souvanna Phouma régime, among other matters. The *Washington Post* (which, in the meantime, had recovered from its own invasion syndrome) commented editorially that "the State Department White Paper would be more convincing if it reflected less eternal rectitude," [34] but the important point, buried at the end of the text, was that the Eisenhower Administration was now willing to find a solution to the Laos tangle "in the spirit of the Geneva agreement" of 1954—a far cry from the more sanguine statements made earlier. To be sure, the old position could not be fully abandoned overnight, nor need it be

[33] Becker, Jim, "Philippines see SEATO Flop as Anti-Red Force," A.P. dispatch in The *Washington Post*, February 8, 1961.
[34] The *Washington Post*, January 12, 1961.

since a new administration was to take over in Washington within a few days. A few old planes with no strategic potential were sent to Laos, while the Soviet Union and Red China, apparently both in doubt (and in all probability in disagreement) on how to handle the Laos problem, in turn approved or disapproved neutral proposals for calling various types of international conferences designed to settle the Laos problem.[35]

In the meantime (and far faster than in 1959), most foreign newspapers with correspondents in Vientiane now openly accused the Boun Oum government of having "lied" (The *New York Times*), or having "fabricated" (The *Washington Post* and The *Chicago Daily News*) the whole invasion scare. Bouavan Norasing, the Laos Minister of Information, candidly pleaded guilty to the charge but explained that his country had given out false information in order to be able to prove to its citizens that it "could count on the aid of its outside friends." This attitude was completely misunderstood, for in all truth, the fact that outside invasion had not taken place in no way diminished the dangers inherent in the Laotian situation.

The change of administrations in Washington on January 20, 1961, brought about a hiatus as well as a *détente* in American preoccupations with Laos. On the communist side, the fact that Russia, and not Red China, apparently was in control of operations was taken as a reassuring factor as long as the view prevailed that Khrushchev was willing to give the new American administration a chance of turning over a new leaf in its relations with the Soviet Union.[36] Also, both the State of the Union message of President John F. Kennedy ("We seek in Laos . . . freedom for the people and independence for their government . . .") and the first press conference of Secretary of State Dean Rusk (". . . 'neutral' means—to me—first, independence;

---

[35] The following conferences were proposed at one time or another: (a) outright neutralization of Laos and Cambodia by joint agreement of the Big Powers ("Sihanouk Plan" of September 1960); (b) reconvening of the Geneva Agreement countries, variously proposed by the USSR, Red China, and Britain; (c) the reconvening pure and simple of the ICSC, proposed by India; and (d) a fourteen-nation conference of all interested powers, proposed in January 1961 by Cambodia.

[36] Middleton, Drew, "British see Laos as Test of Soviet," The *New York Times*, February 1, 1961.

without the kind of commitments to either side . . . which would cause that country to become a battleground of contending forces . . .") seemed to indicate that the new administration was quite willing to see a *modus vivendi* develop on the basis of effective non-commitment to either side. The fact that American military commanders in the Far East came to the conclusion that a war involving American troops in Laos might well become a bottomless pit similar to the wars in Korea and Indochina, might also have had its influence in the decision.[37]

Finally, the Laotians themselves came to realize what a full-scale war on their territory would mean for them. Vientiane's *Voix du Peuple* (which represents the views of a large part of the Laotian legislature) in recent weeks openly declared that it was "better to obtain an immediate compromise than a general war inspired by other powers," even if the compromise entailed abandoning all or parts of three northeastern provinces to a Pathet Lao régime for "several years." [38] And that, as will be remembered, was where the Laos tangle had begun in 1954.

On February 19, 1961, in an extraordinary statement delivered by the king himself in French in front of the Laos government and all the diplomats stationed in Vientiane, Laos formally proclaimed once more its adherence to a policy of "true neutrality," without foreign military alliances and without the stationing of foreign troops on its soil. The king then offered to have Laos' neutrality supervised by a commission composed of representatives from Burma, Cambodia and Malaya, whose duty it would be to "make public all foreign intervention . . . open or camouflaged." Washington was quick to hail the declaration as "constructive" and "promising." Had it been acceptable to the Soviet bloc, it might possibly have offered an acceptable solution. As of mid-March 1961, with Prince Souvanna Phouma endorsing at least tacitly the Kong-Lê–Souphanouvong combination by a visit to the rebel headquarters at Xieng Khouang, it appears that the lines are hardening again. Likewise, the resumption of Soviet arms shipments to the Pathet Lao seems to indicate that the USSR is not yet ready for hard bargaining; or—in the

[37] See, e.g., *Time*, January 6, 1961.
[38] *Voix du Peuple*, Vientiane, January 31, 1961.

view of the Pentagon—feels that political headway can still be made by raising the military ante.[39] [Fall was overly pessimistic about the possibilities for international agreement on the situation in Laos in the early 1960's. By 1962 another Geneva Conference was held, which set up a coalition government for Laos. See Selections 13, 14 and 21 in this volume—eds.]

VI

One can only marvel at the number and extent of wrong policies adopted at one time or another by some of the powers involved in Laos since 1957. Or, more precisely, at the number and extent of policies based upon erroneous premises or on misinformation pure and simple. The policies of the United States, in view of the considerable extent of her moral, financial and military commitments in that small country, seem particularly misguided.

To anyone who was in Laos during the disturbances of 1959 (as this writer was), it was inconceivable how those very minor engagements, almost never involving more than a few dozen men, could have been mistaken as an "invasion." It is even less comprehensible that anyone would have been willing to rush headlong—and blindfolded—into an exact repetition one year later, considering that the Laos government issuing those claims had no effective control whatever over the regions it claimed had been invaded. It must also be considered as surprising that no concerted Allied policy had been developed to cover precisely the contingency of such a situation—for the absence of such pre-coordination treated the world to the spectacle of intra-Allied bickering almost unmatched since the somber days of Suez. There should have been sufficient "hard intelligence" available about events in Laos (if only on the basis of past experience) to allow the three Western powers to come to a mutually acceptable concensus.

[39] Baldwin, Hanson W., "The Realities of Laos—View is that Rise in Communist Arms will make U.S. 'Put up or Shut Up,'" the *New York Times,* March 7, 1961.

A policy, in order to be effective, must have a clearly defined objective—in the case of Laos either the total integration into the SEATO bloc at the risk of war with North Vietnam; or effective neutrality with perhaps a pro-Western cultural and economic "slant" as in the case of Austria and Finland. In Laos, such a policy decision (with all its implications) was never made on the Western side, thus creating an atmosphere of drift and uncertainty in which the Laotian leaders in Vientiane or their communist opponents were left far too free to surmise what Western policy in Laos really stood for.

Since similar situations are bound to occur with increasing frequency in other areas of the world as the old power systems collapse or undergo radical changes—the Congo and Cuba come to mind—it would be an element of considerable reassurance to know that the lessons learned in Laos have not been entirely forgotten.

11

The Vientiane Agreements (1957)*

JOINT COMMUNIQUE BY H.H. PRINCE
SOUVANNA PHOUMA AND H.H. PRINCE
SOUPHANOUVONG

In the higher interest of the nation, in order to comply
with the deep aspirations of the people, for the peace and for
the general reconciliation between all the Laotians, in conformity with the recommendations of the Geneva agreement and in
implementation of the joint declarations of August 5 and 10,
1956, the joint communique of December 28, 1956 and various agreements reached.

H.H. Prince Souvanna Phouma, Prime Minister of the Royal
Government, and H.H. Prince Souphanouvong, Representative
of the fighting units of Pathet Lao, exchanged views during the
talks which were marked with cordiality.

The Prime Minister of the Royal Government and the representative of the fighting units of the Pathet Lao agree on the
formation, by enlarging the present Cabinet, of a Government
of a large National Union comprising of previous members of
Pathet Lao. The presentation of the new Government will be
preceded by the official handing over to the Royal Government
of the Provinces of Phong Saly and Sam Neua and the fighting
units of the Pathet Lao. . . .

The Prime Minister of the Royal Government and the Representative of the fighting units of the Pathet Lao agree to admit
the Neo Lao Hak Sat as a political party which will enjoy the
same rights and which will be subject to the same obligations as
the other political parties legally formed in the kingdom, as

* From *Fourth Interim Report of the International Commission for
Supervision and Control in Laos* (Laos, No. 1 [1958], Command Paper,
541). London: Great Britain Parliamentary Sessional Papers, XXXIV
(1958/1959), pp. 57–67.

soon as the formalities of its creation are completed in conformity with the laws and regulations in force.

The Prime Minister of the Royal Government and the Representative of the fighting units of the Pathet Lao agree to reestablish effectively the Royal Administration in the provinces of Phong Saly and Sam Neua and to integrate the officials and the combatants of the fighting units of the Pathet Lao in conformity with the modalities to be determined by the political and military committees; this integration will entail the *de facto* and *de jure* disappearance of the fighting units of the Pathet Lao.

Regarding the combatants of the fighting units of the Pathet Lao, the Royal Government undertakes to integrate them all in the National Army. Within the limits of the budget provisions, those who wish to continue their services in the Army will enroll themselves in the active service of the National Army, in accordance with the conditions determined by the regulations in force. Those who would wish to leave the service in order to return to their homes will be integrated in the reserves of the National Army. The Royal Government agrees to provide them, as well as their families, with necessary means of transport so that they would return to their villages, as well as all facilities in order to enable them to earn their livelihood.

The Representative of the fighting units of the Pathet Lao agrees to hand over to the Royal Government the totality of the war equipment, more particularly the arms and ammunition held by the fighting units of the Pathet Lao.

Regarding the civil employees of the fighting units of the Pathet Lao who fulfil the conditions required by the rules pertaining to public service, the Royal Government agrees to appoint them to suitable posts in the various administrative and technical services of the kingdom according to the modalities of implementation which will be determined by the political committee.

The Prime Minister of the Royal Government and the Representative of the fighting units of the Pathet Lao admit by common consent that the agreement on the cessation of hostile acts signed on October 31, 1956, no longer fulfils the needs of the changed situation. The present situation demands that the cessation of hostile acts to be more effective. With this aim, the military committee will determine urgent measures aiming to realise immediately the absolute ceasefire and will increase the number and the means of the mobile sub-committees.

The Prime Minister of the Royal Government and the Representative of the fighting units of the Pathet Lao recognise that the difficulties of implementation still exist and the general reconciliation yet remains a complex task. As there is complete agreement on principles they consider that the time has come to settle in every small detail through settlement under negotiation the practical methods of implementation. Substantial progress has been already made by the political and military committees since the recent resumption of talks. The agreement at present under discussion deals more specially with the steps of a practical nature to be adopted for the *de facto* reestablishment of the royal administration in the provinces of Phong Saly and Sam Neua and for the integration of the officials and combatants of the fighting units of the Pathet Lao. These texts will bring the talks to an end. The Prime Minister of the Royal Government and the Representative of the fighting units of the Pathet Lao recommend therefore to the two committees to continue actively and resolutely their task and expect from them that the settlement under negotiations be terminated in the earliest possible time.

The Prime Minister of the Royal Government and the Representative of the fighting units of the Pathet Lao are satisfied with the results of their present talks which seem to augur the complete and early success of the general reconciliation.

The Prime Minister of the Royal Government and the Representative of the fighting units of the Pathet Lao are firmly confident of the goodwill, sincerity and the efforts of the two parties and hope that the talks will end very soon in final agreements.

Done at Vientiane, November 2, 1957.

[signed] H.H. PRINCE SOU-
VANNA PHOUMA

[signed] H.H. PRINCE SOU-
PHANOUVONG

In the name of the Royal Government.

In the name of the Fighting Units of the Pathet Lao.

THE AGREEMENTS

Preliminary Note

In the spirit of this agreement, the term "Government" means the Government of His Majesty the King.

The expression "Former officials of the fighting units of the Pathet Lao" means the officials formerly employed by the fighting units of the Pathet Lao.

*Agreement Reached Between the Political Delegation
of the Royal Government and the Political Delegation
of the Fighting Units of the Pathet Lao*

In conformity with the provisions of the joint declaration, dated December 28, 1956, of H.H. Prince Souvanna Phouma, Prime Minister of the Royal Government, and H.H. Prince Souphanouvong, Head of the Delegation of the fighting units of the Pathet Lao, declaration which follows the talks between the two parties and which concerns the integration of all Lao citizens into the national community,

The political delegation of the Royal Government and the political delegation of the fighting units of the Pathet Lao . . . met at Vientiane from September 16, 1957 to October 22, 1957, in an atmosphere marked with cordiality and mutual understanding.

The two delegations affirm that the formation of a Government of National Union, the settlement of the administrative and military problem and the integration of the members of the fighting units of the Pathet Lao into the national community are to be considered as necessary phases for the reestablishment of the national unity and constitute at the same time the implementation of the clauses of the Geneva agreement, the Joint Declaration of December 28, 1956, and the previous agreements approved by the National Assembly in its session of May 29, 1957.

The two delegations affirm, besides, that the national reconciliation constitutes the basis for peace, for the safeguard of democracy, independence and progress. Imbued with this idea, the two delegations have agreed on the following:

Chapter One: Administrative Reorganisation of the Provinces of Sam Neua and Phong Saly

A) ADMINISTRATION

   Article 1: From the date of publication of the declaration of handing over of the two provinces to the Royal Government, the two provinces shall effectively be placed under the dependence of the kingdom. All the laws in force in the kingdom shall be applied there. They shall be governed by the Constitution and the laws of the kingdom.

   Article 2: In order to show the good faith of the two parties, the administration of the provinces of Sam Neua and Phong Saly shall be ensured by officials of the Royal Government and former officials of the fighting units of the Pathet Lao in the conditions determined as under:

> The province of Sam Neua shall be headed by a Chaokhoueng[2] of the Royal Government; the province of Phong Saly shall be headed by a former official of the fighting units of the Pathet Lao.
>
> The Chaokhoueng of Sam Neua shall be assisted by a former official of the fighting units of the Pathet Lao; the Chaokhoueng of Phong Saly shall be assisted by an official of the Royal Government.
>
> The Chaomuong, the officials of the khoueng and muong offices as well as the officials of the other services shall be nominated, for half of the strength, among the former officials of the fighting units of the Pathet Lao. Their posting shall be announced by the Royal Government on the proposals of a special commission.

   [2] Provincial Chief—eds.

The duties of chaomuong of the chief town of Sam Neua shall be ensured by a former official of the fighting units of the Pathet Lao. The functions of chaomuong of the chief town of Phong Saly shall be ensured by a functionary of the Royal Government.

The strength and ranks of the officials are those already fixed by the Government who is at liberty to modify them, by reduction or increase, according to the needs of the service.

Temporarily the tasseng and naibans shall continue to assume their duties till new regular elections. These shall take place within a maximum delay of three months with effect from the date of handing over of the two provinces to the kingdom.

B) OFFICIALS

Article 3: In conformity with paragraph three of the above article two, the two delegations shall appoint a Special Commission which will receive the former officials of the fighting units of the Pathet Lao and distribute them in the various services according to a list, to be provided by the delegation of the fighting units of the Pathet Lao.

Article 4: The officials who previously belonged to the cadres of the kingdom shall be reintegrated in their original cadre. If they have changed their situation the Government shall endeavor to maintain them in their new position provided that they possess the required ability.

Their services done outside the cadres of the kingdom shall be considered by the Royal Government as effective services in respect of their rights to pension.

Their promotion shall be subjected to the rules which govern presently the amelioration and revision of the public service regulation.

Within the cadre of the regulations on the public service in the kingdom, the officials and the agents formed by the fighting units of the Pathet Lao shall be as far as possible maintained in the present duties.

Article 5: During the period of three months corresponding to the period of integration of the members of the fighting units of the Pathet Lao into the national community, the Government shall take into account their present situation. They shall not be transferred except for health reason or on their request.

Article 6: Prior to their joining duty the former officials of the fighting units of the Pathet Lao integrated into the cadres of the kingdom shall take an oath of fidelity to the king and the Constitution.

Article 7: The former officials of the fighting units of the Pathet Lao who will not wish to be integrated in the cadres of the kingdom and who want to return home as free citizens shall receive as well as their families aid and assistance from the Government so that they can rejoin their native village. The Government shall help them in the first instance, in finding means of existence.

Chapter Two

Article 8: Prior to the Government of National Union being presented to the National Assembly for a vote of investiture, the head of the fighting units of the Pathet Lao shall make a declaration of handing over to His Majesty the King the provinces of Phong Saly and Sam Neua as well as the military units and officials.

Article 9: The Prime Minister of the Royal Government gives its accord for the functioning of the patriotic front called Neo Lao Haksat with all the rights, freedoms and responsibilities enjoyed by the other political parties formed in the territory of the kingdom on the condition that the statutes of the Neo Lao Haksat are in conformity with the laws at present in force.

Article 10: After the formation of the Government of National Union, the Government shall institute in each of the two provinces a commission charged with the handing over of the services to the Chaokhoueng, Chaomuong and head of the technical services as specified in articles two and three of this agreement.

The handing over of the services shall be carried out on the basis of the provisions of the article eight above.

Article 11: After the handing over of the services, the commission shall proceed to the installation of the officials of the cadres of the kingdom and the former officials of the fighting units of the Pathet Lao nominated and appointed by the Government, informing them that they shall henceforth exercise legally their duties pending the publication of the ordinance or decree sanctioning their new status.

After the installation of the officials an effective handing over of the services including all registers and records shall be done. The taking over of registers and records shall be recorded by administrative minutes.

The handing over of the services at the level of the muong [village] shall take place in similar conditions.

Article 12: Movable and real estates held by the fighting units of the Pathet Lao shall be handed over to the Government, compensations and subventions in favor of the populations of the two provinces will be the responsibility of the Government according to the rules at present in force.

Article 13: The transportation up to their place of origin of the persons assembled by the fighting units of the Pathet Lao in the province of Phong Saly and Sam Neua shall devolve upon the Government on proposal by *ad hoc* commission.

Article 14: The Government shall ensure the publication of this agreement in the whole of the kingdom so that everybody, officials, policemen, soldiers, populations, be informed of the integration of all the Laotians into the national community and the return to the peace through reconciliation.

Article 15: This agreement shall enter into force with effect from the date of its signature.

Article 16: The Government shall prepare supplementary elections which shall take place in the whole of the kingdom within a period of four months.

Done at Vientiane on November 2, 1957.

[signed] THAO TAN CHOU-LAMONTRI *The Head of the Fighting Units of the Pathet Lao*

[signed] PHOUMI VONG-VICHIT *The Prime Minister of the Royal Laotian Government*

[signed] PRINCE SOUPHAN-OUVONG

[signed] PRINCE SOU-VANNA PHOUMA

Military Agreement on the Integration of the Fighting Units of the Pathet Lao Forces into the National Army

The Joint Military Committee, created as a result of the joint declaration of August 5, 1956, made by His Highness Prince Souvanna Phouma, Prime Minister of the Royal Government and H.H. Prince Souphanouvong, President of the fighting units of the Pathet Lao delegation. . . .

The two delegations having proceeded with the exhaustive and detailed exchange of views from October 7 to November 1, 1957, in an atmosphere marked with cordiality and mutual understanding,

Referring to the agreements already reached between the Royal Government and the Representative of the fighting units of the Pathet Lao, . . .

Prompted by the desire to put an end to fratricidal strifes and to contribute thus to the reconciliation of all the Laotians and the reunification of the fatherland,

Have unanimously adopted the following agreement:

ARTICLE 1

The Royal Government undertakes to integrate the fighting units of the Pathet Lao into the National Army by taking over the entire personnel of these units and the entire equipment held by them.

Within the limits of the budget provisions, the combatants of the fighting units of the Pathet Lao who wish to continue their service in the Army shall enroll themselves in the active service of the National Army in conformity with the clauses of the present agreement. Those who wish to leave the service and return home shall be integrated into the Reserves of the National Army.

ARTICLE 2

The combatants of the Pathet Lao fighting units integrated into the National Army in conformity with the clauses of the present agreement shall be treated without discrimination. They shall enjoy the same moral and material rights as their colleagues in the National Army, within the limit of the rules in force in this army.

ARTICLE 3

(a) Taking into account the ceiling limit of the budgetary strength of the National Army in 1957 and in 1958, the strength of the combatants of the Pathet Lao fighting units which can be integrated into the National Army cannot be more than 1,500 men (Officers—NCOs—rank and file).

The distribution of the strength which is to be integrated according to the ranks shall be worked out in conformity with the clauses of article nine below.

(b) The units newly formed from the Pathet Lao fighting units shall be organized according to the norms in force in the National Army.

During the transition period, pending a perfect understanding and collaboration between the various units, the combatants of the Pathet Lao fighting units shall remain grouped in units created at the time of the integration. Nevertheless, transfers in the National Army can be decided by the General Staff of the Armed Forces in order to obtain more control in the matter of administration and command.

(c) The units composed of Pathet Lao fighting units shall be posted in the military area of their origin, that is if these units consist of a majority belonging to that region.

(d) The cadres and the specialists of the Pathet Lao fighting units integrated into the National Army shall be posted in the new units formed from the Pathet Lao fighting units in conformity with the strength rosters of the National Army and the budgetary strength of this army. The remaining shall be integrated in the National Army as far as possible.

(e) The General Staff of the Armed Forces shall appoint a certain number of cadres and specialists who shall collaborate with the integrated cadres and specialists as soon as the operations of the integration are carried out, in order to create harmony between the units of the National Army and those of the new formation in the matter of command and administration.

ARTICLE 4

The cadres and the troops of the Pathet Lao fighting units who shall not be integrated, shall be put in the position of the Reserves of the National Army, relieved from military service and sent to their homes in conformity with the clauses of the present agreement. During the releasing operation and till they reach their selected destination they shall be dependent on the National Army. They shall be in possession of an individual certificate of release, worked out on the model used in the National Army.

ARTICLE 5

The rightful claimants of the combatants of the Pathet Lao fighting units who sacrificed their life shall be entitled for the assistance from the Royal Government and their widows to pensions, pensions to orphans or parents in the conditions determined by the rules in force regarding military pensions in the kingdom. The combatants of the Pathet Lao fighting units disabled or wounded during the war shall be entitled to the same moral and material assistance as those disabled or wounded during the war in the National Army.

ARTICLE 6

In order to avoid any incident, all kinds of forces of the National Army stationed in the province of Phong Saly and Sam Neua shall remain in their positions until the end of the period fixed by the present agreement for the completion of the operations of integration of the fighting units of the Pathet Lao. After this period the responsibility for guarding the frontiers and for the security in the provinces of Phong Saly and Sam Neua shall devolve, on the high authority of the Royal Government, and upon the command of the National Army. This command will be empowered to take in these two provinces as in the other provinces of the kingdom, measures in conformity with the law and fit to ensure the defence of the territory of the fatherland, the safeguard of the national independence, the security of the properties and the life of the population and the respect of the Royal Government's authority.

ARTICLE 7

Modalities of handing over to the National Army of the fighting units of Pathet Lao which are to be integrated.

In order to facilitate the operations of integration and the transportation of the released personnel and their families to their selected destinations, the fighting units of the Pathet Lao shall assemble at the four following centers:

Province of Phong Saly . . . Ban Nam Saleng Muong Khoua

Province of Sam Neua . . . Sam Neua Saleui

ARTICLE 8

Periods: The period for assembling and integration is fixed at sixty days with effect from the day of the formation of the Government of National Union.

The operations of assembling, of normal preparation, of integration, of handing over of arms and equipment, the moves of the fighting units of the Pathet Lao shall be within the limit of sixty days, compulsory time limit. Serious incidents shall be settled by the Royal Government.

ARTICLE 9

(a) After the signature of the present agreement and the formation of the Government of National Union, the Joint Military Sub-Committees shall be posted in the four regroupment centers.

The International Commission will have access to these centers.

(b) 1. The handing over to the representatives of the High Command of the National Army of the list of the personnel, equipment, registers, arms, depots, ammunition, tools and other means shall be carried out by the representatives of the fighting units of the Pathet Lao on the same day on which the official handing over of the administration of the two provinces to the Royal Government will take place.

2. In order to organize the reception of the combatants of the fighting units of the Pathet Lao and the movement of the released personnel, a detailed list will be supplied to the Joint Military Sub-Committees in each of the four regroupment centers, basing on the above said overall list, and taking into

account the strength of the fighting units of the Pathet Lao to be integrated in each center.

(c) The actual handing over of the arms and equipment will be carried out in stages, in the presence of the members of the International Commission for Supervision and Control in Laos.

(d) The released personnel will be handed over to the Joint Military Sub-Committee. They shall benefit of the means of transport and will be in possession of individual certificate of release on the model in use in the National Army. The release shall take place in stages in accordance with the delays necessary to integration operations.

(e) The military personnel of the fighting units of the Pathet Lao who will be integrated in the active service of the National Army will be handed over to the Joint Military Sub-Committee on presentation by the Pathet Lao Command in conformity with the strength rosters of the National Army.

The formalities of integration fulfilled, the Joint Sub-Committee will inform the Joint Military Committee which will fix the date of the ceremony of the handing over of the integrated units to the National Army.

The ceremony of handing over will be held by corps and the oath taking will be held in the traditional way.

After the above mentioned ceremony, the movements of the integrated units will be decided by the General Staff of the National Army.

(f) Arms and equipment will be taken over by the Joint Military Sub-Committees of regroupment centers.

(g) All the integrated and released military personnel of the fighting units of the Pathet Lao will be dependent on the Pathet Lao from the day of signature of the present agreement to their arrival at the regroupment centers.

From the day of their arrival in the regroupment centers (Ban Nam Saleng—Muong Khoua—Sam Neua—Ban Saleui) they as well as their families will become the responsibility of the National Army until they reach their homes.

ARTICLE 10
Priorities will be given to the old people, ladies, children,

to the disabled combatants, to the wounded or sick for their transport by plane, vehicles, boats or pirogues to their place of destination.

The Royal Government and the High Command of the National Army shall take all appropriate measures so that the movements of the detachments of the fighting units of the Pathet Lao directed towards their homes are carried out in all security. The utilisation of the routes and the access to the quarters at the halting places put at the disposal of these detachments shall be prohibited to armed persons.

The Royal Government shall issue orders to the military and administrative authories as well as to the national police for the strict implementation of the present agreement so that the authorities give their help and accord facilities to the home-bound combatants of the fighting units of the Pathet Lao as well as to their movement and the means of earning their livelihood, in conformity with the modalities implemented as regards the military men released from the National Army. The regional authorities, khoueng and muong, shall give them all facilities and shall take appropriate steps for the reception, means of road transport so that the detachment of the released men and their families reach their homes with all facilities and in security.

ARTICLE 11

(a) Four military sub-committees shall be formed in order to implement the agreement reached and to ensure the security and to facilitate the operations of integration.

Besides, they shall ensure the transport and transfers of the military personnel and of the released Pathet Lao fighting units who are admitted in the reserves as well as the transfer of their families until they reach their homes.

(b) The Joint Military Committee shall institute the teams which are deemed necessary for the help, protection and security during the travels and all facilities for the soldiers under transfer till they complete their journey.

ARTICLE 12

The implementation of the present agreement within the time

limit determined in article eight, realises entirely in a military point of view, the settlement foreseen in the article fourteen of the Geneva agreement on the cessation of hostilities in Laos.

ARTICLE 13

The present agreement shall be widely published in the Kingdom of Laos.

ARTICLE 14

The present agreement shall come into force on the date of the formation of the Government of National Union.

Done at Vientiane, November 2, 1957.

[signed] OUAN RATHI-KOUN
President of the Military Delegation of the Royal Government

[signed] PRINCE SOU-PHANOUVONG
Head of the Delegation of the Fighting Units of the Pathet Lao

[signed] PRINCE SOU-VANNA PHOUMA
Prime Minister

[signed] CHAO KROM MANES
President of the Council of Ministers of the Royal Government

12

Anti-Communism: The Rationale for US Aid*

MR. HARDY. Before we proceed I want to read a brief statement that I have prepared.

For several months this subcommittee has been making a comprehensive study of the US aid program for the Southeast Asian Kingdom of Laos. We have sought to find particular answers to broad questions which have arisen out of other studies by the subcommittee—questions such as the basis for the establishment of force objectives and the translation of these objectives into levels of aid. This morning we will begin hearings in furtherance of this study.

A great deal of emphasis has been placed on the military aspect of our aid program. Yet, just as essential to sound mutual security is the economic and political stability of a country which will enable it to develop and maintain free institutions and the national solidarity essential to oppose both external aggression and internal subversion.

Military forces are not economically productive in any country, and in a small, less developed country a relatively large military force must necessarily retard capital growth and impair economic well-being. Also, particularly in younger nations, a large military force may have a strong sense of self-perpetuation which could encourage resistance to direction by political authority.

Laos is the only country in the world where we support the entire military budget. Some eighty-five percent or more of our total aid to Laos goes into support of a 25,000 man military

* United States Aid Operations in Laos, *Hearings Before the Subcommittee on Foreign Operations and Monetary Affairs of the Committee on Government Operations, House of Representatives* [Rep. Porter Hardy, Jr., Chairman], Eighty-sixth Congress, First Session, May–June, 1959 (Washington, D.C.: U.S. Government Printing Office, 1959), pp. 1–2, 180–1, 182–5, 190–2, 193–5.

force. I have seen different figures but the 25,000 figure is the most recent I have seen. Yet, I believe it is generally agreed that an army of this size is far beyond the capacity of Laos to support unaided now or any time in the foreseeable future. The heavy cost of this operation to the American taxpayer can only be justified to the extent that accomplishments meet objectives.

It is, of course, no secret that our military assistance programs have political objectives. This is one of the stated purposes of the Mutual Security Act. From the reading of testimony given by responsible executive branch witnesses before congressional committees, I have recognized what seems to be a sharp divergence of views as to whether we are attaining our political objectives in Laos or whether we are further removed from their attainment today than we were at the inception of our aid program in that country. That bothers me. We shall inquire into this, among other subjects during these hearings, in an attempt to establish the facts. If it develops that we are failing in our political objectives we will seek to determine whether this failure is related directly or indirectly to the nature or administration of our aid program.

Economic objectives of the US aid program in Laos have never been clearly specified, perhaps obscured by our preoccupation with political and military goals. Quite often these several types of objectives are mutually inconsistent, and determining whether this is the case in Laos will be another one of the subjects of our inquiry. . . .

STATEMENT OF HON. WALTER S. ROBERTSON,[1] ACCOMPANIED BY HON. JAMES GRAHAM PARSONS[2]

MR. ROBERTSON. Thank you, Mr. Chairman and members of the subcommittee.

I welcome the opportunity to appear before this subcommittee to discuss the policy aspects of our mutual security program in Laos. In my opinion, the prospects for that country have clearly

[1] Assistant Secretary of State for Far Eastern Affairs.
[2] U.S. Ambassador to Laos, May, 1956 to February, 1958; later Deputy Assistant Secretary of State for Far Eastern Affairs—eds.

improved in the past year and our policy objectives have been furthered. These favorable developments are the result of a considerable effort on the part of the patriotic leaders of Laos, an effort that could not have been attempted with any chance of success without the material support of our mutual security program.

Our policy objectives in relation to Laos have been and are to assist the Lao:

1: In keeping the communists from taking over Laos;

2: In strengthening their association with the free world; and

3: In developing and maintaining a stable and independent government willing and able to resist communist aggression or subversion.

The major instrument in the execution of our policy is the mutual security program. Despite the many complicated problems which developed in the administration of this program, I believe a frank appraisal of the record of the past year shows that it has been effective in furthering our objectives.

The degree of progress which has been made toward keeping the communist[s] from taking over Laos may be measured by the degree to which communist potential in this direction diminished in the past year. The government placed in office on August 18, 1958, by a freely elected National Assembly including opposition elements, excluded the two communist ministers who had been admitted by the political agreement of late 1957. . . .

Progress toward development of a stable, independent government willing and able to resist communist aggression or subversion may be measured, I believe, by the action of the Royal Lao Government since August 18, 1958. Toward the end of 1958 there were frequent rumors that the government in Vientiane would resort to extra-legal or unconstitutional measures in order to cope with its many problems. The fact that by January 14, 1959, the government was able to obtain full powers through parliamentary procedures is a gratifying indication of its growing strength. Without our active support and the aid received under the mutual security program such progress would not have been possible.

In spite of what has been accomplished, however, many problems still remain due to the very nature of the peculiar conditions existing in Laos. I wish to stress that 1: our mutual security program has been vital to the survival of this small nation threatened by the forces of international communism; and 2: our aid and support must continue if Laos is to remain free. . . .

MR. HARDY. There was an evaluation, shortly after the election in Laos, in which there was an indication that the army had played a pretty substantial part in the election and would probably continue to be a strong political force in the future. Is it a reasonable assumption that this accomplishment on January 14 may have been affected somewhat by the provision of the army?

MR. ROBERTSON. I think it is possible, Mr. Chairman. I was thinking, while you were talking, the army is probably the most important force in the country in combating communism. The army there, as in most of the Asian countries is oriented to the free world rather than to the communist world. And in this little country of Laos, the army is one of the principal administrative arms of the government.

MR. HARDY. But is it not a fact that wherever the army becomes a dominant power in the political arena, it likely presages a military dictatorship?

MR. ROBERTSON. I am not qualified to say whether that has always been so or not, but I do say that I think that in Laos, as well as in Indonesia, in Burma and in Thailand, the military forces represent the most effective forces in the country in combating the takeover of those countries by the communists. And surely when they are taken over by the communists there is no dictatorship that can begin to match their dictatorship.

MR. HARDY. But if you get communist control, or if you should get an improper leadership at the top, you have a pretty serious situation if the army takes over the functions which are normally expected of civilians in a democracy.

MR. ROBERTSON. I think we must keep in mind the difficulty of applying our standards of democracy to these little countries that have only had their independence for a few years.

MR. HARDY. Of course, you know and I know that we have been going through some of the same situations in Latin America for a long, long time. It is the strength of the military forces down there that usually determines who will be the president, even if you call it a democracy.

MR. ROBERTSON. Mr. Chairman, this isn't an abstract difficulty; it is a very real one. These peoples are largely illiterate. Eight out of the eleven of the countries in the Far East have achieved their independence since 1945; these people since 1955. They had no civil services, no technicians, no administrators, no experience, and they suddenly had put upon them all the problems of running an independent country. It is perfectly true that in many of them the processes of democracy have broken down because of their large illiterate masses.

The communists come in and exploit them very successfully —make them think they are poor and illiterate because they have been exploited by the Western countries. Their standard of living and their lot is so miserable that almost any kind of a change might seem desirable to them. The communists are very quick to exploit this situation. It is one of the very real problems we have in the area everywhere.

MR. HARDY. It is disturbing to me if, in this kind of a situation, the army, which is depending entirely on us for its support, has become the key political factor in that country. The ANL is now an important political factor which will have to be reckoned with by all politicians.

Under the present situation, do we have the same Prime Minister that we had prior to the expulsion of the two communists from the Cabinet?

MR. ROBERTSON. No. Souvanna Phouma was the Prime Minister when the communists had two ministers in the Cabinet; the Prime Minister now is a man named Phoui Sananikone.

MR. HARDY. So he doesn't have a brother who is a leader in the Communist movement?

MR. ROBERTSON. Oh, no. The former Prime Minister's half brother was negotiator for the Communists, who negotiated the coalition government.

MR. HARDY. We developed some of that the other day.

MR. REDDAN.[3] Didn't he also become Minister of Plans?

MR. ROBERTSON. Yes. He became the Minister of Planning in the coalition government, the man who negotiated for the communists.

---

[3] Chief Counsel for the Subcommittee—eds.

MR. HARDY. Go ahead.

MR. ROBERTSON. Mr. Chairman, if I may, speaking about this question of democracy in these countries, I would like to remind ourselves that when we formed our own government we probably had one of the most politically literate people that has ever existed in this country. And, even so, we didn't form a democracy, we formed a republic. There was no such thing as voting just because you had lived for twenty-one years. There were qualifications for voting in every one of thirteen states. We didn't elect the president by popular vote. Even I can remember when we began to elect the senators by popular vote. So we set up a republic here because we were fearful of just what a pure democracy might lead to.

If we, without highly literate political people, put certain limitations upon the powers of the individual, it is not very surprising to me that in a situation there, where they have nothing even remotely comparable to what we started with, that situations do develop where powers that are seeking law and order and trying to preserve the independence of the country have to take measures which ordinarily they wouldn't take.

MR. HARDY. Certainly I don't want anything I have said to imply that I have suggested that we ought to insist on pure democracy in a country like Laos. In fact, sometimes I am inclined to believe that perhaps here our qualifications for voting are too lax. Perhaps even in our own country there is an inclination in that direction which I don't think necessarily leads us to the best government. Certainly it would not be expected that the people of Laos have reached a point of political responsibility where they could exercise a degree of self-government which we consider ourselves capable of doing here.

But when the army becomes a dominant factor, and when we have a comparison that was made here yesterday, I am not sure that the status of the army is much better than that of the rank and file of people insofar as political responsibility with respect to self-government is concerned.

Just yesterday I believe Admiral O'Donnel in his prepared statement made a comparison of the coolie with the privates in the army, the enlisted personnel, not directly but to indicate that comparatively their pay scales were not any better than that of the coolie. Maybe their degree of political competence isn't much better either. If that is the case, we are leaning on a weak reed.

MR. ROBERTSON. I think we are leaning on the best reed we have and we have to deal with that situation as it is, not as we would like to have it.

MR. HARDY. All of this leads me to one question, whether we are going to be permanently the fairy godfather of a government in Laos.

MR. ROBERTSON. I don't think that is what we are doing now, Mr. Chairman. We are trying to keep Laos in the free world. If you will look at the map—

MR. HARDY. I have. I have studied it very carefully.

MR. ROBERTSON. I am sure you have. I say, when you look at the map you will see that Laos is a finger thrust right down into the heart of Southeast Asia. And Southeast Asia is one of the prime objectives of the international communists in Asia because it is rich in raw materials and has excess food. If they can add Southeast Asia with its raw materials and excess food to the manpower of China, and to the industrial capacity of Japan —and they are working terribly hard, without ceasing, to get Japan—we will really have to pull up stakes and come home, because the battle will be lost.

We are not in Laos to be a fairy godfather to Laos; we are in there for one sole reason, and that is to try to keep this little country from being taken over by the communists.

MR. MONAGAN. That is a defensive matter.

MR. ROBERTSON. It is a part of the effort we are making for the collective security of the free world. Every time you lose a country, every time you give up to them, they become correspondingly stronger and the free world becomes weaker.

This isn't only happening in this little country of Laos, it is happening all over the world, everywhere. We are engaged in a struggle for the survival of what we call a free civilization. The communists probe first in Europe, then in the Middle East, in Africa, Taiwan, in Laos—wherever they think they can find a soft spot. They are always probing trying to find it, because this is an expansionist movement and they are dedicated to taking over the world.

MR. HARDY. Certainly I think anyone realizes that this is the fundamental of the whole communist philosophy. Otherwise, we wouldn't have done a lot of things that we have to try to safeguard our own way of life, all of which seems to me brings into sharper focus the necessity for trying to make the very most we can out of what we are spending and not spread ourselves so thin and provide so much latitude for misuse of funds that we may cause our own undoing. . . .

MR. REDDAN. Mr. Robertson, last March—March 28—when you appeared before the Senate Foreign Relations Committee, at pages 323 and 324 of the hearings, you were asked about the Geneva accords, and at that time you stated:

> A delicate situation exists in Laos. The 1954 Geneva accords provide for unification of the country under the central government. The communist-dominated Pathet Lao, however, refused to turn over to the Royal Government the two provinces under their armed control, using their defiance of this international agreement to negotiate successfully in the November, 1957, coalition government which netted them two cabinet positions, other administrative participation, and legal status as a political party. This may extend communist influence dangerously in Laos.

Did subsequent developments change your opinion?

MR. ROBERTSON. No. I have just stated that the things that I feared most didn't come to pass. We very much feared when they took the communists into the government that the same thing would happen to Laos as happened to Czechoslovakia. Jan Masaryk thought he could deal with them and ended up by jumping or being pushed out of a window and the communists took over his country. We very much feared the communist coalition would bring the communists dangerously into the country.

The reason we are encouraged, and very much encouraged by

what has happened is that they did unify the country. They started off with the coalition but it lasted only a few months. They have gotten rid of the coalition and now have a government in which no communists are represented.

MR. HARDY. They started off with a coalition and then had an election which had a lot of people disturbed. That is the one which took place in May, I believe.

MR. ROBERTSON. That's right.

MR. HARDY. And the communists actually were pretty successful in that election, as I remember.

MR. ROBERTSON. Mr. Chairman, the situation was this, and it has been very much misunderstood. In the results, they were unsuccessful, but the facts were these. There were twenty-one seats at stake. They were increasing the National Assembly from thirty-eight to fifty-nine seats. There were twenty-one new seats at stake. The anti-communist forces polled about sixty-five percent of the popular vote, but ran eighty-five candidates for twenty-one seats.

So, getting sixty-five percent of the vote, they ended up with only eight out of the twenty-one seats, whereas the communists concentrated on twenty-one candidates for twenty-one seats— I mean, the leftist forces. And so with thirty-five percent of the vote they got thirteen out of the twenty-one seats. That was the thing, the very thing that we had warned the Government would happen if they didn't get together and agree upon candidates.

They had a number of these parties. They should have agreed between them on a candidate for each seat, regardless of which party he belonged to if he was a non-communist candidate. They didn't do that. So, while getting popular support they only won a little more than a third of the seats.

MR. HARDY. I understand. Of course, we know what happens here sometimes, too, if you have too many candidates in a particular contest. But the fact remains that when the votes were counted and your certificates of election, if they issue them, were issued, the communists won that election.

MR. ROBERTSON. That's right.

MR. HARDY. Then subsequently—and I believe it was in July or August—there was a coalition of the non-communist ele-

ments in the Government which was successful in getting rid
of the communist ministers.

The thing that I was trying to get at is this: What took place
to bring that about?

MR. ROBERTSON. I think they got a tremendous jolt when
they ended up by losing those elections.

MR. HARDY. It wasn't anything that we did?

MR. ROBERTSON. Nothing that we did, no. As a matter of fact,
they went contrary to our advice in the elections. We strongly
urged them to agree on twenty-one candidates and consolidate
their forces for the twenty-one seats. They didn't do that and
thereby lost the elections. It was a tremendous jolt to them.

MR. PARSONS. May I supplement that? We did do something
in this matter although it was not a concrete act, which is what
Mr. Robertson must have had in mind.

The Prime Minister, in forming the government which contained the two communists, said that the life of the government
would last only until the partial general elections were over, then
a new government would be formed. As soon as he said that I,
and every other free-world representative in Laos, was pointing
out to the Prime Minister, here is your golden opportunity; you
win this election, you win enough seats in the election to make
sure that you can form a non-communist government afterward,
with no communists in it. [. . . Security deletion]

MR. HARDY. I am delighted to get that explanation because
actually I had been worried. It is the first time I have seen anything that happened in these countries that looked like it was an
advantage to us that we didn't claim full credit for.

I am surprised nobody in the State Department has claimed
that they were completely responsible for the coalition of the
non-communist parties because every other statement we have
had has been so high-poweredly optimistic; all your boys seem
to get their best foot forward in fine shape when talking to the
committees, especially the Foreign Affairs Committee. I don't
see how you missed this one. It was a wonderful opportunity. . . .

This is a good time to illustrate a point that I was trying to
make a moment ago, and to put out the point which seemed

to me to reflect at least disagreement if not inconsistency in statements which you two gentlemen made last year.

Mr. Reddan read one made by the Secretary before the Senate Foreign Relations Committee.

Just a matter of a few weeks later Mr. Parsons made a statement before the House Appropriations Committee.

In your statement, Mr. Secretary, you were pointing out the seriousness of the situation in Laos and the delicacy of this whole election proposition. A few weeks later Mr. Parsons, successfully putting his best foot forward during the appropriations hearings, made a statement that doesn't seem to tie in with yours. Maybe I don't read into them the purport that I should.

This testimony before the House Subcommittee on Appropriations was:

> The program has maintained the independence of Laos up to the present time. I have heard no one say that Laos could remain independent without the program. I would point out further that this is the only area that I can think of at the present moment where territory has been recovered from the communists; two provinces of Laos which were behind the Bamboo Curtain are now in the kingdom.

To interject at this particular point, that has been one that some of us, and some of you people in the Department of State, had viewed with considerable concern. Mr. Parsons at this time seemed to be taking it as an asset.

To continue with the statement:

> This, in a sense, was a divided country. It is no longer a divided country. The communists are still contesting for it. They never give up contesting for any country, but this is a country where the aid program is responsible in very large part for not only maintaining its independence, but for making it possible for the government to reunite the country

and to work toward consolidating the reunified
country

Maybe I don't understand these things. But I had thought
that in all of the other material I had seen, and the other comments that had been made by responsible representatives of the
Department of State, that we suffered something of a blow when
the Pathet Lao was brought in and put two ministers in the
Cabinet and when the election came up, which at least in the
final analysis produced more communist ministers than they had
had before.

Here, a matter of a few weeks after the election, Mr. Parsons
views it as an asset. This is the kind of thing that bothers me
and prompted the observation that I made a moment ago. If
you have any comments, if I am reading it wrong, I would like
to be corrected. But I don't think that you two gentlemen were
actually presenting the same kind of picture to the Congress at
approximately the same time in history.

MR. PARSONS. Mr. Chairman, I would like to make just a very
brief comment on that. As you read the statement, I do not know
what it was in reply to. But everything in that statement is a
statement of fact and I would stand by it today just as I stood by
it then.

MR. HARDY. It is a matter of interpretation, I think.

MR. PARSONS. There is not much interpretation there, sir, if I
may correct you. Further than that, I don't think that one particular statement is sufficient to indicate that I had no concern
about Laos.

MR. HARDY. I didn't mean to imply that.

MR. PARSONS. I dare say that I have worried about Laos more
than any man in this room.

MR. HARDY. I didn't mean to imply that you had no concern
about it.

MR. PARSONS. And I am still concerned about Laos; still
worried about the future of Laos. It would be foolish of me or
any one else to be unconcerned about a situation in a country
located geographically where Laos is, so devoid of material assets
and experience and virtually everything else which goes into the
maintenance of independence.

MR. HARDY. Let me say this to you, and this will sum up my reaction to it, which does not imply any lack of concern. If I interpret these two statements correctly, Mr. Robertson was saying, in effect, that the coalition was a community victory, and you were saying, in effect, that it was a victory for us. Maybe I don't interpret it correctly. But that is the way it sounds to me. And that is why I have a little trouble reconciling those two views from people who have the stature that you two gentlemen have in the Department.

MR. PARSONS. Mr. Chairman, you have my statement before you. I don't. I don't think I said anywhere there that coalition was a victory for the United States. I struggled for sixteen months to prevent a coalition.

13

Declaration on the Neutrality of Laos (1962)*

The Governments of the Union of Burma, the Kingdom of Cambodia, Canada, the People's Republic of China, the Democratic Republic of Vietnam, the Republic of France, the Republic of India, the Polish People's Republic, the Republic of Vietnam, the Kingdom of Thailand, the Union of Soviet Socialist Republics, the United Kingdom of Great Britain and Northern Ireland and the United States of America, whose representatives took part in the International Conference on the Settlement of the Laotian Question, 1961–1962;

Welcoming the presentation of the statement of neutrality by the Royal Government of Laos of July 9, 1962, and taking note of this statement, which is, with the concurrence of the Royal Government of Laos, incorporated in the present Declaration as an integral part thereof, and the text of which is as follows:

> THE ROYAL GOVERNMENT OF LAOS,
>
> Being resolved to follow the path of peace and neutrality in conformity with the interests and aspirations of the Laotian people, as well as the principles of the Joint Communiqué of Zurich dated June 22, 1961, and of the Geneva agreements of 1954, in order to build a peaceful, neutral, independent, democratic, unified and prosperous Laos, Solemnly declares that:
>
> (1) It will resolutely apply the five principles of peaceful coexistence in foreign relations, and will develop friendly relations and establish diplomatic

* *International Conference on the Settlement of the Laotian Question, 1961–1962* (Laos no. 1 [1962], Command Paper, 1828). London: Great Britain Parliamentary Sessional Papers, XXXVII (1961/1962), pp. 16–18.

relations with all countries, the neighboring countries first and foremost, on the basis of equality and of respect for the independence and sovereignty of Laos;

(2) It is the will of the Laotian people to protect and ensure respect for the sovereignty, independence, neutrality, unity, and territorial integrity of Laos;

(3) It will not resort to the use or threat of force in any way which might impair the peace of other countries, and will not interfere in the internal affairs of other countries;

(4) It will not enter into any military alliance or into any agreement, whether military or otherwise, which is inconsistent with the neutrality of the Kingdom of Laos; it will not allow the establishment of any foreign military base on Laotian territory, nor allow any country to use Laotian territory for military purposes or for the purposes of interference in the internal affairs of other countries, nor recognize the protection of any alliance or military coalition, including SEATO;

(5) It will not allow any foreign interference in the internal affairs of the Kingdom of Laos in any form whatsoever;

(6) Subject to the provisions of article five of the Protocol, it will require the withdrawal from Laos of all foreign troops and military personnel, and will not allow any foreign troops or military personnel to be introduced into Laos;

(7) It will accept direct and unconditional aid from all countries that wish to help the Kingdom of Laos build up an independent and autonomous national economy on the basis of respect for the sovereignty of Laos;

(8) It will respect the treaties and agreements signed in conformity with the interests of the Laotian people and of the policy of peace and neutrality

of the Kingdom, in particular the Geneva agreements of 1962, and will abrogate all treaties and agreements which are contrary to those principles.

This statement of neutrality by the Royal Government of Laos shall be promulgated constitutionally and shall have the force of law.

The Kingdom of Laos appeals to all the States participating in the International Conference on the Settlement of the Laotian Question, and to all other States, to recognize the sovereignty, independence, neutrality, unity, and territorial integrity of Laos, to conform to these principles in all respects, and to refrain from any action inconsistent therewith.

Confirming the principles of respect for the sovereignty, independence, unity and territorial integrity of the Kingdom of Laos and non-interference in its internal affairs which are embodied in the Geneva agreements of 1954;

Emphasizing the principle of respect for the neutrality of the Kingdom of Laos;

Agreeing that the above-mentioned principles constitute a basis for the peaceful settlement of the Laotian question;

Profoundly convinced that the independence and neutrality of the Kingdom of Laos will assist the peaceful democratic development of the Kingdom of Laos and the achievement of national accord and unity in that country, as well as the strengthening of peace and security in Southeast Asia:

1. Solemnly declare, in accordance with the will of the Government and people of the Kingdom of Laos, as expressed in the statement of neutrality by the Royal Government of Laos of July 9, 1962, that they recognize and will respect and observe in every way the sovereignty, independence, neutrality, unity and territorial integrity of the Kingdom of Laos.

2. Undertake, in particular, that

(*a*) they will not commit or participate in

any way in any act which might directly or indirectly impair the sovereignty, independence, neutrality, unity or territorial integrity of the Kingdom of Laos;

(b) they will not resort to the use or threat of force or any other measure which might impair the peace of the Kingdom of Laos;

(c) they will refrain from all direct or indirect interference in the internal affairs of the Kingdom of Laos;

(d) they will not attach conditions of a political nature to any assistance which they may offer or which the Kingdom of Laos may seek;

(e) they will not bring the Kingdom of Laos in any way into any military alliance or any other agreement, whether military or otherwise, which is inconsistent with her neutrality, nor invite or encourage her to enter into any such alliance or to conclude any such agreement;

(f) they will respect the wish of the Kingdom of Laos not to recognize the protection of any alliance or military coalition, including SEATO;

(g) they will not introduce into the Kingdom of Laos foreign troops or military personnel in any form whatsoever, nor will they in any way facilitate or connive at the introduction of any foreign troops or military personnel;

(h) they will not establish nor will they in any way facilitate or connive at the establishment in the Kingdom of Laos of any foreign military base, foreign strong point or other foreign military installation of any kind;

(*i*) they will not use the territory of the Kingdom of Laos for interference in the internal affairs of other countries;

(*j*) they will not use the territory of any country, including their own, for interference in the internal affairs of the Kingdom of Laos.

3. Appeal to all other States to recognize, respect and observe in every way the sovereignty, independence and neutrality, and also the unity and territorial integrity, of the Kingdom of Laos and to refrain from any action inconsistent with these principles or with other provisions of the present Declaration.

4. Undertake, in the event of a violation or threat of violation of the sovereignty, independence, neutrality, unity or territorial integrity of the Kingdom of Laos, to consult jointly with the Royal Government of Laos and among themselves in order to consider measures which might prove to be necessary to ensure the observance of these principles and the other provisions of the present Declaration.

5. The present Declaration shall enter into force on signature and together with the statement of neutrality by the Royal Government of Laos of July 9, 1962 shall be regarded as constituting an international agreement. The present Declaration shall be deposited in the archives of the Governments of the United Kingdom and the Union of Soviet Socialist Republics, which shall furnish certified copies thereof to the other signatory States and to all the other States of the world.

In witness whereof, the undersigned Plenipotentiaries have signed the present Declaration.

Done in two copies in Geneva this twenty-third day of July one thousand nine hundred and sixty-two in the English, Chinese, French, Laotian and Russian languages, each text being equally authoritative.

For the Union of Burma:
U THI HAN

For the Kingdom of Cambodia:
NHIEK TIOULONG

For Canada:
H. C. GREEN
CHESTER RONNING

For the People's Republic of China:
CHEN YI

For the Democratic Republic of Vietnam:
UNG-VAN-KHIEM

For the Republic of France:
M. COUVE DE MURVILLE
JACQUES ROUX

For the Republic of India:
V. K. KRISHNA MENON

For the Polish People's Republic:
A. RAPACKI

For the Republic of Vietnam:
VU VAN MAU
THANH

For the Kingdom of Thailand:
DIRECK JAYANÁMA

For the Union of Soviet Socialist Republics:
A. GROMYKO

For the United Kingdom of Great Britain and Northern Ireland:
HOME
MALCOLM MACDONALD

For the United States of America:
DEAN RUSK
W. AVERELL HARRIMAN

14

Protocol to the Declaration on the Neutrality of Laos (1962)*

The Governments of the Union of Burma, the Kingdom of Cambodia, Canada, the People's Republic of China, the Democratic Republic of Vietnam, the Republic of France, the Republic of India, the Kingdom of Laos, the Polish People's Republic, the Republic of Vietnam, the Kingdom of Thailand, the Union of Soviet Socialist Republics, the United Kingdom of Great Britain and Northern Ireland and the United States of America;

Having regard to the Declaration on the Neutrality of Laos of July 23, 1962;

Have agreed as follows:

Article 1

For the purposes of this Protocol
>   (*a*) the term "foreign military personnel" shall include members of foreign military missions, foreign military advisers, experts, instructors, consultants, technicians, observers and any other foreign military persons, including those serving in any armed forces in Laos, and foreign civilians connected with the supply, maintenance, storing and utilization of war materials;
>   (*b*) the term "the Commission" shall mean the International Commission for Supervision and Control in Laos set up by virtue of the Geneva

* *International Conference on the Settlement of the Laotian Question, 1961–1962* (Laos no. 1[1962], Command Paper, 1828). London: Great Britain Parliamentary Sessional Papers, XXXVII (1961/1962), pp. 19–24.

agreements of 1954 and composed of the representatives of Canada, India and Poland, with the representative of India as Chairman;

(c) the term "the Co-Chairmen" shall mean the Co-Chairmen of the International Conference for the Settlement of the Laotian Question, 1961–1962, and their successors in the offices of Her Britannic Majesty's Principal Secretary of State for Foreign Affairs and Minister for Foreign Affairs of the Union of Soviet Socialist Republics respectively;

(d) the term "the members of the Conference" shall mean the Governments of countries which took part in the International Conference for the Settlement of the Laotian Question, 1961–1962.

Article 2

All foreign regular and irregular troops, foreign para-military formations and foreign military personnel shall be withdrawn from Laos in the shortest time possible and in any case the withdrawal shall be completed not later than thirty days after the Commission has notified the Royal Government of Laos that in accordance with article three and ten of this Protocol its inspection teams are present at all points of withdrawal from Laos. These points shall be determined by the Royal Government of Laos in accordance with article three within thirty days after the entry into force of this Protocol. The inspection teams shall be present at these points and the Commission shall notify the Royal Government of Laos thereof within fifteen days after the points have been determined.

Article 3

The withdrawal of foreign regular and irregular troops, foreign para-military formations and foreign military personnel shall take place only along such routes and through such points as shall be determined by the Royal Government of Laos in consultation with the Commission. The Commission shall be notified in advance of the point and time of all such withdrawals.

Article 4

The introduction of foreign regular and irregular troops, foreign para-military formations and foreign military personnel into Laos is prohibited.

Article 5

Note is taken that the French and Laotian Governments will conclude as soon as possible an arrangement to transfer the French military installations in Laos to the Royal Government of Laos.

If the Laotian Government considers it necessary, the French Government may as an exception leave in Laos for a limited period of time a precisely limited number of French military instructors for the purpose of training the armed forces of Laos.

The French and Laotian Governments shall inform the members of the Conference, through the Co-Chairmen, of their agreement on the question of the transfer of the French military installations in Laos and of the employment of French military instructors by the Laotian Government.

Article 6

The introduction into Laos of armaments, munitions and war material generally, except such quantities of conventional armaments as the Royal Government of Laos may consider necessary for the national defence of Laos, is prohibited.

Article 7

All foreign military persons and civilians captured or interned during the course of hostilities in Laos shall be released within thirty days after the entry into force of this Protocol and handed over by the Royal Government of Laos to the representatives of the Governments of the countries of which they are nationals in order that they may proceed to the destination of their choice.

Article 8

The Co-Chairmen shall periodically receive reports from the Commission. In addition the Commission shall immediately report to the Co-Chairmen any violations or threats of violations of this Protocol, all significant steps which it takes in pursuance of this Protocol, and also any other important information which may assist the Co-Chairmen in carrying out their functions. The Commission may at any time seek help from the Co-Chairmen in the performance of its duties, and the Co-Chairmen may at any time make recommendations to the Commission exercising general guidance.

The Co-Chairmen shall circulate the reports and any other important information from the Commission to the members of the Conference.

The Co-Chairmen shall exercise supervision over the observance of this Protocol and the Declaration on the Neutrality of Laos.

The Co-Chairmen will keep the members of the Conference constantly informed and when appropriate will consult with them.

Article 9

The Commission shall, with the concurrence of the Royal Government of Laos, supervise and control the ceasefire in Laos.

The Commission shall exercise these functions in full co-operation with the Royal Government of Laos and within the framework of the Ceasefire Agreement or ceasefire arrangements made by the three political forces in Laos, or the Royal Government of Laos. It is understood that responsibility for the execution of the ceasefire shall rest with the three parties concerned and with the Royal Government of Laos after its formation.

Article 10

The Commission shall supervise and control the withdrawal of foreign regular and irregular troops, foreign para-
military formations and foreign military personnel. Inspection
teams sent by the Commission for these purposes shall be present
for the period of the withdrawal at all points of withdrawal from
Laos determined by the Royal Government of Laos in consultation with the Commission in accordance with article three of
this Protocol.

Article 11

The Commission shall investigate cases where there are
reasonable grounds for considering that a violation of the provisions of article four of this Protocol has occurred.

It is understood that in the exercise of this function the Commission is acting with the concurrence of the Royal Government
of Laos. It shall carry out its investigations in full cooperation
with the Royal Government of Laos and shall immediately inform the Co-Chairmen of any violations or threats of violations
of article four, and also of all significant steps which it takes in
pursuance of this article in accordance with article eight.

Article 12

The Commission shall assist the Royal Government of Laos
in cases where the Royal Government of Laos considers that a
violation of article six of this Protocol may have taken place.
This assistance will be rendered at the request of the Royal
Government of Laos and in full cooperation with it.

Article 13

The Commission shall exercise its functions under this
Protocol in close cooperation with the Royal Government of
Laos. It is understood that the Royal Government of Laos at
all levels will render the Commission all possible assistance in
the performance by the Commission of these functions and also

will take all necessary measures to ensure the security of the Commission and its inspection teams during their activities in Laos.

Article 14

The Commission functions as a single organ of the International Conference for the Settlement of the Laotian Question, 1961–1962. The members of the Commission will work harmoniously and in cooperation with each other with the aim of solving all questions within the terms of reference of the Commission.

Decisions of the Commission on questions relating to violations of articles two, three, four and six of this Protocol or of the ceasefire referred to in article nine, conclusions on major questions sent to the Co-Chairmen and all recommendations by the Commission shall be adopted unanimously. On other questions, including procedural questions, and also questions relating to the initiation and carrying out of investigations (article fifteen), decisions of the Commission shall be adopted by majority vote.

Article 15

In the exercise of its specific functions which are laid down in the relevant articles of this Protocol the Commission shall conduct investigations (directly or by sending inspection teams), when there are reasonable grounds for considering that a violation has occurred. These investigations shall be carried out at the request of the Royal Government of Laos or on the initiative of the Commission, which is acting with the concurrence of the Royal Government of Laos.

In the latter case decisions on initiating and carrying out such investigations shall be taken in the Commission by majority vote.

The Commission shall submit agreed reports on investigations in which differences which may emerge between members of the Commission on particular questions may be expressed.

The conclusions and recommendations of the Commission resulting from investigations shall be adopted unanimously.

Article 16

For the exercise of its functions the Commission shall, as necessary, set up inspection teams, on which the three member-States of the Commission shall be equally represented. Each member-State of the Commission shall ensure the presence of its own representatives both on the Commission and on the inspection teams, and shall promptly replace them in the event of their being unable to perform their duties.

It is understood that the dispatch of inspection teams to carry out various specific tasks takes place with the concurrence of the Royal Government of Laos. The points to which the Commission and its inspection teams go for the purposes of investigation and their length of stay at those points shall be determined in relation to the requirements of the particular investigation.

Article 17

The Commission shall have at its disposal the means of communication and transport required for the performance of its duties. These as a rule will be provided to the Commission by the Royal Government of Laos for payment on mutually acceptable terms, and those which the Royal Government of Laos cannot provide will be acquired by the Commission from other sources. It is understood that the means of communication and transport will be under the administrative control of the Commission.

Article 18

The costs of the operations of the commission shall be borne by the members of the Conference in accordance with the provisions of this article.

> (*a*) The Governments of Canada, India and Poland shall pay the personal salaries and allow-

ances of their nationals who are members of their delegations to the Commission and its subsidiary organs.

(b) The primary responsibility for the provision of accommodation for the Commission and its subsidiary organs shall rest with the Royal Government of Laos, which shall also provide such other local services as may be appropriate. The Commission shall charge to the Fund referred to in sub-paragraph (c) below any local expenses not borne by the Royal Government of Laos.

(c) All other capital or running expenses incurred by the Commission in the exercise of its functions shall be met from a Fund to which all the members of the Conference shall contribute in the following proportions:

The Governments of the People's Republic of China, France, the Union of Soviet Socialist Republics, the United Kingdom and the United States of America shall contribute 17.6 percent each.

The Governments of Burma, Cambodia, the Democratic Republic of Vietnam, Laos, the Republic of Vietnam and Thailand shall contribute 1.5 percent each.

The Governments of Canada, India and Poland as members of the Commission shall contribute one percent each.

Article 19

The Co-Chairmen shall at any time, if the Royal Government of Laos so requests, and in any case not later than three years after the entry into force of this Protocol, present a report with appropriate recommendations on the question of the termination of the Commission to the members of the Conference for their consideration. Before making such a report the Co-

Chairmen shall hold consultations with the Royal Government of Laos and the Commission.

Article 20

This Protocol shall enter into force on signature.

It shall be deposited in the archives of the Governments of the United Kingdom and the Union of Soviet Socialist Republics, which shall furnish certified copies thereof to the other signatory States and to all other States of the world.

In witness whereof, the undersigned Plenipotentiaries have signed this Protocol.

Done in two copies in Geneva this twenty-third day of July one thousand nine hundred and sixty-two in the English, Chinese, French, Laotian and Russian languages, each text being equally authoritative.

For the Union of Burma:
U THI HAN

For the Kingdom of Cambodia:
NHIEK TIOULONG

For Canada:
H. C. GREEN
CHESTER RONNING

For the People's Republic of China:
CHEN YI

For the Democratic Republic of Vietnam:
UNG-VAN-KHIEM

For the Republic of France:
M. COUVE DE MURVILLE
JACQUES ROUX

For the Republic of India:
V. K. KRISHNA MENON

For the Kingdom of Laos:
Q. PHOLSENA

For the Polish People's Republic:
A. RAPACKI

For the Republic of Vietnam:
VU VAN MAU
THANH

For the Kingdom of Thailand:
DIRECK JAYANÂMA

For the Union of Soviet Socialist Republics:
A. GROMYKO

For the United Kingdom of Great Britain and Northern Ireland:
HOME
MALCOLM MACDONALD

For the United States of America:
DEAN RUSK
W. AVERELL HARRIMAN

15

Statement by His Highness Prince Souvanna Phouma Prime Minister of the Royal Government of Laos (1962)*

After persistent efforts the work of the Conference on the Laotian question is finished at last. After so many years of suffering, the Laotian people sees at last its dearest hopes realized in peace, national reconciliation and neutrality.

On this day, at this moment which will remain for ever engraved in the history of Laos, I cannot help expressing once again my profound regret at not seeing amongst us here the architect of the agreement which we are going to sign, on whose initiative this Conference was convened: that great statesman, His Royal Highness Prince Norodom Sihanouk. His onerous duties prevent him from honoring with his illustrious presence the end of the work which he began and which, thanks to his support, has been successfully completed. I venture to send to His Royal Highness and to the Cambodian people the warm and brotherly thanks of the people of Laos.

I also venture to express our thanks to our Co-Chairmen, who sometimes in very delicate situations have ungrudgingly given their time and effort so that this Conference might come to the happy conclusion which we see today. Nor must I forget the delegates and their staff, well knowing the work that they have always willingly accomplished even in the most difficult times. I likewise heartily thank the Swiss Government and the

* *International Conference on the Settlement of the Laotian Question, 1961–1962* (Laos no. 1[1962], Command Paper, 1828). London: Great Britain Parliamentary Sessional Papers, XXXVII (1961/1962), pp. 12–14.

City of Geneva, who have enabled this Conference to work towards the settlement of our national problem.

For the first time, different political ideologies have agreed on the settlement of an international problem. It was inevitable that there should be conflicts; it was obvious that innumerable difficulties would have to be overcome. But they were overcome, and the result is here, tangible, indisputable: an agreement has been reached between fourteen nations of different race, customs, religion, and political outlook. Is not this a wonderful promise for the future? Is it not the beginning of a new era in which threats of war will give place to negotiation? Does not the successful completion of your work prove that, with goodwill and readiness to grant mutual concessions, statesmen and common men can understand one another and live together in peace?

If your performance sets an example for the solution of other international problems, particularly those of Southeast Asia, Laos will not have suffered in vain, and her children will have shed their blood for the greatest of all causes.

Personally, I do not think that the new agreement is at all utopian, and I can assure you that Laos will apply its clauses in all strictness, and also those of the Joint Communiqué of Zurich,[1] in particular those prescribing the immediate tasks of

[1] JOINT COMMUNIQUE OF THE THREE PRINCES ON THE PROBLEM OF ACHIEVING NATIONAL CONCORD BY THE FORMATION OF A GOVERNMENT OF NATIONAL UNION

As agreed between them on June 18 last, the three Princes, Souvanna Phouma, Boun Oum and Souphanouvong, being the high representatives of the three parties in Laos, met at Zurich on June 19 and thereafter to discuss the problem of achieving national concord by the formation of a Government of National Union. The three Princes discussed successively the political programme of the provisional Government of National Union and its immediate tasks.

With regard to these two matters, the three Princes agreed as follows:

I.—POLITICAL PROGRAM

The Kingdom of Laos is resolved to follow the path of peace and neutrality in conformity with the interests and aspirations of the Laotian people and with the Geneva agreements of 1954, in order to build a peaceful, neutral, independent, democratic, unified and prosperous Laos. A provisional Government of National Union will be formed, which will give effect to this policy of peace and neutrality, by carrying out the following political program:

Domestic Policy:

(1) To implement the ceasefire agreement concluded between the three parties concerned in Laos and to see that peace is restored in the country.

(2) To give full effect to democratic freedoms for the benefit of the people and to abrogate all provisions contrary to such freedoms; to bring back into force the law on the democratic freedoms of citizens and the electoral law approved by the National Assembly in 1957.

(3) To preserve the unity, neutrality, independence and sovereignty of the nation.

(4) To ensure justice and peace for all citizens of the kingdom with a view to appeasement and national concord without discrimination as to origin or political allegiance.

(5) To bring about the unification of the armed forces of the three parties in a single National Army in accordance with a program agreed between the parties.

(6) To develop agriculture, industry and crafts, to provide means of communication and transport, to promote culture and to concentrate attention on improving the standard of living of the people.

Foreign Policy:

(1) Resolutely to apply the five principles of peaceful coexistence in foreign relations, to establish friendly relations and to develop diplomatic relations with all countries, the neighboring countries first and foremost, on the basis of equality and the sovereignty of Laos.

(2) Not to join in any alliance or military coalition and not to allow the establishment of any foreign military base on Laotian territory, it being understood that a special study will be made of what is provided in the Geneva agreements of 1954; not to allow any country to use Laotian territory for military purposes; and not to recognize the protection of any alliance or military coalition.

(3) Not to allow any foreign interference in the internal affairs of Laos in any form whatsoever; to require the withdrawal from Laos of all foreign troops and military personnel, and not to allow any foreign troops or military personnel to be introduced into Laos.

(4) To accept direct and unconditional aid from all countries that wish to help Laos build up an independent and autonomous national economy on the basis of respect for Laotian sovereignty.

(5) To respect the treaties and agreements signed in conformity with the interests of the Laotian people and of the policy of peace and neutrality of the kingdom, in particular the Geneva agreements of 1954, and to abrogate all treaties and agreements which are contrary to those principles.

II.—IMMEDIATE TASKS

The provisional Government of National Union will carry out the following immediate tasks:

(1) Formation of a Government delegation to take part in the

the Government of National Union, as defined in the Joint Communiqué and in my statement of June 23,[2] when I pre-

---

International Conference on the settlement of the Laotian question.

(2) Implementation of the ceasefire and restoration of peace throughout the country.

(3) Fulfilment of the undertakings entered into on behalf of Laos at the International Conference on the settlement of the Laotian question and faithful execution of the agreements concluded between the three parties concerned in Laos.

(4) Release of all political prisoners and detainees.

(5) Holding of general elections to the National Assembly for the formation of the definitive Government.

(6) During the transitional period, the administrative organs set up during the hostilities will be provisionally left in being.

As regards the formation of the Government of National Union the three Princes agreed on the following principles:

(1) The Government of National Union will include representatives of the three parties and will be provisional.

(2) It will be formed in accordance with a special procedure by direct designation and nomination by His Majesty the King, without reference to the National Assembly.

Exchanges of views on this matter will be continued between the three Princes at further meetings, in order to achieve national reconciliation as soon as possible.

Done at Zurich, this twenty-second day of June 1961.

[Signed:] Prince Souvanna Phouma   Prince Boun Oum
                        Prince Souphanouvong

[2] EXTRACT FROM THE STATEMENT BY HIS HIGHNESS PRINCE SOUVANNA PHOUMA ON JUNE 23, 1962, WHEN PRESENTING THE PROVISIONAL GOVERNMENT OF NATIONAL UNION TO HIS MAJESTY THE KING OF LAOS

The Provisional Government of National Union will carry out the following immediate tasks:

(1) Formation of a Government delegation to take part in the International Conference on the settlement of the Laotian question.

(2) Fulfilment of the undertakings entered into on behalf of Laos at the International Conference for the settlement of the Laotian question, and faithful execution of the Geneva Agreements of 1962 and the agreements concluded by the three parties in Laos.

(3) Implementation of the ceasefire, and restoration of peace throughout the country and the raising of the standard of living of the people.

(4) Release of all political prisoners and detainees.

(5) Unification of the organs of administration throughout the country, under the authority and direction of the Government of National Union following a plan to be agreed between the parties.

(6) Unification of the armed forces of the three parties in a single

sented my Government to His Majesty the King of Laos. As you know, these tasks comprise the restoration of national unity, harmony and peace by military and civil integration and by wiping out the rancours of the recent past.

I am profoundly convinced that all the participants at this Conference will comply in all points with the provisions of the document that is to be signed the day after tomorrow, Monday, July 23. I am sure that the states other than the signatories will also comply with them, and will recognize the neutrality, unity and national integrity of Laos. Thus we face the future with confidence. Our country will now be able to take the road of progress and freedom; it can set to work to rebuild its ruins, and to establish its economy together with those who wish to give us help unfettered by conditions.

We do not delude ourselves. The work before us is long and difficult; but we shall tackle it with courage and persistence.

All those near and far who have helped us to achieve our aim should know that the Laotian people are profoundly grateful. Gentlemen—our Co-Chairmen, your Excellencies, representatives—I thank you.

---

national army following the program to be fixed between the parties.

(7) Preparation for the holding of general elections for the National Assembly in order to set up a definitive Government.

(8) Linking of diplomatic relations, establishment of friendly relations and development of economic and cultural exchanges with various countries, in the first place with neighboring countries, on the basis of equality and reciprocity.

16

Action Program
of the Neo Lao Hak Sat*

1. To unite all the people, unite various nationalities [tribal groups], strata, religious communities, political parties, patriotic personalities, and intellectuals, including individuals in the royal family and Buddhist monks and nuns who favor peace and neutrality, regardless of their political tendencies, beliefs and religion, also organizations and individuals who were formerly forced by the United States to follow it but now favor a policy of peace and neutrality; and to strive to consolidate and strengthen the alliance and mutual assistance between the Neo Lao Hak Sat and the patriotic neutralist forces.

2. To struggle against the United States imperialists and their followers—the traitors—for a correct implementation of the 1962 Geneva agreements and the agreements reached among the three parties of Laos; to defend and consolidate the coalition government so as to fully carry out the political program aimed at restoring peace, building national concord, and consolidating the independence of the country; first of all to demand that the United States imperialists and their satellites withdraw all their troops from Laos, stop the introduction of weapons and war materiel into Laos and all acts of intervention in Lao affairs under whatever form and in whatever fields, and not set up military bases on Lao territory; to demand that the Phoumi Nosavan group put an end to aiding operations encroaching upon and terrorizing the people and withdraw their troops to the positions existing when the 1962 Geneva agreements were signed; to demand that the Phoumi Nosavan group

* Adopted at the Second National Congress of the Neo Lao Hak Sat in Sam Neua Province, April 6–11, 1964, and reported by Vietnam News Agency (Hanoi), April 13, 1964, reprinted in Arthur J. Dommen, *Conflict in Laos: The Politics of Neutralization* (New York, 1965), pp. 319–21.

strictly implement the agreements concluded among the three parties: first of all to organize the mixed police and to neutralize Vientiane and Luang Prabang so as to restore the normal activities of the coalition government, and then to continue the tripartite negotiations in order to settle pending questions and other problems of the fatherland and people.

3. To correctly carry out the policy of peace and neutrality ensured by the Geneva agreements, implement the independent foreign policy on the basis of the five principles of peaceful coexistence, to establish diplomatic relations with all countries on an equal footing, receive aid without any conditions attached from all countries regardless of their political regimes, provided the latter respect the sovereignty and independence of Laos and sincerely help Laos' national construction; to actively support all movements for peace, democracy, and social progress, and the national liberation movement of all the Asian, African, and Latin American countries, and actively contribute to the safeguarding of peace in Southeast Asia and the world.

4. To heighten the spirit of self-reliance and at the same time make full use of assistance without any conditions attached from various countries to build an independent and self-supporting economy under the leadership and unified management of the coalition government; to wipe out the vestige of local despots and trade monopolies, and at the same time to help people develop production, tap forest products and natural resources, expand exchanges of goods, develop handicrafts, and build industry; to eliminate speculation and hoarding, oppose corruption and misuse of power to grab goods and economic monopolies; to help the peasants develop cultivation and livestock breeding; to encourage the improvement of cultivation and protection of crops, thus helping the peasants to raise their income; to help the workers to get jobs, to improve their living conditions, and create a regime of social insurance so as to enable them to restore and develop the national economy; to stimulate and help the traders and industrialists to invest in construction and commerce which benefit the national economy and the people's life; to create conditions for students and pupils to study and develop their abilities to serve the father-

land; to provide intellectuals, office employees, cultural workers, and artists with suitable jobs and security so that they may serve the people.

5. To organize and build a national army and police force to defend the independence of the fatherland and the security of the people; to help soldiers and policemen to come close to and help the people; to forbid all repression of the people by the army and the police; to ensure political rights and due pay for soldiers; to cancel the regime of ill treatment of soldiers and policemen; to work out a policy to improve the living conditions of wounded soldiers' and war martyrs' families.

6. To carry out all the democratic rights of the citizens as provided for by the 1947 Constitution, thus enabling them to devote all their abilities to serve national construction; first of all to release all political detainees and ensure the life and property of the people; to stop all acts of discrimination and reprisal against patriotic individuals and organizations in the areas temporarily controlled by the Phoumi Nosavan group, especially Vientiane.

7. To respect and defend the Throne, build and consolidate national solidarity, and realize national harmony and unification; to carry out the policy of national union, thus helping the various nationalities [tribal groups] to live on an equal footing and carry out mutual assistance, improving their living standards, helping each other in studying; to oppose all schemes of sowing discord among the nationalities [tribal groups] and ensure the legitimate rights of foreign residents in Laos.

8. To assure equality between men and women; help women in all fields so as to enable them to develop their ability to catch up with men; to help confined mothers and protect children.

9. To develop progressive national culture; to devote attention to education and develop both primary and secondary educational systems and other popular educational schools; to help all the people, especially the mountain people, to learn to read and write; to protect and develop good ethics; to strictly oppose the depraved and obscurantist culture of the United States and its henchmen; to eliminate gambling and other social vices; to respect freedom of belief, oppose all schemes to sabo-

tage and split up religions; to protect pagodas and respect
Buddhist priests.

10. While the United States imperialists have not yet given
up their schemes to eliminate the Neo Lao Hak Sat and other
patriotic forces, to turn Laos into a neo-colony, a war-provoca-
tive base, and to turn the Lao people into their slaves, all the
people of Laos have the task of defending and consolidating
the liberated areas, strengthening the Neo Lao Hak Sat forces,
helping to consolidate the other patriotic forces, resolutely
smashing all schemes to encroach upon and occupy the liberated
areas and to send bandits to disturb and sabotage these areas.
The people of Laos must actively carry out all tasks which
benefit the people and must bring them a happy life so as to
help them build the liberated areas into a firm basis for the
people's struggle for peace, neutrality, independence, democracy, unity, and prosperity.

PART IV

THE STRUGGLE
FOR NEUTRALITY
IN CAMBODIA

Introduction

In the late eighteenth century, America as a "new nation" found it necessary to divorce itself from the international power rivalries of the time. Britain and France were locked in an epochal struggle, which, to the participants, was no less than a battle between liberty and despotism. The principals looked with disdain upon nations who affected "neutrality." America in particular earned the ire of the great European powers for its presumptuous belief that it could be "above the battle," and for its insufferable pose of moral superiority.[1]

By the mid-twentieth century this situation was ironically changed. American policy makers refused to allow the new nations emerging after the Second World War the opportunity to seek genuine neutrality amidst cold war contentions. John Foster Dulles, a major architect of US Asian policies in the 1950's, considered neutralism to be "immoral," and "an obsolete conception."[2] But for the new nations of the twentieth century, as well as for comparable states in earlier epochs, nonalignment with great power blocs seemed to be the only way in which these states could retain a semblance of independence.

Historical analogies are often misleading, but the parallel between early American neutrality and the post World War II Cambodian foreign policy is close and striking. In both countries, nonalignment was not only a fortuitous circumstance of geography, but the conscious aim of policy.

While Americans feared that "entangling alliances" would hinder their experiment in democracy, for Cambodians neu-

---

[1] On early American neutrality, see Thomas A. Bailey, *A Diplomatic History of the American People* (6th ed., New York, 1958), ch. VII; R. W. Van Alstyne, *The Rising American Empire* (Oxford, 1960), p. 5; Alan F. Westin, "We, too, Were Once a New Nation," The *New York Times Magazine* (August 19, 1962).

[2] Dulles, "Confident of Our Future," *Department of State Bulletin,* XXXIII (October 24, 1955), p. 642. Cf. Cecil V. Crabb, Jr., *The Elephants and the Grass: A Study of Nonalignment* (New York, 1965), p. 14.

trality became essential for survival. The latter recognized that once their country became embroiled in an alliance, it would no longer be able to maintain its independence. As Prince Norodom Sihanouk expressed it, neutrality was simply a requisite of continued existence.[3]

For almost sixteen years Prince Sihanouk managed to keep his nation out of direct involvement with the holocaust which was destroying Vietnam and Laos. This accomplishment is a testimony to his dedication and to his ability as a leader. All along he was confronted with American hostility, ranging from pressure of various sorts to plots designed to overthrow his rule.[4] China, by contrast, showed a continued willingness to accept a neutral Cambodia.[5] In the end Sihanouk would be overthrown and a pro-American government installed, placing Cambodia at the mercy of its traditional enemies, Thailand and (South) Vietnam.[6] Its territory a battleground, its countryside slowly being destroyed, Cambodia now, for the first time since the nineteenth century, faces the prospect of obliteration of its identity as a nation.

[3] See Selection 18, this volume.
[4] Roger Smith, *Cambodia's Foreign Policy* (Ithaca, N.Y.: Cornell University Press, 1965), pp. 91–104, 199–200.
[5] George Mc T. Kahin, *The Asian-African Conference* (Ithaca, N.Y.: Cornell University Press, 1956), p. 26.
[6] See Part VI, this volume.

17

Dynamics of Power in Cambodia

PHILIPPE DEVILLERS *

Among the five "Buddhist nations" of South and Southeast Asia Cambodia occupies a very special place. It achieved independence in 1953 without war or violence and has subsequently set out upon an original political path which has no equivalent in Ceylon, Burma, Siam or Laos. It is true that in comparison with at least three of those countries Cambodia enjoys the undoubted advantage of not being an ethnic mosaic and not being acquainted with "communalism."

The recent political evolution of Cambodia has just been the subject in France of an excellent study,[1] so this paper will only aim at marking the outstanding points of that evolution and at formulating in a summary and unintegrated fashion some reflections evoked by the Khmer experience to consider whether or not it has the value of an example in Asia.

I

Cambodia has not experienced a popular independence movement analogous or comparable to those which were seen in countries like India, Vietnam or Burma. Perhaps one may find an explanation of this feature in the origins of the French protectorate in Cambodia. That protectorate had not been imposed by force. French help had been requested by the Cam-

* From Saul Rose, ed., *Politics in Southern Asia* London: St. Martin's Press, 1963. By permission. Philippe Devillers is a long-time student of Indochinese affairs, author of the standard *Histoire du Vietnam de 1940 á 1952* (Paris, 1952), "The Struggle for Unification of Vietnam," *China Quarterly* [London], No. 9 (January–March, 1962), and other important books and articles—eds.

[1] Philippe Preschez, *Esai sur la Démocratie au Cambodge*, Paris: Centre d'Étude des Relations Internationales (Fondation Nationale des Sciences politiques), 1961.

bodians themselves who felt themselves threatened by the rival ambitions of Vietnam and Siam. That alliance for safeguarding the independence of the kingdom has not lost its *raison d'être*. The Khmers still remain today very conscious of their relative weakness in face of their dynamic neighbors and of their need to rely upon a power which is capable of inspiring fear and respect.

The absence of a nationalist movement may perhaps also be explained by two other facts. The first is the manner in which the colonial authorities generally respected the traditional Khmer institutions (the rebellion of 1885–7 had demonstrated that it was dangerous to try to touch them). The reality of political and economic power was certainly transferred to French hands, but all the appearances in relation to both the monarch and the Buddhist religion remained. The traditional framework of Khmer life was scarcely affected. National self respect and patriotism were not affronted. The relations between French and Cambodians were generally good.

The second fact that some would advance as an explanation of the first is the slight importance of French public and private interests in Cambodia: no substantial agricultural colonization apart from some large rice-growing estates (Battembang) and some big rubber plantations (created out of deserted forests), no industry worth the name, a competent administration but insubstantial and remote. Cambodia was a part of that somewhat forgotten Indochina where the pleasantness of living, the sparseness of the population, the absence of pressing social or political problems had the effect of producing a kind of torpor. It is rare for a virulent nationalism to develop in such circumstances.

II

No serious social tension resulted from the European impact. The economic activity of the Europeans only affected the population indirectly and, except on the planations, in an almost invisible manner. In Cambodia the French traded mostly with the Chinese and relied for administrative work on immigrant Vietnamese. No class of the Khmer population was tied by any economic interest to the "colonizer." Granting that at some stage the latter might arouse, by their attitude or their policy, an opposition, it could only take a nationalist character and could not be diverted to more revolutionary methods of struggle and include among its objectives the elimination of foreign "puppets" or "agents."

The foreign grip which was most resented was not that of the French. The presence of ethnic minorities of Chams and Phnong did not present any serious problems. That was not a question of foreigners but of Cambodians of different race. On the other hand the position which had been secured by the Vietnamese (in the administration and as artisans) and by the Chinese (in commerce and industry) created fears that one day or other the Cambodian people might no longer be completely masters of their destiny, and the only visible resentment that some Cambodians showed sometimes towards the French presence was directed at their having too much favored the Chinese and Vietnamese grip on the economy and the administration. To this the French replied that they had not any choice and that the Khmer "nonchalance" had compelled them to have recourse to more dynamic personnel.

The Khmer people remained profoundly attached to their customs, to their ancestral way of life and to their framework of traditional institutions. They retained a respectful loyalty to their monarchy and their rulers. The Buddhist religion left a deep imprint on personal and collective life. The monks (*bhikku*), grouped in two orders, enjoyed undoubted consideration and respect. In the villages the pagoda was the real center of the community, the meeting place for everybody where matters of common interest were discussed.

The country did not experience overpopulation (quite the contrary), nor special difficulties resulting from the infertility of the soil or from lack of space. The population nevertheless suffered from ills which were also traditional, resulting from national sociological conditions and not from the French presence: a chronic agrarian indebtedness, prohibitive interest rates (usury) exacted by the Chinese moneylenders, some peculation and corruption by civil servants, high and low, poor production techniques, high infantile mortality rate, and so on. The efforts of the colonial administration had achieved some results but much remained to be done.

III

Political awakening in Cambodia is a very recent phenomenon. It dates in fact from the last war and its origins go back to the ferment in religious circles provoked in 1941–42 by some measures of modernization ordered by the French administration (adoption of the Gregorian calendar, attempted at Romanization of Khmer writing). A small group of laymen who were associated with the Buddhist Institute and whose leader was the young Son Ngoc Thanh took an active part in this agitation in which there was also some Japanese influence. The stifling of the movement (almost in embryo) and the subsequent flight of Son Ngoc Thanh to Japan produced a respite of three years.

The Japanese *coup* in March 1945 by cutting off the top of the French administration opened out other possibilities. On March 12, 1945, the Japanese arranged the proclamation of the independence of Cambodia by the young king, Norodom Sihanouk, who had come to the throne in 1941, and a certain number of responsible political and administrative posts were transferred to Cambodians (who were assured of the enlightened assistance of Japanese counselors). But the political character of Cambodian public life only assumed real breadth with the nomination as prime minister in June 1945 of Son Ngoc Thanh who had returned from Japan, and the collection around him of a small group—more anti-Western than nationalist—who were determined, mainly for personal reasons, to oppose a return to the previous regime.

IV

However, the reestablishment of French authority in Cambodia was accomplished without great difficulty shortly after the Japanese surrender. When the Japanese had been disarmed and repatriated by the British, Son Ngoc Thanh was arrested, taken to France and placed under surveillance. His followers —the *Khmer Issarak* or free Khmers—took to the jungle or fled to Siam. A new pro-allied government, headed by the uncle of the king, Prince Monireth, was established.

France had declared herself ready to grant internal autonomy to Cambodia immediately, and a Franco-Khmer *modus vivendi* signed at Phnonpenh on January 7, 1946, laid down the framework. Essential political and administrative responsibility remained in Cambodian hands.[1] The French theoretically held the position of counselors, yet France still retained very extensive powers going well beyond the reserved field of foreign affairs and defense and including practically everything which should in principle belong to future federal institutions (currency, economic planning, customs, telecommunications, immigration, the protection of minorities and so on). Nevertheless a long step had been taken which would allow new forces to make their appearance on the Cambodian political scene.

V

The political movement quickened with the return from France at the beginning of 1946 of a small group of young Cambodians (not more than thirty) who were animated by a keen desire to modernize the kingdom by providing it with, above all, institutions of a Western type. Since King Sihanouk for his part indicated his intention to put an end to the absolute monarchy and to grant a constitution, the main topic in the speeches and discussions of Khmer ruling circles was the "next" constitution.

In fact, behind the more or less theoretical discussions about

[1] It is interesting to note that at the time (January, 1946) well informed observers estimated the number of Cambodians who had received a modern secondary education and were capable of taking a certain amount of responsibility at 150. Compared with the population of that time (about four million) this figure highlights the terrifying lack of cadres from which the kingdom was suffering and the magnitude of the task to be accomplished.

the value of such a type of regime or about the amount of "civil liberties" which could be conceded to the Khmer people there was immediately to be discerned a conflict of forces, a struggle for power between the upholders of the traditional order on the one hand (the noble families, the high religious dignitaries, largest landed proprietors, the senior civil servants) and those on the other hand who, often with a thought for their career, placed their hopes in a change (junior and middle civil servants, students, educated elements among the personnel of the agricultural, industrial, and commercial enterprises). The former grouped themselves mainly under the banner of a "Liberal Party," of which the leader was Prince Norindeth. The latter came together in a modern-type party, the "Democratic Party" which was formed in April, 1946, by a group of young men returning from France and was organized with masterly skill by its dynamic general secretary, Chhean Vam (who was also headmaster of the Phnompenh High School). Its supreme head was Prince Youthevong, a man of great culture, very Westernized, with numerous relations in France where he had lived for a very long time.[2]

The Democratic Party discovered in a few months how to inject politics into Khmer public life and provoke a general agitation. It was able particularly to make use of the profound desire for modernization which animated the younger generation (which had been marked by the youth organizations of the Admiral Decoux regime and the Japanese period) and the coolness of the civil servants towards the regime set up by the Franco-Khmer *modus vivendi*. The civil servants for the most part were on the side of the Democrats and their influence on the countryside swung the balance heavily in favor of that party which emerged triumphant from the elections of September, 1946. From the summer of 1946 to the summer of 1955, that is to say for nine years, the Democratic Party was to dominate continuously the Cambodian political scene, though under various forms.

[2] He had also been a member of the French delegation to the IPR [Institute for Pacific Relations] conference at Hot Springs in 1945.

VI

For five years, from 1947 to 1952, the scene was occupied by a conflict, more or less open at different times, between the Palace and the Democratic Party.

The clear victory of the party at the elections in September, 1946, the fact that the government was entrusted to it at the beginning of 1947, delayed for a long period the equilibrium which, it had been hoped, would be established between the forces of tradition and the forces which we may call progressive. Apparently given an overwhelming majority by an electorate dominated by the civil servants, and controlling the Assembly, the Democrats were quickly to transcend the framework in which some had wished to confine the first Assembly. The constitution of May, 1947, which was to be granted by the king, was in fact their work. Largely inspired by the French constitution of 1946, it was to bring Cambodia from absolute monarchy to constitutional monarchy much more quickly than the King, though liberal, had wished, and to give it moreover parliamentary institutions hardly corresponding to the stage of the country's political and social evolution.

The powers of the sovereign were ostensibly preserved. According to the constitution all powers theoretically emanated from the king but he exercised them by the intermediary of the Council of Ministers. All the acts of the king had to be countersigned by the prime minister. The prime minister was nominated by the king but he could only constitute his government after receiving the investiture of the Assembly, to which the government was responsible.

The preponderance of the Democratic Party in the Assembly was such that the regime under which Cambodia was to live could be compared with that of a single party. For an underdeveloped country this was not in itself a bad thing provided that it brought the country stability, unity and firmness of direction, mobilization of energy, coordination of effort, participation of the masses, efficient economic and social activity and so on. Cambodia did not enjoy any of these advantages under the Democratic regime.

The Democratic Party was quickly weakened by the death, in July, 1947, of its leader, Prince Youthevong, who headed the government. It was unable to preserve its unity. While the left wing adopted blustering anti-colonialist attitudes which were desperately negative and showed itself very susceptible to the influence of the *Khmer Issarak* and the followers of Son Ngoc Thanh, the center and the right wing indulged rather in activities of a less political but often more profitable nature. The rivalry of persons and clans and the "auction" which resulted from it made any political definition or serious action impossible. The quasi-sovereign Assembly was to make and un-make governments, and ministerial instability was to become one of the principal characteristics of the new Cambodian democracy.

King Norodom Sihanouk, who had allowed the experiment to begin and develop without resisting, in spite of pressure which was exerted upon him by conservative circles, became gradually conscious of the reality of the danger. The Democratic Party, besides, systematically blocked legislation proposed by the king; so he decided to enter the fray and to profit by the dissensions of the Democrats for the progressive reestablishment of his authority.

The government of Yem Sembaur, which was formed in February, 1949, was no longer the kind of government which the framers of the constitution had envisaged. Yem Sembaur was a dissident Democrat who enjoyed only an intermittent and limited confidence in the Assembly, which he had alarmed by his temperament and his taste for authority. In fact, conflicts were numerous, but ended this time not in the overthrow of the government but in the dissolution of the Assembly. Insecurity did not permit the holding of fresh elections, and the government continued to govern without Parliament.

From 1949 to 1951, therefore, the Democratic Party lost its hold on power to the profit in the first instance of one of its own members who had gone over to the camp of the king, and then, when parties had multiplied, to a government of national union which the king even presided over for a month. In spite of the absence of an Assembly the conflict between the king and the main party continued behind the scenes, made sharper by the fact that the Democratic Party criticized strongly the Franco-Khmer treaty of 1949 (which recognized the independence of the kingdom but enmeshed it in a multiplicity of obligations) and reproached the king and Yem Sembaur for playing the French game.

The victory of the Democratic Party in the elections of September, 1951, consequently resulted in a return to the parliamentary regime, the results of which were no better than during the earlier period. The dissensions within the ruling party and the obstruction produced were of the same kind. The Democratic Party, now strongly organized with a hierarchy, governed in a partisan fashion, penetrating and disorganizing the administration where it tried to appoint its friends and so arousing much dissatisfaction. Another factor also intervened: the return to Cambodia of Son Ngoc Thanh who was freed by the French in October, 1951, on the request of the king, who was trying to appease the opposition. Almost at once Son Ngoc Thanh became the rallying point of a virulent nationalism. He re-grouped the whole of the left wing of the Democratic Party and renewed contact with the *Khmer Issarak* of the maquis, leading Cambodia progressively towards an open conflict with France.

On June 15, 1952, the king, in weariness, dismissed the Democratic cabinet of Huy Kanthoul and took upon himself the executive power. In a message to the people published on the same day as this "legal *coup d'état*" he allowed himself three years to obtain full and satisfactory independence, accomplish the pacification of the country and its unity and clean up the finances and ensure economic recovery.

The underground opposition of the Democratic Party to the new policy was to lead the king to take still more radical measures; in fact to put an end to the parliamentary regime. The Assembly was dissolved on January 13, 1953, and the nation was declared "in danger." All the regulations for the summoning of electors to elect a new Assembly within a given time were suspended.

So the conflict which had been foreseeable from the start between the dominant party, which claimed to represent the people, and the sovereign, ended provisionally in the victory of the latter. The artificial character of political activity born of parliamentarism became evident to almost everybody. In fact, the parties whose nature, significance and objects still remained practically foreign to the peasant masses had established themselves mainly as new privileged castes, as associations for furthering careers. The parties had made the constitution, but in their thirst for power, believing that they could keep the control of affairs for a very long time, they had neglected the fact that the monarchy remained, in the hearts of the people, the very essence of the nation—the great refuge, the great protector—and that it was to the monarchy and not to the parties that popular hopes turned in the end. In opposing the monarchy it is probable that the Democratic Party sealed its own fate.

VII

An important factor in the opposition of the king to the Democratic Party was the denunciation, made implicitly by the party and explicitly by its attachments abroad, of the "collusion" between the king and the French. The Democratic Party was basically trying to do what the Vietminh was doing in Vietnam: by discrediting the monarchy, by showing what an outworn institution it was, a mere instrument of the colonial power which consequently could not have any desire to achieve real independence, the Democratic Party (or its left wing) had touched the king to the quick and awakened in him a lasting and personal animosity against the people who had dared to cast doubt upon his patriotism.

This surely explains why the king came forward as the champion of nationalism and devoted most of his energy during the first two years of the "royal mandate" to obtaining independence. After a series of solemn warnings, diplomatic journeys, dramatic reversals, and spectacular withdrawals to half-dissident areas which marked the year 1953, he succeeded in obtaining the treaty of November, 1953, which really marks the recognition by France of the "full and satisfactory" independence of Cambodia.

That independence was to be internationally acknowledged in the following year by the Geneva agreements (July, 1954) which put an end to the war in Indochina. Cambodia was the most successful at the Geneva Conference through knowing how to exploit cleverly the Anglo-Indian anxiety for the external security of Malaya and Burma, and Chinese and Soviet haste to conclude with M. Mendès-France a satisfactory arrangement of a kind which would exclude any American intervention. While Vietnam emerged from the war exhausted, war-torn and partitioned, and the internal unity of Laos was gravely damaged, Cambodia emerged little weakened, neither ravaged nor divided, independent and accepted (or recognized) by the two blocs, free from all ties, having been able to obtain from its opponent unconditional evacuation.

This unexpected result was due essentially to the policy of the king and his team, among whom Sam Sary was prominent. Among the basic facts in the Cambodia of today the first is this: it was the king who personally restored to the Khmer people their independence: ninety-nine percent of the electorate recognized this in 1955. The prestige of the monarchy, which had appeared for a moment to be somewhat weakened, was completely restored.

During this decisive period the king became aware of his role as the real leader of the nation, and of his ascendancy over the people (contact revealed it to him and this new role inspired him more than the one to which he had been destined, that of remote and hieratic sovereign), as well as of his international audience. It was clear thenceforward that he would not reconcile himself to resuming the background functions of a constitutional monarch. He had suspended parliamentarism and reverted to a tradition of an active monarchy, which was probably that of the Angkor kings, and anyway that of all enlightened Buddhist sovereigns. The king was very deeply impressed by this experience. The "royal mandate" marks a real turning-point in the history of modern Cambodia.

VIII

By the end of the war, the Geneva agreements contained in embryo (and perhaps with still more danger than before) the revival of the party system, and this time probably of parties still more "popular" and demogogic than the Democratic Party. The agreements did indeed envisage an amnesty for the rebels and their reintegration in national public life, the restoration of democratic liberties and fresh elections. The nation was no longer "in danger." It was going to be necessary again to take account of the parties and Parliament. In view of the favor with which anti-colonialist movements (Democrats or others) were regarded by the international bodies (especially the supervisory commission) the king foresaw that in spite of his prestige there was a risk that he might be outflanked.

He immediately set to work to oppose a return purely and simply to the previous constitutional regime; on February 19, 1955, he proposed a constitutional reform of which the main feature was to make the cabinet responsible no longer to the Assembly but to the king. This proposal had very little democratic appeal, and for that reason was received with coolness and reserve not only by Cambodian "political circles" (where the Democrats were again dominant with Son Ngoc Thanh back from the maquis) but also in diplomatic circles.

This time the king threw himself into the arena with the knowledge that it was the best method left to him of preventing the Democrats' return to power. He abdicated in favor of his father (March 2, 1955) and soon afterwards, with Sam Sary and some others, formed the Popular Socialist Community (Sangkum Reastr Niyum) henceforward known by the name of Sangkum. The scheduled elections were postponed to September. They gave the Sangkum an overwhelming victory: eighty-two percent of the votes, as against twelve percent for the Democrats and three percent for the Communists (Pracheachon), and almost all the seats in the Assembly.[3] From that time Cambodia has lived under the Sangkum regime.

IX

More illuminating than an analysis of the form and functions of present day institutions in Cambodia would be an in-

[3] Out of 761,958 votes cast the Sangkum obtained 630,625; the Democratic Party 93,919; the Pracheachon 29,509; the Liberal Party 5,488.

quiry into the intentions and motives of the Samdech (Prince)
Norodom Sihanouk. This seems the best way to approach an
understanding of the dynamics of power in Cambodia.

In the first place, the formation of the Sangkum accords with
a clear and simple aim enunciated by the king at the time of his
abdication, that of "making democracy comprehensible to the
people." Of recent years the parliamentary game has been played
out on a plane wholly inaccessible to the masses. The prince
intends to restore real, effective, and live contact between leaders and populace.

There is considerable sincerity in this declared aim, but an
element of political calculation also enters into it. The new
structure of the Sangkum had for its object not only to allow
the people to express themselves but also to resolve finally the
conflict between the throne and the parties, or rather the party.
The Sangkum itself was not a new party, it was the grouping of
all active patriotic Cambodian citizens who wanted to work
for the greatness and prosperity of their country; but to be admitted to the Sangkum it was necessary not to belong to any
political party (article six of the statutes).

By creating the Sangkum the prince outflanked all the parties,
broke through the screen which they had set up, and aimed at
establishing direct contact with what he called "the real people,
the great mass of the little people who symbolize the Khmer
nation." He was not wrong in thinking that his personal prestige,
the confidence that he inspired and the contact which he knew
how to establish and foster with those who listened to or spoke
with him, would guarantee an overwhelming victory for the
Sangkum. The majorities which were obtained enabled him to
say that the Sangkum alone represented and interpreted the
Khmer people, and that the parties which remained represented
practically nothing. Plebiscitary regime with a single movement?
The problem was not there. The essential fact was that there
was no longer a duality or dyarchy or dichotomy in Khmer political life. "Communion" was reestablished between the people
and the throne. The prince was the incarnation of that union.
His person still had a sacred character yet very human, and he
wanted to take the leadership of the great popular grouping. He
also took from the Democrats their main trump: the support of

the class of civil servants. Having scented the wind they rallied massively to the Sangkum, of which they constituted more or less the framework, and they contributed much to the remarkable penetration of the movement among the masses. Whether through idealism, enthusiasm or opportunism, the fact is that the civil servants played the Sangkum card and consequently any possible opposition could only show itself with difficulty.

However, Prince Norodom Sihanouk did not lose sight of the fact that to prevent his opponents (the Democrats) from getting the upper hand or from benefiting by popular support was not enough. He had to go further and outflank both the Parliament and the bureaucracy if he was not to fall into their hands.

When in India several weeks after his abdication, the prince declared that he felt that his duty as sovereign had come to an end once independence had been achieved, and that the task for the future was

> the solution of social problems and the fostering of a truly democratic regime to put an end to a situation in which the powers of the government were concentrated in the hands of a small group of privileged people who one could not say represented, in any sense, the real interests of the people whom in fact they exploited, . . .

and he added "My object is to see to it that those powers are exercised by the people themselves."

In its statutes the Sangkum described itself after April, 1955, as a "national rally which fights against injustice, corruption, exaction, oppression and treason which are committed against the people and the country." It was in order to supervise from below (that is to say by his allies, "the little people,") the "exploiters" that the prince introduced new institutions and rules: the possibility for electors to recall their deputy (by a majority of three-quarters), personal responsibility of civil servants (whom the people might question in certain circumstances and even have transferred or dismissed), popular provincial assemblies, election of *Mekhums* (chiefs of basic local groups) by universal suffrage, and finally, and above all, the National Congress, where twice a year the assembled people came to hear the record of government action, to discuss with the prince affairs of state, to question ministers and senior civil servants and so on. It was a variation on direct democracy recalling the *Landesgemeinde* of the small Swiss cantons.

X

To what extent did the Popular Socialist regime (SRN) remedy the ills from which Cambodia had suffered during the preceding period?

It appears to have succeeded largely in enabling the people to participate in political life, in giving them at least the illusion of a kind of sovereignty. Also it created an outlet for grievances or complaints of all kinds and that contributed very much to clearing the atmosphere—all the more since the Samdech, leader of the Sangkum, undertook in some sense, and this time more closely, the fundamental royal function of protector of the people, of great dispenser of justice and redresser of wrongs.

It has also brought about a real mobilization of popular energy for the purpose of collective improvement of the standard of living and of economic development. A journey to people's China revealed to the prince the efficacy of voluntary manual labor practiced on a large scale. This idea adapted to Cambodia took the form of digging pits and wells almost everywhere, the building of roads, bridges, dikes and barrages and of hospitals and schools, etc. The Khmer people were aware that under the aegis of the Sangkum and the prince they were making progress and modifying little by little the aspect of the country.

There were there some very positive elements. But the record also showed some darker spots.

Contrary to what might have been expected, the new regime did not bring the country ministerial stability. One might have thought that with the overwhelming majorities obtained at the elections of 1955 and 1958 the Sangkum would have a stable ministerial team putting into effect a definite policy without having to worry about parliamentary harassment or demagogic bidding. That hope was disappointed. Numerous Sangkum governments followed one another and were overthrown or compelled to resign by the Assembly.

It must be recalled here that the parliamentary regime continued and that the government was still responsible to the Assembly. In the first legislature (1955–58) the government had been composed of members with little experience and often of a mediocre quality. But the better quality of the chamber elected in 1958 did not prevent it from falling into the same bad ways: personal rivalries, clannishness, submission to narrow particular interests and so on. All the deputies, or nearly all of them, belonged to the Sangkum so there was no room in Parliament for ideological debates, and it became clear that there is no real Parliament without parties and without ideas. The parliamentary experience of the Sangkum period was unhappy. But one should not conclude from that, as some have done, that there was a duplication between the Assembly and the National Congresses. The two institutions had their value and their utility. It is correct to think that the efficacy of the Khmer Parliament would have been very much improved if the Sangkum had a better constructed executive committee with a sounder doctrine capable of imposing strict discipline on the parliamentary group. The Assembly would then have exercised, during the interval between the National Congresses, the necessary supervision over government action.

Rivalries and corruption continued, opposing clans were not disarmed, but the opposition, being unable to succeed by parliamentary maneuver, adopted the classical method employed in a more or less unanimous regime, of plotting. On several occasions since 1955 plots have been discovered in which there were implicated elements belonging either to evicted parties, like the Democratic Party, or to groups more or less manipulated by foreign services. It was here that foreign policy intervened. Its relationship with internal policy was indeed close.

XI

At the Geneva Conference of 1954 Cambodia had refused any neutralization of her territory. She wanted to preserve complete liberty of action which at that moment had a very precise significance: it was a matter of being able to continue to benefit from American aid and to have whatever relations she wished with the United States.

The following year, in 1955 at Bandung, Cambodia discovered the virtues of neutrality. A certain number of facts led her rulers to proceed to a fresh analysis of the situation. It was realized at Phnompenh that American aid was not unconditional. It implied on the part of the recipient an alignment on certain fundamental positions, in the first place consistent anti-communism. In this context the Khmers understood that between South Vietnam and Thailand, both of them anti-communist and large beneficiaries of American aid, they would never have more than crumbs, and above all that the interest of South Vietnam or Thailand would always take priority, almost certainly, over those of Cambodia.

Prince Sihanouk, who had already been very sensitive to the campaign of the Democratic left which in 1949–51 had depicted him as a tool of the French, showed himself in 1955 no less sensitive to the campaign of the Pracheachon (communist) Party, and to certain Democrats who now accused him of being the instrument of the Americans and of sacrificing the independence of the country for dollars. The Indian seduction (the visit to New Delhi) also contributed to modify the outlook of the prince.

The result was that Cambodia publicly affirmed her desire to be neutral and to pursue a policy totally independent of the two blocs, declaring herself ready to accept help from anybody providing that it was unconditional. Certain American pressures only resulted in reinforcing Cambodia in that determination. After being admitted to the UN in November, 1955, Cambodia, supported by France, was able to pursue with success this policy of total independence which she wanted.

However, the establishment of diplomatic relations with Moscow, Peking and the European satellites of the USSR cooled the relations of the kingdom with the USA and strained its relations with South Vietnam. The visits of the prince to the USSR and China and the visits of Russian and Chinese personalities to Phnompenh, the economic and technical aid which the communist bloc began to give Cambodia from 1957, soon led Bangkok and Saigon to regard Khmer neutrality as the communist Trojan horse in the region. Pressure to put an end to this orientation, which was regarded as dangerous, has scarcely ceased since 1956–57. The various plots that have been disclosed have shown that behind the groups which proposed to overthrow the Sangkum regime there were always Siamese or Vietnamese shadows. As in the nineteenth century, before the French intervention, Cambodia found herself thenceforward threatened, within the regime itself, by intrigues fomented by her neighbors, who wanted to secure a *de facto* protectorate at Phnompenh.

The influence of foreign policy on Cambodian internal policy was complex. It was above all in order to disarm the left wing opposition that Prince Sihanouk turned towards neutrality. But that neutrality brought with it, among other advantages, the power to neutralize, at least provisionally, communism in Cambodia. China and the USSR had no interest in supporting the handful of Cambodian communists (for that would drive the prince back towards the USA) so long as Khmer neutrality allowed them to demonstrate to good account, right in the heart of the SEATO zone, their generosity and pacifism.[4] The policy of Prince Sihanouk obtained in this respect results analogous to Mr. Nehru in India or Colonel Nasser in Egypt (until recently): anti-communism was tolerated by Moscow provided that it was not, or was no longer, "Atlantic."

On the other hand, this neutrality provoked sharp reaction from the Siamese and Vietnamese (and also Americans). There, too, it was the Sangkum which was the real beneficiary of the situation. The proof which it provided of the intervention of Bangkok and Saigon in Khmer affairs enabled it to intensify to the utmost the traditional Cambodian distrust of their neighbors and to discredit all groups or individuals who worked in liaison with them. All the adversaries of the Sangkum could now be classed as foreign agents or enemies of the throne, of religion, or of the country. Thus foreign policy (including foreign economic aid) continued powerfully to raise still higher the prestige

[4] The USA and France for their part continued to give substantial aid.

of the prince and to consolidate, at least in appearance, the re-gime.

XII

The policy of Prince Sihanouk and the Sangkum was not pure empiricism. Nor did it merely aim at altering the balance of forces in Cambodia. If in its appearance it closely resembled the policy of certain French kings who invoked the aid of the people to defeat or subdue the feudal powers, it was anchored basically in the Cambodian past. The ideology of the Sangkum existed. It was "Khmer socialism" and it now found for itself some antecedents which enabled it to place its activities in the process of evolution of the Khmer nation.

Certain theorists of the Sangkum, after specifying that for them Marxism was only one form of socialism and not the whole of socialism which "has existed in one form or another for centuries and in all human societies," explained why they had chosen socialism and oriented the Sangkum towards it. They accepted as a definition of socialism the following:

> the system in which the state assumes the direction of the national economy and protects the citizen from the exploitation of his labor by a privileged class and assures him his existence and dignity and aims at giving him the material means to find hap-piness.[5]

If the Sangkum chose socialism it was because "this path is a continuation of that which was followed by our kings for a thousand years, corresponds to our Buddhist ethic and alone will permit us to advance our country and give greater well-being to our people."

This Khmer socialism, according to these theorists, was not Marxist, first because it was national and because the Khmers

---

[5] *Considération sur le socialisme Khmer*, Paris: Cambodian Embassy 1961. 14 pp.

could not accept that "a philosophic doctrine and even an ethic could take on a character of universality," and then because Marxism was almost inapplicable to Cambodia, taking into account above all the class structure. Cambodia created "without difficulty" its own socialism, which was essentially pragmatic and adapted itself gradually to the evolution of the country.

The roots of Khmer socialism went back, they said, as far as the Angkor kings who immortalized their names by great works of economic and social value. Buddhism was besides both "the most precious guide in the elaboration of this socialism considered from the moral and philosophical angle" and also a "cornerstone." Buddhism taught indeed that "man must rely on his own powers to reach the truth and the liberation from all alienations. . . . Buddhism is socialist in its aspect of struggle against evil and social injustice. . . . Buddhism is also struggle against suffering in all its forms. Thus it may be seen that Khmer socialism derives from profoundly religious sources.

For the theorists of the Sangkum, the Cambodian people and particularly the rural communities were already living and applying socialism in their daily lives: they had the habit of working in common (for example there was no other way of achieving irrigation works), of helping one another and of living in an atmosphere of equality. The tools of this "natural" socialism would be perfected by the new regime, but the spirit was to remain.

As for economic development it was to be sought in the framework of a plan of which the essential objective would be to harmonize efforts. Taking into account the state of the country, the coexistence of private and public enterprise would be permitted for a long time.

Khmer socialism, impregnated with Buddhist thought, is opposed to violence. It does not think in terms of "revolution." It chooses to realize itself by means of persuasion and not by authoritarian measures or by constraint.

As may be seen, the new Cambodian regime did not neglect the ideological field but it did not go much further than giving to an essentially national reality a name which was well known and enabled it to take a better position on the world's ideological chessboard and to describe as "reactionary" and "anti-popular" any opposition. Moreover, it only wanted to modify that reality cautiously because it considered that it had no basic structural faults and that it needed above all to be developed and modernized. Here again Prince Sihanouk had an insight into what would please both the people and the elite, by loyalty to the best national traditions and also through the desire to progress and to reach an equal footing with more advanced nations.

XIII

The new Cambodian regime presented the original feature of being the only one in Asia where the king himself took direction of the democratic movement. It may be wondered whether in doing so he did not modify the traditional image of the monarchy in the minds of the Cambodians. The fact that he was no longer king but at the same time head of the state, head of the government (for the time being) and head of the Sangkum, showed to what extent power in present day Cambodia was personalized. Indeed there was something like a reversion to ancient forms of power in that country. The Angkor kings, to whose glory there is such frequent reference today, also exercised personal power, it is said, and through their ministers, counselors and civil servants, they had—at least some of them—a real contact with the people.

However attractive it may appear (particularly through the spontaneous, direct, sympathetic and relaxed character of the frequent encounters between power and the people) the Khmer experiment, nevertheless, leaves with observers an impression of fragility. It is impossible to avoid the thought that in reality its success or failure depends on the fate of one man, Samdech, Prince Sihanouk. Would the machine operate without him? Has the Sangkum penetrated deeply enough among the masses, has it inspired them to the point where they are now capable of producing cadres and elites dynamic enough to take over from the "mandarins," the civil servants of the old school or of the democratic school? Will powerful personalities arise in the shadow of the prince to whom the supreme responsibilities of the Sangkum and of the state may one day be entrusted without conflict or deadly rivalries? There are so many questions posed by the internal situation in Cambodia today.

But there are others. In Asia, where ancient rivalries and hatreds which had been more or less stifled by the Western presence are reappearing on all sides, and where the recourse to force is more and more attractive (particularly against the weak) can neutral Cambodia resist for long the pressure of her threatening neighbors? Prince Sihanouk is so conscious of this danger that he has already taken practical steps to prevent it: his recent *rapprochement* with Communist China constitutes his response to a more distinct menace. In the years to come will China succeed France as guarantor and protector of Cambodian independence? This would be a serious matter with grave consequences for the whole Southeast Asia.

If external threats oblige the Khmers to close their ranks about the throne, they also set up a tension which is harmful to the success of the task that has been undertaken. The new democratic experiment, to succeed, needs peace. For there remains a great deal to be done internally to free the people from injustice, from exactions, from exploitation and from suffering, to bring them a better life.

18

Cambodia Neutral: The Dictate of Necessity

PRINCE NORODOM SIHANOUK *

Certain misconceptions have arisen from insufficient knowledge of the true situation in my country since it attained independence in November, 1953. Although I am convinced that the leaders of the United States Government and the State Department's experts on Southeast Asia are fully conversant with Cambodian policy, I do not feel that the public has always been accurately informed about us. Americans will have learned, from the type of magazine that serves up complex world problems in palatable and easily digested form, that Cambodia has more or less cast off its former friends in order to seek new ones further east, that it practices a "pro-Red neutralism," is "rotten" with communist propaganda and constitutes a "breach" in the front of the "free nations." I have received a number of touchingly naïve letters from American citizens imploring me to end this state of affairs and warning me of the dangers that would face my country if it put its trust in a certain "bloc."

I would like our American friends to know how mistaken they are in such appraisals. I can think of no better way of convincing them than by giving a frank account of Cambodia's present situation, its difficulties and the way in which it is trying to overcome them.

Cambodia is a country of six million inhabitants, including 400,000 Vietnamese and 350,000 Chinese. Our army—and this is important to remember—numbers only 25,000 men. After Laos, which has a population of two million, we are the smallest state in the Indochinese Peninsula. But at least we are united. With our long-standing tradition of monarchy, we are drawn together by the Throne. As sincere democrats, we hate disorder,

* From *Foreign Affairs,* (July, 1958), pp. 582–86.

and as exponents of a purely national form of socialism, we can only be indifferent to foreign ideologies. We go our own national way, unswervingly.

First and foremost we are Cambodians, and lackeys of foreign powers have no hope of success here. Since we achieved independence, our policy has always been suited to our national needs. In our foreign relations we have favored neutrality, which in the United States is all too often confused with "neutralism," although it is fundamentally different. We are neutral in the same way Switzerland and Sweden are neutral—not neutralist like Egypt or Indonesia. Let anyone examine our votes in the United Nations; they are not often "aligned" with those of the bloc of "neutralist" nations.

Our neutrality has been imposed on us by necessity. A glance at a map of our part of the world will show that we are wedged in between two medium-sized nations of the Western bloc and only thinly screened by Laos from the scrutiny of two countries of the Eastern bloc, North Vietnam and the vast People's Republic of China. What choice have we but to try to maintain an equal balance between the "blocs"?

Furthermore, how could our neutrality be taken seriously if we had persisted in maintaining diplomatic, commercial and other relations exclusively with the Western bloc? As it is, we have refrained from recognizing the non-unified countries. The United Kingdom has an embassy at Peking; we have not. France has a general delegation at Hanoi; we have not. Our connections with these countries are limited to economic, commercial and cultural relations.

We are receiving some $25,000,000 in economic aid from China over a period of two years, with no conditions attached. But we do not forget that American economic and military aid amounted to almost $40,000,000 for the 1957–58 budgetary year and that it was also offered unconditionally, as is the aid afforded by France for equipment.

Assuredly all these aid programs are of great help to us. We feel particularly indebted to the United States for underwriting a great part of the maintenance of our army; for constructing the highway which will directly connect the seaport of Kompong-Som with our capital of Phnompenh; for the teacher training school of Kompong Kantout; and for the projected police academy and important irrigation schemes.

It is true that we wish this aid might be less "rigid" in its conception; more flexibility is desirable so that we can face unforeseen needs and situations. Finally—why not say it?—we would like to be reassured about the continuity of aid, especially for the army, which is of such vital importance to the security of our country.

Chinese aid has been granted us for only two years. But it is very flexible. On a grant basis, we receive from China consumer goods which are used both to meet the requirements of the population and at the same time to provide our government with much needed revenue. Thus, from the sale of aid goods received from China, we have been able to dig wells, build dams, furnish schools, construct administration buildings and help victims of national disasters. In addition, the Chinese are building three factories in Cambodia which they will equip and donate to us. Furthermore, the Soviet Union has promised to build a 500-bed hospital in Phnompenh entirely equipped and provided with consultation services.

As to France, she maintains a military mission which provides advisers and instructors for our army. A French economic mission puts exports at our disposal and offers numerous scholarships to our students and military personnel. France has undertaken to provide us with a seaport at Kompong-Som and a modern airport at Phnompenh with longer and more adequate runways. Several other important projects are under study, but whether they can be undertaken depends on the French financial situation.

By far the most important aid is that from the United States, since its purpose is to provide us with the framework of a modern state. For this reason American aid is conceived in anticipation of the future. Our elite understands this. The poor, however, are less sympathetic to it because what they think about above all is the quick and easy satisfaction of their most pressing needs. This is the reason why other aid programs, more tangible because they are in response to present demands, perhaps bring higher returns to their authors.

We have nothing to reproach ourselves with in so far as our

old friends are concerned. Most of our students and soldiers receive their basic or advanced training in the West. Our elite has retained its French culture and many of the younger generation are learning English as well. Our foreign experts and military instructors are from the West. No Westerner has ever met with the slightest hostility here and all our visitors speak favorably of our hospitality, even "Eastern" diplomats and travellers, who seem to appreciate the atmosphere of freedom they find here.

Are we "pro-Red"? Our neutrality is neither complacence nor surrender to anyone. When a great power tries to submerge us beneath a flood of propaganda or to tempt our youth away from its duty to king and country, we take a firm stand. I have twice had occasion to put my compatriots on their guard against such attempts, regardless of the consequences. And our people have approved and supported me wholeheartedly on both occasions. In these circumstances it will be difficult, if not impossible, to "corrupt" us.

We are taking all the necessary precautions—and we will go to considerable lengths if necessary—to prevent anything of the kind. Besides, the loyalty of our people would doom any such dividing tactics to failure from the start. As for the foreign minorities living in Cambodia, we shall, without ever repressing them, see that they respect our neutrality and security. In that regard we are far more vigilant than is generally believed.

I have sometimes been represented to the American public as trying to "flirt with the Reds." The fact is, I abdicated in 1955 to save the monarchy—not to abandon it. However strongly democratic, I am sure that the citizens of the United States can appreciate that, short of being mentally deranged, a prince and former king must be well aware that the first concern of the communists is to get rid of the king and natural elite of any country they succeed in laying hands on. By that I do not mean to imply that the communists wish to take possession of Cambodia; that may not enter into their plans at all and, for the moment at least, they have far weightier matters to occupy them. But I am not overlooking any possibilities, and that one is quite enough to deter me from any "flirtation."

If I have no particular liking for communism, neither have I any cause or means to join a crusade—even a moral one—

against the nations that have adopted that ideology and which since 1954 have not given my country sufficient grounds for complaint. It would be absurd to suppose that a tiny country like mine, geographically situated as it is, would risk provoking the Chinese and Soviet colossi now that planes fly so fast and rockets so far.

We are not a "breach" in the Western bloc merely because we cannot be a "rampart." In the event of a world conflict, we might very well become one of the first victims of a harsh occupation. In that case, the "free world" would have other things to do besides undertaking our liberation—or rather the liberation of what little remained of us.

Are we selfish or "wrong-minded" in thinking as we do? I maintain that we are merely being realistic. By practicing a genuine neutrality which eliminates any pretext for aggression we have a chance of not bringing down a storm on our heads; and a storm can be dangerous where there is no lightning-conductor.

Our precautions may be to no avail and we may one day be invaded notwithstanding them (I am not afraid of internal subversion which stands no chance here). If, in spite of our manifest good intentions and our utter propriety in respect to the blocs, one of these should attack us, then I would be the first to advocate reconsidering our policy and invoking aid from the opponents of our aggressors. I profoundly hope that our country will never have to take such a step.

[For earlier statements by Sihanouk on Cambodian neutrality see Selections 5 and 8 in this volume—eds.]

19

Cambodian Neutrality

WILLIAM E. WILLMOTT *

Viewed from the west, Cambodia's foreign policy has often seemed contradictory and unpredictable. Norodom Sihanouk, Cambodia head-of-state, launches a verbal attack on the United States one day and says nasty things about the Soviet Union the next. While complaining bitterly of the imperialist intentions of North Vietnam, he has opposed the various anti-communist regimes that have followed each other in South Vietnam. In addition, his statements on Chinese intentions for Southeast Asia have been quoted extensively in our press.[1]

In terms of the cold-war global concepts prevalent in North America, these statements do not add up to a consistent policy. In terms of the central issue facing Cambodia, however, Sihanouk's statements appear not only consistent, but well conceived. The central issue is the preservation of the integrity and independence of the Cambodian nation in the face of its much larger neighbors and the world powers who see Southeast Asia as one of the battlefields for their own confrontation.

This issue has been analyzed by an American observer in four categories:

1) Cambodia hopes "to avert a confrontation between the Cold War powers on her soil";

2) "Cambodia wishes to avoid any relationship with a stronger power which may compromise her independence";

* From William E. Willmott, "Cambodian Neutrality," *Current History,* LII (January, 1967), pp. 36–40, 52–3. By permission. Willmott is Associate Professor of Anthropology at the University of British Columbia, Canada. He did research in Cambodia in 1962–3, and is the author of "Cambodia," *New Left Review* [London], No. 25 (May–June, 1964) and *The Chinese in Cambodia* (Vancouver, B.C., 1967).

[1] See, for instance, the quotation in John Armstrong, *Sihanouk Speaks* (New York: Walker & Co., 1964), p. 123.

3) "She wishes to preserve the sanctity of her borders . . . against . . . the imperialistic ambitions of . . . Thailand and Vietnam";
4) "Cambodia would like again to be able to exert some influence upon international events." [2]

While all four are important, the first three are most cogent in shaping Cambodian policy.

Sihanouk's preoccupation with national integrity can be seen in the persistent struggle he undertook for Cambodian independence from the French. While the independence movements of most other Southeast Asian countries did not gain the sympathy of the indigenous aristocracy (with the exception of Malaya, of course), Cambodia won statehood primarily through the actions of its monarch, Norodom Sihanouk, who spurred a "royal crusade" for independence. His concern, and that of the Khmer elite which supported him, can be understood only in terms of their fear that if the Vietminh were victorious in Vietnam while Cambodia remained under French "protection," it would be dominated by an independent Vietnam under Ho Chi Minh. To avoid this unhappy future, Sihanouk went to great lengths to achieve independence before that imminent victory. At Geneva in 1954 he strongly (and successfully) opposed Vietminh claims for a Cambodian communist representative.

Traditionally, Cambodia has seen its two large neighbors as the main threats to its national integrity. For four centuries, the armies of Thailand (Siam) and Vietnam (Annam) have fought on Cambodian territory; each has exerted suzerainty over Cambodia at various times; and both have occupied large tracts of Cambodian territory, either temporarily or permanently. Throughout pre-French history, conflicts within Cambodia have been exploited by one more powerful neighbor or the other to win further concessions from the Khmer court. From their own history, then, Cambodians believe they have good reason to distrust Thai and Vietnamese intentions.

Nor are these suspicions founded merely on history: Cambodia today suffers continual harassment along both her Thai and

[2] Roger Smith, *Cambodia's Foreign Policy* (Ithaca: Cornell University Press, 1965), p. 87.

Vietnamese borders. In the first five months of 1965 alone, the International Control Commission reported 385 border incidents with South Vietnam, while the *New York Times* reported yet another Thai attack on Cambodian territory on April 27, 1966.[3] Such incidents reinforce Cambodian concern for the future of the Khmer nation.

It seems evident that Cambodian foreign policy is guided by the overriding issue of national integrity. Before turning to foreign policy, however, a brief look at internal policy will illustrate how important this issue is for all aspects of Cambodian politics. For instance, the emphasis upon the throne, at a time when monarchy appears increasingly anachronistic to outside observers, represents an attempt to maintain a unifying symbol to stand above political divisions within the country. Where but in Cambodia would one find a "royal socialist youth" (*Jeunesse Socialiste Royale Khmère*) movement?

Cambodian "Buddhist socialism" can also be understood in this light. The government is faced with the problem of developing a socialist economy without antagonizing groups that might encourage intervention on their behalf. Accordingly, it has carefully avoided expropriation. The nationalization of banking and foreign trade, announced in December, 1963, is an example of this policy: rather than expropriating private firms, the government ordered them to move their capital out of these sectors; they were free to export their capital out of Cambodia altogether —as some did—or to invest it in private industrial production, where it would serve not only their own interests but the interests of national economic development as well.[4] The five year plan that begins in 1967 is to move further in this direction, providing for the establishment of an increasing state sector without diminishing the operation or role of private investment in industry.

Cambodia is in a better position than many developing countries in this regard, because agriculture does not present urgent problems. Unlike South Vietnam, Cambodia suffers no problem

---

[3] The *New York Times,* May 5, 1966.

[4] The results of this policy are already evident in rising figures of industrial capacity. In the year 1963–64, private investment in industry increased by more than 140 percent, with 380 new privately owned industrial concerns set up. *Kambuja,* Phnompenh, No. 3 (June 15, 1965), p. 42.

of landlordism, for 95 percent of the Khmer peasants own the land they till.[5] Unlike Java, it suffers no overpopulation problem, for its arable land could maintain twice the current Khmer population without technological advance. It suffers little from drought, for the rains are dependable, and the Great Lake provides an incredible natural system of water conservation, maintaining the water table in the dry season and absorbing the peak floods. The priorities of development in Cambodia's first decade of independence have therefore been placed on education and health, with results that are clearly visible to the peasant.[6] Now that the emphasis will be shifted to economic development in the first five year plan, the government can rely on a backlog of strong support. It will be interesting to see how Buddhist socialism attacks the difficult and universal problem of agricultural productivity.

NONALIGNMENT

On the international scene, Cambodian policy is one of announced neutrality. By this is meant nonalignment, the avoidance of any involvement in the global conflict between power blocs espousing differing ideologies. It does not mean neutralism —the espousing of yet a third ideological position or the alignment with a third bloc in opposition to the other two. Cambodia has been careful to eschew neutralism, for it believes that any alignment will diminish its ability to maneuver in its own interests. Cambodia's rejection of SEATO protection at a time when Sihanouk was strongly oriented toward the West is an example ·

---

[5] Jean Delvert, *Le paysan cambodgien* (Paris: Mouton & Co., 1961), p. 501. Delvert reports that in the area he investigated, which involved most of the ricelands of Cambodia, 770,000 of 806,000 peasants owned their own land.

[6] See statistics on health facilities, *Le Sangkum*, Phnompenh, No. 12 (July, 1966), p. 39, and in *Kambuja*, No. 4 (July 15, 1965), pp. 68–79. Between 1955 and 1965, hospitals increased from sixteen to thirty-six, infirmaries from 100 to 387, midwifery stations from sixty to 518, with even greater increases in medical personnel. Primary schools have increased from 2500 to 3700 in ten years, while secondary schools have gone up from seven to eighty-seven, with corresponding increases in enrollment (*Kambuja*, No. 3, pp. 68–69). See also *Cambodge* (Phnompenh: Ministry of Information, 1962), pp. 111–131.

of this neutrality. Its refusal to provide material to the National Liberation Front in South Vietnam at a time when Sihanouk is friendly with China is another.

But neutrality does not imply silence on world affairs. On the contrary, Cambodia's lack of commitment to either side permits Sihanouk to present his views in the frankest terms. The problem Cambodia poses for the West is its vehemently anti-Western neutrality—and this from a country that was a pro-Western neutral only a decade ago. In May, 1955, Cambodia signed a military aid agreement with the United States which gave to the Americans the responsibility of equipping and training the Cambodian armed forces (with some French participation in training). An agreement for economic aid was also signed that year. Although the International Control Commission set up by the Geneva Conference concluded unanimously that this did not violate the Geneva agreements,[7] the aid agreement itself testifies that Cambodia at that time looked to the West for protection of its independence. Yet ten years later, in May, 1965, Cambodia broke diplomatic relations with the United States. It is instructive to examine how this great shift has come about.

Cambodians argue that their "disillusionment" with the United States is a direct result of American actions over the past decade. For instance, Cambodians believe that, in 1958, an attempted coup d'etat was planned and supported by the United States Central Intelligence Agency, and they claim to have a letter from President Dwight D. Eisenhower to the leader of the coup, Dap Chuon, offering American recognition and aid if it succeeded.[8] Part of the plan was an attempt on Sihanouk's life; a bomb which arrived through the mails killed the two palace servants who opened it.

US ALLIES

Fundamental to Cambodian antagonism for the United States is the fact that the governments of both its neighboring

[7] *Progress Report of the International Commission for Supervision and Control in Cambodia*, No. 3 (London: HMSO Cmd. 9579, 1955), pp. 5–6.

[8] *Le Sangkum*, No. 2 (September, 1965), p. 18.

traditional enemies are today firmly allied to the United States. While in 1950 a threat to Cambodia might have come from a Vietnam that everyone at Geneva assumed would be communist, today it comes from a South Vietnam, or more particularly a Thailand, that enjoys the closest ties with the United States. Since both these countries have massive armies supplied with American equipment and "advisors" (Thailand counts about 130,000 men, Saigon about 300,000; Cambodia has 33,500 men in its combined armed forces), Cambodians therefore see the United States as partially responsible for this double threat.

Unfortunately, the United States has been less than diplomatic in ignoring Cambodian claims against her neighbors. In 1961, Sihanouk said the following in an interview for *Figaro:*

> Vietnam's claims on the small coastal islands of Cambodia appear negligible in a (world policy) conceived in Washington, as does the episode of Preah Vihear (the temple returned to Cambodia by World Court decision in 1962). . . . Since the "friends of our enemies are our enemies as well," it is not surprising that Cambodia judges Washington's policy by the behavior of its proteges.[9]

Cambodia's mistrust of United States intentions is further compounded by the presence in both South Vietnam and Thailand of an active anti-Sihanouk movement, apparently with the tolerance if not the encouragement of the governments concerned. This movement, known as the Khmer Serei (Free Khmer) and led by Cambodian exiles Son Ngoc Thanh and Sam Sari, calls for the overthrow of the Cambodian government and the abandonment of its "pro-communist policies." It broadcasts radio programs in Khmer from both Thailand and South Vietnam, an operation that obviously could be stopped were these governments willing to stop it. Cambodia charges that the radio equipment was provided by American agents and that the exiles have the same sort of support as did Dap Chuon in 1958. The refusal of the United States government to take action against the Khmer Serei (on the grounds that these were matters in-

---

[9] Quoted in Armstrong, *Sihanouk Speaks,* pp. 23–24.

ternal to the states of South Vietnam and Thailand) was the occasion for the rejection of United States aid by Cambodia in November, 1963.

Finally, Cambodia considers the United States military action in Vietnam to be a threat to her internal security and peace. As the American direct involvement increases, the expansion of the war into Cambodia appears ever more imminent to that small country. The "domino theory" works in reverse in this case: the longer the American presence remains in Vietnam, the closer become the relations between Cambodia and China. When in December, 1965, American field commanders were authorized to fire into and even cross into Cambodian territory "in case of clear self-defense," Cambodian response was to seek stronger guarantees of Chinese protection. In April, 1966, three American jets bombed Kompong Batras, and a helicopter straffed Kompong Trach some days later. Then on July 31 and August 2, Thlok Trach was bombed, inflicting civilian deaths and casualties; American authorities hedged about the attack, and finally expressed regret on August 16. Cambodians are fearful that the incidents presage an escalation of the war in Vietnam into Cambodian territory.[10]

CHINESE AID

Faced with what they believe to be a hostile United States, the Cambodians have moved to strengthen their relations with China. Having first exchanged diplomatic recognition in 1958, Cambodia and China signed a treaty of friendship and non-aggression at the end of 1960. Chinese aid has been accepted

[10] Pentagon statements that military action against Cambodia is justified because of Cambodian support to the N.L.F., in particular by the existence of the "Sihanouk Trail," have been discounted by various authorities in the United States. See for instance Seymour Topping in the *New York Times,* October 14, 1965. See also Stanley Karnow's articles in the *Washington Post.* Prince Sihanouk has invited American journalists to investigate freely the areas where the "Sihanouk Trail" is supposed to exist. See his recent interview with Sam Jaffe of the ABC, published in *Kambuja,* No. 17 (August 15, 1966), pp. 14–18. The interview is an eloquent exposition of the Cambodian view of neutrality.

by Cambodia since 1961, when China offered to build four factories. After its unilateral renunciation of United States aid at the end of 1963, Cambodia turned to China for assistance in military training and arms. However, Cambodia has sought material from all over the world in an attempt to diversify her military aid portfolio.

Chinese aid to Cambodia, although offered "without strings," has encouraged Cambodia to support Peking's cause in the United Nations and elsewhere. It is clear from Sihanouk's refusal to consider acting as a mediator in Vietnam that Cambodia now supports Peking's "hard line" against negotiations rather than Hanoi's slightly more liberal approach.[11]

Paradoxically, China, the country most dogmatic in its announced attachment to ideology, is able to maneuver to take advantage of local antagonisms to win friends in its global struggle, while the United States, the country known for the "death of ideology," has remained so intransigently wed to a policy of global anti-communism that it has lost possible friends by ignoring local circumstances!

The rapprochement between Cambodia and China may lead some observers to conclude that Cambodia no longer adheres to a policy of neutrality. This is not true. While disillusioned by American support for South Vietnam and Thailand, Cambodia has attempted to maintain relations with the West by developing ever closer ties with France. Because Cambodia won its independence without an armed struggle against the French, relations between the two countries have never been ruptured. The Khmer elite feels a strong identification with things French, but even this identification does not adequately explain the tumultuous and ceremoniously splendid reception accorded French President Charles De Gaulle during his recent visit to Cambodia. It exceeded by far the official reception for China's President Liu Shao-chi in 1963. Sihanouk was making it abundantly clear to China that he has no intention of joining its "camp." Increasing trade and cultural relations with Japan indicate the same thing.[12]

Unfortunately for Cambodia, the Soviet Union recently has

[11] See, for example, *Le Sangkum,* No. 2 (September, 1965), p. 21.
[12] See *Le Sangkum,* No. 6, p. 19. Japan is today the largest exporter to Cambodia.

made it difficult to maintain the cordial relations that have until now existed between the two countries. In the first decade of independence, Cambodia received more aid from the Soviet Union than from any other country but the United States and France.[13] Since the end of the Khmer American military aid agreement, the Cambodian Royal Air Force has obtained several Russian MIG's. On October 8, 1965, however, during a state visit to North Korea, whence he intended to proceed to the Soviet Union at the invitation of the Kremlin, Sihanouk received a most cavalier note from the Russian ambassador cancelling the invitation until a new date could be fixed "through diplomatic channels." [14] This incident, which Cambodians refer to as the "Pyong Yang coup," has soured relations somewhat, suggesting to left wing Cambodians that the Russians suffer from the same white supremacist disease as the Americans.[15] Sihanouk considers that the Soviet Union has also neglected its duties as co-chairman of the Geneva Conference in failing to act on his repeated suggestions that the conference be reconvened.

That Cambodian policies are independent of Peking is clearly demonstrated in its attitude toward the Laotian tangle. In June, 1966, Radio Phnompenh announced that a spokesman for the Communist Neo Lao Hak Sat (Patriotic Laotian Front) had claimed part of the Cambodian province of Stung Treng as Laotian territory. "The Laotian communists reveal themselves as annexationist candidates whose territorial lust demands all our vigilance," said the statement.[16] It went on to compare these claims with the activities of the Vietminh in 1953–54, when it sought international recognition for its claim to control part of Cambodia. In contrast, the Laotian prime minister, Prince Souvanna Phouma, announced his government's position that the border between Laos and Cambodia had been settled completely and finally before independence and that he made no claims on Stung Treng. Although left wing Cambodians con-

---

[13] Smith, *Cambodia's Foreign Policy*, p. 123. The figures (in US dollars) on foreign aid for the decade 1955–1964 are the following: US, $310 million; France, $53 million, Soviet Union, $49 million; China, $48 million; aid from all other countries totals less than $30 million.

[14] *Le Sangkum*, No. 4, p. 31.

[15] *Ibid.*, p. 9.

[16] *Le Sangkum*, No. 11, p. 27; No. 12, p. 44. See also the *New York Times*, July 27, p. 2.

tinually chide Souvanna Phouma privately and in print, there is no doubt that relations between Cambodia and Laos have been improved by this statement.

Recognition of North Vietnam by Cambodia can also be understood in this light. Cambodia has long mistrusted the intentions of Vietnamese communists with regard to its country, for early Vietminh statements clearly indicated that they expected to assume the mantle of power for the whole of French Indochina. The First Indochinese War was fought on that basis, not as a merely Vietnamese war. Until this year, North Vietnam was represented in Cambodia by nothing more than a press representative and a trade mission. Diplomatic recognition of North Vietnam was finally extended by Cambodia in 1965 and an embassy was opened in Phnompenh in April, 1966. The text published by Cambodia of the talks in September, 1964, between Prince Sihanouk and North Vietnamese Prime Minister Pham Van Dong indicates that, at Sihanouk's insistence, the primary question discussed was a final settlement of the Vietnamese-Cambodian border. He pointed out that recognition by his government of North Vietnam and the National Liberation Front was a "dangerous position for Cambodia," and he returned again and again to the question of settling the border, particularly with regard to the offshore islands claimed by South Vietnam. It is clear that the renunciation of any Vietnamese claims on Cambodian territory was an essential prior condition for the exchange of diplomatic representatives.[17]

In a recent article in a quasi-official publication, Prince Sihanouk has compared the activities of the Khmer Serei today with those of the Khmer Vietminh during the First Indochinese War. Since one of these movements is of the right and one of the left, it is evident that the issue Sihanouk is raising has little to do with communism. Rather, the similarity between the two movements in Cambodian eyes is their close attachment to Vietnamese sources of power and influence. In the case of the Khmer Serei, this is compounded by its reliance on Thailand as well. Cambodians see the major danger to their peaceful development in the regimes next door.

There have been some recent indications that the United States

[17] *Le Sangkum*, No. 1, pp. 38ff., esp. p. 42.

State Department is beginning to recognize this fact. In a news conference at the end of May, 1966, Secretary of State Dean Rusk expressed his doubts about the Defense Department's statements concerning Cambodian military aid to the National Liberation Front, stating also that he knew of no evidence of Vietcong in Cambodia.[18] On June 16, the *New York Times* announced that the United States was reviewing its Cambodian policy with a view to improving relations between the two countries. And in August, Dean Rusk complimented Prince Sihanouk for having "done a very constructive and positive job in the development of his own country," all the more noteworthy because Cambodia lies "in an area which is in flames at the present time." Unfortunately, these moves have been paralleled by the military actions against Cambodian territory mentioned above. The Cambodian reaction could have been predicted.

One of the few hopeful signs for a Cambodian-American rapprochement is the naming of the "Boulevard Senator Mansfield" in Phnompenh on July 24, 1966. That our hopes should be reduced to such miniscule signs, in a nation whose friendship for the West—and in particular for the United States—was strong only ten years ago, is indeed unfortunate. That the nation involved is one of the few in the world developing entirely independently, peacefully and somewhat democratically, is a tragedy of American foreign policy.

[18] The *New York Times*, May 28, p. 1. See also note 10 above.

PART V

THE FURTIVE WAR IN LAOS

Introduction

In this book there is little direct discussion of events in neighboring Vietnam, though the war there has come to be the most significant fact of life for Laotians and Cambodians. It has been the failure of United States military power to crush the communist insurgency in Vietnam that has brought about "escalation" into Laos, and, most recently, Cambodia.[1] The causes of that failure in Vietnam are instructive, for as the philosopher Santayana once said, those who refuse to learn from history are doomed to repeat it.

Essentially, what the United States tried to do in Vietnam in the late 1950's and 1960's was to counteract an indigenous movement for national liberation. The fact that in Asia these nationalist movements were usually led by native communists explains the repeated rebuffs they have received from the Western, capitalist nations. For example, when Ho Chi Minh pleaded with the delegates to the Versailles Peace Conference at the end of World War I to make the principle of self-determination a reality for the Indochinese, he got no satisfaction.[2] In 1946 the French revoked their promise of independence for Vietnam. By the time America took over, after 1954,[3] Ho Chi Minh was the universally recognized leader of the country, a symbol of its victorious struggle against colonial domination. The Americans seized the opportunity of the supposedly temporary partition of the country to foster a non-communist Vietnam. But the leaders whom the US chose, or who came to power by intrigues that were possible because of the American presence, could count on

[1] See Part VI, this volume, for recent developments in Cambodia.

[2] See his letter and appeal (under the pseudonym, "Nguyen Ai Quoc") to US Secretary of State Robert Lansing, 1919, in the National Archives, Washington, D.C., reprinted in Marvin E. Gettleman, ed., *Vietnam: History, Documents and Opinions* (2nd ed., New York, 1970), Selections 3 and 4.

[3] On the significance of this transfer of power, see George McT. Kahin and John W. Lewis, *The United States in Vietnam* (New York, 1967), chs. IV and V.

no popular following.[4] In the face of a powerful resistance movement the puppet government resorted to terror. They called on their American protectors for help when they were unable to cope with the insurgents, thus fanning the flames of revolution. America quickly responded to an appeal made by the very government it had created and installed, but just as the local Vietnamese elite were unable to wean the people away from the insurgents, their American sponsors could do little better.

At first the American leaders hoped that the esoteric strategy of counterinsurgency would successfully defeat the revolutionaries. US military officers pored over the writings of Mao Tsetung, Che Guevara and Vo Nguyen Giap to discover the key to revolutionary warfare. Once the tactics had been identified they could be used by "our" side against the revolutionaries, or so the theory went.[5] But the theory did not work. Revolutionary tactics could not easily be separated from revolutionary goals, and no matter how earnestly the Americans claimed to be in favor of "genuine revolution," [6] their actions in support of right wing military regimes belied these claims. Another strategy had to be found.

The answer has been massive firepower "to compensate for and transcend [America's] . . . unavoidable political weakness in its Vietnam adventure." [7] But even with an infusion of firepower that staggers the imagination, the tenacity of the Vietnamese resistance has been the incalculable factor that US military leaders could not control. In exasperation, the United States enlarged the theater of war, so as to dilute the bitter draught of defeat.[8] It is in this context of defeat, despite overwhelming

[4] On the vagaries of South Vietnamese internal leadership in the 1950's and 1960's, see *ibid.*, ch. VII.

[5] See the insightful discussions of the "counterinsurgency" fad during the Kennedy administration, in I. F. Stone, *In Time of Torment* (New York: Random House, 1967), ch. VIII.

[6] See, for example, "The Real Revolution in South Vietnam," *Foreign Affairs*, XLII (April, 1965), by CIA official George A. Carver, Jr.

[7] Gabriel Kolko, "War Crimes and the Nature of the Vietnam War," in Gettleman, ed., *Vietnam,* Selection 77.

[8] For the best account of the cycle of defeat-and-escalation, see Franz Schurmann, Peter Dale Scott and Reginald Zelnick, *The Politics of Escalation in Vietnam* (Boston and New York, 1967).

military advantage, that the furtive war in Laos must be understood.

Beginning long before the bombing of North Vietnam in the spring of 1965, secret American air operations in Laos have been an integral part of the US war effort in Indochina.[9] The repeated attempts of the CIA and other US governmental agencies to overthrow the neutralist regimes in Laos have been hidden from the American people. So blatant were the violations of solemn treaties, international agreements, and the announced principles of US policy, that an important aspect of the Laotian struggle became the attempt to keep it covert. The veil was slightly lifted during the Symington Committee hearings in the fall of 1969,[10] but much is still obscure. MIT professor Noam Chomsky recently returned from Laos with a report of the genocidal destruction of life and civilization there by American firepower which, if the precious capability of outrage is still possible, should call up a massive cry of protest from all people.[11]

The secret nature of the Laotian war, an extension of the often covert struggle in Vietnam, suggests that US policy makers are apprehensive about domestic public reaction. And well they might be, for the American anti-war movement has escalated its protest in response to the escalating Indochinese war. In the past the anti-war movement was beset by a number of illusions that prevented its development into a more significant social force. One of these was the idea that American intervention in Asia was simply a lamentable "mistake," and that if policy-makers could be shown that it was not in the nation's interest to wage war on the people of Indochina, they would desist. Thus, innumerable letters were written to the White House, frequent newspaper advertisements addressed themselves to "Dear Mr. President," and many academics left their customary research fields to learn about Asia, and to discuss US

[9] See Peter Dale Scott, "Air America: Flying the US into Laos," *Ramparts,* VIII (February, 1970).

[10] See Selection 23, this volume, for excerpts from these hearings.

[11] Chomsky, "Destroying Laos," *New York Review of Books,* XV (July 23, 1970).

policy with their colleagues and students at "teach-ins," forums and rallies.[12]

This educational work is important and must continue, but in a spirit of greater realism. The installation of a reactionary regime in Cambodia in the spring of 1970, and the dispatch of American troops there, has convinced many Americans that the United States is not a benevolent nation gone astray, but rather an imperialist power whose policies are formulated and administered by a ruling class that has interests of its own. This radicalism has been reinforced by the increased repression of segments of our own population. As the Indochinese have discovered that their struggle against imperial domination has had to be a revolutionary one, so growing numbers of Americans are becoming aware of the no less revolutionary task of transforming America.

The revolutionaries of Indochina, who are in direct, daily contact with the lethal American war machine, distinguish between the people and the leaders of the United States.[13] It is a crucial distinction, because it allows us to penetrate the mystification that shrouds the American-directed counterrevolutionary terror in Indochina.

[12] A valuable record of this period in the anti-war movement is Louis Menashe and Ronald Radosh, eds., *Teach-Ins USA* (New York, 1967).

[13] See the statement by Prince Souphanouvong (March, 1970), Selection 25 in this volume.

20

The Situation in Laos: The Case for Escalation (March 6, 1970)

RICHARD M. NIXON *

In light of the increasingly massive presence of North Vietnamese troops and their recent offensives in Laos, I have written letters today to British Prime Minister Wilson and Soviet Premier Kosygin asking their help in restoring the 1962 Geneva agreements for that country.

As co-chairmen of that Conference, the United Kingdom and the Soviet Union have particular responsibilities for seeing that its provisions are honored. My letters note the persistent North Vietnamese violations of the accords and their current offensives; support the Laotian prime minister's own current appeal to the co-chairmen for consultations; urge the co-chairmen to work with other signatories of the Geneva accords; and pledge full United States cooperation.

Hanoi's most recent military build-up in Laos has been particularly escalatory. They have poured over 13,000 additional troops into Laos during the past few months, raising their total in Laos to over 67,000. Thirty North Vietnamese battalions from regular division units participated in the current campaign in the Plain of Jars with tanks, armored cars, and long-range artillery. The indigenous Laotian communists, the Pathet Lao, are playing an insignificant role.

North Vietnam's military escalation in Laos has intensified public discussion in this country. The purpose of this statement is to set forth the record of what we found in January, 1969 and the policy of this administration since that time.

* From *Weekly Compilation of Presidential Documents,* March 9, 1970.

I. WHAT WE FOUND

A. The 1962 Accords

When we came into office, this administration found a highly precarious situation in Laos. Its basic legal framework had been established by the 1962 accords entered into by the Kennedy administration.

Laos has been a battleground for most of the past twenty years. In 1949 it became a semi-independent state within the French union. The Pathet Lao communists rebelled against the government in the early 1950's, and fighting continued until the 1954 Geneva settlements ended the Indochina War. Laos at that time became an independent neutral state. The indigenous communists, the Pathet Lao, nevertheless retained control of the two northern provinces.

Since then, this small country has been the victim of persistent subversion and finally invasion by the North Vietnamese.

By 1961 North Vietnamese involvement became marked, the communist forces made great advances, and a serious situation confronted the Kennedy administration. In his news conference of March, 1961, President Kennedy said, "Laos is far away from America, but the world is small. . . . The security of all Southeast Asia will be endangered if Laos loses its neutral independence."

In May, 1961 negotiations for a Laotian settlement opened in Geneva, with Governor Harriman as the chief American negotiator. During the course of those long negotiations fighting continued and the Communists made further advances. Faced with a potential threat to Thailand, President Kennedy ordered 5,000 Marines to that country in May, 1962.

Finally, in July, 1962, after fourteen months of negotiations, fourteen nations signed the Geneva accords providing for the neutralization of Laos. Other signatories besides the United States included the Soviet Union, Communist China, North Vietnam, the United Kingdom, France, the Southeast Asian nations most directly involved, and the members of the International Control Commission—Canada, India and Poland.

These accords came one month after the three contending forces within Laos announced agreement on the details of a coalition government composed of the three major political factions and headed by the neutralist, Prince Souvanna Phouma. North Vietnam claimed that it favored a coalition government. Both North Vietnam and the Soviet Union backed Prince Souvanna for his new post. The present government of Laos thus has been the one originally proposed by the communists. In approving the 1962 arrangements, the Kennedy administration in effect accepted the basic formulation which had been advanced by North Vietnam and the Soviet Union for a Laotian political settlement.

B. The Record 1962–1969

Before the ink was dry on the 1962 Geneva documents, and despite the fact that they embodied most of its own proposals, North Vietnam started violating them. In compliance with the accords, the 666 Americans who had been assisting the Royal Lao Government withdrew under ICC supervision. In contrast, the North Vietnamese passed only a token forty men through ICC checkpoints and left over 6,000 troops in the country.

A steadily growing number of North Vietnamese troops have remained there ever since, in flagrant violation of the Geneva accords. They climbed to about 33,000 in mid-1967, 46,000 in mid-1968, and 55,000 in mid-1969. Today they are at an all-time high of some 67,000 men.

These are not advisers or technicians or attaches. They are line units of the North Vietnamese army conducting open aggression against a neighbor that poses no threat to Hanoi.

In addition, since 1964, over 500,000 North Vietnamese troops have crossed the "Ho Chi Minh Trail" in Laos to invade South Vietnam. This infiltration route provides the great bulk of men and supplies for the war in South Vietnam.

The political arrangements for a three-way government survived only until April, 1963, when the Pathet Lao communist leaders departed from the capital and left their cabinet posts vacant. Fighting soon resumed and since then, there have been cycles of communist offensives and Royal Laotian Government counteroffensives. The enemy forces have been led and dominated throughout by the North Vietnamese. In recent years Hanoi has provided the great majority of communist troops in Laos.

North Vietnam appears to have two aims in Laos. The first is to insure its ability to use Laos as a supply route for North Vietnamese forces in South Vietnam. The second is to weaken and subvert the Royal Lao Government—originally established at its urging—to hinder it from interfering with North Vietnamese use of Laotian territory, and to pave the way for the eventual establishment of a government more amenable to communist control.

Prime Minister Souvanna Phouma has tried a variety of diplomatic efforts to restore peace in Laos. He has repeatedly appealed to the co-chairmen and others to help arrange for restoration of the 1962 accords. He and the International Control Commission, hampered by lack of authority, have reported and publicized North Vietnamese violations of the accords. And Prime Minister Souvanna Phouma has made several attempts to achieve political reconciliation with the Pathet Lao and to reconstitute a tripartite government.

None of these efforts has borne fruit. Frustrated in his diplomatic efforts and confronted with continuing outside aggression, Souvanna has called upon three American administrations to assist his government in preserving Laotian neutrality and integrity.

By early 1963 the North Vietnamese and Pathet Lao had openly breached the 1962 agreements by attacking the neutralist government forces in north Laos and by occupying and fortifying the area in southeast Laos along what came to be known as the Ho Chi Minh Trail. In these circumstances, the Laotian Prime Minister requested American aid in the form of supplies and munitions. The Kennedy administration provided this assistance in line with the Laotian government's right under the Geneva accords to seek help in its self-defense.

In mid-May, 1964, the Pathet Lao, supported by the North Vietnamese, attacked Prime Minister Souvanna Phouma's neutralist military forces on the Plain of Jars. North Vietnam also began to increase its use of the Ho Chi Minh Trail to further its aggression against South Vietnam. The Johnson administration responded to Royal Laotian Government requests to meet this escalation by increasing our training and logistic support to the Royal Lao Government. In May, 1964, as North Vietnamese presence increased, the United States, at Royal Lao Government request, began flying certain interdictory missions against invaders who were violating Lao neutrality.

Thus, when this administration came into office we faced a chronically serious situation in Laos. There had been six years of seasonal communist attacks, and growing US involvement at the request of the Royal Laotian Government. The North Vietnamese had steadily increased both their infiltration through Laos into South Vietnam and their troop presence in Laos itself. Any facade of native Pathet Lao independence had been stripped away. In January, 1969, we thus had a military assistance program reaching back over six years, and air operations dating over four years.

II. THE POLICY OF THIS ADMINISTRATION

Since this administration has been in office, North Vietnamese pressure has continued. Last spring, the North Vietnamese mounted a campaign which threatened the royal capital and moved beyond the areas previously occupied by communists. A counterattack by the Lao Government forces, intended to relieve this military pressure and cut off supply lines, caught the enemy by surprise and succeeded beyond expectations in pushing them off the strategic central plain in north Laos known as the Plain of Jars.

The North Vietnamese left behind huge stores of arms, ammunition, and other supplies cached on the Plain. During their operations in the Plain of Jars last summer and fall, Lao Government forces captured almost 8,000 tons of communist equipment, supplies and weapons, including tanks, armored cars, artillery pieces, machine guns, and thousands of individual weapons including about 4,000 tons of ammunition. The size and nature of these supply caches the communists had emplaced on the Plain by the summer of 1969 show clearly that many months ago the North Vietnamese were preparing for major offensive actions on Laotian territory against the Royal Lao Government.

During the final months of 1969 and January, 1970, Hanoi sent over 13,000 additional troops into Laos and rebuilt their stocks and supply lines. They also introduced tanks and long-range artillery.

During January and February, Prime Minister Souvanna Phouma proposed to the other side that the Plain of Jars be neutralized. The communists' response was to launch their current offensive which has recaptured the Plain of Jars and is threatening to go beyond the furthest line of past communist advances.

The Prime Minister is now once again trying to obtain consultations among all the parties to the Geneva accords, envisaged under Article IV when there is a violation of Lao sovereignty, independence, neutrality, or territorial integrity.

In this situation, our purposes remain straightforward.

We are trying above all to save American and allied lives in South Vietnam which are threatened. By the continual infiltration of North Vietnamese troops and supplies along the Ho Chi Minh Trail, Hanoi has infiltrated over 100,000 men through Laos since this administration took office and over 500,000 altogether. Our air strikes have destroyed weapons and supplies over the past four years which would have taken thousands of American lives.

We are also supporting the independence and neutrality of Laos as set forth in the 1962 Geneva agreements. Our assistance has always been at the request of the legitimate government of Prime Minister Souvanna Phouma which the North Vietnamese helped establish; it is directly related to North Vietnamese violations of the agreement.

We continue to be hopeful of eventual progress in the negotiations in Paris. But serious doubts are raised as to Hanoi's intentions if it is simultaneously violating the Geneva agreements on Laos which we reached with them largely on the basis of their own proposals. What we do in Laos has thus as its aim to bring about conditions for progress toward peace in the entire Indochinese peninsula.

I turn now to the precise nature of our aid to Laos.

In response to press conference questions on September 26, December 8 and January 30, I have indicated:

—That the United States has no ground combat forces in Laos.

—That there were 50,000 North Vietnamese troops in Laos and that "more perhaps are coming."

—That, at the request of the Royal Laotian Government which was set up by the Geneva accords of 1962, we have provided logistical and other assistance to that government for the purpose of helping it to prevent the communist conquest of Laos.

—That we have used air power for the purpose of interdicting the flow of North Vietnamese troops and supplies on that part of the Ho Chi Minh Trail which runs through Laos.

—That, at the request of the Royal Laotian Government, we have flown reconnaissance missions in Northern Laos in support of the Laotian Government's efforts to defend itself against North Vietnamese aggression and that we were engaged in "some other activities."

It would, of course, have posed no political problem for me to have disclosed in greater detail those military support activities which had been initiated by two previous administrations and which have been continued by this administration.

I have not considered it in the national interest to do so because of our concern that putting emphasis on American activities in Laos might hinder the efforts of Prime Minister Souvanna Phouma to bring about adherence to the Geneva agreements by the Communist signatories.

In recent days, however, there has been intense public speculation to the effect that the United States involvement in Laos has substantially increased in violation of the Geneva accords, that American ground forces are engaged in combat in Laos and that our air activity has had the effect of escalating the conflict.

Because these reports are grossly inaccurate, I have concluded that our national interest will be served by putting the subject into perspective through a precise description of our current activities in Laos.

These are the facts:

—There are no American ground combat troops in Laos.

—We have no plans for introducing ground combat forces into Laos.

—The total number of Americans directly employed by the US Government in Laos is 616. In addition, there are 424 Americans employed on contract to the government or to government contractors. Of these 1,040 Americans, the total number, military and civilian, engaged in a military advisory or military training capacity numbers 320. Logistics personnel number 323.

—No American stationed in Laos has ever been killed in ground combat operations.

—US personnel in Laos during the past year has not increased while during the past few monts, North Vietnam has sent over 13,000 additional combat ground troops in Laos.

—When requested by the Royal Laotian Government, we have continued to provide military assistance to regular and irregular Laotian forces in the form of equipment, training and logistics. The levels of our assistance have risen in response to the growth of North Vietnamese combat activities.

—We have continued to conduct air operations. Our first priority for such operations is to interdict the continued flow of troops and supplies across Laotian territory on the Ho Chi Minh Trail. As Commander-in-Chief of our armed forces, I consider it my responsibility to use our air power to interdict this flow of supplies and men into South Vietnam and thereby avoid a heavy toll of American and allied lives.

—In addition to these air operations on the Ho Chi Minh Trail, we have continued to carry out reconnaissance flights in Northern Laos and to fly combat support missions for Laotian forces when requested to do so by the Royal Laotian Government.

—In every instance our combat air operations have taken place only over those parts of Laos occupied and contested by North Vietnamese and other communist forces. They have been flown only when requested by the Laotian Government. The level of our air operations has been increased only as the number of North Vietnamese in Laos and the level of their aggression has increased.

Our goal in Laos has been and continues to be to reduce American involvement and not to increase it, to bring peace in accordance with the 1962 accords and not to prolong the war.

That is the picture of our current aid to Laos. It is limited. It is requested. It is supportive and defensive. It continues the purposes and operations of two previous administrations. It has been necessary to protect American lives in Vietnam and to preserve a precarious but important balance in Laos.

III. THE FUTURE

Peace remains the highest priority of this administration. We will continue our search for it in Vietnam. I hope my appeal today to the Geneva Conference co-chairmen will help in Laos. Our policy for that torn country will continue to rest on some basic principles:

—We will cooperate fully with all diplomatic efforts to restore the 1962 Geneva agreements.

—We will continue to support the legitimate government of Prime Minister Souvanna Phouma and his efforts to deescalate the conflict and reach political understandings.

—Our air interdiction efforts are designed to protect American and allied lives in Vietnam. Our support efforts have the one purpose of helping prevent the recognized Laotian government from being overwhelmed by larger communist forces dominated by the North Vietnamese.

—We will continue to give the American people the fullest possible information on our involvement, consistent with national security.

I hope that a genuine quest for peace in Indochina can now begin. For Laos, this will require the efforts of the Geneva Conference co-chairmen and the signatory countries.

But most of all it will require realism and reasonableness from Hanoi. For it is the North Vietnamese, not we, who have escalated the fighting. Today there are 67,000 North Vietnamese troops in this small country. There are no American troops there. Hanoi is not threatened by Laos; it runs risks only when it moves its forces across borders.

We desire nothing more in Laos than to see a return to the Geneva agreements and the withdrawal of North Vietnamese troops, leaving the Lao people to settle their own differences in a peaceful manner.

In the search for peace we stand ready to cooperate in every way with the other countries involved. That search prompted my letters today to the British Prime Minister and the Soviet Premier. That search will continue to guide our policy.

NOTE: The statement was released at Key Biscayne, Fla.

21

Laos: The Story Nixon Won't Tell

PETER DALE SCOTT *

President Nixon cannot expect peace in Vietnam while escalating the war in Laos. His Key Biscayne statement on Laos of March 6 [1970] itself draws attention to the connection between the two conflicts, which has since been underlined by Vice President Agnew. In reality the so-called "Vietnamization" [1] in 1969 of the ground war in South Vietnam was balanced by a sharp escalation of the US air war in Laos, beyond the range of inquisitive TV camera teams. This escalation is now rationalized (though not admitted) by the President's statement on Laos, which puts forth a grossly misleading history of North Vietnamese "persistent subversion" and "invasion."

This story was put together long before the present administration. Many of its allegations were supplied years ago by US intelligence sources, who had a stake in misrepresenting the Laotian war which they had themselves largely helped to create. The statement must however be answered, since it is at least as misleading as the intelligence reports of North Vietnamese and Chinese aggression in South Vietnam, which preceded our air war in that country. Of course, the escalation in the long run will involve two sides, and some day historians can analyze

* From The *New York Review of Books*, XIV (April 9, 1970), pp. 35–41. By permission. Peter Dale Scott, co-author of *The Politics of Escalation in Vietnam* (Boston and New York: Beacon Press and Fawcett, 1966), teaches English at the University of California at Berkeley.

[1] "Vietnamization" refers to the policy announced by President Richard Nixon on November 3, 1969, which ostensibly dedicated America to eventual withdrawal from Vietnam by the substitution of South Vietnamese troops for US armed forces. See Nixon's speech in Marvin E. Gettleman, ed., *Vietnam: History, Documents and Opinions* 2d ed., New York, 1970, Selection 74. Most observers agree that "Vietnamization," despite well-publicized token withdrawals of US troops, is little more than mystifying "cover" for deeper American involvement. See also Selection 33 in this volume.

the whole involvement in Laos of Thailand, the Philippines, South Vietnam, North Vietnam, the United States, Taiwan, and China.

It is important, however, to see that it has been not North Vietnam but the United States, and more particularly its apparatus of civil and military intelligence agencies, which has been consistently guilty of the *initial* subversion of whatever order has been established in Laos through international agreements. Thus the President's statement should be examined in the light of indubitable CIA and US Air Force activities that he wholly leaves out.

Although the present war in Laos dates back to 1959, the President's statement is totally silent about the 1959–61 period. This is understandable, since virtually every independent observer has condemned the subversive activities in Laos of the CIA and other US agencies during the period when Mr. Nixon was Vice-President. A Rand Corporation report on Laos concluded, for example, that in 1959 it was not the pro-communist Pathet Lao but the right wing Sananikone government (which had been installed by US intrigue and was counseled by US advisers) that "precipitated the final crisis which led to war in Laos."

This "final crisis" followed a probe by a government patrol into the small but sensitive disputed area of Huong Lap on the North Vietnamese border, which had been governed as part of Vietnam in the days of the French. When the patrol was, predictably, fired upon, the government charged the North Vietnamese with frontier incursions and claimed that this was related to a planned insurrection by the Pathet Lao. It then obtained a vote of emergency powers from the Assembly, and soon ordered the two remaining battalions of the Pathet Lao to be integrated forthwith into the national army.

The Pathet Lao had previously (in November, 1957) agreed to this integration, as part of a political settlement in which they received two Cabinet posts and were permitted to participate in elections for specially created seats in the National Assembly. In this election the Pathet Lao and their allies (the party of left-leaning neutralist Quinim Pholsena) obtained thirty-two percent of the votes and thirteen of the twenty-one contested seats, showing that they had grown considerably in

popularity in the four years since the 1954 [Geneva] agreements. (Prince Souphanouvong, the Pathet Lao leader and half-
brother of the then Premier Prince Souvanna Phouma, received more votes than any other candidate.)

Arthur Schlesinger, Jr., in *A Thousand Days,* has recorded
the response of the US to the election:

> Washington decided to install a reliably pro-West-
> ern regime. CIA spooks put in their appearance,
> set up a Committee for the Defense of National
> Interest (CDNI) and brought back from France as
> its chief an energetic, ambitious and devious of-
> ficer named Phoumi Nosavan. Prince Souvanna,
> who had shown himself an honest and respected if
> impulsive leader, was forced out of office [by a
> withholding of US aid and CIA encouragement of
> a parliamentary crisis, allegedly through the use of
> bribes] . . . a veteran politician named Phoumi
> Sananikone took his place.

The Pathet Lao were then excluded from the new Cabinet approved on August 18, 1958.

In May, 1959, one Pathet Lao battalion refused, understand-
ably, to be assimilated under the new right wing government,
and it decamped to a valley on the North Vietnamese border.
The Sananikone government then declared that the Pathet Lao
had committed an act of open rebellion and that only a military
solution appeared possible. It thus by its own actions deflected
the Pathet Lao from the role of political opposition into a military insurgency for which it was poorly prepared, and hence it
was forced increasingly to depend on North Vietnamese support.
(By 1969 this included regular units of the North Vietnamese
Army.)

In August, 1959, the government itself received a large increase in US military support by claiming, falsely, that it had
been "invaded" by a North Vietnamese force of as many as
eleven battalions. (In February the government had given itself
the right to receive this support by declaring unilaterally, with
US approval, that it would no longer be bound by the limitations on foreign military aid which it had accepted at Geneva

in 1954.) Bernard Fall and the British historian Hugh Toye linked the phony invasion scare to a US Congressional exposé at this time of major scandals in the Laos aid program, and the very real risk that US military aid would be curtailed.[2]

It is frequently claimed that the Pathet Lao was never more than a front for North Vietnamese ambitions in Laos; but this is contradicted by the election results of 1958 (the last honest elections in Laos). Though before 1954 Souphanouvong and his cadres had fought with the Vietminh against the French, the indubitable growth in popularity of the Pathet Lao between 1954 and 1958, by which time it had established a country-wide network of cells at the village level, must be attributed to its own talent for organization, particularly in exploiting the resentment of the many hill tribes against the dominant Lao population in the lowlands and cities.

Let us examine the President's statement itself:

1) *Statement:* "By 1961 North Vietnamese involvement became marked, the communist forces made great advances, and a serious situation confronted the Kennedy Administration."

Comment: The crisis facing President Kennedy in early 1961

---

[2] For the preceding paragraphs, see: Halpern, A. M., and Friedman, H. B., *Communist Strategy in Laos,* Rand, RM-2561, p. 51; cited and amplified in Bernard Fall, *Anatomy of a Crisis,* Garden City: Doubleday, 1969, p. 108; Arthur Schlesinger, Jr., *A Thousand Days,* Boston: Houghton Mifflin, 1965, pp. 325–26; Hugh Toye, *Laos: Buffer State or Battleground,* Oxford, 1968, pp. 113–31; US Congress, House, Committee on Government Operations, *United States Aid Operations in Laos: Seventh Report,* June 15, 1969, 86th Cong., 1st Sess.

Denis Warner heard some of the witnesses to the "invasion" that was alleged to have taken place on August 30, 1959, and reported that the responsible Laotian general "accepted as fact what the most junior western staff officer would have rejected as fiction" (*The Last Confucian,* New York: Macmillan, 1963, p. 210). But Joseph Alsop, a former US staff officer under General Chennault, heard the same allegations and reported them as fact to Washington, where (during Eisenhower's temporary seclusion in Scotland) willing believers dispatched a series of secret orders (never yet disclosed) to US armed forces in the Pacific. Bernard Fall (p. 36) implies that the evidence was not merely false, it was deliberately staged.

was the armed conflict following the successful displacement from the capital city of Vientiane of Souvanna Phouma's neutralist government (which we officially recognized) by the CIA-supported right wing insurrectionary forces of General Phoumi Nosavan. His rebellion against Souvanna had from the outset received logistical support from the CIA-linked airline, Air America, Inc. With the help of Air America, Phoumi's Royal Laotian Army drove the neutralist troops of General Kong Le, Souvanna's military chief, to the north and into a temporary alliance with the pro-communist Pathet Lao. After Kong Le captured the Plain of Jars from Phoumi's troops, the Pathet Lao moved south to join him. Souvanna Phouma and Kong Le, genuine neutralists who feared North Vietnamese influence, nevertheless had been forced to seek communist support in order to survive Phoumi's attack. Thus CIA-sponsored subversion was itself directly responsible for the communists' "great advances." [3]

It is true that in late 1960 Souvanna Phouma's government, faced with US encouragement of a rebellion against it, did in response invite in Russian, North Vietnamese, and Chinese "advisers," thus creating the first known North Vietnamese presence in Laos since the 1954 Geneva agreements. However, in his well-informed book, *Conflict in Laos,* A. J. Dommen dates the presence of North Vietnamese combat troops (along "the

[3] Text of the President's statement as printed in the *San Francisco Chronicle,* March 6, 1970, p. 9. [See Selection No. 28 in this volume—eds.]. The late Bernard Fall observed of the CIA's policy of deliberate "polarization" in Laos in this period that "it had thrown into communism's arms a great many people who essentially were *not* communists (just as in 1946 many Vietnamese who at first merely wanted the French to get out as colonial masters in Vietnam were finally pushed into Ho Chi Minh's Vietminh) but who, by deliberate action on our side, were left with no alternative." (Fall, *Anatomy of a Crisis,* p. 199; cf. p. 189.)

  Cf. also Arthur Schlesinger, Jr., *A Thousand Days,* p. 328. "The Eisenhower Administration, by rejecting the neutralist alternative, had driven the neutralists into reluctant alliance with the communists and provoked (and in many eyes legitimized) open Soviet aid to the Pathet Lao. All this was done without serious consultation with the incoming administration which would shortly inherit the problem." For further details, see Toye, *Laos,* pp. 145–64; Peter Dale Scott, "Air America: Flying the U.S. into Laos," *Ramparts,* January, 1970, pp. 39–54.

Laos-Vietnam border") from July–August 1962, and contrasts them with "the technical experts and cadres that North Vietnam had maintained in Laos since the end of 1960." [4] Bernard Fall estimated that

> The fighting in Laos in 1960–62 involved relatively small forces from the [North Vietnamese] 335th and 316th divisions, many of whose men were of the same Thai *montagnard* stock as the tribesmen on the Laotian side.

The British observer Hugh Toye writes that "On balance, participation by Vietminh infantry, as opposed to cadres and support detachments, in the skirmishes of 1961–2 is unlikely." [5] But by early 1961 the US had brought in AT-6's armed with bombs and rockets, US pilots to fly them, and Special Forces "White Star" teams to encourage guerrilla activity by Meo tribesmen behind the Pathet Lao lines. Furthermore, Air America was using American helicopters and American pilots to move Phoumi's troops into battle. At this time the Joint Chiefs of Staff pressed for a military showdown over Laos, including the possible use of tactical nuclear weapons; while Richard Nixon himself, in a meeting with Kennedy, urged "a commitment of American air power." [6]

2) *Statement:* "[In 1962] During the course of those long negotiations [at Geneva for a Laotian settlement] fighting continued and the communists made further advances."

[4] Arthur J. Dommen, *Conflict in Laos,* Praeger, 1964, p. 238. Even though he conceded that North Vietnam in 1962 was "very probably" moved by fear of the 5,000 US troops airlifted into Thailand, Dommen was no apologist for the North Vietnamese presence in Laos. On the contrary, his book (prepared with assistance from the Council on Foreign Relations staff) urged "the sudden encirclement of one of the Vietnamese border patrol battalions . . . and its noiseless liquidation by a determined and highly trained [US] Special Forces unit." This, he argued, "would have a tremendous shock effect in Hanoi" (p. 301).
[5] Bernard Fall, *Anatomy of a Crisis,* pp. 249–50; Toye, *Laos,* p. 178.
[6] Roger Hilsman, *To Move a Nation,* Garden City: Doubleday, 1967, p. 127; The *New York Times,* March 25, 1961, p. 2; Fall, *Anatomy of a Crisis,* p. 206; *Fortune,* Sept. 1961, p. 94; Schlesinger, pp. 336–7.

Comment: This is misleading, since both the delays and the renewal of fighting in 1962 were again clearly attributable to Phoumi Nosavan, not to the communists. For months President Kennedy and his special envoy Averell Harriman had been attempting to restore Laotian neutrality and bring about the withdrawal of foreign military elements, by working to establish a tripartite coalition government (Phoumist, neutralist, and Pathet Lao). Phoumi continued to resist Harriman's efforts to involve him in such a coalition for months after Kennedy attempted to coerce him by cutting off his subsidy of $3 million a month. In contravention of the May 1961 ceasefire, and against US official advice, Phoumi also built up a garrison at Nam Tha (only fifteen miles from the Chinese border) to a strength of 5,000, and began to probe into enemy territory.

When the Pathet Lao, after giving repeated warnings, fired on Nam Tha in May, Phoumi's troops withdrew precipitously into Thailand. Thus the "further advances" of the Pathet Lao were achieved "after a flurry of firefights but no Pathet Lao attack." [7] The Thai government now requested SEATO aid; and the United States responded by sending troops in accordance with the Thanat-Rusk memorandum, signed just two months before, which provided for unilateral US assistance to Thailand. By all accounts "the Royal Lao Army ran from Nam Tha as soon as the first shells started to fall," claiming falsely (as they had done and continued to do in other crises) that they had been attacked by North Vietnamese and Chinese troops.[8]

This deliberate flight was what President Nixon now calls "a potential threat to Thailand." Phoumi's purposes at Nam Tha were by most accounts not military but political, to thwart the Geneva negotiations and further involve the United States. According to the *London Times,* the CIA had again encouraged Phoumi to resist the establishment of a neutral government in Laos; made up out of its own funds the subsidy which Kennedy had withheld; and urged Phoumi to build up the Nam Tha garrison in spite of contrary US official advice.[9] A State Department spokesman denied the story, and others suggest that

[7] Toye, *Laos,* p. 182; cf. Hilsman, *To Move a Nation,* p. 140.
[8] Denis Warner, *The Last Confucian,* New York: Macmillan, 1963, pp. 217–18.

the subsidy may have been paid by Phoumi's kinsman, Sarit Thanarat of Thailand, or by Ngo Dinh Diem.

There are however disturbing similarities between the Nam Tha build-up and the CIA's "Quemoy plot" of 1954, when without doubt it encouraged Chiang to build up offensive forces on the offshore islands, again in spite of official US advice. One such common feature was the activity of Chinese Nationalist KMT troops, apparently armed and supplied by the CIA and Air America, in the Nam Tha area.[10]

3) *Statement:* "In approving the 1962 [Geneva agreements] the Kennedy Administration in effect accepted the basic formulation which had been advanced by North Vietnam and the Soviet Union for a Laotian political settlement. . . . The 666 Americans who had been assisting the Royal Lao Government withdrew under ICC supervision. In contrast, the North Vietnamese passed only a token forty men through ICC checkpoints and left over 6,000 troops in the country."

Comment: As part of the 1962 Geneva agreements, the Government of Laos declared that it would "not allow any foreign interference in the internal affairs of the Kingdom of Laos"; while the other signing governments agreed to the prohibition of all foreign troops and "paramilitary formations" in Laos, including "advisers" (except for "a precisely limited number of French military instructors"). President Nixon's picture of North Vietnamese violation is created by referring to intelligence reports of 6,000 North Vietnamese troops in Laos, which (as we have seen) objective scholars such as Toye do not accept.

It does appear that at about this time North Vietnamese border patrol battalions began to move into positions on the Laotian side of the frontier passes; but Dommen and Toye suggest that this action was primarily defensive, in reaction to the 5,000

[9] The *London Times,* May 24, 1962; May 31, 1962. A story in the *Saturday Evening Post* (April 7, 1962, pp. 87–88) also identified a "handful" of CIA and MAAG members as working "industriously to undermine our present policy in Laos."

[10] President Kennedy made another effort to have the KMT troops removed from the area in the spring of 1961; but at least 800 were reported to have insisted on remaining in Laos and Thailand.

US troops which had been flown into Thailand. Meanwhile Kennedy's acceptance of the 1962 agreements was violated by the US in Laos in at least two respects:

a) Roger Hilsman, then State Department intelligence chief, records that the President and National Security Council agreed with Harriman's contention that "the United States should comply with both the letter and the spirit of the agreements in every detail . . . and thereafter there should be no . . . 'black' [covert] reconnaissance flights to confirm whether the North Vietnamese had actually withdrawn." [11]

Yet within one or two weeks after the agreements were signed such reconnaissance was carried out at low levels over Pathet Lao camps by USAF intelligence using RF-101 Voodoo jets. According to Dommen this was part of "regular aerial surveillance of northern Laos in connection with contingency planning related to the deployment of American troops in Thailand." [12] One RF-101 was hit over the Plain of Jars on August 13, 1964, but made it back to its base in Bangkok. The reconnaissance flights continued until May 1964, when they were belatedly authorized by the new administrations which had come to power in both the United States and Laos.

These overflights seem from the outset to have been concerned less with the Ho Chi Minh Trail in southern Laos than with the Plain of Jars some 200 miles to the northwest. This was the area in which the CIA and Air America had since 1960–61 armed, trained, and supplied Meo guerrillas, the Meos being hill tribesmen on both sides of the border with little sympathy for either their Lao or their North Vietnamese rulers.

b) Inasmuch as the Pathet Lao objected vigorously to the support by the CIA and Special Forces of the Meo guerilla tribesmen inside the Pathet Lao area of Northeast Laos, the agreements called for the withdrawal of "foreign military advisers, experts, instructors . . . and foreign civilians connected with the supply . . . of war materials." [13] Yet Air America

[11] Hilsman, *To Move a Nation*, pp. 152–53.

[12] Dommen, *Conflict in Laos*, p. 238; Grant Wolfkill, *Reported to be Alive* (W. H. Allen, 1966), pp. 273–74.

[13] *Protocol to the Declaration on the Neutrality of Laos;* Articles 1(a), 2, 4; see Selection 14, this volume.

continued its airlift into Northeast Laos, if only because (as Roger Hilsman observes) "arming the tribesmen engendered an obligation not only to feed them . . . but also to protect them from vengeance." [14] The Pathet Lao and some neutralists objected violently to Air America's airlift in support of their recent enemies; they objected even more violently to Air America's overt airlift of October, 1962, to Kong Le.

The first military incident in the breakdown of the 1962 agreements was the shooting down on November 27, 1962, of an Air America C-123 plane over the Plain of Jars. The plane, it soon developed, had not been shot down by the Pathet Lao, but by a new left-leaning neutralist faction, under Colonel Deuane, which now opposed Kong Le and his increasing dependence on the Americans.[15]

So far as Air America's airlift is concerned, the President's assertion that "our assistance has always been at the request of the legitimate government of Prime Minister Souvanna Phouma" is false. The government (which was a tripartite coalition) had not been consulted; Souvanna himself, as Dommen writes,

> had neither endorsed the Air America airlift (the contract was a carryover from [Phoumi's right-wing] government, and had merely been initialled for the coalition by Keo Vithakone, Secretary of State for Social Welfare, a Phoumist) nor prohibited it.[16]

Nor apparently was Souvanna consulted about reconnaissance overflights until May, 1964.

These US violations of the 1962 agreements were not in response to North Vietnamese activity; they date back to the signing of the agreements themselves, one month before the date set for the withdrawal of foreign troops. (In this respect the President's claim that "our assistance . . . is directly related to North Vietnamese violations of the agreements" suggests a

[14] Hilsman, *To Move a Nation*, p. 115; cf. Bernard Fall, *Street Without Joy* (Stackpole, 1964), p. 340; Dommen, *Conflict in Laos*, p. 233.

[15] The *New York Times*, December 5, 1962, p. 3; Dommen, *Conflict in Laos*, p. 243.

[16] Dommen, *Conflict in Laos*, p. 244.

time sequence of causality which is the reverse of the truth.) In effect, in August, 1962, our military and civilian intelligence services invited the other side to violate the newly signed agreements by proving conspicuously to them (though not of course to the US public) that the agreements would be violated on our side.

In addition, it appears that the "withdrawal" of US military advisers was illusory. It has just been revealed that for "several years" several hundred members of the "civilian" US AID mission (working out of the mission's "rural development annex") have been former Special Forces and US Army servicemen responsible to the CIA station chief and working in Northeast Laos with the CIA-supported Meo guerrillas of General Vang Pao.[17] Vang Pao's *Armée Clandestine* is reportedly not even answerable to the Royal Lao Government or Army, being entirely financed and supported by the CIA.

Dommen's carefully qualified description of US compliance with the 1962 agreements ("Not a single American military man was left in Laos *in uniform*") says nothing to refute the Pathet Lao charge which has now been confirmed by American reporters in Laos: that the Meo's Special Forces "advisers" simply remained, or soon returned, to work for the CIA in the guise of civilian AID officials.[18]

One country embarrassed by these provocations was the Soviet Union. In 1962, as in 1954, Moscow had helped to persuade its Asian allies to accept a negotiated settlement which the Americans would not honor. The Soviet Union soon moved to extricate itself from its Laotian involvement, since its support of Souvanna now caused it to lose favor not only in Peking but also in Hanoi.

[17] See discussion of this figure in Selection 23, this volume.
[18] Jack Foisie, San Francisco *Chronicle*, March 10, 1970, p. 16; Dommen, *Conflict in Laos*, p. 239, italics added. According to Foisie, "There is the possibility that some [annex] men have gained temporary leave from the Armed Forces and can return to the military after their contract expires." Some of the US "civilian" pilots working in Laos are also reported to have been recruited from the USAF on this basis.

On March 13 Senator Fulbright reported that Richard Helms, Director of Central Intelligence, had "generally confirmed" the accuracy of news dispatches from Laos reporting the CIA activity (The *New York Times*, March 14, 1970).

4) *Statement:* "The political arrangements for a three-way government survived only until April, 1963, when the Pathet Lao communist leaders departed from the capital and left their cabinet posts vacant. Fighting soon resumed."

Comment: The Pathet Lao leaders did not resign their Cabinet posts in the coalition government; two of their four ministers withdrew from Vientiane, giving the very good reason that, on April 1 and April 12, two of their allies in Colonel Deuane's left-neutralist faction (one of them Quinim Pholsena, the Laotian Foreign Minister) had been assassinated. The Pathet Lao has since attributed these murders to a CIA assassination team recruited by the Laotian Military Police Chief Siho. It is known not only that the CIA was using such teams in Vietnam but that in 1963 it was responsible for collaborating with Siho in training his cadres. But the murders can also be attributed to the growing factionalism between Kong Le and Deuane in the neutralist forces. (One of Deuane's men on February 12 killed Kong Le's deputy commander, a few weeks after the murder of a left-oriented Chinese merchant.)

It seems clear that the resumed fighting on the plain of Jars in April, 1963, was chiefly, if not entirely, between the two neutralist factions, rather than with the Pathet Lao. Moreover, Kong Le's faction, with the support of his old enemy Phoumi, was able to capture certain key outposts, such as Tha Thom, controlling a road north into the Plain of Jars.[19] But the negotiations between Souvanna Phouma and Souphanouvong in April and May, 1964 (after the opening of a new French peace initiative) suggest that the 1962 political arrangements did not break down irrevocably for almost two years.

5) *Statement:* "In mid-May, 1964, the Pathet Lao supported by the North Vietnamese attacked Prime Minister Souvanna Phouma's neutralist military forces on the Plain of Jars."

[19] As late as May 4, 1964, William Bundy could tell a House Committee that the power change since July 1962 in the Plain of Jars area had "been favorable . . . to the non-communist elements of the Government"; House Committee on Appropriations, *Foreign Operations Appropriations for 1965, Hearings Before a Subcommittee*, 88th Congress, 2nd Session, p. 414.

Comment: Dommen confirms that in May, 1964, Kong Le's men were attacked by the left-neutralist followers of Colonel Deuane. The Pathet Lao shelled the positions of Phoumist troops flown in since 1962, while the North Vietnamese may have played a supporting role, as did the United States with Kong Le. The result of Deuane's initial attacks was roughly to restore the *status quo ante* April, 1963: the town of Tha Thom in particular was recaptured by his men. By the end of May, Deuane's men and the Pathet Lao held virtually all the territory occupied by the neutralists and the Pathet Lao in June, 1962, but no more.[20] It is essential to understand these specific events, inasmuch as they were used as a pretext for launching the US bombing of Laos in May, a new policy which soon was extended to both North and South Vietnam.

What Nixon omits to say is that the fighting in May was, once again, preceded not by a left-wing but by a right wing initiative. On April 19 a right wing faction headed by Police Chief Siho staged a coup against Souvanna Phouma—a coup which caused the final collapse of the tripartite coalition government, a restructuring of the Cabinet to shift it to the right, the disapperance of an independent neutralist faction, and the eventual decline and fall of the former right-wing leader Phoumi Nosavan. Thus it is not true, as the President's statement claims, that "the present government of Laos . . . has been the one originally proposed by the communists": the 1962 political settlement broke down altogether when the Cabinet was reconstituted without Pathet Lao permission or participation. It is thus not unreasonable for the Pathet Lao to ask (as it did recently) for a conference of all parties to establish a new coalition government (The *New York Times,* March 10, 1970).

The day before Chief Siho's coup, on April 18, Souvanna and

---

[20] Dommen, *Conflict in Laos,* p. 256: "On May 16, the dissident followers of Colonel Deuane Siphaseuth, with Pathet Lao and North Vietnamese support, compelled Kong Le to abandon a number of positions on the Plain and to evacuate his Muong Phanh command post. . . . By the end of May, the Pathet Lao and the "true neutralists" [under Deuane] occupied virtually all the ground that had been held jointly by themselves and Kong Le . . . in June, 1962"; cf. Toye, *Laos,* p. 193.

Phoumi had met with Pathet Lao leader Prince Souphanouvong on the Plain of Jars, reportedly to work out the details of a new agreement to neutralize the royal capital of Luang Prabang and reunite the coalition government there.

Though the details are unclear, it seems that the coup was at least in part designed to prevent the restoration of the neutralist coalition. No one has denied Denis Warner's report that Siho "used the acquiescence of Souvanna Phouma and Phoumi Nosavan in the neutralization of the royal capital of Luang Prabang as the excuse" for the coup.[21] Ambassador Unger and William Bundy of the State Department personally persuaded Siho to release Souvanna and restore him as Prime Minister; but the reconstitution of the Laotian army under a new general staff consisting of nine rightist generals and only one neutralist indicated the real shift of power to the right.[22] The new command then ordered the neutralist troops on the Plain of Jars to be integrated with the right under its authority.

This order was too much for many of Kong Le's men on the Plain of Jars and, instead of complying, six battalions of troops defected, some of them to Deuane's left-neutralist faction. Warner confirms that "the resulting mass defections . . . led [in May] to the rout of Kong Le's troops and the fall of the Plain of Jars." [23] Again, as at Nam Tha in 1962, many troops withdrew, amid charges of a North Vietnamese and Chinese Communist invasion, without ever having been directly attacked.[24]

These right wing maneuvers in Laos, whether or not they were directly encouraged by irresponsible American advisers, cannot but have been indirectly encouraged by the highly publicized debate in Washington over Vietnam. It was known that in early 1964 many generals were calling for US air strikes against "communist bases" in the north, including the bomb-

---

[21] Denis Warner, *Reporting Southeast Asia* (Angus and Robertson, 1966), p. 190.

[22] The *New York Times,* May 14, 1964, p. 11; May 19, 1964, p. 5; Fall, *Street Without Joy,* p. 341.

[23] Warner, *Reporting Southeast Asia,* p. 191. The integration order recalled a similar rightist order in 1959 to the Pathet Lao, an order which was instrumental in triggering the Laotian war.

[24] The *New York Times,* May 16, 1964, p. 2; May 28, 1964, p. 10.

ing of the Ho Chi Minh Trail in Laos. The result of Siho's April coup, if not the intention, was to make way for the initiation of this bombing policy.

6) *Statement:* "In May, 1964, as North Vietnamese presence increased, the United States, at Royal Lao Government request, began flying certain interdictory missions against invaders who were violating Lao neutrality."

Comment: By this important admission it is now for the first time conceded that the US assumed a combat role in Laos in May, 1964, at a time when the North Vietnamese army was still engaged in a support role comparable to that of Air America. (North Vietnam was not formally accused by the US of violating the Geneva agreements until June 29, 1964.) The air attacks were first carried out by US "civilian" pilots in T-28 fighter-bombers based in Thailand but carrying Laotian markings. On June 11, 1964, one of these T-28's attacked the Chinese cultural and economic mission at the Pathet Lao capital on the Plain of Jars, killing at least one Chinese. The United States at that time denied responsibility, though the State Department revealed that Thai pilots also flew the T-28's and had been involved.[25]

On May 21, 1964, the United States admitted for the first time that "unarmed United States jets" were flying reconnaissance missions over Laos. Dean Rusk later explained that this was in response to Souvanna Phouma's general request for assistance; but Souvanna Phouma refused to comment on the matter of reconnaissance flights for the next three weeks. In fact these flights had been conducted regularly since at least as early as August, 1962. What was new was that in mid-May President Johnson, at the insistence of the Chief of Naval Operations, authorized accompanying escorts of armed jet fighters. These were ordered not to bomb or strafe Laotian installations

[25] Dommen, *Conflict in Laos,* p. 259; Toye, *Laos,* p. 194. The first substantial reports of North Vietnamese infiltration followed the new US bombing policy. Cf. T. D. Allman (*Far Eastern Economic Review,* January 1, 1970, p. 21): "When the Vientiane government permitted the Americans to start the bombing, the North Vietnamese committed increasing amounts of troops in an effort to discredit that government."

until and unless United States planes were damaged.[26] When a Navy RF-8 was shot down on June 6, President Johnson ordered retaliatory strikes.

At this point Souvanna Phouma finally commented publicly on the reconnaissance flights: he reportedly asked that they cease altogether forthwith. (The New York Times on June 10 published a report that he had not agreed to the use of armed escorts.) On June 12 Souvanna announced that the reconnaissance flights would continue; this suggested to some observers that since the April 19 coup and the collapse of the neutralists Souvanna was no longer his own master.[27] His reluctant ex post facto acquiescence in the use of jet fighter escorts for reconnaissance is the closest approximation in the public record to what President Nixon now calls a "Royal Lao Government request" for interdictory missions one month earlier.

It has never been explained why the US reconnaissance pilots were ordered to conduct their flights over Laos at low altitudes and slow speeds, when (as they informed their superiors) with their modern equipment they could obtain photographs of equal quality if they were permitted to fly higher.[28] The orders seem to reflect the determination of certain Air Force and Navy officials either to coerce the other side by a US air presence,

[26] Joseph C. Goulden, Truth Is the First Casualty: The Gulf of Tonkin Affair—Illusion and Reality (Rand McNally, 1969), p. 97.

[27] Toye, Laos, p. 194; Dommen, Conflict in Laos, p. 258: "Souvanna . . . became daily more of a figurehead in a situation over which he had little control." In response to the news of Souvanna's objections, the United States announced that it was suspending the reconnaissance flights "for at least 48 hours"; but at the same time the State Department announced the flights would continue "subject to consultation." This was by no means the first time that the United States had treated Souvanna in so humiliating a fashion; cf. Fall, Anatomy of a Crisis, pp. 193ff., 223.

[28] Goulden, Truth is First Casualty, p. 97. Grant Wolfkill, then a prisoner of the Pathet Lao, testifies to the lowness of the flights (Reported to Be Alive, pp. 273–74): "Flying at a thousand feet, it [an unmarked jet F-101] whipped through the valley and swung around leisurely at one end. I could see the pilot's head as the plane turned. . . . Three days later the F-101 returned. . . . Every gun in the camp blazed away at it this time. With arrogant indifference the jet maintained its course." Statement of Secretary Rusk, July 30, 1964, in US State Department, American Foreign Policy, 1964, p. 943; see also Dommen, Conflict in Laos, p. 258.

or alternatively to obtain a suitable provocation, as was finally supplied by the Tonkin Gulf incidents, for the bombing of North Vietnam.

The withdrawals from the Plain of Jars in 1964 produced what Phoumi had failed to obtain by his withdrawal from Nam Tha in 1962—a direct armed US intervention in Laos and the frustration of a new initiative (this time by the French) to restore peace in that country. The similarities between the two withdrawals—the gratuitous right wing provocations, the flight before being attacked, and the incredible stories of Chinese Communist invasion—have been attributed by some to Laotian lack of discipline.

Toye, however, will not accept this explanation for 1962[29] and there are disturbing indications that in 1964 Laotian and US hawks were still intriguing together to bring about a further Americanization of the war. Perhaps the chief indication was the dispatch in May of US Navy aircraft carriers into the Tonkin Gulf area for the purpose of conducting "reconnaissance" flights and air strikes against Laos (even the new armed flights could easily have been initiated, as in the past, by the USAF in Thailand).

By the time the US jet air strikes got under way in June, the rainy season in Laos had begun, the panic was over, and there was no prospect of ground military activity in Laos for the next several months. Yet many observers (including Melvin Laird, who had his own Pentagon channels) predicted accurately that the aircraft carriers moved in against Laos might soon be used against North Vietnam. As *Aviation Week* reported on June 22, 1964, President Johnson appeared to be awaiting reactions to the Laotian air strikes ("the first US offensive military action since Korea") before taking "the next big step on the escalation scale." On June 3, 1964, a *New York Times* correspondent reported "a sense of crisis and foreboding" in Southeast Asia, attributed "more to the statements of US Government officials than to any immediate emergency in Laos, South Vietnam or Cambodia."

Congress would do well to investigate the crucial decisions

[29] Toye, *Laos,* p. 182.

made during the period preceding the Tonkin Gulf incidents, for the present period, as we shall see, offers disturbing parallels to the withdrawals of 1962 and 1964.

7) *Statement:* "Since this Administration has been in office, North Vietnamese pressure has continued. Last spring, the North Vietnamese mounted a campaign which threatened the royal capital and moved beyond the areas previously occupied by communists. A counterattack by the Lao government forces, intended to relieve this military pressure and cut off supply lines, caught the enemy by surprise and succeeded beyond expectations in pushing them off the . . . Plain of Jars."

Comment: Though it is too early to analyze authoritatively the events of the last year in Laos, it is clear that this statement leaves out the biggest recent development of all. Shortly after November, 1968 (when it halted the bombing of North Vietnam) the US began to apply to combat zones in Laos the tactic of massive bombardment which hitherto had been reserved for Vietnam and the region of the Ho Chi Minh Trail in the Laotian panhandle. According to Senator Cranston, air strikes against Laos have increased from 4,500 sorties a month (before the November, 1968 halt to the bombing of North Vietnam) to between 12,500 and 15,000 sorties a month today. (Other sources suggest a much more dramatic increase.)[30]

This new policy has led to the total annihilation of many Laotian towns (at first briefly, but falsely, attributed to a North Vietnamese "scorched earth" policy). It has also been accompanied by the evacuation and resettlement (apparently sometimes by coercion) of between 500,000 and 600,000 Laotians, or about one-quarter of the total population. (See *The Nation,* Jan. 26, 1970; The *New York Times,* Mar. 12, 1970, p. 3.)

With this new tactic, General Vang Pao's CIA-advised Meo guerrillas have been ordered to withdraw rather than suffer serious casualties in attempting to hold forward positions: their function is rather to engage the enemy and thus expose them

---

[30] T. D. Allman reported in the *Far Eastern Economic Review* (January 1, 1970), p. 21, that "the US now flies as many as 20,000 bombing sorties a month in Laos"; Richard Dudman (St. Louis *Post-Dispatch,* December 23, 1969) put the level one year earlier at 1,000 a month.

to heavy losses through air strikes. These are the tactics alleged by our generals to be succeeding in South Vietnam: attrition of the enemy by massive bombardment, rather than serious attempts to hold territory. The new tactics (like the original covert US military involvements eight years earlier) were inaugurated during the "lame-duck" period of a changeover in administrations. In December, 1968, the Pathet Lao protested to the International Control Commission that US planes were dropping four or five times as many bombs in Laos as they had done two months earlier.[31]

In accordance with their orders to engage the enemy while avoiding heavy casualties, Vang Pao's guerrillas have twice in the last year made spectacular advances into the enemy Plain of Jars area (on one occasion to about thirty miles from the North Vietnamese border) and then withdrawn from key outposts like Xieng Khouang and Ban Ban without waiting for the enemy to attack in strength. Just as with General Phoumi in 1962, these withdrawals from isolated advance positions in the face of enemy probes have been widely publicized and used as arguments for US escalation. The Kennedy Administration did not take this bait; apparently the Nixon Administration (with its recent B-52 strikes) has.

In the wake of the reported bombing increase, there has also been a reported rise in Pathet Lao and North Vietnamese ground activity. Apparently none of this activity has violated the 1961–62 ceasefire line as seriously as Vang Pao's unprecedented forays of April–May and August–September into the Xieng Khouang–Ban Ban area. Most of the Pathet Lao activity in the northeast has been directed against Meo outposts within their base area, notably the forward communications post of Na Khang, which was used for the all-weather bombing of North Vietnam, and the US-Thai base at Muong Soui, which was used to support the Meo outposts. On August 25, 1969, The New York Times said that "If Vang Vieng falls . . . the Laotian government will have been pushed behind the ceasefire line of 1961"; but even Vang Vieng was still on the Pathet Lao side of the line.

[31] The New York Times, December 31, 1968, p. 6.

There are disturbing indications that in 1969 (as in 1962 and 1964) right wing provocations and escalations were deliberately intended to frustrate Souvanna Phouma's continuing efforts to restore peace and a neutralist coalition government. In May, 1969, Souvanna Phouma saw the North Vietnamese ambassador to Laos (at the latter's invitation) for the first time in over four years. On May 15 he announced he was hopeful that the Laotian problem could be solved even before the end of the Vietnam war. It was later revealed that he had offered a formula for the termination of US bombing comparable to that used in Vietnam: a gradual reduction in the bombing in return for a gradual withdrawal of North Vietnamese troops. Souvanna said that he would accept the continued use of the Ho Chi Minh Trail by the North Vietnamese troops "with the condition that those troops withdrew" elsewhere.[32] (I have been informed that in September, four months after this proposal by Souvanna, the North Vietnamese withdrew altogether from the Plain of Jars.)

Four days later, on May 19, The *New York Times* reported that with the advent of the rainy season, Laos was "suddenly quiet." Pathet Lao pressure had tapered off: "Where there is any action Government forces appear to be taking the initiative." Only one day later "fierce fighting" was reported from the Plain of Jars: Vang Pao's CIA-supported guerrillas had clashed with the enemy thirteen miles from Xieng Khouang. On May 27 Vang Pao was reported to have withdrawn from Xieng Khouang (which he had held for one month) "following orders . . . not to risk heavy casualties." The next day his troops seized Ban Ban, about thirty miles from North Vietnam, "as Laotian and American bombers continued devastating attacks on North Vietnamese soldiers and supply lines all over northeastern Laos."[33]

This chronology recalls the depressing sequence of occasions in the Vietnam war when a new diplomatic initiative was followed by a new escalation or an intensification of the bombing,

[32] The *New York Times,* May 15, 1969, p. 13; May 17, p. 3; *Far Eastern Economic Review* (June 5, 1969), p. 569; The *San Francisco Chronicle* (March 6, 1970), p. 26.

[33] The *New York Times,* May 19, 1969, p. 6; May 20, p. 3; May 27, p. 5; May 28, p. 9.

instead of a hoped-for reduction.[34] This pattern of a "politics of escalation" appeared to repeat itself in February of this year. In early February

> Souvanna Phouma startled the diplomatic community by publicly offering to go to Hanoi to negotiate an end to the conflict. . . . Souvanna was ready, so he said, to agree to the neutralization of the Plain of Jars . . . and . . . promised that his government would "close its eyes" to what goes along the Ho Chi Minh Trail.[35]

On February 17, the Associated Press reported "some of the heaviest air raids ever flown in Southeast Asia" and on February 19, the first "massive air strikes by US B-52 bombers in the Plain of Jars region." On February 22 the AP fed the American public the typical kind of panic story that has been emanating from Northeast Laos ever since the phony "offensive" of August 1959. Vang Pao's guerrillas, it said, had been "swept from the Plain of Jars by an overwhelming North Vietnamese blow . . . with a third of its force dead or missing. . . . The government garrison of 1,500 men based at Xieng Khouang was hit by 6,000 North Vietnamese supported by tanks."

On the next day came the typical corrective story: the attack had been made by 400 troops, not 6,000; the defenders (who had falsely inflated their strength "for payday purposes") had withdrawn with "very little close-in action." It would appear that once again wildly exaggerated tales from remote areas had resulted in the frustration of a peace initiative, by what was (as Senator Mansfield warned) a significant escalation of the bombing.[36]

[34] Franz Schurmann, Peter Dale Scott, Reginald Zelnik, *The Politics of Escalation in Vietnam* (Beacon Press/Fawcett, 1966); David Kraslow and Stuart H. Loory, *The Secret Search for Peace in Vietnam* (Random House, 1968), pp. 3–74; *Ramparts* (March 1968), pp. 56–58; The *New York Times*, January 6, 1968, p. 28.

[35] *Newsweek,* February 16, 1970, p. 37.

[36] The *San Francisco Chronicle,* February 17, 1970; Feb. 19; Feb. 22; Feb. 23.

In August 1969, there was also the mysterious episode of the tribal

8) *Statement:* "We are trying above all to save American and Allied lives in South Vietnam which are threatened by the continual infiltration of North Vietnamese troops and supplies along the Ho Chi Minh Trail. . . . Today there are 67,000 North Vietnamese troops in [Laos]. There are no American troops there. Hanoi is not threatened by Laos; it runs risks only when it moves its forces across borders."

Comment: The CIA's persistent support, guidance, and encouragement of Meo guerilla activities in northeast Laos cannot be rationalized by references to the Ho Chi Minh Trail. As anyone can see by looking at a map, the Ho Chi Minh Trail runs south from the Mu Gia pass in the southern portion of the Laotian panhandle, 200 miles to the southeast of the Plain of Jars. These Meo tribesmen were first trained by the French for paramilitary activities inside what is now North Vietnam, where some of them continued to operate for years after the 1954 Geneva agreements, almost to the time when their French officers were replaced by CIA "Special Forces." [37] Veterans of the Special Forces, now "civilians" working for the CIA, are still working with the Meos behind enemy lines; Air America, and more recently Continental Air Services, have never ceased to airlift and supply them.

Hanoi is indeed directly threatened by these CIA activities just across the Laotian border. Heavily fortified Meo outposts at Pa Thi and Na Khang were developed as forward communications centers for the all-weather pinpoint bombing of North Vietnam.[38] On November 21, 1968, the *Far Eastern Economic Review* reported

> . . . evidence that American aircraft, including jets, were flying from a secret base in northern

double-agent who, on Vang Pao's instruction, sold a map of the secret Meo headquarters at Long Cheng to six members of the North Vietnamese Embassy. According to T. D. Allman, "The Affair . . . appeared to be at least in part a right wing effort to reduce the Prime Minister's room to maneuver and perhaps even force a break in diplomatic relations between the two countries." *Far Eastern Economic Review* (September 11, 1969), p. 648.

[37] Fall, *Street Without Joy,* p. 341.

[38] Robert Shaplen, *Time Out of Hand* (Harper & Row, 1969), p. 346; The *New York Times,* Oct. 26, 1969, p. 24.

Laos . . . about fifty miles from the North Vietnam border.

It is difficult to explain the tenacity of the CIA's ground operations behind enemy lines in northeast Laos, or the recent conversion of the Plain of Jars into an evacuated "free strike" zone for F-4's, F-105's, and B-52's, except as part of a "forward strategy," to remind North Vietnam of the threat that the United States might resume bombing it. The President's statement indeed suggests that the US hopes to use its escalation in Laos as a means of imposing its peace formula on Vietnam. ("What we do in Laos has thus as its aim to bring about the conditions for progress toward peace in the entire Indochinese Peninsula.")

One cannot confirm or refute the current intelligence estimates of 67,000 North Vietnamese in Laos. What is clear is that the intelligence estimates have themselves sharply "escalated" from the figure of 50,000 that was used by the Pentagon as late as last month. One is reminded of the similar "escalation" of infiltration estimates for South Vietnam in January, 1965. The claims then put forward as to the presence of regular North Vietnamese army units in South Vietnam, including at least a battalion if not a division, were tacitly refuted only six months later by no less an authority than McNamara.[39] Six months later it was of course too late. The regular bombing of North and South Vietnam had been initiated; the full "Americanization" of the Vietnam war had been achieved.

[39] Secretary McNamara on June 17, 1965, *Department of State Bulletin*, July 5, 1965, p. 18; cf. *Department of State Bulletin*, March 22, 1965, p. 414; May 17, 1965, pp. 750, 753; Theodore Draper, "How Not to Negotiate," *New York Review of Books*, May 4, 1967, p. 27n; Theodore Draper, *Abuse of Power* (Viking, 1967), pp. 76–77; Schurmann, Scott, and Zelnik, *Escalation*, p. 47n.

With respect to the current estimate of 67,000 North Vietnamese troops in Laos, one needs to know how many of these are involved in the Ho Chi Minh Trail and how many are border guards sent in defensively (as in the past) to occupy the Laotian side of the border passes. One also needs to know the sources and reliability of the information. The months of January and February have repeatedly seen highly questionable US escalations of infiltration estimates followed by escalations of the bombing. One is reminded not only of the 1965 White Paper but also of the bombing escalation in February 1967.

The President's statement on Laos is an alarming document, alarming above all not because of what it misrepresents, but because of what it may portend. In its skillful retelling of events known only to a few, it resembles the State Department's White Paper of February, 1965,[40] on Vietnam. The White Paper, which also relied heavily on intelligence "estimates," was not really an effort to understand the true developments of the past. It was instead the ominous harbinger for a new strategy of victory through American air power, a document aimed not at serious students of Southeast Asia (who swiftly saw through it) but at the "silent majority" of that era.

What further new strategy of escalation can still attract the Nixon Administration in 1970 is unclear, since American air power has failed to achieve with conventional weapons the results which its advocates promised. As it stands, however, the Key Biscayne statement on Laos is not only an argument for our present murderous bombing policy, it is an argument which, if believed, would lead logically to escalation. The argument is false; and it is urgent that it be refuted.

[40] See Marvin E. Gettleman, ed., *Vietnam: History, Documents and Opinions* (2d ed. New York: New American Library, 1970), Selection 57—eds.

22

Laotian Tragedy: The Long March

CARL STROCK *

Vientiane: After twenty years of sporadic, semi-secret warfare, Laos has a serious refugee problem. At least half the population of three million has been displaced by the fighting, according to government officials in Vientiane. At least 180,000 are living in "refugee villages."

At the end of 1968, American bombers were diverted from North Vietnam to Laos and began systematically depopulating Pathet Lao-controlled territory. Air strikes were no longer limited to the network of North Vietnamese supply routes twisting through the sparsely inhabited mountains of eastern Laos on their way to South Vietnam (the Ho Chi Minh Trail), nor confined to "combat support missions," as President Nixon would have it. Everything that stood and was not controlled by the government became a target. Tribesmen and peasants began to flee to the relative safety of the government-controlled lowlands. The US Embassy, having persuaded itself that the people were escaping "communist terrorism," was enthusiastic about this "voting-with-the-feet." Yet it was not—and is not yet—eager to advertise the refugee situation.

In mid-1969 air strikes were escalated to their present high level of 15,000 sorties a month. In support of a secrecy-shrouded offensive by the CIA-financed "Clandestine Army" of Meo mercenaries, the US carried out a saturation bombing campaign on the Pathet Lao-controlled Plain of Jars in northeastern Laos. After seizing the Plain, the Clandestine Army rounded up the inhabitants, culled out the prosperous farmers and merchants—the main contributors to Pathet Lao tax coffers—and shipped them to the Vientiane lowlands. The poor peas-

* From *The New Republic* [Washington, D.C.] CLXII (May 9, 1970), pp. 12–13. By permission. Carl Strock, correspondent for Dispatch News Service, spent three years covering Southeast Asia.

ants were allowed to remain behind, not in their original homes, which had been reduced to rubble by the bombing, but in the "refugee villages."

I asked a young man what happened when the Clandestine Army took over his village. "The soldiers gathered us together," he said. "They told us we had one hour to leave. We didn't know where we were going. The soldiers took whatever they wanted from our houses, and then they burned the village down. An officer told us that if anyone asked, we should say we were escaping from the communists. We walked twenty miles to an airstrip, and then American planes brought us here. I was lucky. I'm half-Chinese, so they didn't make me join the army. The Lao boys were drafted right there. I haven't seen them since."

When the dry season came at the end of last year, intelligence reports indicated that the North Vietnamese and the Pathet Lao were planning a counteroffensive to recapture the Plain of Jars. No one believed that the rag-tag Clandestine Army could hold off a determined communist advance, but the US Embassy here wanted two guarantees: that the peasant-refugees—indispensable producers of rice—would not again be available to benefit the Pathet Lao; and that American bombers would have a free hand to pound the oncoming troops. So it was decided to evacuate all civilians from the Plain of Jars.

Between February 5 and 11, some 15,000 bedraggled Laotian peasants were loaded onto Air American cargo planes and shipped to new "refugee villages" in the Mekong lowlands. The Plain of Jars became a free-strike zone. The US-Vientiane planners, unable to carry their government to the people, had chosen the Vietnam-tried course of bringing the people to the government. "We could work in the fields only at night; by day we slept underground in the bunkers," explained one old woman in a camp near Vientiane. "Everything that moved was bombed. Our village was bombed three times. The second time my daughter was killed. Then we left and went to live in the forest. It's very difficult to live there. There's not enough to eat."

Though more people live under government control since the bombing, American officials here deny that was the intent of the bombing. They claim that "Communist terrorism" is responsible for the influx of refugees. When the mass evacuation from the Plain of Jars was begun in February, US AID officials who supervised the operation maintained that the people all freely chose to leave their homes. Other US AID officials, who do not wish to be identified, now admit, however, that the decision was made in Vietiane and that the people were moved regardless of their wishes. Naturally, when confronted with the choice of being bombed at home or surviving in a far-away camp, many people chose the latter. But it seems devious to call that choice "free."

The plight of refugees here is not yet as grim as that of their counterparts in Vietnam. Camps are small and usually contiguous to an established village. The idea is that the old villagers will help dispossessed newcomers; so far it has worked well, to the great credit of the Lao villagers. But refugees do not have enough land to support themselves, and the land they do receive is usually the least fertile. The thatched, barrack housing is depressing even to peasants accustomed to primitive conditions. Medical care is rare; so is schooling. US AID this year will spend some $7 million on refugee relief (about one thirty-fifth of the estimated $250 million spent to wage the war); most of that will be used for rice crops.

The worst suffering is not in the camps. By the time people reach them, the worst is over. Their villages have been destroyed; their relatives killed or drafted; they have walked, sometimes for months, through some of the most rugged country in the world. Only the lucky ones ride Air America. The others, by the tens of thousands, put their belongings on their backs and set out across the hills on foot. It is an agony difficult for an outsider to imagine. American and Laotian officials estimate that over the last ten years twenty percent of the people of northeastern Laos have died in these refugee marches. The verdant limestone mountains that seem to have been lifted from a delicate Chinese scroll are a cemetery for 100,000 peasants! Random air strikes are always a threat; countless unexploded bombs lie scattered half-buried in the hills; exhaustion claims the weaker marchers; epidemics, especially of measles, are common; and of course there is never enough food.

The US Embassy downplays the dimension of the tragedy by counting only those currently living on relief in recognized "refugee villages"—the 180,000 I have mentioned. The Laotian government, however, reports 543,000 refugees and says there are at least another 150,000 unregistered. Now—because of heavy fighting and bombing near the Plain of Jars—another 100,000 are trudging southward through the roadless mountains to safety. One out of five will probably die before reaching the lowlands.

23

Exploring the U.S. Role in Laos: Hearings of the Symington Committee (October, 1969)*

WHY SECRECY ABOUT U.S. ACTIVITIES IN LAOS WHEN IT IS IN PUBLIC PRESS?

SENATOR SYMINGTON: Why is the Government so determined to pretend all this [U.S. bombing raids in Laos] does not take place, even though we consistently have these stories in the press? . . .

MR. SULLIVAN. [William H. Sullivan, Deputy Assistant Secretary of State for East Asian and Pacific Affairs] I think that this is . . . a matter of major concern of this committee, and I think something that we do want to consider in some detail as to why it is that the United States is reluctant to place on the public record through the statements of officials precise definition of what the US involvement or operations in Laos have entailed. The original understanding between my predecessor and the Prime Minister of Laos was premised upon statements being limited, admissions publicly stated being very carefully structured.

This, I think, has two or three reasons: First of all, it is the intention and the desire of the Prime Minister and of the Lao to maintain the, and establish as best they can a, neutral status. Now, by neutral, particularly when the nation is under attack, they have had to contort considerably to develop what their

* United States Security Agreements and Commitments Abroad: Kingdom of Laos, *Hearings Before the Subcommittee on United States Security Agreements and Commitments Abroad* [Senator Stuart Symington, Missouri, Chairman] *of the Committee on Foreign Relations, United States Senate*, Ninety-First Congress, First Session, October, 1969 (Washington, D.C.: U.S. Government Printing Office, 1970), pp. 398–405, 463–5, 536–40, 541–8, 592–3.

neutral stand would be. But a senior Soviet official, for example, has said that insofar as he reads things in newspapers or hears statements and allegations about US operations, he does not have to take any official cognizance of them. But if they are made directly by US officials he does have to take cognizance of them, and this will color, to some extent, the Soviet attitude toward Souvanna Phouma's neutrality and toward the retention of the understandings which underlie the agreement between ourselves and the Soviets for the neutrality of Laos.

One other feature that enters into this was the fact that the Chairman just mentioned, that the mechanism for determining and bringing to public attention gross violations by the North Vietnamese of the Lao neutrality are frustrated because the ICC [International Commission for Supervision and Control] are not able to move into the areas and ascertain exactly what is going on there.

The North Vietnamese operate with enormous numbers of forces in Laos, totally clandestinely. They deny that their people are there, and this, therefore, in terms of the mechanism of the 1962 agreements, gives them a totally unfair, totally legal protection. Part of the concern being our desire to maintain the framework of the 1962 agreements, so that eventually they can reestablish and put back into function, we have therefore been concerned in attempting to avoid those actions or those statements which would result in the mechanism being deployed in relation to us.

COMMITTEE AND CONGRESS HAVE RIGHT TO KNOW TRUTH

SENATOR SYMINGTON. I can understand your concern about the Russians, but do you not think this committee and the American people have equal interest in what is going on?

MR. SULLIVAN. I think certainly this committee has every right or need to know, and over the year we have consistently talked with committee members about these matters.

SENATOR FULBRIGHT. You have said there is nothing this

committee or this Congress has done to authorize action in Laos. There is no legal commitment, and then it comes down to a practical, pragmatic matter of the defense of South Vietnam as to what you are doing in Laos.

STEADY BUILDUP IN LAOS AS IN VIETNAM

SENATOR SYMINGTON. There has been this steady buildup of our not admitting we were doing various things, and the North Vietnamese not admitting they were doing various things, and regardless of who started it, in effect, that is exactly what is going on in Laos now. That is why this sub-committee is worried. I am sure the American people would be very worried if they knew the facts; whether, in effect, we could run into the same kind of escalation in Laos we did in Vietnam.

MR. SULLIVAN. I certainly recognize your concern, and it is certainly alluded to in my statement.

SENATOR FULBRIGHT. It seems to me a very anomalous situation. We pretend it is a sovereign and independent country. We say we want to keep it sovereign and independent, but without any treaty or authorization I can think of, as you have already stated. But we do intervene in a major way, supply them with bombers, bombing people on their territory, and responding to General Vang Pao's request,[1] and so on, as if he had a full-fledged treaty, very much as if he were a member of NATO.

CONSULTATION WITH CONGRESSIONAL COMMITTEES

Is this a reflection of the previous Administration's attitude that the Constitution is of no consequence after all, that is out-

[1] General Vang Pao of the Royal Laotian Army, had repeatedly called for U.S. bombing raids in Laos—eds.

moded? You remember Mr. Katzenbach's famous testimony that the Constitution is outmoded.[2]

MR. SULLIVAN. I read Mr. Katzenbach's testimony; yes, sir.

SENATOR FULBRIGHT. It seems to me if you really think this is an independent country that there ought to be some kind of authorization of your actions in Laos other than what is apparently a verbal agreement with your predecessor. You meant with your ambassador there.

MR. SULLIVAN. Yes.

SENATOR FULBRIGHT. Who was that?

MR. SULLIVAN. Ambassador Unger.

SENATOR FULBRIGHT. Unger. Did he have a conversation with Souvanna Phouma and they agreed to keep it secret; is that what you testified to?

MR. SULLIVAN. I think I can assure you that Ambassador Unger's conversation and requests were referred back here to Washington, and the decisions taken here in Washington were taken at departmental levels. I am not sure that there was any consultation with any committees.

SENATOR FULBRIGHT. You have no evidence that this committee was advised of it, do you?

MR. SULLIVAN. I do not know, sir.

SENATOR FULBRIGHT. If there is any would you ask your associates to supply it? I would be curious to know whether or not we were advised of it.

(The information referred to follows.)

> *Was this committee advised re the Lao requests for assistance?*
>
> Answer: Although a search of the files before 1965 fails to reveal whether the Senate Foreign Relations Committee was specifically briefed on the late 1962 RLG request for military assistance, the Department of Defense in February 1963 presented the Military Assistance Program for Laos to the four Congressional Committees concerned: Senate Foreign Relations, House Foreign Affairs, Senate

[2] Nicholas J. Katzenbach was Attorney General under Lyndon Johnson—eds.

and House Appropriations. On 23 June 1964, Secretary of Defense McNamara testified before Congress on the Laos program. Since Service funding was initiated in 1966, there has been a separate line entry for military assistance to Laos in each Defense appropriations bill.

Ambassador Sullivan testified on Laos before the Senate Foreign Relations Committee in March, 1968. From 1965 through 1968, Ambassador Sullivan briefed on US operations in Laos, either in Laos or Udorn, the following members of the Foreign Relations Committee: Senators Mansfield, Symington, Aiken, Dodd, and McGee. Some of these Senators visited Laos more than once during that period.

SENATOR FULBRIGHT. One reason we may be unduly concerned about it is the recent discovery of the contingency plan in Thailand signed by the Prime Minister, and the reluctance, in fact, refusal, of the Defense Department to make it available to this committee, and the State Department pleading, in effect, that it was in the custody of the Joint Chiefs and they did not have it, which is also a new development in international relations.

Formerly, it was considered that agreements involving prime ministers and governments were a matter for the State Department, wouldn't you say?

MR. SULLIVAN. I think they still are, sir.

SENATOR FULBRIGHT. You do?

SENATOR SYMINGTON. If the Senator would yield, in an open hearing Ambassador Martin testified that the contingency plan in question was handled under his direct supervision, but Secretary of State Rogers reportedly said the contingency plan was not in the State Department. So we asked Ambassador Martin whether he had sent this plan, made under his "direct supervision" to the State Department. The Ambassador said he could not give a categorical answer to that question.

SENATOR FULBRIGHT. Where is Ambassador Unger now?

MR. SULLIVAN. He is in Thailand. Bangkok.

DOES LAO GOVERNMENT FEEL U.S. COMMITMENT THERE?

SENATOR FULBRIGHT. Do you think the Laotian Government, Souvanna Phouma, believes he has a commitment from our Government to support him?

MR. SULLIVAN. No, sir; I do not think so.

SENATOR FULBRIGHT. You do not think so?

MR. SULLIVAN. No, because Souvanna Phouma has had some —he has had a series of associations with the United States, and I think he is a man without any illusions.

SENATOR FULBRIGHT. Without what?

MR. SULLIVAN. Without any illusions in terms of what these arrangements would signify. In other words, he was at one time Prime Minister, and I would say fell from favor with the United States.

SENATOR FULBRIGHT. Is that when we said he was a communist?

MR. SULLIVAN. Some people said.

SENATOR FULBRIGHT. I did not. I just made the statement.

MR. SULLIVAN. My feeling, quite frankly, is that the Lao, having been buffeted around by circumstances over a number of years, have become very pragmatic and quite understanding that there is a coldness in this which does not transcend the—

SENATOR FULBRIGHT. This means if we decided it was no longer in our interest to continue this bombing program, and so on, in Laos about which we read in the paper, that he would feel no resentment or even surprise that we should decide to cease those raids?

MR. SULLIVAN. [Deleted][3] the question you asked me was whether he felt he had a commitment from us.

SENATOR FULBRIGHT. Yes, and I think you indicated properly that he, having had previous experience with our Government, he would not be surprised—

---

[3] Sections of these hearings have been deleted "at the request of the Department of State and the Department of Defense"—eds.

MR. SULLIVAN. I did not say he would not be surprised, but I said he had no illusions.

SENATOR FULBRIGHT. He has no illusions about it.

IS IT IN U.S. INTERESTS TO CONTINUE ACTIVITY IN LAOS?

Which brings me back again to my central question, and that is, is it in our interest to continue this activity in this secret —I guess, I am not quite sure of the right word to call it, it is not really secret, it is well known in the press—unacknowledged, officially unacknowledged, activity? Is this really in our interest to continue it? It certainly is not disassociated from the Vietnam War.

It is my understanding that the official attitude of the present Administration—I am not sure I am clear about this because it is a complicated matter, and it is hard for me to decipher it— but I have a feeling we wish to disengage from South Vietnam. It is not now considered in the national interests of the United States to occupy and retain control of South Vietnam. I guess that is the policy, is it not?

MR. SULLIVAN. I think the President has made it quite clear that he would very much wish to be able to disengage US forces from Vietnam under appropriate conditions.

SENATOR FULBRIGHT. That being so, it seems to me it would be wise to begin to liquidate the activity in Laos. Wouldn't you think so?

MR. SULLIVAN. I think that the two are interrelated, as you said earlier, sir, and I think the action with respect to one would have an influence with respect to the other.

SENATOR FULBRIGHT. It seems to me it would be, if that is true, it would be in our interest to discuss this matter publicly, I mean, to make the Congress and this committee aware of what we are doing there, to honestly acknowledge it.

You said, you talked about its effect on the Russians. I do not know why it would. The Russians know it. What in the world would the Russians do, could or would they do, if you acknowledged tomorrow morning exactly what you are doing? We acknowledge we were bombing North Vietnam, didn't we? We did not pretend we were not bombing North Vietnam, and the Russians didn't do any more than they were doing, that is, they give them the assistance they thought appropriate. What do you think they would be doing in Laos?

MR. SULLIVAN. I think our concern would be primarily with the attitude of the Soviets toward continuing a respect for the Prime Minister of Laos as a neutralist.

"NEUTRALITY" OF SOUVANNA PHOUMA

SENATOR FULBRIGHT. He is not really a neutralist, is he?

MR. SULLIVAN. He is a nationalist, and nationalists would not wish to be alined with either system.

SENATOR FULBRIGHT. You know, there is something about this pretense that is a little offensive to me. You undoubtedly have heard about the credibility gap which has afflicted us for a long time, and I do not like this idea. I do not like to be a party to it. He is not a neutralist. He is an ally except we do not have a treaty with him, but we are helping him, we are giving him money, we are giving him assistance, and so on. He is not neutral as between the North Vietnamese and ourselves, is he? He does not profess that?

MR. SULLIVAN. No, but I think we give money and assistance and help to a great many countries such as India, which I would accept as a neutralist country. I do not believe they would be categorized—

SENATOR SYMINGTON. If the Senator would yield, why is it that we do not allow bombing in North Vietnam, preferring to work it out with ground troops in South Vietnam but do not have ground troops in Laos, preferring to work it out with bombing? It is sort of—

MR. SULLIVAN. I do not think I am competent—

SENATOR SYMINGTON. You directed this war for several years to my certain knowledge.

MR. SULLIVAN. First of all, I was not aware we were not bombing our enemy in South Vietnam.

SENATOR SYMINGTON. I was referring to North Vietnam. In 1965 you told me you were opposed to bombing in North Vietnam, so why do we bomb in Laos? We are losing money and lives in an unpopular war; and our losses are far greater because we refrain from bombing in North Vietnam. Why is it proper to bomb the enemy in one place where your people are fighting, but not in another? As I remember when we talked in 1965, you were for ground troops going into North Vietnam, but against the use of air.

SENATOR FULBRIGHT. Let me review this just a little more. I am not quite satisfied with the analogy with India. In the first place, when China attacked her she called for help, and we did not give it to her. She is not all that neutral. But we are not fighting a war. We do not have bombers there. We are only giving them economic aid. Now, she could accept economic aid from the Russians, too. In fact, the Russians have made quite an effort there in building a steel mill, etc. Doesn't Souvanna Phouma accept aid from Russia and China?

MR. SULLIVAN. Yes, sir; he gets aid from Russians.

SENATOR FULBRIGHT. Now?

MR. SULLIVAN. Yes, sir. He gets—

SENATOR FULBRIGHT. What does he get?

MR. SULLIVAN. He does not get any aid from China.

SENATOR FULBRIGHT. What does he get from Russia?

MR. SULLIVAN. It is mostly technical assistance and primarily, I think, in terms of working with his meteorological services, and they do provide scholarships and assistance for students.

SENATOR FULBRIGHT. Yet the Russians, at the same time, are supporting the North Vietnamese and say they are not there.

MR. SULLIVAN. Yes, sir.

UNITED STATES FIGHTING AN UNACKNOWLEDGED WAR

SENATOR FULBRIGHT. Doesn't this ever strike you as sort of an absurdity? They are pretending they are not there and we are pretending we are not there. What does it all lead to? We give the impression not only to foreign people but to many of our own people that we are mad. Why isn't it better to go and say what we are doing and give a reason for it and say the reason you give, which I think is the only possible reason, the support of the war in Vietnam, that we have just gone in and are doing what we think is assisting in the war in Vietnam. That makes some sense. I do not quite see the persuasiveness of your reasons.

MR. SULLIVAN. Well, my answers may not be persuasive, but I go back and state our concern has been, and it still is, to try to establish those conditions which would permit the 1962 neutrality agreements to apply, and in doing that I think it was encumbent upon us to maintain that initial understanding we have had with the Soviets—

AMERICAN PEOPLE ARE BEING DECEIVED

SENATOR FULBRIGHT. In the meantime you are deceiving the American people and the Congress, and they do not know what to think, and I think you have created a situation which could become very difficult.

Supposing the President should change his policy or the force of pressure from people in this country who wished to increase the pressure. We can get into another full scale war up there. I do not know, I would think these are complex matters, and it is much better to be open and above board with it and, at least, the Congress and the people participate in the decisions which result in their undoing.

You cannot leave them free of it. I think they have a legitimate complaint now that they really do not know what is going on, just as the complaint I have, and I think the only legitimate complaint I have, aside from my own failure, is that I think I was deceived by the Administration in what they told this committee at the time of the incidents in the Gulf of Tonkin. I think it was an outright misrepresentation of what actually happened and, therefore, I did not have a free chance to exercise a judgment because I made a judgment and went on the floor and defended a course of action which was not justified by the reported facts, and I have always resented it.

I think the American people resent it, too, if they are not told what is going on there, and if Congress is not told. We appropriate vast sums and we send over people and we are fighting a war that is unacknowledged, fighting part of a war that is unacknowledged. I do not really think it is justified.

I do not know why this should not be made public. We could discuss it on the floor of the Senate and see if they want to support it. In the absence of any real strong and well-clarified national interest that would justify it, I think it is a very close case whether you are justified in doing what you are doing in Laos. I doubt that we are because I think we are prolonging and making more difficult an already difficult situation, and it is tied in with Thailand and with Vietnam. I think we are protecting them by doing this. Don't you think they think that?

MR. SULLIVAN. I think the Thai have always considered that Laos is a territory between them and the North Vietnamese and offers a protective buffer to them.

WHY ARE THAI NERVOUS ABOUT THEIR SECURITY?

SENATOR FULBRIGHT. Well, I do not think it is our duty to protect the Thai. I think it is their duty to have created a government that appeals to their own people and that will be strong with their own people. I expect they would resist this because it would require some greater participation by the people in the government, I expect. Why should they be so nervous about their security? They have been there a long time, a lot longer than the United States has been here, if it is not that they are conscious that this government is not very appealing to the people.

MR. SULLIVAN. Well, I think they have an experience in recent years with the forces that have been directed against their side.

SENATOR FULBRIGHT. But those forces are relatively small.

MR. SULLIVAN. Relatively small.

SENATOR FULBRIGHT. How large an army do they have, isn't it roughly 100,000?

MR. SULLIVAN. Roughly that.

SENATOR FULBRIGHT. And they are nervous about 2,000 or 3,000. That does not make a lot of sense to me.

MR. SULLIVAN. But I think they are up against a country or a territory which they see is being inimical to them, the Chinese.

SENATOR FULBRIGHT. Then it comes back to China.

MR. SULLIVAN. As far as the Thai are concerned, I think they are very much concerned about China.

SENATOR FULBRIGHT. Well, I do not know. I am very, very reluctant to accept the decision that this activity has to be secret, that we cannot talk about it and cannot consider it out in the open in the same way we do other matters that involve our troops.

You have already gone over, I guess, how many troops we have there and how many we have operating in Laos?

MR. SULLIVAN. Yes.

SENATOR SYMINGTON. Mr. Chairman, counsel has a great many questions he is going to ask this afternoon.

SENATOR FULBRIGHT. I will desist. I have a man from Cambodia who wants to see me. I do not know what about. Have we got any agreements with Cambodia? . . .

[The next day the subcommittee questioned US Air Force Colonel Robert L. F. Tyrrell, US Air Attaché to the Royal Laotian Government, Vietiane. Roland A. Paul, Subcommittee counsel, did some of the questioning.]

MR. PAUL. My question is are some preplanned targets for the US Air Force consummated without being referred to the Laotian military commanders?

COLONEL TYRRELL. Yes, sir; in certain areas not accessible to the Lao in the interdiction phase.

MR. PAUL. In Northern Laos?

COLONEL TYRRELL. In Northern Laos, although they would be aware of it because they are briefed on all USAF activities in that area on a daily basis.

MR. PAUL. But in that case, just so that I understand, Colonel, that would in some cases be after the strike rather than before the strike.

COLONEL TYRRELL. The frag[4] that we spoke of is forwarded to the AOC [Air Operations Center] the evening before the next day's operation on a daily basis, and the forward air controllers, of course, FAC [authorize] most of these flights, and it is coordinated at that time at the AOC's, but it is not formally coordinated in all cases, say, eastern part of Route 7, for instance, that is strictly an interdiction area, the Lao will request that we interdict the road. We will tell them where we have set up interdiction points. But as far as briefing on a daily basis we only keep them informed of the results primarily, but as far as being aware of specific points, no, the request in this case comes in on a general nature, but on closer targets, yes, they are very aware.

ACCELERATION OF US STRIKES AGAINST NORTH LAOS

SENATOR SYMINGTON. Before we go on with your statement, Colonel, the figures for North Laos we have shown a rapid recent acceleration of our strikes against North Laos, something on the order of roughly [deleted] a month to [deleted] a month, correct?

COLONEL TYRRELL. That is correct; yes, sir.

SENATOR SYMINGTON. I think the word "heavy" would be better than rapid.

Also, so far as the Ho Chi Minh Trail goes there has been a heavy decline in South Laos from January to September of 1969.

At the same time there has been a heavy acceleration of the hitting of North Laos—in some months in 1969 the strikes doubled, in others, tripled—there has been a marked deceleration in US efforts against the Ho Chi Minh Trail, correct?

COLONEL TYRRELL. Yes.

SENATOR SYMINGTON. Why?

COLONEL TYRRELL. Well, the reason for that, starting in June —and this was the beginning of the rainy season—and the intensity of truck traffic fell off on the Ho Chi Minh Trail.

---

[4] Military jargon, referring to an official order for an air strike— eds.

Normally, in past years, the activity would have fallen off in Northern Laos about the same time, but this particular year the North Vietnamese intensified their offensive operations during the rainy season. . . .

[On the following day, Assistant Secretary Sullivan again testified, along with Col. Peter T. Russell, US Army "Adviser" in Thailand.]

OTHER COUNTRIES KNOW OF US ACTIVITIES IN LAOS

SENATOR SYMINGTON. Mr. Secretary, you say in view of the provisions of the Geneva accords the existence of an overt military organization in Laos was impossible. You should have added one word, "therefore." It is obvious why there was created an organization known as Deputy JUSMAG [Joint US Military Advisory Group] Thailand, as an integral part of the JUSMAG headquarters.

That type and character of covert operation may be withheld from the American people because of the nature of our Government, but it cannot possibly be withheld from the military attaches of all the other countries; therefore you have a situation which surfaces time and again since I have been a member of this committee, namely the other countries know what we are doing, and actually the only people who do not know what is going on are the American people.

I do not think I ever saw clearer proof of this than the way your statement is worded.

SENATOR FULBRIGHT. Following that up, Mr. Chairman, then what you find in the public sphere at least is that these other countries are reluctant to make a negotiation with us, to trust us at all and the American people are completely frustrated. The American people think we are such good, God-fearing, righteous people and we are the only good people and all other people are bad. They do not know what we are doing. But the other people do. You participated in drawing up the Geneva accords and now you are doing everything to subvert them and go around them and ignore them. You do it surreptitiously and you do it with the highest motives of serving your country. How do you think this appeals to the Russians? You know the Russians know you are doing it. You do not think for a moment the Russians do not know what you are doing in Laos, do you?

MR. SULLIVAN. I think the Russians are pretty well informed.

SENATOR FULBRIGHT. You told us the other day that you did.

MR. SULLIVAN. That is right.

SENATOR FULBRIGHT. But the American people do not know it, they just think we are living up to the agreement. Every now and then some very patriotic Senator will make a speech about how those so-and-so communists never live up to a single treaty they ever made but we, of course, never breach one, we do everything according to the Bible.

This is very confusing to our politics. It is very hard to make any sense of our politics at all and Americans get very impatient with delays in reaching agreements. They do not know that the others know we are doubledealing just like they are. I do not mean that they are not, too. They probably are doing the same thing, but I do not see why you do not, both you and the Russians, go on and do it aboveboard.

SENATOR SYMINGTON. . . . Coming down to page three of your statement, is this $3,940 million [sic] pay to the Thai Express Transportation Organization—who owns the Thai Express Transportation Organization?

COLONEL RUSSELL. The Royal Thai Government. It is a Government monopoly.

SENATOR FULBRIGHT. Is the Prime Minister the principal stockholder, or the Government?

COLONEL RUSSELL. I have no idea, sir.

SENATOR FULBRIGHT. You do not know whether it is private or not?

COLONEL RUSSELL. No, sir.

SENATOR FULBRIGHT. You do not know any more about that than you do your noncommissioned officers clubs, do you?

COLONEL RUSSELL. No, sir.

SENATOR FULBRIGHT. You never made an audit of it?

COLONEL RUSSELL. No, sir.

SENATOR FULBRIGHT. You do not know what the proper charges should be?

COLONEL RUSSELL. All of our services are provided under a contract that was negotiated with the Royal Thai Government by the US Army Support Command based in Korat.

SENATOR FULBRIGHT. Did anybody ever audit this? Do you have an audit of the profits of this Thai Express Transportation Co.?

COLONEL RUSSELL. I am only a user of the facility and not a negotiator or a supervisor of the ETO.

SENATOR FULBRIGHT. What I am getting at is this: the corruption we find within our own body and then in connection with doing business with these foreign companies is becoming a scandal. It seems to me there ought to be some idea of whether we pay these express charges, do we not?

COLONEL RUSSELL. Yes, sir.

SENATOR FULBRIGHT. This $3.9 million [*sic*] went to this express company?

COLONEL RUSSELL. Yes, sir.

SENATOR FULBRIGHT. For carrying ammunition to save Thailand. It is really to save Thailand, is that not the excuse you are fighting in Laos? Is it not?

COLONEL RUSSELL. I am not qualified to answer it.

SENATOR FULBRIGHT. Is it, Mr. Sullivan?

MR. SULLIVAN. I think we had testimony here in the last couple of days that there are several reasons why we are in Laos.

SENATOR FULBRIGHT. That is one of them?

MR. SULLIVAN. That is included as one of them.

SENATOR FULBRIGHT. Probably the principal one.

MR. SULLIVAN. I would not think it is the principal one, no, sir.

SENATOR FULBRIGHT. What is the principal one?

MR. SULLIVAN. Well, the scale of activity in Laos, I think is relative to our concern with Vietnam.

SENATOR FULBRIGHT. Do you also pay a Lao organization transportation charges to transport these ammunition and goods across the river?

COLONEL RUSSELL. No, sir. That is done under the same contract.

SENATOR FULBRIGHT. The same contract, you pay the Thais? You do not have a similar organization in Laos?

COLONEL RUSSELL. I have no operations inside Laos.

SENATOR FULBRIGHT. Is there one, Mr. Ambassador?

MR. SULLIVAN. Goods are transported by the ETO to depots and warehouses on the Lao side of the river and at that stage they become the property of the Lao Armed Forces, and Lao Armed Forces undertake their own disposition of movement of them from there on.

SENATOR FULBRIGHT. Is there a ferry charge across the river included in the ETO charge?

MR. SULLIVAN. I believe it is included in the contract.

COLONEL RUSSELL. Yes.

SENATOR FULBRIGHT. Is that ferry a Lao ferry or a Thai ferry?

COLONEL RUSSELL. I do not know, but I believe they are Thai ferries or a combination.

MR. SULLIVAN. I believe it is a Lao company.

SENATOR FULBRIGHT. Do you know who owns it? Do you know who owns the ferry?

COLONEL RUSSELL. No, sir, I do not.

SENATOR FULBRIGHT. And you do not know who owns the ETO?

COLONEL RUSSELL. I believe the Thai Government owns the ETO.

SENATOR FULBRIGHT. Do you have any real evidence? You believe that. Do you have any evidence rather than just a vague belief?

COLONEL RUSSELL. No, sir, but I can provide it for the record.

SENATOR FULBRIGHT. I think it ought to be.

(The material requested follows.)

Khamsouk Luangkhot, a Lao national Assemblyman, is the principal director of the Lao Transport Association (LTA), which has the monopoly to transport commercial goods coming to Laos from Thailand.

A Lao company, *La Société de Gestion d'Outillage Public de la Province de Vientiane,* leases the Nongkhai-Thadena ferry. The company is more frequently known by its initials SOGOV. It is a joint government/private transportation enterprise. The government owns one-third of the stock. Khamsouk Luangkhot also owns the ferry that SOGOV leases.

OWNERSHIP OF THE EXPRESS
TRANSPORTATION ORGANIZATION

ETO, since 1956, has been the only concern authorized by Thai law to transport in-transit and re-export cargo. It is wholly Thai government owned; its profits go to the Thai treasury. The Chairman of its Board of Directors is always the current Thai Minister of Communications—currently Air Chief Marshall Dawee Chullaspya. The Director of its Executive Committee is Lieutenant General Jitt Sundhanond, Chief Executive Officer of the ETO and Director, Defense Fuel Organization.

TOO MUCH PROFIT BY LOCAL
OFFICIALS ASSERTED

SENATOR FULBRIGHT. I think the continuation of these arrangements that are tainted with profit by the officials of these governments obviously creates a situation where they never want us to leave and they bring all the pressure they can to keep us there.

There is just too much profit in it for them. What happens in the war, I think it is quite incidental to them, is it not, in Laos, to those who become involved in the moneymaking aspect of it?

COLONEL RUSSELL. I do not know the answer.

SENATOR FULBRIGHT. You do not know the answer.

You are familiar, however, with the revelation in recent weeks of the corruption within the Army itself, are you not?

COLONEL RUSSELL. Some of it, yes, sir.

SENATOR FULBRIGHT. Some of it. You read the newspapers, don't you?

COLONEL RUSSELL. Yes, sir.

SENATOR FULBRIGHT. Do you not think it is a rather disturbing development?

COLONEL RUSSELL. It is to me, sir.

SENATOR FULBRIGHT. It was to me. I never dreamed this went on in our own Armed Forces. Did you?

COLONEL RUSSELL. No, sir.

SENATOR FULBRIGHT. I thought it rather shocking, and I do not like to be part of similar activities in Thailand. It is bad enough to discover it within our own Army, in fact it is worse, but this is a classic case of where we are being exploited by some people in Thailand. . . .

MR. SULLIVAN. If I could speak to the issue in Laos. I think our basic concern, as I said the other day, is to attempt to preserve, even though it may be pretty badly torn, preserve the substance of the 1962 agreements so that eventually we could have a reversion to the conditions which made those agreements possible and on which they were predicated.

Now, the agreements have been violated strenuously by the other side in a clandestine way, which they have never admitted. There is a mechanism to make public these violations, which has been frustrated by the actions of those who are our adversaries and, particularly in this instance the Poles.

SENATOR SYMINGTON. Have they tried to make public all of our violations?

MR. SULLIVAN. Yes, sir.

Now the question is whether these violations, having taken place, we should ignore them entirely or whether we should adopt what has been the guidance of the policy of the past two administrations. [Deleted.] That is to take certain responsive actions because of the fact that the violations have occurred from the other side. But taking those actions in a form in which we would come out publicly and state we were doing them, would leave the matter very one-sided, and we might end up with the Geneva agreements being completely disavowed by the other side and particularly by the Soviet Union, which had been, after all, the primary partner with us in attempting to establish an agreement in Laos.

If that were to happen, our feeling would be that we would have a polarized situation in Laos. We would then have probably a government in Laos that, bereft of its current abstention from calling upon SEATO for assistance, might feel that it was free to call upon SEATO for assistance, and we would have a greater obligation and a greater immersion of American presence and pressure to go into Laos.

So that this has been a very, very difficult and perplexing problem for us. Our feeling is that the American people deserve to know as much as they can about our foreign policy. But if we tell them in a manner which makes it possible for our adversaries to use the information contrary to our interests, then, it seems to us, that a better course would be to resort to telling the representatives of the American people and the Congress and the Senate about this subject. . . .

WHY PRETEND GENEVA AGREEMENTS ARE OF VALUE?

SENATOR FULBRIGHT. If both sides are not living up to the Geneva agreements, what is the use of pretending it is of any value?

MR. SULLIVAN. I think our consideration is that the value would be in the future when negotiations are started. Our effort is to try to get negotiations resumed on this and reestablish it. I think our chances of doing this depend, as you said the other day, to some great extent on the outcome of the situation in Vietnam, and if there is a situation which would permit the reestablishment of the 1962 agreements, and permit a neutral regime to obtain in Laos, that we hope would lead to a situation in which we could quietly disengage from the military activities that are currently there.

SENATOR AIKEN. Wouldn't the accords be completely divorced from SEATO?

MR. SULLIVAN. There is—1962 agreements. There is a provision in the 1962 agreements, you see, in which the Royal Lao Government says that it will not exercise its right to call upon SEATO, and the SEATO members who happen to be parties to the 1962 agreements said they would respect that decision by the Royal Lao Government.

SENATOR FULBRIGHT. But that was a unilateral announcement.

MR. SULLIVAN. That is the point I make. If this regime collapsed, a polarized government, a right wing government, if we can call it that, would call upon SEATO.

SENATOR SYMINGTON. Do you think any member of SEATO besides us would answer the call?

MR. SULLIVAN. I imagine the Thai would be responsive.

SENATOR SYMINGTON. In effect, that would be because of us, would it not?

MR. SULLIVAN. Well, sir, I think there is a difference between bodies and lives and dollars, and I think that in the instance of payments that are made to offset contributions by lives—

SENATOR SYMINGTON. I just meant that whatever happened we would finance Thailand. They have helped us very little in Vietnam and except for Korea, and to a lesser extent Australia, who else has really helped?

MR. SULLIVAN. The question I was addressing was would the United States have a greater obligation then, and in theory I think we would. As I have said constantly here, currently we believe we have no commitment in Laos. Our actions could be reversible today. They could, perhaps, be reversible more because they are not matters of the public record, than they could be if they were. That is another consideration.

But our primary concern is to try to preserve the possibility of returning to what we had hoped in 1962 was going to be a settlement that would arrange to get everybody out of Laos, and leave the Lao to their own devices. . . .

ARE OUR ACTIONS THAT
OF AN OPEN SOCIETY?

SENATOR SYMINGTON. We incur hundreds of thousands of US casualties because we are opposed to a closed society. We say we are an open society, and the enemy is a closed society.

Accepting that premise, it would appear logical for them not to tell their people; but it is sort of a twist on our basic philosophy about the importance of containing communism.

Here we are telling Americans they must fight and die to maintain an open society, but not telling our people what we are doing. That would seem the characteristic of a closed society. We are fighting a big war in Laos, even if we do not have ground troops there. Testimony for three days has been to that effect, yet we are still trying to hide it not only from the people but also from the Congress. I do not see why this Administration believes there is any responsibility on their part to mask all this to the same degree and nature it has been masked in past years.

MR. SULLIVAN. I must say, Mr. Chairman, that I consider these hearings as a very sincere token of an open society. In other words that we are telling the representatives of the people, and the question then is whether the security interests or the national interests—

SENATOR SYMINGTON. You would not go so far as to say we were holding them because the State Department had been urging us to hold them, would you?

MR. SULLIVAN. No, sir. But I would say that every Senator, every Congressman, who has ever come to Laos any time I was there was fully and completely informed on all our actions, and what we did—I have appeared before this committee at other times.

SENATOR SYMINGTON. I understand that, but it is a non sequitur as against what we have been talking about.

MR. SULLIVAN. All right, sir.

PREVIOUS TESTIMONY TO COMMITTEE

SENATOR FULBRIGHT. When did our operation begin? Has it been going on just a few weeks or when did the support of the Air Force and bombing become significant?

MR. SULLIVAN. I think the testimony we have had over the past few days, sir, has traced that from 1964, the incidence of first air action over Laos.

SENATOR FULBRIGHT. 1964.

Well, you have just said that your reports to this committee are evidence of our open society. I was under the impression that we did not have an advisory or military training organization in Laos much less that we were carrying on bombing raids.

MR. SULLIVAN. Well, I have testified before this committee in the past, I believe, on the same subject.

SENATOR FULBRIGHT. I thought your testimony before was to the effect that we did not have advisory organizations in Laos or military training.

MR. SULLIVAN. We have not had advisory organizations in Laos, and the training that we are talking about is being undertaken in Thailand.

SENATOR FULBRIGHT. Or military action by our Air Force there. I thought that was the testimony.

MR. SULLIVAN. I do not recall ever having given any testimony to that effect. I have given testimony concerning—

SENATOR FULBRIGHT. I misunderstood it, I guess.

In your own testimony in 1968 before this committee, Senator Cooper was questioning, and I quote from page nineteen:

> According to newspaper accounts, three or four thousand troops advised and trained by the US advisers, equipped with howitzers and Wessons, and ammunition, according to the newspaper reports, these troops just fled and abandoned the howitzers and abandoned the ammunition and no fight at all after five or six years of our training.

Then he said:

> You said a while ago that Souvanna Phouma was
> considered and accepted as a nationalist and fight-
> ing for that country. How do you explain the fact
> that these people flee again after they are trained?

Your answer then was this:

> Ambassador Sullivan. I would like just to correct
> the record, we do not have a military training and
> advisory organization in Laos.
> And we, therefore, do not have advisers with
> these troops. We don't have advisers with them.
> However, some of these units probably had been
> trained in Thailand under American supervision,
> but we don't have people with them. We don't have
> a military advisory group there.

I learned yesterday that we do have a very substantial group
of military people there.

MR. SULLIVAN. No, sir. I think if you will read what I said
we do not have advisers with the units, and they do not go out
into combat action with the units.

SENATOR FULBRIGHT. I did not have any idea that we were
doing anything like we are. What is a better way to describe
what we are doing? We are just fighting our own war?

MR. SULLIVAN. No, sir. There are—the Americans who fly in
aircraft certainly on many occasions engage in combat.

AMERICAN ARMY PERSONNEL IN LAOS

SENATOR FULBRIGHT. How many people? I thought it was
the other day, wasn't it, when it was mentioned that over 700
American personnel and more than 100 Army people in Laos?

MR. SULLIVAN. I would have to get it. What is the Army
figure?

SENATOR FULBRIGHT. What do they do there, do they just

spend all the time in the officers' club? Don't they do something? Don't they advise and train and do something? What do they do?

MR. SULLIVAN. As Colonel Duskin testified the other day we have [delete] Army personnel at each of the five regional headquarters.

SENATOR FULBRIGHT. What do they do?

MR. SULLIVAN. Well, Colonel Duskin, perhaps, can give a breakdown of their activities.

COLONEL DUSKIN.[5] I would like to testify on that. The personnel at the military regional headquarters do provide advice insofar as key personnel can at the individual level. But these are sizable areas in Laos, and this is—the only people involved in this role are those people at the regional level. I have also a sizable communications facility that is provided. It provides work in Vientiane and through operations and intelligence.

SENATOR FULBRIGHT. But they do not ever give them advice?

COLONEL DUSKIN. I did not say that.

SENATOR FULBRIGHT. I am asking you, do they or don't they?

COLONEL DUSKIN. My personnel at regional level do provide advice, yes.

SENATOR FULBRIGHT. Then what is an advisory group?

COLONEL DUSKIN. An advisory group, sir, is an organization that is constituted for the sole mission to provide advice to include it down to lower unit levels.

SENATOR FULBRIGHT. So if they do anything else they are not advisory. We are getting so technical with your semantics it is impossible for us to understand. If they give advice it does not matter whether they are in an organized group, solely and exclusively in such an organization, is it? What I think this testimony tends to do is to mislead the committee when you rely upon these fine-spun theories as to how you describe them. You are in there in force, aren't you, and you are working with the Lao. You are bombing for them, protecting their troops whenever they are attacked; is that not true?

COLONEL DUSKIN. I said there is an air campaign which is conducted in Laos.

[5] Lt. Col. Edward Duskin, U.S. "adviser" in Laos—eds.

COMMITTEE MEMBERS FELT NOTHING
OF SIGNIFICANCE BEING DONE IN LAOS

SENATOR FULBRIGHT. I think in all fairness too, Mr. Sullivan, when you look at the whole record of this testimony you presented to this committee in 1968, I think we were justified in coming away from that hearing with a feeling that we were not doing anything of any significance in Laos; that it was very minor, that we had no advisory groups there.

Then later on the impression is quite clear, on page twenty-three, that we were not doing any bombing; that whatever was being done, was being done by the Lao Air Force. I will read you what you said. This is your statement:

Senator Symington asked you as follows:

> Mr. Ambassador, we have been all over this before many times, and this is not a record that is published on any basis and I would just ask respectfully, but very sincerely, how far would they have to succeed before we would have to begin to move our own military forces in there, if we wanted to save the country, on a different basis than we are operating today with your people [deleted] and so forth.
>
> AMBASSADOR SULLIVAN. That would be a very serious judgment, as you know, that would require looking at a lot of circumstances.
>
> SENATOR SYMINGTON. I ask this because we had another witness who will come before this committee on Tuesday, and I was distressed to see the extent of the map that was colored showing the amount that still was under control of the Pathet Lao and the communists.
>
> AMBASSADOR SULLIVAN. Well, certainly, it is fairly extensive. As you know, the population live very largely in the river valley, the Mekong valley, and I would say between seventy-five and eighty

percent of the population are under government control. The Pathet Lao, however, and the North Vietnamese are able to wander through these hills up in the area contiguous to North Vietnam.

If they came down into the valley, if they came out of the hills and came down in conventional force to the valley in the first place they, the communists, would have to come down in quite considerable force, I believe, because they would have to come down out of those areas into an area where they would be susceptible to air action because the Lao Air Force can and has blunted them when they have come down before into the valley, and if they came down and established themselves in the valley and constituted by their presence there is a direct threat to Thailand, they would be deliberately upsetting the balance, upsetting the apple cart, changing the picture and it would present the President with a very, very serious situation.

That very clearly leaves the impression that the Lao Air Force, not the US Air Force, is doing what is being done.

In going through this hearing in 1968, there was a tentative probing on our part to see what we were doing, and I would think it is a fair interpretation of this whole record that you indicated we were not doing much, if anything, directly.

LITTLE COMMUNICATION BETWEEN COMMITTEE AND EXECUTIVE BRANCH

Mr. Sullivan, you cited this as evidence of ours being an open society, your coming and testifying before this committee in 1968. If you knew how very little this committee has been enlightened from time to time by the Department of State, I think you would think twice before you say that, because there has been very little communication.

The previous Secretary of State [Dean Rusk] refused to come over for two years, come at all. The present Secretary of State has been here once in open session, and I think twice in secret session. . . .

SENATOR FULBRIGHT. But he has agreed to come later. I did not insist on it earlier because he was a new man and he had not had any previous experience. But there is a minimum of enlightenment of this committee by anybody in the executive. I do not know whether they tell other committees any more or not, but I doubt it. I think this 1968 record of yours—a secret record—does not reveal anything like what you have revealed in these statements this week to this subcommittee.

The testimony of these Army officers, and this statement I mentioned a moment ago, go much further as to what we are actually doing there than I have ever been exposed to before.

MR. SULLIVAN. I do not have that record in front of me, Mr. Chairman.

SENATOR FULBRIGHT. You are welcome to look at it.

MR. SULLIVAN. But if there were any direct questions asked of me about US air operations—

SENATOR FULBRIGHT. You see, we did not know enough to ask those direct questions, and this is what I meant about quibbling about whether the US role in Laos is exclusively advisory. When you take a group of Senators who are primarily concerned with their own states, and only incidentally in this foreign affairs area, the responsibility for which we are given by the Senate, we do not know enough to ask you these questions unless you are willing to volunteer the information. There is no way for us to ask you questions about things we don't know you are doing.

MR. SULLIVAN. I assume in that discussion I did talk about US air operations in Laos, but the specific mention there—

SENATOR FULBRIGHT. If you did the staff has not discovered it. Is there anything in there? Well, I will say this, I think the surprise that is evidenced by the Chairman of the subcommittee and others, that they did not know the extent of this involvement until these hearings, is pretty clear evidence that we were not aware of these activities, although we had had some hearings on it.

I would not wish to be too critical of you in saying that you were not asked and you did not give an incorrect answer, because we did not ask the right questions. The only way for us to get the information is if you volunteer it or to have a study like this with our staff people going out to find the information first and give it to the committee.

So I would not say there is anything to brag about on the openness of the society if what you have given to these committees is the evidence of it. Very limited information is given to us.

I do not know whether we know all of it now. I have no idea whether we do or not. But what we do know, it seems to me, ought to be made public. . . .[6]

---

[6] Although these hearings were held in October, 1969, they were not published until April of the following year, and only after considerable material had been deleted.—eds.

24

Lao Patriotic Front's "Five Points" (March 6, 1970)*

For many years now, the US imperialists have carried out a policy of unceasing intervention and aggression in Laos in an attempt to turn it into a new colony and a military base of the United States in Southeast Asia.

In defiance of its obligations under the 1954 Geneva agreements and the 1962 Geneva agreements on Laos, the United States has trampled upon the independence and sovereignty and undermined the peace and neutrality of Laos. Over the past eight years, its intervention and aggression in Laos have grown ever more brazen. The United States, through a military *putsch,* has toppled the National Union Government which received investiture from the King and recognition from the 1962 Geneva agreements on Laos, and rigged up a stooge administration headed by Prince Souvanna Phouma and following a so-called policy of "peace and neutrality" by the agency of that administration, it has conducted a "special war" in Laos, it has launched bombing raids against the Laos territory, and used the Lao puppet army for repeated nibbling attacks on the areas under the control of the Lao Patriotic Forces.

True to the Lao people's aspirations for a peaceful, independent, neutral, democratic, unified and prosperous Laos, the Lao Patriotic Front has always correctly implemented the 1962 Geneva agreements on Laos. In close alliance with the Lao Patriotic Neutralist Forces, it has exercised along with the people its legitimate right of self-defense, it has resolutely fought against the US "special war"; it has opposed the nibbling attacks of the Americans and their stooges; it has inflicted on them fitting blows, and has recorded increasing victories.

* Statement of the Central Committee of the Neo Lao Hak Sat [Lao Patriotic Front], broadcast in English by Pathet Lao clandestine radio, March 9, 1970.

While fighting against the US intervention and aggression, the Lao Patriotic Front has repeatedly demonstrated its good will with regard to a peaceful settlement of the Lao problem. . . .

Yet the United States and the Vientiane Administration have ignored all reasonable and logical proposals made by the Lao Patriotic Front. Since notably Nixon took office as President of the United States, the United States has intensified the war in Laos with even greater obstination.

The United States has brought more US and Thailand military personnel, weapons and war materiel into Laos; it has strengthened the puppet army and the special forces under Vang Pao's command; it has launched repeated nibbling attacks against many places controlled by the patriotic [as received] from the north to the south of the country. It has also put in action a modern air force for saturation bombings against the territory of Laos, thus perpetrating extremely barbarous crimes against the Lao people.

Beginning August, 1969, it mustered about fifty battalions of puppet troops and Thailand mercenaries, conducted operation "Kukiet" to nibble at the Plain of Jars–Xieng Khouang area. Meanwhile, it launched several nibbling operations against the liberated zone in central and southern Laos. What is particularly serious, since February 17, 1970, the United States has used B-52 and planes of the types for mass bombings against the Plain of Jars—Xieng Khouang area, as well as against central and southern Laos, destroying hundreds of villages and savagely massacring the civilian population.

But the armed forces and people, resolved to defend the liberated areas, have smashed the nibbling attack of the United States and its agents in the Plain of Jars–Xieng Khouang area as well as other places. They have wiped out an important part of the US commanded and fostered "special forces" and dealt a heavy blow at the "prestige" of the US Air Force.

To cover up the Nixon Administration's "escalation" of the war in Laos, the United States and the Vientiane Administration have launched a campaign of slander against the Lao Patriotic Front and the Democratic Republic of Vietnam. At the same time, they have resorted to deceitful allegations about "peace" in an attempt to fool US and world public opinion which is condemning the Nixon war of aggression in Laos.

The Nixon Administration's attempt to "escalate" the aggressive war has brought about the present tension in Laos, and poses an extremely serious threat to peace and security in Indochina and Southeast Asia.

In face of the tension in Laos, the Lao Patriotic Front affirms the necessity of ending the US war and finding a political solution to the Lao problem.

The position of the Lao Patriotic Front is: The peaceful settlement of the Lao problem must be based on the 1962 Geneva agreements on Laos and on the actual situation in Laos. In more concrete terms:

> 1. All countries respect the sovereignty, independence, neutrality, unity and territorial integrity of the Kingdom of Laos, as provided for in the 1962 Geneva agreements on Laos. The United States must put an end to its intervention and aggression in Laos, stop escalating the war, completely cease the bombing of the Lao territory, withdraw from Laos all US advisers and military personnel as well as all US weapons and war materiel, and stop using military bases in Thailand and Thailand mercenaries for purposes of aggression against Laos. It must stop using Lao territory for intervention and aggression against other countries.
>
> 2. In accordance with the 1962 Geneva agreements, the Kingdom of Laos refrains from joining any military alliance with foreign countries, and from allowing foreign countries to establish military bases in Laos and to introduce troops and military personnel into its territory.
>
> The Kingdom of Laos follows a foreign policy of peace and neutrality, establishes relations with other countries in accordance with the five principles of peaceful coexistence, and accepts aid with no political conditions attached from all countries. With the other Indochinese countries, it establishes

friendly and good neighbour relations on the basis of the five principles of peaceful coexistence and of the principles of the 1954 Geneva agreements on Indochina and the 1962 Geneva agreements on Laos.

With regard to the Democratic Republic of Vietnam and the Republic of South Vietnam, it respects Vietnam's independence, sovereignty, unity and territorial integrity. With regard to the Kingdom of Cambodia, it respects the latter's independence, sovereignty, neutrality and territorial integrity within its present borders.

3. To respect to the throne, to hold free and democratic general elections, to elect a national assembly and to set up a democratic government on [as received] national union truly representative of the Lao people of all nationalities, to build a peaceful, independent, neutral, democratic, unified, and prosperous Laos.

4. During the period from the restoration of peace to the general elections for setting up the national assembly, the parties concerned shall, in a spirit of national concord, equality and mutual respect, hold a consultative political conference composed of representatives of all Lao parties concerned in order to deal with all the affairs of Laos, and set up a provisional coalition government. The parties shall reach agreement on the establishment of a security zone to ensure the normal functioning of the consultative political conference and the provisional coalition government, free from all attempts at sabotage or pressure by forces from inside or outside Laos.

5. The unification of Laos shall be achieved through consultations between the Lao parties on the principle of equality and national concord. Pending this unification, no party shall use force to encroach upon or nibble at the areas controlled by another. The pro-American forces must withdraw

forthwith from the areas they have illegally occupied, and resettle in their native places those people who have been forcibly removed from there. At the same time, they must pay compensations for damages caused to them. Each party pledges itself to refrain from discrimination and reprisals against those who have collaborated with another party.

The above-mentioned position of the Lao Patriotic Front for the settlement of the Lao problem meets the Lao people's earnest aspirations and is consistent with the interests of peace and security in Indochina, Southeast Asia and the world. It is the just basis of a solution to the Lao problem.

The Lao problem must be settled among the Lao parties concerned. To create conditions for the Lao parties concerned to meet, the United States must, as an immediate step, stop escalating the war, and stop complete [as received] the bombing of Lao territory without posing any condition.

The Lao people deeply aspire for independence, freedom and peace. If the United States obdurately persists in its aggressive schemes, the Lao Patriotic Front, the Lao Patriotic Neutralist Forces and the Lao people are resolved to fight on till total victory.

The Lao Patriotic Front earnestly calls on the Laos people of all nationalities to closely unite around the military alliance between the Lao Patriotic Front and the Lao Patriotic Neutralist forces, to heighten their vigilance, to stand ready and resolved to smash all military plans and deceitful schemes of the United States and its agents with a view to defending the liberated zone, safeguarding their fundamental national rights and contributing to the preservation of peace in Indochina and Southeast Asia.

The Lao Patriotic Front calls on the peace and justice loving governments, the American people and the world's peoples strongly [to] support the Lao people's just struggle, and resolutely demand that the United States stop its war of aggression in Laos, and, as an immediate step, put a complete end to the bombing of Lao territory.

With the broad sympathy and strong support of the world's

peoples, the entire Lao people, closely united, are sure to defeat the US aggressors and their agents, and successfully build a peaceful, independent, neutral, democratic, unified and prosperous Laos.

25

Interview with Prince Souphanouvong in the Liberated Zone of Laos (March, 1970)

MADELINE RIFFAUD *

RIFFAUD: In his March 6, 1970 statement concerning Laos,[1] Nixon claimed that he was only pursuing the policy of previous US administrations. May I ask Your Highness for his opinion on this subject?

SOUPHANOUVONG: Recently international opinion and especially American opinion has expressed great concern about the situation in Laos, which might develop into "a second Vietnam," and strongly criticized Nixon's adventurist policy. Faced with this situation, Nixon has been forced to provide a hasty explanation of both the situation in Laos and US policy there. In this explanation Nixon indeed stated that he was only pursuing the policy of previous US administrations. He thus aimed at absolving himself of responsibility for the war escalation in Laos and also at reassuring public opinion.

THE UNITED STATES HAS SABOTAGED
THE 1962 GENEVA AGREEMENTS

Let us look back for a while at the previous US administrations' policy concerning Laos. In Eisenhower's time, as early as the fifties, Nixon was among the most frantic advocates of Eisenhower's policy of aggression and intervention. That administration forced Laos to accept the protective umbrella of

---

* From L'Humanité [Paris], March 26, 1970. [Broadcast by Pathet Lao Radio, April 2, 1970] slightly condensed, by permission.

[1] See Selection 20 in this volume—eds.

SEATO, provided aid amounting to three hundred million dollars (until the end of 1960) for the Laotian reactionaries, eighty-five percent of this aid being for military purposes, and overthrew the National Coalition Government established in 1957 with Pathet Lao participation. In the days of Kennedy and Johnson, as a result of its military defeats and political isolation, the United States was forced to accept the 1962 Geneva agreements concerning Laos and to recognize Laos's independence, sovereignty, and neutrality. However, the US administration soon shamelessly sabotaged these Geneva agreements, overthrew the tripartite national coalition government, and established in Vientiane a puppet administration as an instrument for pursuing its aggressive war in Laos under the guise of a "special war."

It is, therefore, obvious that US policy toward Laos, from Eisenhower to Johnson, was neither more nor less than a policy of intervention and aggression.

HOW NIXON INTENSIFIED THE WAR

By stating that the present government is only continuing the policy pursued by previous governments, Nixon wished to camouflage his war escalation in Laos on the one hand, and on the other acknowledged for the first time, in his capacity as US President, the existence of the US Air Force activities, the presence of American military specialists in Laos, and so forth.

This was a public admission that the United States was waging war in Laos and was sabotaging the 1962 Geneva agreements on Laos. Previous US administrations had always denied all this or tried to conceal it by means of thousands of subterfuges.

Thus pursuing the aggressive policy of the US administrations which he has replaced, Nixon has intensified the escalation since his accession to power and increased the violence of the war in Laos to a degree unknown in the days of previous administrations.

Some 12,000 US military "advisers," including 1,200 Green

Berets, have arrived in Laos. Furthermore, since Nixon's accession to power, several units of mercenary Thai troops have been brought in by the United States with a view to using them in the fighting in Laos. The Lao puppet armed forces have been reorganized and brought to strength, in particular the Vang Pao special forces whose strength has been increased from 15,000 to 20,000 men. The Americans organize, equip, feed, and control these forces directly and they consider them to be completely reliable shock troops intended for waging their long-term aggressive war in Laos.

Thus the Nixon administration has not only increased both the ground and other forces in Laos but also intensified the use of the air force for bombing and machine gunning Laotian territory and for spreading harmful chemical products over it on a large scale and with unprecedented violence.

And there is a still graver danger: The American B-52's extended the escalation to northern Laos at a time when the puppet troops were sustaining heavy defeats in the Xieng Khouang region and on the Plain of Jars in February, 1970. Even American and Western press agencies have published the information that at the end of 1969 and the beginning of 1970 US strategic and tactical planes of various types dropped 3,000 tons of bombs daily over Laotian territory.

During an offensive campaign against the Xieng Khouang region and the Plain of Jars, which have been controlled by the patriotic Laotian forces since August, 1969, the American puppets have escalated the war in Laos to a degree of fierceness which is fraught with the most dangerous consequences.

During this military operation the United States mobilized major ground forces (about fifty battalions) and the Vang Pao special forces, with the participation of the US Green Berets and Thai mercenary units. These forces received the greatest possible air support from the US Air Force, including the strategic B-52 planes whose mass bombing destroyed almost all the localities and populous sectors of this region.

One may say that this was a very large-scale operation and that it was the fiercest, most horrible, and longest. It was unprecedented in the annals of the US war of aggression in Laos.

Nixon applied in Laos the formula "puppet land forces supported by the greatest possible US fire power."

THE PATRIOTIC FORCES'
COUNTERATTACKS

However, this greatest possible US fire power which even comprised the use of B-52 planes was unable to save the puppet ground forces. After a series of fierce counterattacks which took place on February 10 through 24, 1970, the Lao patriotic forces broke this operation staged by the American puppets and reoccupied completely both the Xieng Khouang region and the Plain of Jars. Therefore, this also means that the notorious US "formula" failed for the first time in Laos and that a fatal blow was struck by the patriotic armed forces and the Lao population against the so-called "Nixon doctrine for Asia."

Despite the fact that it had suffered these defeats and been condemned by public opinion, the Nixon Administration has continued to prove obstinate. Did Nixon not say at random in his statement that the United States' own interests are forcing it to reconsider its present activities in Laos? Laos is an independent and sovereign country, a fact which the Geneva agreements concerning Laos have recognized. Nixon cannot invoke the "interests of the United States" in order to interfere in the internal affairs of Laos.

It is obvious that Nixon's statement on Laos only amounts to a fallacious self-defense full of deceitful arguments which conceal the extremely dangerous new war escalation started by the Nixon Administration in Laos. Indeed these escalations have made the situation in Laos more tense than ever and thus seriously endanger peace in Indochina and Southeast Asia.

THE UNITED STATES MUST CEASE
ITS BOMBINGS

RIFFAUD: What would be, in your opinion, the conditions which would permit a just solution to the Laotian problem to be found in the present context?

SOUPHANOUVONG: Events in Laos have evolved in an extremely dangerous situation as a result of the Nixon Administration's new escalations of the war. The most urgent problem which is presently facing our nation is to put an end as soon as possible to this criminal war of aggression of the United States.

The conditions currently necessary for a settlement of the Laotian problem are contained in our March 6, 1970, declaration, in which we have stressed that a peaceful settlement of the Laotian problem must be based on the 1962 Geneva agreement, as well as on the concrete realities of the present situation in Laos, and that it must be effected between the interested Laotian parties.

In order to create the conditions enabling the interested Laotian parties to meet and resolve the internal affairs of Laos, the United States must immediately put an end to its escalation of the war and completely cease the bombing of Laotian territory, without posing any conditions.

It is only through the cessation of American interference and aggression aaginst our country that a fully guaranteed peace can be restored and a national agreement achieved in Laos: In fact, the increasingly more dangerous course taken by the situation with every passing day is due to American interference and aggression.

Our five-point political solution[2] amply shows all our goodwill and our sincere desire to resolve the Laotian problem. It is both reasonable and in accordance with the concrete realities of the domestic and external situation, and it responds well to the aspirations of the Laotian people and of international opinion. Should the United States and the Vientiane Administration turn a deaf ear or seek in a roundabout way to avoid replying to the five-point political solution advanced by the Laotian Patriotic Front, they would thus assume the entire responsibility themselves.

[2] Selection 24—eds.

RAPPROCHEMENT BETWEEN LAOTIANS
FOR A PEACEFUL SETTLEMENT

RIFFAUD: Your messenger has by now reached Souvanna Phouma in Vientiane. Could you clarify, for the benefit of our readers, the reasons which have induced the Laotian Patriotic Front, currently engaged in a victorious counteroffensive, to make this gesture of appeasement?

SOUPHANOUVONG: We will let pass no occasion and we will spare no effort in order to arrive at a peaceful settlement of the Laotian problem. Thus, following the publication of our five-point political solution for the settlement of the Laotian problem, I have sent my messenger to Vientiane, on behalf of the Laotian Patriotic Front, in order to deliver my letter, together with the declaration of the Laotian Patriotic Front Central Committee containing the five-point solution, to Prince Souvanna Phouma. I have done the same as regards Mr. Khamsouk Keola, Chairman of the Committee of Alliance of the Laotian Patriotic Neutralist Forces.

These are gestures that we have considered necessary to open the way for a meeting between the interested Laotian parties in order to talk about the peaceful settlement of the Laotian problem on the basis of the five-point political solution approved by the Laotian Patriotic Front. A meeting will take place soon between the Laotian Patriotic Front and the Committee of Alliance of the Patriotic Neutralist Forces so as to proceed toward an exchange of views on this solution. . . .

THE AMERICAN PEOPLE

I would like to address to the American people, who are fundamentally attached to freedom, peace, and justice, the cordial greetings of solidarity of the Laotian people. We greatly appreciate the determined struggle movement of the American people against the atrocious war waged by the yankee imperialists in South Vietnam, which has caused so many losses and so much grief to the Nixon Administration, which is intensifying its escalation of the war in Laos. American progressive opinion is seeking by all means to prevent the Nixon Administration from further aggravating the situation to the point of transforming it into a "second Vietnam war."

Our Laotian people are fully capable of distinguishing between the belligerent American leaders who have been constantly stirring up the tension in Laos over the past fifteen years, on the one hand, and the American people who are sympathetically supporting the just struggle of the Laotian people, on the other.

I hope that the American people and all progressive forces in the United States will give concrete and energetic support to the Laotian Patriotic Front's five-point political solution, with the aim of putting an end to the war waged by the Nixon Administration and to the bombing of Laotian territory by the US Air Force, so that the interested Laotian parties may settle the affairs of Laos among themselves.

PART VI

THE WAR
SPREADS
TO CAMBODIA

Introduction

The expansion of the Vietnam war into Cambodia came as a shock and a disappointment to an American public which had been lulled by promises of withdrawal. "Operation Total Victory," however, represented yet another stage in the steady escalation of American involvement that has occurred periodically since 1954, when we replaced the French as the opponents of Vietnamese independence.

In many ways the invasion of Cambodia is just one more bloody episode in a war that has revealed the true character of American foreign policy translated into military terms. For years we have been witnessing saturation bombing, napalm attacks, bulldozing of hamlets, relocation of inhabitants into refugee camps—in a word, genocide committed against Asians. Having given up at an early stage the concept of "counter-insurgency," [1] the American approach to guerrilla warfare has been to destroy all potential guerrilla support; this is accomplished by rendering huge areas of the countryside uninhabitable. Survivors are forced to flee their homes and settle as refugees in overcrowded cities, where America's "allies," the mercenary soldiers, maintain their control.

Laos, a country where American military activities are neither officially acknowledged, nor publicized, is gradually being destroyed. At the time of this writing there are over 600,000 refugees out of a total population of less than three million— or nearly a quarter of the populace.[2] A similar fate awaits Cambodia.

Connected with every war are the propaganda and distortions disseminated by governments in defense of their actions. President Nixon's justification for the "incursion" into Cambodia in terms of eliminating sanctuaries and capturing the secret enemy headquarters (COSVN) was contradicted by his own officials

---

[1] See the Introduction to Part V, this volume—eds.
[2] See Selections 21, 22, this volume.

even before he spoke, and bore no relationship to actual intentions.[3] Indeed, the President's statement that an invasion of Cambodia by American troops would save American lives is a contradiction in terms remarkable for its callousness. It is obvious that American lives would most effectively be saved by immediate withdrawal from Indochina; implicit also in his statement is the assumption that American soldiers are worth more than the hundreds of thousands of Cambodian civilians who will surely perish before the war ends. In Laos and Cambodia, as in Vietnam, the unforgivable immorality of United States policy is exceeded only by its ruthlessness.

With this new escalation of the fighting comes a further weakening of American society. Wars have always had the effect of hindering the operations of democratic institutions and infringing upon civil liberties. The Vietnam war has all but eliminated Congress' role of advice and consent in questions of foreign policy. In February, 1965, American planes began bombing a country with which the US was officially at peace. The Cambodian invasion represents the first time in recent years that the United States invaded a country without obtaining Congressional approval or declaring war. President Nixon's almost mystical invocation of his powers as Commander-in-Chief carries dangerous implications for the future.

[3] See Selections 33, 34, 37, this volume, and "Cambodian Decision: Why President Acted," The *New York Times*, June 30, 1970.

26

The Coup in Phnompenh

DANIEL ROY *

On Monday and Tuesday, March 2 and 3, 1970, Phnompenh was the scene of a "votive" ceremony: all the members of the National Assembly, of the High Council of the Kingdom and of the Royal Government, led by Prince Sisowath Sirik Matak, Council President for the interim, called for the swift recovery of Prince Norodom Sihanouk, Chief of State. And the president of the National Assembly, Cheng Heng, exercising, in accordance with the Constitution, the functions of acting Chief of State, affirmed in a solemn speech "the general will to work toward the union of all Khmers around the person of the Chief of State, Prince Norodom Sihanouk."

The Chief of State, Norodom Sihanouk, and the Council President, General Lon Nol, were absent at this time: both of them, separately, were following a course of medical treatment in France.

On March 18, those same deputies of the National Assembly and those same royal counselors unanimously deposed Norodom Sihanouk, and replaced him with Cheng Heng, ex-director of the central prison. But no one was deceived: the real power passed into the hands of General Lon Nol, now back in Cambodia.

This state of affairs at first astounded all those who knew the extraordinary popularity enjoyed by the heir of the kings of Angkor among the Khmer people—how could such a situation so quickly have come about?

Factually speaking, we may note that on Wednesday, March 4, just a day after the traditional votive assembly, Prince Sirik Matak had carried out a ministerial reorganization, something

* Daniel Roy, "Le Coup de Phnompenh," *Le Monde Diplomatique,* (April, 1970), pp. 12–13, translated by Kathy Brown and the editors. The author, who lived in Southeast Asia for fifteen years, is a former press attaché of Prince Norodom Sihanouk.

which passed by unobserved. General Lon Nol, still absent, already Council President and Minister of Defense, received in addition the portfolio of communications—that is, control over television, radio, and the press. Yem Sambaur, Minister of Justice and Foreign Affairs, became Second Vice President of the Council and Prom Thos, Secretary of State, was named Minister of Commerce and Industry. On his return, therefore, General Lon Nol found a changed situation, but it is impossible to know for certain whether he had deliberately engineered it —for he had often refused to listen to the voice of temptation— or whether his friends had to some extent forced his hand. Still, the fact remains that General Lon Nol seems to be "the strong man" of Cambodia while the apparent organizer of the conspiracy, Prince Sisowath Sirik Matak, is a likely candidate for the throne left vacant since the death of King Suramarith.

The present Assembly was elected September 14, 1966, and those elections were profoundly different from the "consultations" of previous years. Formerly, the rites were simple: Prince Sihanouk, as President of the Sangkum Reastr Niyum, the Popular Socialist Community, chose one candidate for each district: this candidate alone could make use of the Sangkum name and he was in fact the official candidate. In designating the candidates, Sihanouk had taken account of the different tendencies comprising this broad aggregation which had never aspired to be a party: thus, he distributed the candidatures so that the tendencies of the left, center and right were represented in the Assembly pretty much in proportion to their influence in the country. This procedure may be surprising to a Westerner, but it is understandable in Cambodia, a country lacking democratic traditions and where an attempt at French-style parliamentarianism had unquestionably failed, carrying the kingdom to the brink of anarchy and disintegration. Besides, anybody could become a candidate; the Cambodian Communist Party tried its luck, obtaining 1.5 percent of the vote but failing to win a single seat. This system at least had the virtue of clarity; the voter knew where he stood: there were Sihanouk's candidates and . . . the others, none of whom got his vote.

In 1966, the voter found himself at a loss, for Sihanouk—

wishing, no doubt, to avoid accusations of personal power and electoral fakery—allowed several "Sangkumian" candidates to compete in each district.

Thus emerged the curious spectacle of several candidates, all with the same program and the same label, demanding the votes of the electorate. In order to differentiate themselves from one another, they resorted to the most demagogic methods, for the most part using arguments only remotely ideological in character. They outdid one another with hard-to-keep promises; there was a shameless extravagance of publications and pamphlets; favors of all kinds were distributed: offices, honors, money. With few exceptions, it was the rich and the feudal who triumphed, and the candidates of a right which would not identify itself as such eliminated all the left and center-left delegates but three: Hu Nim, Hu Huon and Khieu Samphann.

However, these three survivors of the conservative floodtide were soon accused of all sorts of wrongdoing; rightly or wrongly, they were considered as dangerous revolutionaries, communists and Maoists. The three of them were supposed to be using the "Trojan Horse" tactic, opening the gates of the kingdom to the Maoists. They disappeared and their disappearance was never explained: the official version had them joining the Red resistance forces; another story was to emerge whereby they were "suppressed" by General Lon Nol's men. No matter: after that, Cambodia had a right wing Assembly. Its members, however, continued to affirm their loyalty to the person of the Chief of State, for the time had not yet come to change their tune. At that point, this Assembly did not intend to depose Sihanouk; its only objective was to change the direction of his policy, especially in economic matters.

"REDS" AND "BLUES"

The terms "left" and "right" cannot be taken to mean the same thing in Cambodia as they do in France: in Cambodia there are clans—each with their own "clientele," in the Latin sense—which contend for power in order to reap its concrete benefits. However, keeping this reservation in mind, the term "reds" may serve to describe intellectuals of lower class origin, young reformers, the workers—still very few in number, the teachers, and a few liberal individuals concerned primarily with avoiding a foreign policy which would make Cambodia a United States satellite. Those who may be called "blues" include the property-owners, the businessmen hostile to nationalization and social reforms, and the adherents of the American alliance. These "blues" comprise an aggressive right with enormous pecuniary resources at their disposal. Each of these two rival clans is only a narrow fringe at the two extremes of the Sangkum, for the mass of peasants and small landowners rest content with the "middle road" celebrated by Sihanouk, yet are avowedly hostile to communism—for every Cambodian peasant, owner of his parcel of land, is a natural enemy of any collectivist system.

To go back to the right, it was given impulse above all by what might be called "the party of the villa proprietors." When the Americans maintained a large embassy at Phnompenh, complete with a vast number of auxiliary offices for military, economic and technical aid, numerous functionaries arrived from the United States and it was necessary to find them housing. The Cambodians asked the Americans to remit a twelve or eighteen months' advance on their rent and with this money they had villas built in Phnompenh and at the country's two spas for weekends. While these villas were rapidly being constructed, the proprietors put their own houses at the disposal of the American officials, taking a chance on the hospitality of understanding relatives for a stay of several weeks' duration.

And so, in the excitement, structures were erected which had required but little capital on the part of the builders: a few connections, a few special intermediaries placed in the United States embassy—that was enough.

From the same point of view, it is obvious that the Americans' departure ran counter to the interests of certain merchants and businessmen, of a number of go-betweens, and of certain elements of the underworld; thus, a party was organized which had rather self-serving motives for desiring the return of the dollar.

FALSIFIED ACCOUNTS FOR A
GOOD IMPRESSION

To be sure, these dubious elements could not have taken effective action if other factors had not gradually been causing an aggravation of the social situation. It must be admitted that the regime often boasted of successes which were questionable indeed—or which, to be more exact, cut both ways. That is the way it was with education. On paper, it made a ravishing picture: 200,000 pupils in primary schools in 1953, the date of independence; 1,000,000 pupils in 1969, the number of schools having doubled. The same apparent success for secondary education: 3,000 pupils in 1953, 120,000 in 1969. In 1953 the kingdom had eight grammar schools or high schools; today it has 180.

UNEMPLOYED INTELLECTUALS

As for higher education, which had accommodated only 350 students in 1953: at the start of the most recent university term, over 17,000 were admitted. Such a leap forward inevitably ran into a number of snags: there was a dearth of qualified professors and primary school teachers, a falling standard of curriculum, and degrees were awarded too freely. As a result, thousands of young Cambodians, having had an inadequate education, could not find suitable employment: they had learned too much ever to contemplate returning to the soil, and they had learned too little to attain those positions in the civil service —the only career possible—for which they mistakenly believed themselves qualified. These intellectuals and semi-intellectuals, victims of the demagogy of some of their leftish elders, quickly turned either to sponging off their families or to Maoist revolt. Another dubious success was industrialization, described on the left as the panacea which had enabled Japan, without mineral resources, to make itself the equal of the great Western nations. Efforts were made, but their results were greatly over-estimated in a flurry of widely distributed pamphlets. Let us take a specific example: the cement factory at Chakrey-Ting. First we were told that the yearly production was 50,000 tons, then a production of 100,000 tons was predicted and finally an "expert" (French) cited a production of 150,000 tons. In this manner, production statistics in too many sectors were falsified and presented to the Chief of State by servile flatterers, advisers who did not hesitate to double or triple the real total of production. On the surface, everything was going fine; meanwhile, many state or private enterprises were operating at a deficit.

One textile factory on the outskirts of Phnompenh, which had been unable to dispose of its goods—too expensive in comparison with imported fabric—imperturbably published accounts which were as sensational as they were inaccurate. The plywood factory of Dey-Eth was known to be operating at a loss, as was the Chhlong paper factory, but nobody quite dared to admit it. In the statistics, a large hydroelectric dam like Kirirom was put on the same level with a few indeterminate little clay embankments built up in some remote districts. Under a single heading a large oil refinery and a large brewery would be undifferentiated from pre-industrial saw mills, small metalware workshops, and domestic industries weaving fishnets. One cannot help thinking that some informants, more eager to please than to render accurate accounts, were giving the Chief of State a false idea of the economic situation of the country for the sole purpose of advancing themselves.

Nevertheless, important achievements were made: the Phnompenh–Sihanoukville railway, a glassworks, a tire factory, a sugar refinery, a tractor assembly plant. In agriculture, rice production doubled between 1955 and 1968, mechanization was successfully introduced in some regions, there was progress in rubber plant cultivation. On the whole, one can say that the balance is largely on the positive side. But the rightist opposition was able to accentuate the failures and misrepresentations, while at the same time condemning expenditures for purposes of prestige, such as the construction of a national sports stadium, used primarily for mass demonstrations; the grandiose reception given obscure politicians from countries remote from Cambodia in every respect; the folly of a great State Hotel in Sihanouk-ville when already existing motels lay empty; the inordinate attention given by official publications to projects of little national interest: State cinema, hotel swimming pool . . . etc. Even taking all of these observations into account, it must be acknowledged that no other regime could have done better.

A FATAL ERROR

In the face of a rightist Assembly, which was soon to install an extreme right wing government, Sihanouk had several trump cards in his hand. First of all he had—and undoubtedly still does—the support of the common people, in particular the peasantry, representing nine-tenths of the population; he had the prestige of being the former king in a country where the monarchical tradition is seldom contested; and in addition, he had the support of a progressive left which favored his foreign policy. But perhaps he forgot this leftist bulwark when in September, 1967, he ousted from the government two ministers accused of collusion with China. Although one of the two, Sa Nem, minister of public health, was still almost unknown, the other dismissed minister, Chau Seng, was a really outstanding individual. A professor with a BA from Montpellier, married to a Frenchwoman from the region of Bèziers, Chau Seng—today barely forty years old—had already had a brilliant political career. He had been a dynamic Minister of National Education and, conscious of the importance of communications, was Editor-in-Chief of the only daily French-language newspaper published at that time, la Dépêche du Cambodge, a journal whose political director was Sim Var. A relentless worker and ambitious, too, Chau Seng, was able to win the confidence of Sihanouk, who made him head of his Cabinet. Such quick success inevitably made him the target of considerable hostility, all the more so since his frank way of speaking—often characterized as insolent—antagonized the politicians of the old school. It wasn't long before this conscientious reformer was denounced as a pro-Chinese revolutionary and Sim Var, ex-ambassador to Tokyo and said to have been in contact with

Japanese secret societies manipulated by the CIA, entered into open conflict with his Editor-in-Chief. Chau Seng remained at the head of the newspaper, now renamed *la Nouvelle Dépêche,* while Sim Var assembled a right wing group which published a new daily, the *Phnompenh-Presse,* the mouthpiece of General Lon Nol. The two papers engaged in rather crude polemics and Chau Seng, who had a number of informants, learned for a certainty as early as 1966 that the extreme right, emboldened by General Suharto's coup in Indonesia, had chosen the still reticent General Lon Nol as the instrument of a similar operation. Chau Seng intimated his suspicions to Sihanouk, whereupon General Lon Nol demanded that he leave the cabinet. His demand was met. But some months later, Chau Seng won the second round, returning to the government as Minister of State in charge of the economy and of commerce. The attacks against him resumed, and he was imprudent enough to publish a *communiqué* about a Chinese–Khmer Friendship Society dissolved by Prince Sihanouk because of its manifest interference in the internal politics of Cambodia.

A FREE HAND

Sihanouk, irritated by the excesses of Maoist propaganda and—apparently—convinced by the arguments of Lon Nol and his friends, rid himself of Chau Seng, but in doing so rid himself also of the man who three years earlier had put him on his guard against the schemes of the Lon Nol clan. Since then, Chau Seng has joined neither the "Red Khmers," Hanoi, Moscow, nor Peking. He was forced into exile, to be sure, but took refuge in France. The departure of Chau Seng and his friends meant the disappearance of those rare men comprising a governmental and Sihanoukist left: after that, Cambodian progressives were deprived of parliamentary representation, deprived of their press when *la Dépêche* was banned, and deprived of any legal means of influencing the politics of the country. The right had a free hand and the left no longer had any way to make itself heard save open, armed revolt: this was undoubtedly one of the basic causes of the present situation.

In 1963 Sihanouk had carried through a major economic reform, nationalizing the banking and commercial sectors. The activities of foreign banks were suspended and importers-exporters were obliged to operate through the intermediary of two State companies, Sonexim and Sonaprim. The aim of the reform was to "Khmerize" the economic sector, screening it off from cosmopolitan firms and from the highly active Chinese minority which controlled the major portion of commercial transactions. Another objective was to try to put an end to corruption, to the bribery which was rife in Cambodia as it was in the East as a whole.

Corruption, which is not regarded as unlawful by the majority of Cambodians, is the legacy of the Mandarin system. In former times, the mandarins did not receive official salaries and, like the tax-collectors of early France, they lived and enriched themselves on "gifts" paid out by the inhabitants. The same state of mind persists among many officials; they have not really conceded that they are public servants. Rather, they see themselves as rendering services to the people they administer, and they hardly consider it illicit to receive costly presents and fat envelopes in return for the services they perform, especially since their salaries are very low. These practices cannot be ended by decree; they can only be eliminated either by a protracted process of re-education or else by the drastic methods characteristic of totalitarian regimes. The reforms did not suppress corruption, for the officials of the newly-created financial organizations, as well as the representatives of the special corruption control agencies, simply converted the windfall to their own use. Foreign and private capital, in turn, fled the country; investments ceased; and the state companies were clearly insolvent. Perhaps the reforms were excellent in principle but it must be said that they led to depression—or at the very least, to stagnation.

The right wing government of General Lon Nol did not propose to effectuate these reforms nor to improve their application: at the time of his investiture in August, 1969, Lon Nol promised that there would be no more nationalizations and proclaimed that the state enterprises would be transformed or returned to the private sector. It was a return to the old "liberal" system; however, this system too had carried the country to the brink of bankruptcy. Prince Sihanouk, aware of the failure of his statist reforms, was not hostile to some liberalization, but recommended that it be done gradually, and that a third road, lying between state socialism and the old system, be defined. A new three round bout began: first, on November 15, 1969, Op Kim Ang, Minister of the Economy, and Prom Thos, Minister of Commerce, got approval for their plans to put an end to the monopoly of the state companies, Sonexim and Sonaprim, in the import-export sector; to terminate the state monopolies on alcohol, certain industries, and pharmaceutical products; and above all to authorize the activities of private, foreign, investment banks.

Sihanouk won the second round on December 27, 28 and 29 at the National Congress: he denounced "the captains of industry invading Cambodia with their foreign banks in order to corrupt her elites, undermine her economy, and attempt to change her regime." The Congress unanimously pronounced itself against the re-installation of "foreign banks which serve foreign interests more than they do Cambodian interests and which transfer enormous quantities of exchange stock abroad, leaving only a pittance to the state."

Sihanouk was bound to lose the third round, for the Lon Nol government proceeded as if nothing had happened and in the prince's absence, those who had remained loyal to him on this point finally resigned in protest. And so, Ung Hong Sath, a moderate centrist and Second Vice President of the Council, Chuon Saordi, Minister of Agriculture, Srey-Pong, Secretary of State for Industry, and Tep Chhieu Kheng, Secretary of State for Communications, all relinquished, or were dismissed from, their posts. They were not replaced; their prerogatives passed into the hands of the ministers of the Lon Nol clan. And Sirik Matak, who played a leading role in the whole business, explained that this reorganization was in the logic of things, even though Sihanouk had implored the "resigners" to retain their functions until the end of the legislature.

All the businessmen of the country congratulated themselves on the new economic policy, all the more so since in the wake of the resumption of diplomatic relations with the United States the American embassy was reinstalled, and with it came the dispensers of dollars and the agents of the CIA.

In the face of the elimination of the legal left and the continually hardening stance of the governmental right, the North Vietnamese and the Viet Cong considered that they no longer had to act with discretion. For years, of course, NLF elements pursued by American-South Vietnamese forces had been finding sanctuary in the eastern provinces of Cambodia, but these were small groups which melted into the jungle or forest and after a brief transit rejoined the "liberated zones" of Laos or North Vietnam. The Cambodian army could hardly have opposed this infiltration, both because of its lack of adequate manpower and because the Viet Cong had moved discreetly through sparsely inhabited regions, taking care to avoid major villages and skirting around posts held by the Khmer army. In reprisal, American–South Vietnamese forces had bombed a few villages; then calm had returned until the next incident.

But in 1967–8, there was a sudden resumption of terrorist activity by certain Khmer–Vietminh cells organized before 1954 in a number of provinces to fight against the French and deactivated after the Geneva accords; undoubtedly these cells were concerned with preparing themselves for a new struggle should the extreme right take over Phnompenh, as well as with arranging "zones of reception" for North Vietnamese and Viet Cong elements forced to retreat toward the west.

As for the North Vietnamese and Viet Cong incursions, they became more and more numerous, and instead of making their way toward the north as rapidly as possible, the communist forces did everything in their power to implant themselves and even to establish an administration, supplanting that of the Khmer authorities, over vast areas of Cambodia.

All this put Sihanouk in an untenable position, for it had sorely wounded the Cambodians' national pride, their desire for independence, their concern for neutrality, and their wish to have their frontiers universally respected. One might say, in Marxist language, that these communist forces made themselves the objective allies of the Cambodian right. In any case, these communist bases enabled General Lon Nol to issue a shrill report in September, calling for struggle against the "reds:" "The over-all size of these foreign forces stationed on our territory has risen to between 35,000 and 40,000 men. . . . There is no indication that these foreign units will leave our territory in the near future . . ." The communist bases enabled Lon Nol to call on the people to fight against the Vietnamese invaders at the very same moment that Sihanouk was preparing to ask leaders in Moscow and Peking to intervene with the DRVN and the PRG [1] in an effort to put an end to these installations.

The Chief of State had to make haste, for all Cambodians, while not xenophobes, are Vietnamophobes. This feeling arises from racial antagonism, since the Khmer, a proto-Indochinese of the "brown race," with an Indianized civilization, feels himself to be—and is—radically different from the Vietnamese from the north, the "yellow race" with its sinicized civilization. This Vietnamophobia is explicable also for historic reasons: in their slow movement from the north to the fertile south, the Annamites conquered the rich land of Cochinchina—which had been Khmer territory until recently and where a significant Khmer minority lived under the authority of the Saigon government. The Cambodians have always feared the conquering spirit of the Vietnamese—the agriculturists who seized their best land, the fishermen who swarmed the length of their streams, the traders who managed to divide up the greater part of the commercial affairs of the country with the Chinese, the Vietnamese officials the French placed everywhere in their midst at the time of the protectorate. In short, Cambodians have little liking for Vietnamese, whether from the north or the south, communist or not. Thus, Lon Nol appealed to the lowest instincts of the Khmer people, and in presenting Sihanouk as the friend of the Vietnamese, he could have found no better demagogic argument. These communist bases are thus one of the root causes of the crisis.

THE FINAL PREPARATIONS

As early as 1958, an influential general named Dap Chuon

[1] Democratic Republic of Vietnam (DRVN), Provisional Revolutionary Government (PRG).

had attempted a coup with the help of the American and South Vietnamese special services: departing with his troops from his fief, Siem Reap–Angkor, he had intended to march on Phnompenh and form a pro-American government there. Some days later, abandoned by all his erstwhile supporters, he met a rather inglorious death at the turning of a forest path. Now Lon Nol had led the fighting against this traitorous general, and this memory was to weigh heavily on his mind, accounting for his reservations and hesitation in crossing the Rubicon. But once having assured himself the support of the majority of the Assembly and having consolidated his ascendancy over the government, he went on to make the final preparations—or rather, he entrusted them to the care of a sort of triumvirate composed of the three Vice Presidents: Sirik Matak, Yem Sambaur and Op Kim Ang. Sirik Matak, Minister of the Interior, is a prince—a Sisowath (younger branch) and not a Norodom (older branch). It mustn't be forgotten that in 1941, on the death of King Sisowath Manivong, Prince Sisowath Monireth had expected to accede to the throne. The Crown Council and Admiral Decoux had decided otherwise, but it was easy for Prince Sirik Matak—the nephew of Prince Monireth—to see himself in the royal palace.

Yem Sambaur, Second Vice President, an easy-going magistrate, is an experienced politician. Former Council President, he was barred from public affairs for over ten years for having belonged to the *"régime des partis"* prior to the formation of the Sangkum. Confined to the modest functions of Custodian of the National Library, he was bound to feel some rancor. He had a score to settle and never hid his lack of sympathy for Prince Sihanouk nor concealed his pro-American feelings: it would have been difficult to find a better "contact" with the American services, should the need arise.

Op Kim Ang, Third Vice President, performed the functions of provincial governor and in Kompong-Cham had been involved in a complicated tale of embezzlement of public funds whose instigator, a French tax-collector, died in a strange accident. It is difficult to explain the rapid rise of this authoritarian and zealous official except by his devotion to Lon Nol.

These three men already were in possession of inordinate

powers; indeed, they constituted a cabinet unto themselves, accustomed to making decisions in all areas. Against them, Sihanouk held two trump cards: ground defense was entrusted to Colonel Oam Mannorine, and public security to Colonel Sosthene Fernandez—two men close to Sihanouk by virtue of their family relationship with the Princess Sihanouk. Lon Nol could count on neither their cooperation nor their passivity. Therefore, prior to their dismissal on the eve of the coup, there was an attempt to discredit them. At the National Assembly on February 26, on the interpellation of a right wing deputy, they were accused of smuggling. Op Kim Ang, posing as a confederate, was also interrogated: he stated that he had been on the verge of discovering an enormous ring and that he had unmasked the guilty parties . . . Meanwhile, in the background, thanks to his "cover" of Chief of Police, Lon Non, younger brother of Lon Nol and a dedicated intriguer, was hatching his own plot.

As for those deputies who might possibly have disturbed the show of unanimity which was so carefully being prepared, they were intimidated when additional charges of smuggling were brought against an interim Assembly President, a secretary in his department, and two other deputies. It could just as well have been thirty-six as three; they could have been accused of any crime in the book, and everybody knew it . . .

Lon Nol had great influence over the army, but he had to reckon with General Nhek Tioulong, Chief of Staff of the Royal Khmer Armed Forces, a man of proven loyalty to the government. Opportunely enough, it was discovered that he had reached the age limit and that the state of his health barred him from carrying such heavy responsibilities any longer. Other generals and high-ranking officers were dismissed or discharged under various pretexts.

"FIELD TOUR"

At the end of January, Prince Sirik Matak and Op Kim Ang made a "field tour" to visit the northeastern provinces, to encourage the troops in their fight against the "reds," to apprise themselves of the state of mind of the officers and, as Sihanouk's practice had been, to distribute salt and pieces of fabric . . . and perhaps to distribute other things as well. Be that as it may, they couldn't have lacked money, and Sirik Matak will recall that he had a very good friend in Bangkok, a banker of a sort, an adventurer named Songsak who had managed an incredible escape from Cambodia, bribing the French pilot of an aviation club plane and absconding with the club's funds. In Bangkok this Songsak had joined the fascist Son Ngoc Thanh, puppet president of the Cambodian government during the Japanese occupation and today in the service of the CIA. These two men started the Khmer Serei (Free Khmers), a group composed of Cambodians enlisted in the American special forces in South Vietnam and Thailand. Subsequently, many of these Khmer Serei pretended to "rally" to Sihanouk with their arms, vehicles, women and impedimenta. Thanks to the work of Lon Nol, these pseudo-supporters were infiltrated into the army and the police. Again a "Trojan Horse," for one can imagine the sort of activity that could be carried on by these mercenaries—armed, schooled and trained by CIA agents.

All the precautions having been taken, it was time for action: provocation, "spontaneous" demonstrations, deposition.

AN OVERCONFIDENT DILETTANTE

Prince Sihanouk's dual aim was to ensure the survival of the kingdom within its present boundaries and to prevent the country from becoming overly involved in the Vietnamese conflict, even though he was perfectly aware that some repercussions were inevitable. Thanks to his policy of neutrality and equilibrium, Cambodia had known about fifteen years of relative peace, no mean accomplishment; and if now the conflagration is overtaking this former oasis of tranquility, the responsibility lies with the handful of ambitious men who are playing the part of sorcerors' apprentices.

The men now in power at Phnompenh are going to mobilize all of the means of propaganda they have lately appropriated in order to blacken Sihanouk, his family, and his circle. But for what, without a loss of credibility, can the prince be reproached? He is not a greedy man. If his expenditures were excessive it wasn't so much out of personal pride as it was an effort to restore a little of the kingdom's past glory, its Angkorian splendor.

The prince has also been reproached with having given too much publicity to his Ingres violins, of being a *touche-à-tout,* a dilettante. Poet, composer, musician, singer, actor, screenwriter and film producer—where, then, did he find time to concern himself with affairs of state? Indeed, perhaps the columnists were wrong to place too much emphasis on these harmless diversions in their newspapers, but Prince Sihanouk spent many nights over his political papers, and arts and letters are traditionally cultivated by Far Easterners. Would that we could be sure that the March 18 *putschists* are content with equally innocent distractions.

As for the comparison of his wife, Madame Monique Sihanouk, with Madame Nhu, it is a vulgar joke. Princess Monique, a discreet consort, occupied herself mainly with charities, the Cambodian Red Cross in particular. If she promoted the careers of some of her friends and relatives, if she received a few presents —in fact, she smilingly accepted the simple homage of a few flowers as sufficient introduction—to reproach her seriously for this would be exceedingly hypocritical.

Perhaps there are some men in the prince's circle who enriched themselves a bit faster than others—yet there is no cause to believe that the members of the Lon Nol clan are behaving as pure, absolutely disinterested activists.

Sihanouk's most serious fault is that he permitted the development of a conspiracy about which he had been warned three years earlier by Chau Seng and others. How could he have let such a protracted, minutely prepared operation unfold? Why did he gradually abandon the principal levers of governmental control to Lon Nol and his confederates while men loyal to him were being slandered, threatened, removed, pensioned off or dismissed? And above all, why did he stay away from Cambodia for so long when his very presence would have done much to thwart the schemes of the conspirators?

Unless one supposes some sort of Machiavellian design, there is only one plausible answer to these questions: he didn't think it possible.

This excessive confidence in himself and his popular favor is now obliging him to attempt to regain power, with the help of allies of whom—should he succeed—he will have to be just as wary as he is at present of his momentarily victorious enemies.

27

Apology for the Coup

LON NOL *

My dear compatriots: The Salvation Government, through me, wishes to convey to the National Assembly and the Council of the Kingdom its gratitude for the confidence and support which the people's representatives have unanimously given it by voting to grant it full power. I wish also to pay a well-deserved homage to our two assemblies which constitutionally divested Prince Norodom Sihanouk of his function as Chief of State, thus putting an end to a grave political crisis created by the prince in his personal interest. The decisions made reflect the Khmer people's aspirations and meet the supreme interests of our threatened nation.

I solemnly assure our clergy in the two orders, and especially the chiefs of these orders, our people's elected representatives, our civil and military officials, our students, our youth, and people of all walks of life that the government which I have the honor to head will cope with the situation created by the Viet Cong encampments and exactions within our frontiers; that it will officially use all means—including political, diplomatic, and international ones—to insure respect for our national territorial integrity. We intend also to simultaneously devote our efforts to economic and social development in order to improve the well-being of all our countrymen and not just a privileged minority.

The Salvation Government is aware of the many tasks it must implement to insure Cambodia's survival and future. With the contribution of all of you and national unity being restored, I am convinced that we will be successful in this undertaking.

Finally, we must proclaim that the Salvation Government will strictly follow the policy of independence, neutrality, and territorial integrity set forth by the people in full conformity

* Statement broadcast by Radio Phnompenh, March 20, 1970.

with the fatherland's interests. In this spirit we will maintain friendly relations and cooperation with all countries in the world regardless of regime or ideology and—to state it clearly —without adherence to any military pact or ideologic bloc, contrary to all that Prince Sihanouk has ventured to accuse us of. We will defend our right to live independently within our frontiers, and we demand that other countries respect international law. Only in this way can our foreign friendships flourish.

The Salvation Government has already informed Cambodian diplomatic and consular missions abroad, as well as foreign diplomatic and consular missions and international organizations accredited to Cambodia, that Prince Sihanouk was legally divested of his functions as Chief of State on March 18, 1970, at 1300 [hours] by a unanimous vote of the two houses convened in a Congress according to the provisions of the national Constitution.

28

The Aristocratic Basis of the Cambodian Coup

T. D. ALLMAN *

Phnompenh: Cambodia has taken to its new rulers very calmly. The only serious demonstration of hostility towards the overthrow of Prince Sihanouk came last week when a band of youths tried to stage a march from Kompong Cham to the capital.

Two National Assembly delegates were hacked to death. Kompong Cham is some seventy-five miles from Phnompenh, close to the border with South Vietnam. Government forces had no difficulty in dispersing the demonstrators, who suffered some casualties, but the new administration showed its nervousness by closing down the capital's international airport.

What were the underlying causes of Prince Sihanouk's fall? Perhaps familiarity breeds contempt; and too much success makes a nation forget how lucky it has been with its leaders.

Alone among its neighbors, Cambodia during the last six years has remained peaceful, and largely free of foreign intervention. While Vietnam and Laos were being torn apart, Cambodia—thanks to Prince Sihanouk—remained an island of peace.

Perhaps the years empty of real crisis convinced the people around him that the trick was not so difficult because the master had performed it so well for so long. Although Sihanouk never lost the affection of the common people, the small Cambodian elite, through and with whom he governed, began to feel they could do better on their own. That remains, of course, to be seen.

* T. D. Allman, "Cambodia, Sealing Their Own Doom," *Far Eastern Economic Review* [Hong Kong] (April 2, 1970), p. 6. By permission.

MINOR PROBLEMS

There were problems with the economy; problems with the Viet Cong. But compared to the problems of Cambodia's neighbors, they were minor. Prince Sihanouk's very successes in more important areas made these problems seem bigger than they were, and eventually led most of his fellow members of the Cambodian aristocracy to think they could get along without him.

They forgot, eventually, that it was better to have thousands of communist soldiers behaving themselves just inside the Cambodian frontiers than to have them actively fighting against Cambodians. And this, indeed, remains the real choice for Cambodia: a carefully negotiated accommodation with the communists, or a war which is sure to ravage the country and probably result in its being taken over eventually by the communists. Sihanouk never forgot this.

The underlying cause for Sihanouk's fall probably lay in the fact that although he revolutionized Cambodia's foreign policy, and his own relations with the peasants and workers, he left the traditional Khmer elite free to occupy office and eventually use their traditional power against him.

STILL A HERO

The common people continued to revere Sihanouk, but it was an unending insult for any Cambodian of education and ambition to have to kowtow constantly to the egotistical, but always brilliant leader Sihanouk had proved himself to be.

One Cambodian worker said to me: "Sihanouk is our hero. I cannot judge the new leaders because I do not know what is in their hearts."

But a young member of the educated elite had entirely different thoughts: "We were bored with him and humiliated by him. His damn film shows and endless radio speeches in that sing-song voice. If he tries to come back I hope they shoot him at the airport."

The latter statement represents only a tiny minority of thought in Cambodia. But that minority in the end brought Sihanouk down, because those through whom he governed simply no longer could abide his total preeminence.

The irony of course is that it is Sihanouk's hold on the countryside and the peasants which have made insurrection in Cambodia impossible. The new rulers, as they busy themselves taking back in power and financial opportunities what Sihanouk took away from them, doubtlessly will have a much harder time retaining the loyalty of the countryside—where all real Asian revolutions begin and are won.

By biting off the hand which fed them, the tiny group of aristocrats, army officers and businessmen which toppled Sihanouk may have insured its own doom.

29

Message and Solemn Declaration Against the Conspirators, March 23, 1970

NORODOM SIHANOUK *

I pay my highest respects to Her Majesty the Queen, and extend my respectful regards to the Buddhist clergy and my dear compatriots.

I convey to you my most sincere, constant and affectionate feelings.

The handful of reactionary bourgeois elements and princes, who were able to climb to the highest positions thanks to the Sangkum Reastr Niyum and its President and consequently seize all kinds of privileges, have not only expressed their "gratitude" by "deposing" me illegally but moreover have slung mud at me and vilified me with monstrous slanders and base accusations including the accusation of my betrayal of the motherland "to serve foreign interests."

But my grief at these slanders and accusations is not so acute as my grief at the present very unfortunate fate of our country, which is being wantonly ravaged by the group of traitors and renegades who have unbridledly imposed on the nation a dictatorship (after having violated and thrown overboard the Constitution of the Kingdom) and is leading our country straight to anarchism and war provoked by US imperialism. Our country of Khmer had been known in the world as an oasis of peace and stability for many years, up to the eve of the crisis created by men of the March, 1970, coup d'etat.

At present the liberty, democracy, relative prosperity, unity

* Press release kindly supplied by Professor Gabriel Kolko, of York University, Toronto—eds.

and national union which our people enjoyed not long ago have all been destroyed, reduced to nothing.

Our soldiers have been ordered to give up defending the frontiers and the country's territory to set themselves against their own compatriots and ruthlessly repress all those who dare to show even the slightest verbal opposition to the new fascist power which serves US imperialism.

This is not an accusation made by me but an obvious fact seen by all clear-sighted observers in the world.

The Lon Nol–Sisowath Sirik Matak–Cheng Heng clique declared that I was a "traitor" and that I had "sold out" my country to foreign countries, because I wanted to make our nation avoid, on the one hand, losing its good reputation of wisdom and maturity and, on the other, running into great danger in the future by provoking recklessly and with undue hostility socialist Vietnam which the USA, the richest and biggest military power of the world, failed to bring to its knees.

My devotion and loyalty to the nation have become a crime of high treason, owing to the "good will" of my enemies.

However, their "condemnation" does not disturb me much since they themselves are genuine renegades who have insatiable greed for power, wealth and fame, and are mere cowards who only dare to attack Sihanouk in his absence and stab him in the back.

Therefore this despicable clique will not be able to affect me or make me fall back from my unshakable determination to defend the supreme and long-term interests of my motherland and her liberty.

The millions of Khmers at home and the thousands of Khmers abroad will certainly very soon uphold the banner of revolt against the reactionary Lon Nol–Sirik Matak–Cheng Heng clique and its masters—the US imperialists. The patriotic Khmers will overthrow these traitors and drive their accomplices and their US masters out of our country. After victory, our patriots will build up a new Kampuchea whose power will remain forever in the hands of the progressive, industrious and pure working people, who will ensure that our motherland will have a bright future with social justice, equality and fraternity among all Khmers.

The treason, cowardice, slanders, and the despicable attack by the reactionaries have opened my eyes and made me painfully aware of my unpardonable naivete and my misjudgment, which made me believe that a free, democratic, peaceful, prosperous and happy country could be built with the help of such notorious personages, the corrupt bourgeois elements and princes, fascists, and reactionaries as those making up the present "Government" and "Parliament" of Phnompenh.

The "heavy blow" they dealt me and are still dealing me serves as a painful but very useful lesson to me. A lesson I will never forget all my life.

In view of this misjudgment, I should resign the function as Head of State after our people's certain victory over their enemies and reactionary oppressors and their masters—the US imperialists. And on that very occasion I will give our progressive youth and working people the possibility of fully assuming the responsibility of national construction and defense with the cooperation of the entire nation.

In the present circumstances my task has not yet been fulfilled, because I will never allow the treacherous reactionaries, with the backing of the power of US dollars and at bayonet point, to go on wantonly trampling underfoot the ideals, laws and basic principles of the state with impunity.

And it is in this spirit that I solemnly declare as follows:

1. In my capacity as legal Head of State of Cambodia, a supreme position given me by the Khmer people unanimously, I irrevocably dissolve the Lon Nol government and the two Chambers of Parliament who have betrayed their constitutional oaths and the Constitution of the Kingdom.

2. I call on all my compatriots and all the foreigners residing in Cambodia not to recognize and carry out the decrees [Prakas, Kret],* laws [Kram], orders, messages, circulars, judgments, all kinds of decisions, and verdicts, "works" which the Lon Nol–Sirik Matak–Cheng Heng group and their accomplices or servants have produced or are going to produce.

3. A new National Union Government will be established.

* Translator's brackets—eds.

A provisional consultative assembly will also be established (for assisting the government) whose members will be qualified representatives from all circles of the Khmer society (monks, peasants and farmers, workers and other laborers, merchants, industrialists, army men, policemen, provincial guards, youth and intellectuals, functionaries, women etc. . . .)

4. A National Liberation Army will be formed.

5. All Khmer people at home and abroad—the clergy and laymen, army men and civilians, men and women—who cherish the ideals of independence, democracy, neutrality, progress, socialism, Buddhism and nationalism, and stand for territorial integrity of the country within her existing frontiers, anti-imperialism and anti-neocolonialism—will unite, to form a united front under the official name "The National United Front of Kampuchea" (Abbreviation NUFK).

The essential tasks of the NUFK are to:

1. Liberate our motherland from the dictatorship and oppression by the reactionary and pro-imperialist Lon Nol–Sirik Matak–Chenk Heng clique.

2. Struggle against the US imperialists who have invaded our Indochina and are oppressing its peoples and breeding injustice, war and all kinds of calamities, hostility and disunity, troubles, crimes and misery among our three peoples—the Khmers, Vietnamese and Laotians—and this struggle will be waged side by side with the socialist, progressive, anti-imperialist countries and peoples, far and near, with their complete support.

3. Rebuild our country and make her advance as rapidly as possible along the road of progress following our victory over our enemies. This task of reconstruction is to be accomplished by all of us, the Khmers, in comradeship, solidarity and perfect unity as in times of hard fight.

I am longing very much for my beloved motherland which is and will always remain the sole purpose of my life.

I also miss very much my poor mother, our Buddhist clergy and our beloved people.

If I am not to die in the struggle our patriotic and progressive people and ourselves are going to wage together, I will surely salute and embrace them when we win inevitable victory over the imperialists and their lackeys.

In the course of this struggle I call on all those of my children [compatriots], military and civilian, who can no longer endure the unjust oppression by the traitors and who have the courage and patriotic spirit needed for liberating the motherland, to engage in guerrilla warfare in the jungle against our enemies.

If you are armed and have already mastered military skills I will provide you at opportune moments with munitions and new arms. If you do not yet have arms but wish to acquire military skills I will take necessary measures to send you to the military school of the National United Front of our Kampuchea, which is being established way out from your barracks and villages, and this is for the purpose that the enemy will not be able to reach or locate it.

Those of my children [compatriots] who live in and around Europe and wish to serve the motherland and the people by joining the Liberation Army of the National United Front of Kampuchea, please come to call on me in Moscow or Peking.

Long live Cambodia.

30

Joint Declaration of the Summit Conference of the Indochinese Peoples*

Samdech Norodom Sihanouk, Head of State of Cambodia and Chairman of the National United Front of Kampuchea, issued to the press in Peking on April 27 the Joint Declaration of the Summit Conference of the Indochinese Peoples. The Joint Declaration was also made public the same day by the side of the Democratic Republic of Vietnam in Hanoi, by the Laotion side in Sam Neua, and by the side of the Republic of South Vietnam in south Vietnam respectively. The text of the Joint Declaration reads in full as follows:

The Summit Conference of the Indochinese Peoples was held at a place in the frontier region of Laos, Vietnam and China from April 24 to 25, 1970, on the initiative of Samdech Norodom Sihanouk, Head of State of Cambodia and Chairman of the National United Front of Kampuchea. The three peoples of Indochina were represented at the conference by four delegations:

The Delegation of the Cambodian People composed of

—Samdech Norodom Sihanouk, Head of State of Cambodia, Chairman of the National United Front of Kampuchea, Head of the Delegation;
—Samdech Penn Nouth, Private Adviser to the Head of State, Representative of NUFK, Deputy Head of the Delegation;
—Mr. Huot Sambath, Ambassador Extraordinary and Plenipotentiary, Representative of NUFK;
—Mr. Sarin Chhak, Ambassador Extraordinary

* From *Peking Review* [Special Issue] (May 8, 1970).

and Plenipotentiary, Representative of NUFK;
—Mr. Chau Seng, Representative of NUFK;
—Mr. Thiounn Mumm, Representative of NUFK;
—Mr. Roeurng Mach, Representative of NUFK.

The Delegation of the Lao Patriotic Front composed of

—His Highness Prince Souphanouvong, Chairman of the Laotian Patriotic Front, Head of the Delegation;
—Mr. Khamsouk Keola, Chairman of the Committee of Alliance of Patriotic Neutralist Forces in Laos, Deputy Head of the Delegation;
—Mr. Phoumi Vongvichit, General Secretary of the Central Committee of the Laotian Patriotic Front, Deputy Head of the Delegation;
—Mr. Khamphay Boupha, Member of the Central Committee of the Laotian Patriotic Front;
—Mr. Oun Heuan Phounsavath, Deputy Director of the Information Bureau of the Laotian Patriotic Front in Hanoi.

The Delegation of the People of the Republic of South Vietnam composed of

—Lawyer Nguyen Huu Tho, President of the Presidium of the Central Committee of the South Vietnam National Front for Liberation, President of the Advisory Council of the Provisional Revolutionary Government of the Republic of South Vietnam, Head of the Delegation;
—Lawyer Trinh Dinh Thao, President of the Central Committee of the Vietnam Alliance of National, Democratic and Peace Forces, Vice President of the Advisory Council of the Provisional Revolutionary Government of the Republic of South Vietnam, Deputy Head of the Delegation;
—Mme. Nguyen Dinh Chi, Vice President of the Revolutionary People's Committee of Thua

Thien-Hue, Vice President of the Committee of the Alliance of National, Democratic and Peace Forces of the City of Hue, Member of the Advisory Council of the Provisional Revolutionary Government of the Republic of South Vietnam;

—Mr. Le Quang Chanh, Member of the Central Committee of the South Vietnam National Front for Liberation, Vice-Minister of Foreign Affairs of the Provisional Revolutionary Government of the Republic of South Vietnam;

—Professor Nguyen Van Hieu, Member of the Central Committee of the South Vietnam National Front for Liberation, Ambassador of the Republic of South Vietnam to Cambodia;

—Mr. Vo Dong Giang, Member of the Central Committee of the South Vietnam National Front for Liberation.

The Delegation of the People of the Democratic Republic of Vietnam composed of

—Mr. Pham Van Dong, Premier of the Government of the Democratic Republic of Vietnam, Head of the Delegation;

—Mr. Hoang Quoc Viet, Member of the Presidium of the Central Committee of the Vietnam Fatherland Front, Deputy Head of the Delegation;

—Mr. Hoang Minh Giam, Member of the Presidium of the Central Committee of the Vietnam Fatherland Front, Minister of Culture of the Democratic Republic of Vietnam;

—Mr. Nguyen Co Thach, Vice-Minister of Foreign Affairs of the Democratic Republic of Vietnam;

—Mr. Nguyen Thuong, Ambassador of the Democratic Republic of Vietnam to Cambodia.

The conference, after an exchange of views, arrived at a unanimous appraisal of the present situation in Indochina and of the struggle of the three Indochinese peoples against the common enemy, the American imperialist aggressors and their lack-eys.

The three peoples of Cambodia, Laos and Vietnam live to-gether on the Indochina Peninsula; for a long time friendly rela-tions have united them closely. After long years of heroic strug-gle against the French colonialists and the American interven-tionists, they achieved independence, sovereignty, unity and ter-ritorial integrity. These national rights have been recognized and guaranteed under the Geneva agreements of 1954.

Over the past fifteen years, in the hope of realizing their dream of world hegemony, the American imperialists have tried to turn the Indochinese states into colonies of a new type and mili-tary bases, so as to exploit the peoples of Indochina, wipe out the national liberation movement in Indochina and Southeast Asia and oppose the socialist and other independent countries in Asia.

The American imperialists have shamelessly flouted the aspira-tions of the peoples of Cambodia, Laos and south Vietnam for independence, peace and neutrality, grossly violated the sov-ereignty and security of the Democratic Republic of Vietnam, systematically sabotaged the 1954 Geneva agreements on Indo-china and those of 1962 on Laos, and posed a grave menace to peace and security in Southeast Asia and the world.

The American imperialists have launched a most barbarous "local war" against the Vietnamese people, provoked an atro-cious "special war" against the Laotian people, and intensified their treacherous maneuvers of encirclement, provocation and subversion against Cambodia. They have perpetrated crimes of unheard of barbarity on the Indochina Peninsula.

American imperialism is downright neo-fascism, it is the in-ternational gendarme and the most ferocious and dangerous en-emy of the Indochinese peoples and of humanity.

In the face of this common enemy, the peoples of Indochina have fought side by side in defense of their sacred national rights.

Under the leadership of their Head of State Samdech Noro-dom Sihanouk, the Khmer people have frustrated all the ma-neuvers of the American imperialists for encirclement, provoca-tion and subversion against Cambodia and thus foiled their plans for establishing a system of military bases from south Vietnam to Thailand, including Laos and Cambodia. During the past fifteen years, the Khmer people have been able to safeguard an independent, peaceful and neutral Cambodia and devote their strength to the building of an independent economy and the thriving of national culture. The prestige of independent, peaceful and neutral Cambodia has ceaselessly risen in the international arena.

Under the leadership of the Laotian Patriotic Front headed by His Highness Prince Souphanouvong, the Laotian people are engaged in defeating the US "special war" and the encroachment attacks by the US flunkeys; they have built a liberated area which is being daily consolidated. They have waged a valiant and tenacious struggle for the preservation of the 1962 Geneva agreements and against the American imperialist aggressors and their lackeys who, under the signboard of independence and neutrality, have betrayed the supreme interests of the Laotian people; they are advancing with steady strides along the road of building a truly peaceful, independent, neutral, democratic, unified and prosperous Laos.

In response to the sacred appeal for resistance to American aggression and for national salvation issued by venerated President Ho Chi Minh, the Vietnamese people have fought in unity and achieved great victories in their struggle to liberate the south of the country, defend the north and proceed to the peaceful reunification of their fatherland. Under the glorious banner of the National Front for Liberation, the people of south Vietnam have defeated the "special war" and are frustrating the extremely ferocious "local war" launched by the United States and its lackeys. The people in the north, united in the Fatherland Front, have frustrated the American war of destruction while successfully carrying out socialist construction and fulfilling all the obligations to the heroic "great front" incumbent on the "great rear area."

The brilliant victories of the three Indochinese peoples have deflated the arrogance of the American imperialists, the ringleader of imperialism and the most ferocious enemy of all mankind, thus bringing enormous difficulties to them both within the United States and in the world. These victories have proved that with all their brute force, the American imperialists will nevertheless be battered when they encroach upon the sacred right to existence of a people who are united and determined to fight to the end for the independence and freedom of their fatherland. They constitute an important contribution and great encouragement to the struggle of the peoples of the world for independence and peace.

These most important and glorious victories are victories of the ardent patriotism and indomitable fighting spirit of the three Indochinese peoples each of whom possesses a glorious history of struggle against foreign invasion and a brilliant civilization of more than a thousand years. These are victories of the correct and clear-sighted line advocated by the esteemed leaders of the peoples of Cambodia, Laos and Vietnam. These are victories of the fraternal friendship and militant solidarity between the three peoples, friendship and fraternity which have stood many tests and which are being consolidated and strengthened with each passing day. The 1965 conference of the Indochinese peoples and the present Summit Conference of the Indochinese Peoples contribute greatly to the strengthening and consolidation of this fraternal friendship and militant solidarity. These victories of the three Indochinese peoples are also victories of the extensive and powerful sympathy and support of the world's people for their just cause.

In spite of heavy defeats, the American imperialists, obstinate in their schemes, have not abandoned their criminal aims of aggression against the Indochinese peoples. Since Nixon took office, the United States has done its utmost to "Vietnamize" the war so as to prolong it and perpetuate American military occupation of south Vietnam; it has intensified the "special war" in Laos and launched encroachment attacks against the Plain of Jars–Xieng Khoang region and other places of the liberated area in Laos where it has brought in numerous mercenaries from Thailand for intervention; using the Lon Nol–Sirik Matak clique in its pay, the United States engineered the coup d'etat of March 18, 1970, against the Khmer people and against the policy of Head of State Samdech Norodom Sihanouk, which essentially aims at safeguarding the peace, independence and neutrality of Cambodia and at strengthening the solidarity and friendship between the Indochinese peoples. On April 20 this year, Nixon, President of the United States, displaying once more his gross obstinacy, repeated his deceptive talk about peace and again resorted to his treacherous scheme of withdrawal of troops; at the same time, he came out with impudent and tendentious allegations concerning the patriotic struggle of the three Indochinese peoples. These worn-out allegations and schemes decidedly cannot shake the firm determination of the peoples of Vietnam, Cambodia and Laos to strengthen their solidarity and intensify the fight till complete victory. Nor will these allegations ever appease the public opinion in America and in the world which strongly condemns Nixon's policy of "Vietnamizing the war," prolonging the war and extending it to the whole of Indochina and which demands that the Nixon Administration make a quick and complete withdrawal of American troops from Vietnam and cease its intervention and aggression against the Indochinese states. It is obvious that the American imperialists now seek at all costs to prolong and expand the war in Indochina, gravely menacing the peace in Southeast Asia and the world. It is a pressing demand of the day to stop and smash resolutely all the schemes and acts of the American warmongers.

At this historic moment, the Summit Conference of the Indochinese Peoples urgently calls on the three peoples to strengthen their solidarity, fight with heroism and tenacity and defy all hardships and sacrifices with the firm determination to defeat the American imperialists and their lackeys, defend their sacred national rights, defend the fundamental principles of the Geneva agreements of 1954 and 1962, so that Indochina may truly become an area of independence and peace in conformity with the aspirations of the three peoples and with the interests of peace in Southeast Asia and the world.

The Cambodian, Laotian and south Vietnamese parties explicitly affirm their fighting objectives: independence, peace, neutrality, the prohibition of all presence of foreign troops or foreign military bases on their soil, non-participation in any military alliance and the prohibition of the utilization of their territories by any foreign country for aggression against other countries. These are the profound aspirations of the peoples of

Cambodia, Laos and south Vietnam which conform to the fundamental principles of the Geneva agreements of 1954 and 1962 and to the general situation in this part of the world. The people of the Democratic Republic of Vietnam fully respect these legitimate aspirations and support with all their strength the struggle for these noble objectives.

The conference is particularly interested in the present situation in Cambodia. It expresses its resolute support to the heroic struggle of the Khmer people who, in response to the call of Head of State Samdech Norodom Sihanouk, have risen throughout the country and waged a fierce struggle with weapons in hand or in other forms, with the firm determination to expel the Lon Nol–Sirik Matak coup d'etat clique and frustrate the American imperialists' schemes of aggression. It expresses its full support to the five-point declaration of March 23, 1970, of Head of State Samdech Norodom Sihanouk. It condemns the collective massacres of defenseless civilians, Cambodians and Vietnamese and Chinese nationals carried out by the fascist and racist Lon Nol–Sirik Matak clique for the purpose of camouflaging the American imperialists' intervention and aggression. It vigorously condemns all attempts by the United States and its flunkeys as well as reactionaries in Asia to abuse the name of UNO or any international or Asian organization or conference for legalizing the illegal power of the Lon Nol–Sirik Matak reactionaries and intervening in Cambodia. It is deeply convinced that the struggle of the Khmer people for an independent, peaceful and neutral Cambodia will be crowned with glorious victory.

The conference expresses its resolute support to the valiant struggle of the Laotian people under the leadership of the Laotian Patriotic Front against the American imperialists and their flunkeys; it affirms its full support to the five-point declaration of the Central Committee of the Laotian Patriotic Front dated March 6, 1970. The American imperialists must put an end to their war of aggression, completely cease the bombardment of Laotian territory, withdraw from Laos all the American troops and the satellite troops of Thailand and let the Laotian people settle the affairs of Laos by themselves.

The conference expresses its resolute support to the tenacious and heroic struggle of the Vietnamese people against the American imperialist aggressors and their flunkeys and affirms its full support to the ten-point overall solution put forward by the National Front for Liberation and the Provisional Revolutionary Government of the Republic of South Vietnam. The American imperialists must speedily, totally and unconditionally withdraw from south Vietnam the American troops and the troops of foreign countries in the American camp and let the Vietnamese people settle by themselves their own affairs without any foreign interference.

In the face of the treacherous maneuvers of the United States which, with the "Nixon doctrine," attempts to make Asians fight Asians and sow discord and provoke chauvinistic hatreds between the three peoples of Cambodia, Laos and Vietnam, the conference calls on the three peoples to redouble their vigilance, strengthen their solidarity and intensify the struggle against the common enemy—American imperialism and its flunkeys in the three countries—until complete victory.

Inspired by the principle that the liberation and defense of each country is the affair of its own people, the different parties undertake to do everything possible to render mutual support in accordance with the desire of the interested party and on the basis of mutual respect.

The parties affirm their determination to safeguard and develop the fraternal friendship and good neighborly relations between the three countries so as to give mutual support in the struggle against the common enemy and to cooperate in the future and on a long term basis in the building of each country following the road which it finds appropriate. In the relations between the three countries, the parties are determined to apply the Five Principles of Peaceful Coexistence: mutual respect for sovereignty and territorial integrity; non-aggression; mutual respect for each other's political regime and non-interference in internal affairs; equality and mutual benefit; peaceful coexistence. The parties respect the fundamental principles of the 1954 Geneva agreements on Indochina, recognize and undertake to respect the territorial integrity of Cambodia within her present frontiers and respect the 1962 Geneva agreements on Laos. The parties affirm that all problems in the relations between the three countries can be resolved through negotiations in a spirit of mutual respect, mutual understanding and mutual aid.

The parties agree that meetings will take place whenever it is necessary between their highest level leaders or between competent representatives for exchanges of views on problems of common interest.

The Summit Conference of the Indochinese Peoples expresses its sincere and deep gratitude to the peoples of the world for their valuable sympathy and support. The conference calls on the peoples and governments of the socialist countries, of the countries which love peace and justice throughout the world and the American people to strongly oppose, and demand an immediate cessation of, the American imperialist aggression and intervention and to give increased support to the just struggle of the three peoples of Indochina until final victory.

The conference expresses its full support to the struggle of the peoples of the world for peace, independence, democracy and social progress, against the bellicose American imperialist aggressors, against all forms of old and new colonialism; to the struggle of the peoples of Asia, Africa and Latin America for independence and freedom; to the struggle of the Chinese people for recovering Taiwan, inalienable territory of the People's Republic of China; to the struggle of the Korean people against the American imperialist aggressors and for the liberation of the south of the country and the reunification of Korea; to the struggle of the Arab people for their fundamental national rights against the Israeli aggressors in the pay of the American imperialists; to the struggle of the American people against wars of aggression, against racial discrimination and for peace and the true interests of the people of the United States.

The conference holds that the present situation is more favorable than ever to the Indochinese peoples in their struggle against American aggression and for national salvation. Never have the American imperialist aggressors met with so many defeats and difficulties and been so gravely weakened and isolated as now. The Indochinese peoples are fighting for a just cause, they have a correct line, they are animated by an unshakable determination; they have forged an indestructible solidarity; moreover, they possess greater strength and enjoy more vigorous sympathy and support than ever from the peoples of the world. The conference expresses its firm conviction that the three Indochinese peoples on their victorious advance will make full use of their position of having the initiative and being on the offensive and persistently carry on and intensify the struggle in all fields and will certainly win complete victory.

Done on April 25, 1970 in the Khmer, Laotian and Vietnamese languages.

The French text will serve as reference.

The Head of the Delegation
of the Cambodian People,
NORODOM SIHANOUK
*Head of State of Cambodia,
Chairman of the National United
Front of Kampuchea*

The Head of the Delegation
of the Laotian People,
PRINCE SOUPHANOUVONG
Chairman of the Laotian Patriotic Front

The Head of the Delegation
of the People of the Republic of South
Vietnam,
NGUYEN HUU THO
*President of the Presidium of the Central Committee of the South Vietnam
National Front for Liberation,
President of the Advisory Council of
the Provisional Revolutionary Government of the Republic of South Vietnam*

The Head of the Delegation
of the People of the Democratic Republic of Vietnam,
PHAM VAN DONG
*Premier of the Government of the
Democratic Republic of Vietnam*

31

The Situation in Southeast Asia: Apology for the Invasion of Cambodia (April 30, 1970)

RICHARD M. NIXON *

Good evening my fellow Americans.

Ten days ago, in my report to the nation on Vietnam, I announced a decision to withdraw an additional 150,000 Americans from Vietnam over the next year. I said then that I was making that decision despite our concern over increased enemy activity in Laos, in Cambodia, and in South Vietnam.

At that time, I warned that if I concluded that increased enemy activity in any of these areas endangered the lives of Americans remaining in Vietnam, I would not hesitate to take strong and effective measures to deal with that situation.

Despite that warning, North Vietnam has increased its military aggression in all these areas, and particularly in Cambodia.

After full consultation with the National Security Council, Ambassador Bunker, General Abrams, and my other advisers, I have concluded that the actions of the enemy in the last ten days clearly endanger the lives of Americans who are in Vietnam now and would constitute an unacceptable risk to those who will be there after withdrawal of another 150,000.

To protect our men who are in Vietnam and to guarantee the continued success of our withdrawal and Vietnamization programs, I have concluded that the time has come for action.

Tonight, I shall describe the actions of the enemy, the actions I have ordered to deal with that situation, and the reasons for my decision.

Cambodia, a small country of seven million people, has been a

* From *Weekly Compilation of Presidential Documents*, Vol. 6 (May 4, 1970).

neutral nation since the Geneva agreement of 1954—an agreement, incidentally, which was signed by the Government of North Vietnam.

American policy since then has been to scrupulously respect the neutrality of the Cambodian people. We have maintained a skeleton diplomatic mission of fewer than fifteen in Cambodia's capital, and that only since last August. For the previous four years, from 1965 to 1969, we did not have any diplomatic mission whatever in Cambodia. And for the past five years, we have provided no military assistance whatever and no economic assistance to Cambodia.

North Vietnam, however, has not respected that neutrality.

For the past five years—as indicated on this map that you see here—North Vietnam has occupied military sanctuaries all along the Cambodian frontier with South Vietnam. Some of these extend up to twenty miles into Cambodia. The sanctuaries are in red and, as you note, they are on both sides of the border. They are used for hit and run attacks on American and South Vietnamese forces in South Vietnam.

These communist occupied territories contain major base camps, training sites, logistics facilities, weapons and ammunition factories, air strips, and prisoner-of-war compounds.

For five years, neither the United States nor South Vietnam has moved against these enemy sanctuaries because we did not wish to violate the territory of a neutral nation. Even after the Vietnamese communists began to expand these sanctuaries four weeks ago, we counseled patience to our South Vietnamese allies and imposed restraints on our own commanders.

In contrast to our policy, the enemy in the past two weeks has stepped up his guerrilla actions and he is concentrating his main forces in these sanctuaries that you see on this map where they are building up to launch massive attacks on our forces and those of South Vietnam.

North Vietnam in the last two weeks has stripped away all pretense of respecting the sovereignty or the neutrality of Cambodia. Thousands of their soldiers are invading the country from the sanctuaries; they are encircling the capital of Phnompenh. Coming from these sanctuaries, as you see here, they have moved into Cambodia and are encircling the capital.

Cambodia, as a result of this, has sent out a call to the United States, to a number of other nations, for assistance. Because if this enemy effort succeeds, Cambodia would become a vast enemy staging area and a springboard for attacks on South Vietnam along 600 miles of frontier—a refuge where enemy troops could return from combat without fear of retaliation.

North Vietnamese men and supplies could then be poured into that country, jeopardizing not only the lives of our own men but the people of South Vietnam as well.

Now confronted with this situation, we have three options.

First, we can do nothing. Well, the ultimate result of that course of action is clear. Unless we indulge in wishful thinking, the lives of Americans remaining in Vietnam after our next withdrawal of 150,000 would be gravely threatened.

Let us go to the map again. Here is South Vietnam. Here is North Vietnam. North Vietnam already occupies this part of Laos. If North Vietnam also occupied this whole band in Cambodia, or the entire country, it would mean that South Vietnam was completely outflanked and the forces of Americans in this area, as well as the South Vietnamese, would be in an untenable military position.

Our second choice is to provide massive military assistance to Cambodia itself. Now unfortunately, while we deeply sympathize with the plight of seven million Cambodians whose country is being invaded, massive amounts of military assistance could not be rapidly and effectively utilized by the small Cambodian army against the immediate threat.

With other nations, we shall do our best to provide the small arms and other equipment which the Cambodian army of 40,000 needs and can use for its defense. But the aid we will provide will be limited to the purpose of enabling Cambodia to defend its neutrality and not for the purpose of making it an active belligerent on one side or the other.

Our third choice is to go to the heart of the trouble. That means cleaning out major North Vietnamese and Viet Cong occupied territories, these sanctuaries which serve as bases for attacks on both Cambodia and American and South Vietnamese forces in South Vietnam. Some of these, incidentally, are as close to Saigon as Baltimore is to Washington.

This one, for example [*indicating*], is called the Parrot's Beak. It is only thirty-three miles from Saigon.

Now faced with these three options, this is the decision I have made.

In cooperation with the armed forces of South Vietnam, attacks are being launched this week to clean out major enemy sanctuaries on the Cambodian-Vietnam border.

A major responsibility for the ground operations is being assumed by South Vietnamese forces. For example, the attacks in several areas, including the Parrot's Beak that I referred to a moment ago, are exclusively South Vietnamese ground operations under South Vietnamese command with the United States providing air and logistical support.

There is one area, however, immediately above Parrot's Beak, where I have concluded that a combined American and South Vietnamese operation is necessary.

Tonight, American and South Vietnamese units will attack the headquarters for the entire communist military operation in South Vietnam. This key control center has been occupied by the North Vietnamese and Viet Cong for five years in blatant violation of Cambodia's neutrality.

This is not an invasion of Cambodia. The areas in which these attacks will be launched are completely occupied and controlled by North Vietnamese forces. Our purpose is not to occupy the areas. Once enemy forces are driven out of these sanctuaries and once their military supplies are destroyed, we will withdraw.

These actions are in no way directed at the security interests of any nation. Any government that chooses to use these actions as a pretext for harming relations with the United States will be doing so on its own responsibility, and on its own initiative, and we will draw the appropriate conclusions.

Now let me give you the reasons for my decision.

A majority of the American people, a majority of you listening to me, are for the withdrawal of our forces from Vietnam. The action I have taken tonight is indispensable for the continuing success of that withdrawal program.

A majority of the American people want to end this war

rather than to have it drag on interminably. The action I have taken tonight will serve that purpose.

A majority of the American people want to keep the casualties of our brave men in Vietnam at an absolute minimum. The action I take tonight is essential if we are to accomplish that goal.

We take this action not for the purpose of expanding the war into Cambodia but for the purpose of ending the war in Vietnam and winning the just peace we all desire. We have made and we will continue to make every possible effort to end this war through negotiation at the conference table rather than through more fighting on the battlefield.

Let us look again at the record. We have stopped the bombing of North Vietnam. We have cut air operations by over twenty percent. We have announced withdrawal of over 250,000 of our men. We have offered to withdraw all of our men if they will withdraw theirs. We have offered to negotiate all issues with only one condition—and that is that the future of South Vietnam be determined not by North Vietnam, not by the United States, but by the people of South Vietnam themselves.

The answer of the enemy has been intransigence at the conference table, belligerence in Hanoi, massive military aggression in Laos and Cambodia, and stepped-up attacks in South Vietnam, designed to increase American casualties.

This attitude has become intolerable. We will not react to this threat to American lives merely by plaintive diplomatic protests. If we did, the credibility of the United States would be destroyed in every area of the world where only the power of the United States deters aggression.

Tonight, I again warn the North Vietnamese that if they continue to escalate the fighting when the United States is withdrawing its forces, I shall meet my responsibility as Commander-in-Chief of our armed forces to take the action I consider necessary to defend the security of our American men.

The action that I have announced tonight puts the leaders of North Vietnam on notice that we will be patient in working for peace, we will be conciliatory at the conference table, but we will not be humiliated. We will not be defeated. We will not allow American men by the thousands to be killed by an enemy from privileged sanctuaries.

The time came long ago to end this war through peaceful negotiations. We stand ready for those negotiations. We have made major efforts, many of which must remain secret. I say tonight that all the offers and approaches made previously remain on the conference table whenever Hanoi is ready to negotiate seriously.

But if the enemy response to our most conciliatory offers for peaceful negotiation continues to be to increase its attacks and humiliate and defeat us, we shall react accordingly.

My fellow Americans, we live in an age of anarchy both abroad and at home. We see mindless attacks on all the great institutions which have been created by free civilizations in the last 500 years. Even here in the United States, great universities are being systematically destroyed. Small nations all over the world find themselves under attack from within and from without.

If, when the chips are down, the world's most powerful nation, the United States of America, acts like a pitiful, helpless giant, the forces of totalitarianism and anarchy will threaten free nations and free institutions throughout the world.

It is not our power but our will and character that is being tested tonight. The question all Americans must ask and answer tonight is this: Does the richest and strongest nation in the history of the world have the character to meet a direct challenge by a group which rejects every effort to win a just peace, ignores our warning, tramples on solemn agreements, violates the neutrality of an unarmed people, and uses our prisoners as hostages?

If we fail to meet this challenge, all other nations will be on notice that despite its overwhelming power the United States, when a real crisis comes, will be found wanting.

During my campaign for the Presidency, I pledged to bring Americans home from Vietnam. They are coming home.

I promised to end this war. I shall keep that promise.

I promised to win a just peace. I shall keep that promise.

We shall avoid a wider war. But we are also determined to put an end to this war.

In this room, Woodrow Wilson made the great decisions

which led to victory in World War I. Franklin Roosevelt made the decisions which led to our victory in World War II. Dwight D. Eisenhower made decisions which ended the war in Korea and avoided war in the Middle East. John F. Kennedy, in his finest hour, made the great decision which removed Soviet nuclear missiles from Cuba and the Western Hemisphere.

I have noted that there has been a great deal of discussion with regard to this decision that I have made and I should point out that I do not contend that it is in the same magnitude as these decisions that I have just mentioned. But between those decisions and this decision there is a difference that is very fundamental. In those decisions, the American people were not assailed by counsels of doubt and defeat from some of the most widely known opinion leaders of the nation.

I have noted, for example, that a Republican Senator has said that this action I have taken means that my party has lost all chance of winning the November elections. And others are saying today that this move against enemy sanctuaries will make me a one-term President.

No one is more aware than I am of the political consequences of the action I have taken. It is tempting to take the easy political path: to blame this war on previous administrations and to bring all of our men home immediately, regardless of the consequences, even though that would mean defeat for the United States; to desert eighteen million South Vietnamese people, who have put their trust in us and to expose them to the same slaughter and savagery which the leaders of North Vietnam inflicted on hundreds of thousands of North Vietnamese who chose freedom when the communists took over North Vietnam in 1954; to get peace at any price now, even though I know that a peace of humiliation for the United States would lead to a bigger war or surrender later.

I have rejected all political considerations in making this decision.

Whether my party gains in November is nothing compared to the lives of 400,000 brave Americans fighting for our country and for the cause of peace and freedom in Vietnam. Whether I may be a one-term President is insignificant compared to whether by our failure to act in this crisis, the United States proves itself to be unworthy to lead the forces of freedom in this critical period in world history. I would rather be a one-term President and do what I believe is right than to be a two-term President at the cost of seeing America become a second-rate power and to see this nation accept the first defeat in its proud 190-year history.

I realize that in this war there are honest and deep differences in this country about whether we should have become involved, that there are differences as to how the war should have been conducted. But the decision I announce tonight transcends those differences.

For the lives of American men are involved. The opportunity for 150,000 Americans to come home in the next twelve months is involved. The future of eighteen million people in South Vietnam and seven million people in Cambodia is involved. The possibility of winning a just peace in Vietnam and in the Pacific is at stake.

It is customary to conclude a speech from the White House by asking support for the President of the United States. Tonight, I depart from that precedent. What I ask is far more important. I ask for your support for our brave men fighting tonight halfway around the world—not for territory—not for glory—but so that their younger brothers and their sons and your sons can have a chance to grow up in a world of peace and freedom and justice.

Thank you and good night.

NOTE: The President spoke at 9 p.m. in his office at the White House. His remarks were broadcast on radio and television.

32

Reply to Nixon: Condemnation of the American Invasion of Cambodia (May 2, 1970)

PRINCE NORODOM SIHANOUK *

On April 30, 1970, Mr. Nixon, President of the USA, announced in a speech to the American nation that he had ordered the armed forces of the United States and the mercenaries of south Vietnam to invade my country, Cambodia. . . .[1]

Today, I would like once more to draw the attention of all the peoples and governments throughout the world to the absolutely unjustifiable character of the invasion and occupation of my country, Cambodia, by more than 70,000 Yankee troops and south Vietnamese mercenaries belonging to various "arms" (infantry, armored units, artillery, helicopters, etc.) and to the ultra-criminal character of the intensive bombing by US B-52's of many of our provinces, especially Svay Rieng and Kompong Cham.

The aggression from land and air launched by the US imperialists with the tacit agreement of the fascist regime in their service, the usurper of the constitutional power at Phnompenh, has, in the past few days, caused the death and the atrocious mutilation of hundreds of my compatriots, the vast majority of whom are peaceable peasants, including old people, women and children.

In his speech, Mr. Nixon tried to justify his criminal act with the "necessity" of "protecting the lives" of his soldiers fighting in South Vietnam by cleaning out the so-called "Viet Cong and Vietminh sanctuaries" installed in Cambodia.

---

* From *Peking Review,* no. 19 (May 8, 1970).

[1] Selection 31, this volume—eds.

In reality, the criminal intervention in my country by Mr. Nixon's armed forces has no other aim than coming to the rescue of the Lon Nol–Sirik Matak gang which the US Central Intelligence Agency had helped to set up at Phnompenh, a regime of oppression of the Khmer people and the Vietnamese and Chinese nationals residing in Cambodia, peoples who are united with one another by ties of Asian solidarity against imperialism.

In their intrusion into Cambodia, the Yankee troops and the mercenaries have met no other foreign army occupying my country than themselves.

According to the forecasts of the press of the "free world" itself, the Khmer people fighting under the banner of the National United Front of Kampuchea would soon be able to isolate and then recapture Phnompenh, the capital.

Under the repeated demands of the "hawks" in the Pentagon, Nixon has decided to let his army openly take charge of oppressing the Khmer people and colonizing their country in view of the "absolute incapacity"—to use the expression of Western observers—of the Lon Nol mercenaries, armed and paid by the US imperialists, to realize the latter's plan of turning Cambodia into a US colony and a base for aggression against the resistance of the South Vietnamese people and the people of south Laos.

Nixon's television speech is a model of arrogance, cynicism, Machiavellism and barbarism.

He can never succeed in deceiving his compatriots with his sham patriotic and base demagogic "explanations."

The American Congressmen, intellectuals, youth, press and people have not only rejected with disgust these "explanations" but also denounced vehemently their President's dishonesty. They are clearly aware that their "Chief Executive" has deliberately violated the neutrality, territorial integrity, frontiers, independence and sovereignty of Cambodia for which he has on many occasions proclaimed *urbi et orbi* respect and official recognition in the name of the US Government and people. In this regard, Nixon cannot even find an excuse, as in the case of the US armed intervention in south Vietnam and then in Laos, in the so-called appeal for help from the local government, because his valet Lon Nol, who dares not face the anger of the

Khmer people, has done his utmost to make people believe that he had neither demanded nor approved such an invasion and occupation.

The American Congressmen, intellectuals, youth and people have spontaneously denounced the shameless lie of Nixon, who has promised them "de-escalation" of the US war of aggression in Indochina and withdrawal of the US troops from our peninsula. They have also seen that in April, 1970, the lives of the Yankee soldiers in south Vietnam were in no greater "danger" than in the years and months preceding the US invasion of our country.

As for us, Khmers, we shall firmly bear in mind and, at the same time, call the attention of the people the world over to the confession which Nixon has made involuntarily in his "speech" concerning the US refusal to become "a second-rate power." In other words, according to Nixon and his Pentagon, the United States would never agree to give up being an imperialist and neo-colonialist power. To decolonize Thailand, south Vietnam, South Korea, etc., or to renounce the colonization of Laos and Cambodia means, in the eyes of Nixon and the US "hawks," that the United States would become "a second-rate power" and that they would lose a war for the first time in their history (sic).

This is a nice piece of confession for it simply means that the power and grandeur of the United States is based on the aggression, conquest, colonization and maintenance of its domination over the countries and peoples susceptible to becoming its prey in the world.

But the peoples who are victims of US neo-colonialist imperialism do not and will not agree to remain for ever a prey to Nixon and his like.

So far as the Khmer people in particular and the Indochinese peoples in general are concerned, there is no question, and will never be any question, of bowing to or falling on their knees before the US imperialist aggressor and murderer.

Consequently, I request our valiant people and the heroic brother peoples of Vietnam and Laos to strengthen their militant solidarity and intensify to the maximum their struggle against the common enemy in conformity with the resolution of the Summit Conference of the Indochinese peoples.[2]

I speak with absolute certainty that our three peoples, united in a single Indochinese front of war against US imperialism and its valets in Phnompenh, Saigon and Vientiane, will deal heavier and heavier blows at them in the weeks and months to come and will eventually win complete victory over them, thus liberating completely our three Indochinese countries from their intolerable, evil and bloody oppression.

Finally I count on all the peoples worthy of the name and on all the governments not subservient to the imperialists to immediately break off diplomatic and other relations with the antipopular, pro-imperialist Lon Nol–Sirik Matak clique of traitors who are responsible for the loss of the independence, neutrality, peace and territorial integrity of Cambodia in the interests of the Thieu–Ky clique and its master, US imperialism; to severely condemn this imperialism, its criminal invasion and colonization of Cambodia; and to demand that the US Government withdraw immediately, unconditionally and totally all its troops, the units of all arms, and all the military "advisers" not of Khmer nationality from the entire territory of Cambodia.

It is unimaginable that the Khmer, Laotian and Vietnamese peoples could be a menace to the lives of the American youth or the security of the United States half the globe away from Indochina.

Cambodia, Laos and Vietnam have never for a moment, that is to say neither before nor after the signing of the 1954 Geneva Agreements on Indochina, menaced or provoked the United States.

It is the United States alone which has deliberately violated these agreements and which, like a vulture falling on a defenseless prey, has decided brutally to attack our three countries and peoples.

This fact is known to the whole world. Only the governments subservient to the United States pretend not to be aware of it.

The lives of Mr. Nixon's soldiers will no longer be in danger as soon as the said Nixon decides (and the American people

---

[2] See Selection 30, this volume—eds.

give him the full power to do so) to make his country respect the 1954 Geneva agreements and, consequently, withdraws all the US and "allied" forces from Indochina and lets the Indochinese solve among themselves alone the problems existing within their respective countries.

I request all the peoples of the world and their governments to make President Nixon understand this.

33

Cambodia: Why the Generals Won

PETER DALE SCOTT *

President Nixon's ground operations in Cambodia with US troops will likely be over, as he promises, by June 30, 1970. The long-range strategy by which the Cambodian adventure was undertaken almost certainly will not be. For though the invasion itself was unprecedented, all of the prior elements in the scenario were often repeated cliches, from the initial military overthrow of a popular leader by a right wing pro-American clique, to the announced response to an enemy "invasion" at a time when the prospects for ending the war seemed to be increasing. Most characteristic of all is the likelihood that Nixon was pressured by the Joint Chiefs to authorize the Cambodian adventure in great haste, and in such a way as to bypass or overrule most of his civilian advisers, as a response to an "emergency" for which US intelligence agencies and perhaps the Joint Chiefs themselves were largely responsible.

Even if terminated by June 30, the Cambodian adventure has confirmed yet again what some of us have been saying for years: that at present the US military apparatus in Southeast Asia will work to reject a new policy of deescalation as certainly as the human organism will work to reject a transplanted heart. The formula to neutralize this rejection process has unfortunately not yet been discovered.

In other words one cannot understand what has happened recently in Cambodia without understanding the whole history of the Second Indochina War. One cannot for example appreciate Lon Nol's expectations in overthrowing Prince Sihanouk on March 18 without recalling the anti-neutralist military coups of late 1960 and April, 1964, in Laos, or of January, 1964, and

* From *The New York Review of Books*, June 18, 1970, pp. 28–35. By permission.

June, 1965, in Saigon. US personnel were involved in (or at the very least cognizant of) every one of these coups.[1]

Each coup was followed by, and helped to facilitate, an escalation of the US military effort which the overthrown regime would not have tolerated. As my colleagues and I tried to demonstrate in our book, *The Politics of Escalation in Vietnam,* the result (if not the intention) of every one of these escalations was to nullify a real or apparent threat of peace at the time. (I would now add that we failed sufficiently to emphasize the role of our civilian and military intelligence services in bringing about all of the crises in question, as well as the present one.)

The second cliché of the scenario was Lon Nol's deliberate breach of the accommodation hitherto established between the NLF troops in Cambodia and the troops of Phnompenh, followed by a precipitous retreat, in the face of what seem to have been only light enemy probes, back to the outskirts of Phnompenh itself. This gratuitous provocation of a much stronger enemy has been treated as irrational by several well-established American analysts, but it will be seen to have its own Machiavellian logic when compared to similar events in the Second Indochina War. By the same combination of absurd provocation and precipitous withdrawal in previous springs, Laotian troops (and/or their American advisers) secured the first commitment of US combat troops to Thailand—the first in Southeast Asia, for that matter—in May, 1962, and the first bombings of Laos—which

---

[1] Robert Shaplen, a writer close to CIA sources, writes that "There is no evidence that the Americans participated in the [Cambodian] coup or that they were apprised of it until a few hours before it took place, although they were undoubtedly aware of what might happen and did nothing to try to prevent it ("Letter from Indochina," The *New Yorker,* May 9, 1970, p. 138). This is disingenuous. Central in preparing for the March 18 coup were cadres of CIA-trained Khmer Serei guerillas, who were infiltrated in from South Vietnam or Thailand at least ten days before the coup. They are said to have led the confrontations with the NLF on March 8 in the field (to which Shaplen alludes, p. 136), the assault on the embassies on March 11, and the subsequent slaughter of both Vietnamese and Cambodian civilians. Testimony in the Green Beret murder trial in December identified the Khmer Serei as "an organization which plans the political overthrow of the Cambodian government in the future" (The *New York Times,* January 28, 1970, p. 9).

Aviation Week correctly reported to be "the first US offensive military action since Korea"—in May 1964.[2]

Thus Lon Nol's actions, far from being irrational, followed a recipe for US support which by now has been tested many times and never known to fail. The exigent realities of the monsoon season and the US budgetary process encourage an annual cycle of escalation which by now can be not only analyzed but predicted.[3]

The third and most frightening cliché is the phenomenon of the artificially induced "crisis" used as a pretext for hasty executive actions which preempt the rights of Congress to declare wars and advise on foreign policy. The military pressure on Nixon to escalate hastily in Cambodia recalls the pressure on Kennedy to escalate in 1962 and on Johnson to escalate in 1964, first in response to Laos and later in response to the alleged Tonkin Gulf "incident" of August 1964. In all cases, including the present one, a key role was played by our intelligence agencies, who first helped to induce a crisis which they subsequently misreported to the President.

Furthermore, all but the most rudimentary forms of civilian review within the executive branch were suppressed. When the first US arms shipment to Cambodia was announced on April 22 by White House press secretary Ronald Ziegler, his counterpart Robert McCloskey at the State Department admitted that he "knew nothing about it" (The *New York Times,* April 24, 1970,

---

[2] The most objective book in English on Laos (*Laos,* by the former British military attache, Hugh Toye: Oxford University Press, 1968, p. 182) says categorically that the 1962 withdrawal was deliberate: ". . . after a flurry of fire fights but no Pathet Lao attack, Nam Tha was abandoned. This time there could be no doubt about it; General Boun Leut is no poltroon; he had obeyed Phoumi's orders." Phoumi's men in Nam Tha were accompanied by CIA-Special Forces "advisers." Toye (p. 184) also recalls charges made at the time by the *London Times* that the CIA "had deliberately opposed the official American objective of trying to establish a neutral government, had encouraged Phoumi in his reinforcement of Nam Tha [against US official advice], and had negatived the heavy financial pressure brought by the Kennedy administration upon Phoumi by subventions from its own budget."

[3] Cf. my warning against a similar escalation in *The New York Review of Books* ("Laos: The Story Nixon Won't Tell," April 9, 1970), p. 39: "The present period . . . offers disturbing parallels to the [Laotian] withdrawals of 1962 and 1964." [See Selection No. 21 in this volume—eds.]

p. 3). On April 23, the very day that "emergency" meetings of the Special Action Group began to consider the Fishhook invasion, Secretary of State Rogers told a House Appropriations subcommittee that if US troops went into Cambodia "our whole (Vietnamization) program is defeated," and that "we have no incentive to escalate into Cambodia" (The *Washington Post,* May 6, 1970, A1). In the wake of the Fishhook decision ("Operation Prometheus") it was suggested that the Joint Chiefs of Staff had

> . . . pulled an end run in their effort to get the attack against the border areas approved. . . . Some believed Mr. Laird found himself in the final stages of planning for the invasion without being fully consulted and informed during the preliminary planning stages [*Christian Science Monitor,* May 14, 1970].

Perhaps the most embarrassing plight was that of Senate Republican leader Hugh Scott, who was

> . . . cut adrift with White House inspired statements that renewed bombing of the North was a remote contingency at the very time a hundred American planes were dropping bombs across the demilitarized zone.[4]

Constitutional procedures under Nixon, professedly a "strict constructionist," have clearly deteriorated a long way since 1954, when Dulles had to inform Bidault of France that even a single US air strike to relieve Dienbienphu (which they both desired) could not be authorized by the US President "without action by Congress because to do so was beyond the President's constitutional powers."[5] Here the Tonkin Gulf incidents have set an

---

[4] The *New York Times,* May 4, 1970, p. 36.
[5] Chalmers Roberts, "The Day We Didn't Go to War," The *Reporter,* September 14, 1954, p. 35; reprinted in Marvin E. Gettleman, *Vietnam: History, Documents and Opinions* (2d ed., New York, 1970), Selection 24.

unfortunate precedent, not only for unilateral executive action before Congress is consulted, but above all for compressing the review procedures of the National Security Council into a few brief hours.

On April 20, in announcing his projected withdrawal of 150,-000 US troops over the next twelve months, Nixon had assured his audience that "Vietnamization" was stabilizing the situation beyond anyone's expectations: "We finally have in sight the just peace we are seeking." Yet the April 28 decision to invade Cambodia was clearly reached by *emergency* procedures, through meetings of a "Special Action Group" which originally had been created after the US had failed to respond swiftly to the shooting down of an electronics intelligence spy plane by the North Koreans in 1969.[6] Convened by a National Security Council meeting of Wednesday, April 22, the Special Action Group was chaired by Henry Kissinger, the man who as early as the spring of 1969 had "got Nixon to order bombing strikes against communist bases in Cambodia." [7]

The Special Action Group met on April 23 to consider a range of options including the Fishhook invasion plans, of which Secretary Rogers was apparently still unaware, at a time when two of the Joint Chiefs of Staff, apparently worried about the "imminent collapse" of the Lon Nol regime, were reported to

> . . . contend that the President now controls the fate of the new Cambodia government, and that the allies' military success in South Vietnam depends on its survival [The *New York Times,* April 25, 1970, p. 4; April 24, 1970, p. 1].

Nixon himself told the American people on April 30 that the enemy "is concentrating his main forces in these sanctuaries where they are building up to launch massive attacks on our forces" and that in these sanctuaries were concealed the Communist "headquarters." [8]

---

[6] The *New York Times,* May 2, 1970, p. 7.

[7] Harold Munthe-Kaas, in *Far Eastern Economic Review,* December 25, 1969, p. 668.

[8] On April 28, the day of the Fishhook decision and two days before the public and Congress were informed, the President told a small

If the President was told this, he was not only misinformed but probably lied to. Robert Shaplen, among others, knew of "reliable reports" that the famous COSVN [Central Office of the Vietnamese National Liberation Front] headquarters had in fact been moved *out of* the sanctuaries area "at the time of the [March 18] coup against Sihanouk"; [9] field reports soon confirmed that NLF forces, far from being concentrated, had fanned out westward. US military sources in Saigon are reported to have had no knowledge of a Communist build-up in Cambodia (despite Lon Nol's public claims that their numbers had been trebled).[10] Such evidence raises as many questions about the performance of our senior officers and intelligence agencies during this "emergency" as during the "emergencies" of Nam Tha in 1962 and the Tonkin Gulf incidents of 1964. At the very least, it illustrates yet again the old maxim that the objectivity of official intelligence tends to vary inversely with its relevance to impending strategic decisions.

The Special Action Group's recommendations were expected to be discussed at the National Security Council meeting scheduled for Friday, April 24, the day that Ronald Ziegler (again bypassing the State Department) announced that the NLF and North Vietnamese presence in Cambodia constituted "a foreign invasion of a neutral country which cannot be considered in any way a pretense of civil war." One indication of the haste in convening the Special Action Group is that the NSC Friday meeting did not originally list Cambodia on its agenda. (Similarly, the August 4, 1964, meeting, which authorized air strikes against North Vietnam less than two hours after flash reports of a most

group of visitors to the White House (including Admiral W. R. Smedberg III, president of the Retired Officers Association) that the action he was soon to order against the Cambodian sanctuaries "was imperative if we were to escape the probability of total and humiliating defeat in Vietnam" (The *San Francisco Examiner*, May 21, 1970, p. 1).

[9] Shaplen, "Letter from Indochina," The *New York Times*, April 4, 1970, p. 146.

[10] Robert G. Kaiser, The *Washington Post*, May 3, 1970, A18: "Pressed on this point, military analysts . . . could not point to any recent development of this kind." However, the *Wall Street Journal* of April 28, 1970, p. 1, said "Allied intelligence sources" had predicted a "surge of Red attacks in Vietnam, as violent as those of the 1968 Têt offensive," especially "along the Cambodian border."

improbable "attack" had been received in Washington, had been convened to discuss not Southeast Asia but Cyprus.)

To his credit, Nixon waited four days before finally submitting to the pressure from the Joint Chiefs and (apparently) his own White House staff. The National Security Council meeting was postponed to Saturday, April 25, and then took place on Sunday. Decisions at a third meeting on Monday were not made final until Tuesday, April 28, apparently after both Laird and Rogers had voiced their misgivings about an American invasion. According to Flora Lewis of *Newsday* (May 2, 1970) Nixon chose "what appeared to be the middle option" on Cambodia, rejecting a more ambitious proposal supported on April 27 by two of the joint chiefs (Chairman Wheeler and Admiral Moorer) for an amphibious invasion to take control of Sihanoukville.

Nixon's delaying action was consistent with his earlier resistance to pressure from two of the Joint Chiefs before he responded on April 22 to the April 11 request of the Lon Nol regime for aid. One reason for his delay, according to The *New York Times,* was

> . . . the lingering hope that the Soviet Union might be able to persuade North Vietnam and possibly Communist China to participate in a broad peace conference on Indochina.[11]

This "lingering hope" of a peace conference had been rekindled during April by the obvious impasse which the war had reached. As in previous "critical periods" of the US military effort in Indochina, the inefficacy of its military strategies had led both hawks and doves to take more seriously the risk or hope of a diplomatic solution. In this context of uncertainty about the war, the idea of a peace conference had again been put forward by the French Foreign Minister, Maurice Schumann, on April 1, and on April 16 the Soviet delegate to the United Nations, Yakov Malik, was quoted as saying he favored the idea of convening such a conference as the only way to bring a new solution of the Indochina conflict. The next night, in a radio interview, Malik appeared to reject the French idea,

[11] The *New York Times,* April 27, 1970, p. 5.

though in qualified terms, calling it "unrealistic *at the present time*" [author's italics—eds.]. This same qualification (suggesting that in the future a conference might be more propitious) was echoed and to some extent amplified by Madame Binh, the NLF delegate to the Paris talks. Attacking the recent massacre of Vietnamese citizens of Cambodia by Lon Nol's army, Madame Binh went on to say that

> . . . *in these conditions* [author's italics—eds.] we think that the proposal of the French Government cannot contribute to the settlement of these problems.[12]

Neither of these quotations by itself suggests that peace was about to burst upon us, only that there were indications that diplomatic channels remained open to be further explored. This fact does not exclude the possibility, raised by Jean Lacouture and Noam Chomsky, that France's failure to show support for Prince Sihanouk may have been "one of the results of M. Pompidou's trip to the United States" (*The New York Review of Books,* June 4, 1970, p. 45).

What is important in understanding the Cambodian escalation is not so much that the diplomatic prospects existed or were likely to be profitable as the fact that, by all accounts, the President seems to have taken them seriously enough to delay decisions being pressed on him by his Joint Chiefs. Furthermore, the French proposal for a conference was only one of the diplomatic options being explored at this time. Though the Paris talks on the subject of Vietnam itself had been at a standstill since the departure of Lodge, there had been talk for a year of a step-by-step disengagement in Laos, which if matched by the other side could be enlarged to include Vietnam as well. More recently in Washington there had been discussion (with bitter opposition from American military leaders) of

> . . . halting the bombing of the [Ho Chi Minh] Trail in Laos—in return for which Hanoi and . . . the Pathet Lao have indicated their willingness to

[12] The *New York Times,* April 21, 1970, p. 1.

limit military operations in that country and to start political negotiations there.[13]

Since the NLF forces in Cambodia have been cut off from their coastal supply routes through Cambodian ports, they have predictably taken steps to increase their hold over southern portions of the Ho Chi Minh Trail in Laos; and US and South Vietnamese operations (the former in violation of a Congressional budgetary prohibition) have also escalated there. Thus,

> Unfortunately, whatever chances existed for halting the bombing of the Ho Chi Minh Trail—even for a trial period—have been diminished as a result of our intervention in Cambodia. To stop the bombing now, the American military argue, would give the North Vietnamese total freedom to pour supplies and troops not only into Laos and South Vietnam but also into Cambodia.[14]

This talk of a peace initiative, like that of the French, was probably more significant as a symptom of widespread and well-sounded uncertainty about long-range US strategic intentions than as a likely harbinger of peace itself. Unlike earlier periods in the [Second] Indochina War, when similar proposals had emerged on the eve of US escalations, the world was now much more clearly threatened by a global increase of tensions, as a result of which any two of the world's three great military powers might conceivably soon be drawn into conflict. Such desperate periods give new urgency to talk of peace as well as to talk of war, and there are signs in the major capitals of increasing polarization between hawks and doves. The Soviet Union has been talking to the US in Vienna and (since Mao's surprise

[13] Shaplen, "Letter from Indochina," *op. cit.* "Some Americans have felt that a break in the Laotian situation now could produce some movement in the deadlocked peace talks in Paris, and perhaps bring to an end at least some of the fighting in Vietnam." For earlier phases of the recent diplomatic initiative over Laos, and their successive frustration by US-backed escalations, see my [Scott's] article, *The New York Review of Books*, April 9, 1970, pp. 35ff. See Selection 21 in this volume—eds.

[14] *Ibid.*, p. 145.

visit of May 1 to the Soviet *chargé d'affaires*) to the Chinese in
Peking, while giving military assistance to Cairo. (One recalls
that, in 1939, Stalin talked urgently to the Germans on the one
hand and to the Western Allies on the other.)

On April 29, as talks were going on among all three powers,
Undersecretary of State Elliot Richardson flew to a high-level
meeting in New York of US and Soviet citizens with a major
policy address appealing for geographic "spheres of mutual restraint" on the part of the great powers. The *New York Times*
reported:

> Ironically, Mr. Richardson's carefully planned ad-
> dress came only one day after American intelli-
> gence analysts reached the long feared conclusion
> . . . that the Soviet Union had . . . [sent] trained
> Russian pilots to fly combat aircraft on operational
> missions over Egypt.[15]
>
> Mr. Richardson's "constructive speech" was
> amended at the last minute to include "ominous"
> warnings.[16]

The actual importance of this "detailed intelligence information" about Soviet fliers remains to be evaluated. It is interesting
that news of this intelligence was not only received but given to
the US press on April 28, the day of the Fishhook decision, and
one day before the President ordered an "immediate and full"
evaluation of it.[17] There has since been speculation that the
same intelligence was a significant factor in the President's decision to escalate in Cambodia rather than pursue further his
diplomatic options. The President reportedly "had finally gotten
fed up with assaults on the country's 'will,' not only in Cambodia
[*sic*] and Vietnam but in the Middle East as well." [18]

Also cut off by the Cambodian escalation was the prospect,
announced April 27, of renewed US-Chinese ambassadorial talks
at Warsaw on May 20. Even before the Chinese announced that

[15] The *New York Times,* May 3, 1970, IV, p. 3.
[16] *Ibid.*
[17] The *New York Times,* April 30, 1970.
[18] The *New York Times,* May 3, 1970, IV, p. 1.

they would not attend the talks, giving Cambodia as the reason, US journalists had reported that

> . . . the American military operation in Cambodia has crushed any hope the United States may have had for a significant improvement in relations with Communist China.[19]

This diplomatic casualty may well prove the most serious of all, in view of General Gavin's recent warning that the US "incursion" into Cambodia carries the risk of a war with Communist China, and his fear expressed to the Senate Foreign Relations Committee that some American generals may want such an "ultimate confrontation:"

> There is always a military officer somewhere who wants to win a battle by taking one more hill or dropping one more bomb. . . . But what deeply concerns me now is that out of the . . . inability of our tactical commanders to realize victory, there may be those who would be tempted to the ultimate confrontation, the war with Red China.[20]

It is hard to escape the conclusion that for years some US generals and intelligence agencies in Southeast Asia have been working in collaboration with Nationalist Chinese to frustrate an improvement of relations between Peking and Washington. This alarming fear was raised in 1966, when US planes first bombed and strafed Chinese vessels in the Tonkin Gulf, both times within days of two important Warsaw meetings (the 130th and 131st) on May 25 and September 7, 1966. It was revived in early 1969, when the prospect of the first Warsaw meeting in thirteen months came to nought, after the CIA, for unexplained and probably inexplicable reasons, decided to give unusual publicity to the defection of a minor Chinese diplomat in The

---

[19] Charles R. Smith, UPI correspondent in Hong Kong, The *Oakland Tribune,* May 17, 1970.
[20] The San Jose *Mercury,* May 13, 1970; these specific fears of General Gavin were not reported by either the *New York Times* or the *Washington Post.*

Hague.[21] (The CIA's publicity was abetted by that of the Free China Relief Association, a Taiwan affiliate of the Asian People's Anti-Communist League which in the past has admitted chartering planes from Civil Air Transport—that is to say the Taiwan incarnation of the CIA-linked airline Air America—to drop supplies to KMT [Kuomintang] guerrillas on the Burma-Laos border.)

Last summer the United States cut back the Seventh Fleet's patrol in the Taiwan straits to a single radar ship, after broadcasts from Peking hinted that withdrawal of the fleet (without reference to a concomitant dismantling of US bases on Taiwan, as had previously been demanded) could lead to an improvement of US-Chinese relations. But soon after, in October, 1969, the intelligence community resumed the flights of "drones," or pilotless reconnaissance planes, over China, "at a time when the State Department was working to reopen the Warsaw channel." [22] The flights, which might seem redundant in the light of continued satellite surveillance, had been canceled by Johnson in March, 1968, as part of his strategy to start Vietnam peace talks. Their resumption suggested to at least one Washington observer, cited by Joseph Goulden in the *Nation,* that

> . . . military and intelligence commanders in the Far East wanted a *quid pro quo* for dropping the naval patrol—drones for destroyers.

In January, after Peking suddenly agreed to a new round of

[21] For details on this and subsequent incidents, see Joseph Goulden, "Talks with China: the Military Saboteurs," The *Nation,* March 2, 1970, pp. 231–33.

[22]*Ibid.,* p. 232. Beginning October 3, 1969, the State Department representative on the interagency "201 Committee" which approved the flights was Ray Cline, a close friend of Chiang's son Chiang Ching-kuo and former CIA station chief in Taiwan, who in 1962 flew to Washington "with an idea for a 'covert' but large-scale landing on the [Chinese] mainland—a sort of even larger Bay of Pigs" (Roger Hilsman, *To Move a Nation,* Garden City, N.Y.: Doubleday, 1967, p. 314). I. F. Stone heard reports that Madame Chennault, widow of Civil Air Transport's founder Claire Chennault and a close collaborator with the Asian People's Anti-Communist League, had a hand in securing Cline's appointment (*I. F. Stone's Weekly,* October 20, 1969, p. 3); cf. The *Washington Post,* October 4, 1969, A2.

talks to be held on January 20, the US immediately halted the drone spy flights. The talks did take place, but only after a commando raid on January 18 by Nationalist Chinese troops against the mainland, the first such raid in several years. It is highly doubtful whether the US intelligence community is any closer than before to cooperating with the State Department's search for *rapprochement*. On April 13, 1970, four months after the cancellation of the drone flights, and shortly before the announcement of the May 20 meeting scheduled in Warsaw, the *Dallas Morning News* reported an interview with a former Air America pilot, John Wiren:

> American pilots working with the Central Intelligence Agency (CIA) are making low-level, night-time flights over Communist China to further dissension and eventual revolution, the *Dallas News* has been told by a former government flier. "Our boys are doing quite a bit of flying into China," said John Wiren in an interview. "They fly upriver at night in old PBYs. They drop (Chinese Nationalist) guerrillas and supplies put in there to stir things up." Wiren . . . who spent much of the 1960's flying for the CIA-sponsored airline Air America in Laos . . . said the clandestine flights are made into China as part of a long-range strategic plan. "The big plan is for revolution in China," he said.

It is not necessary to believe that Mr. Wiren's "long-range strategic plan" conforms to the officially arrived-at strategic objectives of either the US Government or even the CIA. On the contrary, it seems to be a lingering survival of proposals and operations during the 1950's by Chennault and his private airline CAT Inc. (since renamed Air America) that failed to gain official approval. The cumulative record does however suggest that personnel within the executive branch, and the intelligence agencies in particular, have over the years participated in a continuous effort, which so far has always been successful, to prevent any significant US de-escalation in Southeast Asia, and above all any significant improvement of US-Chinese relations.

It must be clearly understood that since 1950, the year of the Korean War and the China lobby, there has never been a genuine US de-escalation in Southeast Asia. Every apparent de-escalation of the fighting, such as in Vietnam in 1954 and Laos in 1961–62, has been balanced by an escalation, either covert or structural, whose long-range result overshadowed America's previous war effort. In 1954, for example, America's direct involvement in the First Indochina War was limited to a few dozen USAF transport planes and pilots "on loan" to Chennault's airline CAT, plus 200 USAF technicians to service them. Though Dulles, Radford, and Nixon failed to implement their proposals for US air strikes and/or troop intervention, Dulles was able to substitute for the discarded plan for immediate intervention a "proposal for creating a Southeast Asia Treaty Organization." [23] SEATO soon became a cover for US "limited war" games in Southeast Asia, which in turn grew into the first covert US military involvement in Laos in 1959—the start of the Second Indochina War.

In early 1961 Kennedy resisted energetic pressures from his Joint Chiefs to invade Laos openly with up to 60,000 soldiers empowered, if necessary, to use tactical nuclear weapons (Nixon also conferred with Kennedy and again urged, at the least, "a commitment of American air power"). [24] Unwilling with his limited reserves to initiate major operations simultaneously in both Laos and Cuba, Kennedy settled for a political solution in Laos, beginning with a ceasefire which went into effect on May 3, 1961. On May 4 and 5, 1961, Rusk and Kennedy announced the first of a series of measures to strengthen the US military commitment in South Vietnam. The timing suggests that the advocates of a showdown with China in one country had been placated by the *quid pro quo* of a build-up in another. In like manner the final conclusion of the 1962 Geneva agreements on Laos came only after the United States had satisfied Asian and domestic hawks by its first commitment of US combat troops to the area, in Thailand.

In 1968, finally, we now know that the "de-escalation" announced by President Johnson in March and November, in the

[23] Roberts, in Gettleman, ed., *Vietnam*, Selection 24.
[24] Richard Nixon, "Cuba, Castro, and John F. Kennedy," *Reader's Digest* (November, 1964), p. 291.

form of a cessation of the bombing of North Vietnam, was misleading. In fact the same planes were simply diverted from North
Vietnam to Laos: the overall level of bombing, far from de-
creasing, continued to increase.

One has, unhappily, to conclude that there is simply no
precedent for a genuine US de-escalation in Southeast Asia,
though there have been illusory appearances of de-escalation.
This conclusion does not of itself prove that "Vietnamization"
of the war is impossible, or a deception to delude the American
electorate. It does however suggest that a twenty-year search for
a successful war in Southeast Asia will not be easily converted
into a search for the means to withdraw. The Cambodian adventure is only one more proof, for anyone who still needs it,
that our current crisis in Southeast Asia is only the outward
manifestation of a continuing crisis of government at home in
America.

It is symptomatic of the deep division within our country that
Nixon's "Vietnamization" is in essence neither a simple escalation nor a simple de-escalation, but an effort, which in all likelihood is bound to fail, to pursue both courses simultaneously.
Rather like Johnson during his first fourteen months in office,
Nixon has tried to sound like an advocate of peace in Southeast
Asia, while assuring us he will never let us lose there. In both
cases this may be rather more self-deception than a conscious
attempt to delude voters: Nixon, like Johnson before him, is
still putting off the brutal choice between peace and "victory"
through unprecedented escalation. Thus his "Vietnamization"
policy is an attempt to balance certain partial withdrawals of
US combat and support troops (which are probably too limited
to lead to peace) with a real escalation of the air war (an
escalation which, though murderous, is probably too limited to
lead to victory).

The full extent of the expanded air war is a closely kept secret.
Congressional inquiries into the Laotian war have indicated that
in Laos alone the US is flying anywhere between 20,000 and
27,000 sorties a month, perhaps seven times the level of June,
1968. For an indication of what this means, it is important to
remember that in early 1968 there were roughly between 1,000

and 3,500 sorties over Laos a month, yet at that time we had already generated several hundred thousand refugees in a nation of some four million inhabitants, and almost all the Pathet Lao villages which Jacques DeCornoy of *Le Monde* visited at that time were already flattened. (As for Vietnam, the US intends to double the size of the South Vietnamese Air Force between early 1970 and late 1971, to some forty squadrons or 800 planes; yet even after this expansion the US will continue to fly half the combat missions in South Vietnam.)[25]

Why do we thus escalate our punishment of a terrain already demolished? One answer, as Noam Chomsky has pointed out, is the conclusion of theorists like Harvard government professor Samuel Huntington that the enemy's base among the peasantry can be eradicated if there is " 'direct application of mechanical and conventional power' . . . on such a massive scale as to produce a massive migration from countryside to city." [26] But we are also dropping strategic tonnages over sparsely inhabited areas as part of our tactical air support. The precedent for this lies in Air Force General Momyer's tactics of saturation bombing around the isolated Marine outpost of Khe Sanh in early 1968, a bombing unprecedented in the history of warfare:

> In about six weeks, US aircraft had dropped 100,000 tons of bombs [i.e., some five times the equivalent of the device exploded over Hiroshima] and fired 700,000 rounds of machine gun fire into a circular area roughly five miles in diameter. . . . An Air Force colonel . . . said, "The tonnage of ordnance placed in that circle is unbelievable. In mid-February, the area looked like the rest of Vietnam, mountainous and heavily jungled with very little visibility through the jungle canopy. Five weeks later, the jungle had become literally a desert—vast stretches of scarred, bare earth with hardly a tree

[25] The *New York Times,* January 29, 1970, p. 12.
[26] Samuel P. Huntington, "The Bases of Accommodation," *Foreign Affairs* (July, 1968), p. 650; Noam Chomsky, "After Pinkville," *The New York Review of Books,* January 1, 1970.

standing, a landscape of splinters and bomb craters." [27]

After this pounding the North Vietnamese withdrew, an enemy body count in the battlefield was put at 1,200 and the overall number of enemy dead was estimated at more than 10,000.[28]

It is not clear that the North Vietnamese were defeated at Khe Sanh—the US was asking for a "sign" that Hanoi was ready for serious talks, and their withdrawal may well have been in reply. It is however clear that the Pentagon believes it won a decisive military victory. A senior Army general called Khe Sanh "probably the first major ground action won entirely or almost entirely by air power"; and even Townsend Hoopes, ostensibly an opponent of escalation, calls Khe Sanh "the one decisive victory for air power in the Vietnam war." [29] (Richard Barnet, a former State Department official, has charged in a recent speech that Johnson, under pressure from the military, considered using tactical nuclear weapons to relieve Khe Sanh. See *footnote 38* [this Selection—eds.].)

To drop the equivalent of five Hiroshima atomic bombs around Khe Sanh took 24,200 sorties in six weeks, for a rate of a little over 16,000 a month. Comparisons can only be crude (there is a big difference between F-100's and B-52's) but these figures can still help us to understand what is implied by a reported Laotian sortie rate of 27,000 a month. It is uncertain whether the US can win by converting more and more of Indochina into "a landscape of splinters and bomb craters." One result however has already been accomplished. The so-called "firebreak" distinction, which opponents of tactical nuclear weapons had attempted to establish between "conventional" and "limited nuclear war," has been virtually obliterated, leaving

---

[27] Townsend Hoopes, *The Limits of Intervention* (New York: David McKay, 1969), p. 213. The total tonnage dropped on Berlin in the whole of World War II was 77,000; on Hamburg, 22,500.

[28] The highly dubious practice of multiplying by ten to arrive at a kill estimate dates back to the French Indochina War: cf. William Lederer, *Our Own Worst Enemy*, New York: Fawcett, 1968, p. 37.

[29] Hoopes, p. 214.

the way open to an escalation that would be qualitative as well as quantitative.

As General Frederic H. Smith wrote in 1960 in the *Air University Review*:

> Not only can the intelligent use of nuclear fire power in limited war give us the greatest possible opportunity to win such wars at minimum cost . . . it is highly probable that without the use of such weapons, our chances of winning in many areas are slim indeed.[30]

In other words, for the US Air Force, "Vietnamization" is only one more step in a long history of US escalation. It is evident from recent modifications in the conduct of our offensive operations in South Vietnam that the role of ground troops is now less to destroy the enemy than to locate him. Those who believe that major ground actions can be "won entirely or almost entirely by air power" can doubtless argue that Asian troops will suffice for this reduced role, while the US can continue its air actions from Vietnam enclaves, from Thailand, or conceivably even from aircraft carriers.

It was obvious however that this strategy of air power would put a severe and probably intolerable strain on Cambodian neutrality. On the one hand the NLF forces had little choice but to take shelter in this one part of Indochina which was relatively secure from our rain of death. On the other it was predictable that local US commanders would initiate or condone unauthorized operations against Cambodia, long before Nixon (on the urging of Kissinger) had ordered bombing strikes there in the spring of 1969. A US helicopter pilot boasted in a letter to The *San Francisco Chronicle,* May 13, 1970, that

---

[30] Cf., for example, General Thomas S. Power, *Design for Survival,* New York: Coward-McCann, 1965, especially pp. 217–23: "Once we have decided on that objective we must make every effort to attain it and be willing to employ all the military strengths and weapons that may be needed. . . . Protracted limited wars, such as the conflict in South Vietnam, have become prohibitively expensive, drain military strengths and, because of our lack of success, make our deterrent for both nuclear and limited war less credible."

I've been to Cambodia many times in performing my missions—each time I might add at the risk of a court-martial if caught crossing the border.

It is also obvious that this modified ground strategy of "Vietnamization," largely devised by civilians, has met with stubborn resistance from elements in the US Army. This has been evidenced in part by the army's foot-dragging on the actual withdrawals of US forces. Nixon's original hope in the spring of 1969 was to have almost all 250,000 US combat troops out of Vietnam by the end of 1970,[31] but actual reductions have averaged only 10,000 a month for the last eight months (in mid-May, as I write, there are now 428,750 troops, as against 509,800 on August 31, 1969),[32] and Nixon's April 20 announcement of a large but postponed reduction no longer refers specifically to combat troops at all. It is clear moreover that even this latest announcement was as disappointing to many Army generals as it was to the anti-war movement; it is above all by cutting back the army that Nixon plans to achieve his "low profile."

Repeated allusions by civilian officials and advisers (from David Packard to Sir Robert Thompson) to the prospect of a "Korean" standoff in South Vietnam can only further alienate the Army generals whose recommendations for Asian strategy

[31] *US News and World Report,* September 22, 1969. When Clark Clifford called for a withdrawal of *all* combat troops by the end of 1970, Nixon expressed publicly the hope that he could beat this schedule.

This was the first announced withdrawal of US troops from the area since a similar announcement by the Kennedy Administration on October 2, 1963, concerning the probable withdrawal of 1,000 US troops by the end of that year. The Kennedy withdrawals would have been implemented by the decisions of a top-level Honolulu Conference on November 20, 1963; but these decisions seem to have been secretly countermanded—apparently at an unscheduled "emergency" meeting of Johnson and his top advisers on November 24, two days after the Kennedy assassination. cf. *The United States in World Affairs,* Council on Foreign Relations (1963) New York: Harper & Row, 1964, p. 193. The number of US "advisers" dropped for a while by about 500 to 15,500, but soon rose again.

[32] In February, 1968, at the time of the Tet offensive and Johnson's response to it, there were 510,000 troops in Vietnam. When Nixon was elected in November, 1968, there were 538,300. As of March 1, 1969, there were 541,500.

have for fifteen years been based on the slogan "Never Another Korea." By this the so-called "never again" school has not meant the avoidance of all Asian ground wars, as some columnists have suggested, but that US ground troops should never again be committed without a prior commitment to win with whatever weapons are necessary.

From the point of view of air strategy, the Cambodian adventure is indeed, as Senator Tower and others have argued, a logical extension of "Vietnamization," for it aims to get rid of the major enemy refuge from US air power. The ground strategy of "Vietnamization" has just as clearly been negated: Westmoreland's tactic of attempting to "bottle-up" the enemy has at last been revived, two years after its author was relieved of his command and made the present army Chief of Staff. Hitherto the largest single allied war effort (and the most spectacular such failure) had been Operation Junction City in February 1967, with some 25,000 US and South Vietnamese troops.[33] The Fishhook operation alone required the same number of troops.[34] Even as Nixon announced the Cambodian Fishhook operation, Administration spokesmen noted that the US troop withdrawals announced on April 20 "will probably be slowed down." Although announcements of "future" withdrawals are likely to be escalated before the November [1970] elections, practice may be different: by May 14 there had actually been a troop increase, of 3,250 men, over the level of one month before.

On May 8 Nixon said he "would expect that the South Vietnamese would come out [of Cambodia] approximately at the same time that we do." On May 21 General Ky bluntly rejected this suggestion ("We will continue to maintain our military presence in Cambodia") in terms which prompted Senator Mansfield to recall that the South Vietnamese have long had territorial ambitions in this part of Cambodia.[35] In this way an

---

[33] That escalation, like the present one, followed hard on the heels of developments that might have been construed as a "peace threat": the North Vietnamese Foreign Minister's hint of January 28, 1967, that there "could" be discussion between North Vietnam and the United States.

[34] The *Wall Street Journal,* May 11, 1970, p. 1.

[35] In June, 1958, South Vietnamese troops invaded Cambodia's Stung Treng Province: the United States then not only refused to condemn

Indonesian-style massacre of ethnic Vietnamese in Cambodia by our reactionary proteges in Phnompenh is likely to be followed by a permanent invasion by our reactionary proteges in Saigon. These details are however not likely to deter the Nixon Administration from continuing to aver that its only goals in Indochina are to prevent a bloodbath and external aggression in South Vietnam.

Viewed in the context of previous US escalations, both the Cambodian adventure and the evolution of the "Vietnamization" strategy confirm an alarming thesis. There is not today, and indeed there has not been for some time, a civilian government in Washington with the will or power to enforce a cutback of our operations in Southeast Asia. On the contrary, those operations have in their intensity already reached the upper limits of what can reasonably be called a "limited war," so that Washington's increasing hints and rumors about tactical nuclear weapons no longer seem fantastic. Far from having reached a level of stability, this heightened and enlarged war threatens to expand still further outward. In the wake of the first announcement of US military advisers fighting in the Laotian panhandle, columnist Jack Anderson reported that "President Nixon had on his desk detailed contingency plans calling for US troops to cross into North Vietnam" (The *San Francisco Chronicle,* May 14, 1970, p. 43).

In the face of this crisis, it is not enough to repeat Acheson's observation to Johnson that "with all due respect . . . the Joint Chiefs of Staff don't know what they're talking about." [36] Even the Joint Chiefs realize the likelihood that any one of these escalations will sooner or later bring us into direct confrontation with Communist China. In their tendency to grasp at ever bigger solutions they do not seem to face serious opposition from the President,[37] who on May 8 stressed that the Cambodian invasion

the invasion, it even reminded Sihanouk "that the arms he had received from us were meant for use only against the communists" (Robert Shaplen, *Time Out of Hand,* New York: Harper & Row, 1969, p. 311).

[36] Hoopes, *Limits of Intervention,* p. 204.

[37] They must realize, furthermore, that such a course is not likely to be ratified by the electorate of 1972. Probably only a few of us were disturbed last fall when I. F. Stone reported that generals in Washing-

was a "decisive move" and added that if the enemy escalated in the future "we will move decisively and not step by step."

This is the man who on March 17, 1955, as Vice President, told the Executives Club of Chicago:

> Our artillery and our tactical air force in the Pacific are now equipped with atomic explosives which can and will be used on military targets with precision and effectiveness. It is foolish to talk about the possibility that the weapons which might be used in the event war breaks out in the Pacific would be limited to the conventional Korean and World War II types of explosives. Our forces could not fight an effective war in the Pacific with those types of explosives if they wanted to. Tactical atomic explosives are now conventional and will be used against the military targets of any aggressive force.[38]

What should be studied closely in the next weeks is not the withdrawal of US ground troops from Cambodia, which may well be speeded up in response to dissent and the falling stock market (while the South Vietnamese dig in for an indefinite stay). Instead we should watch for the first signs of the next "decisive" escalation. For the crisis we face at present derives not from a single mistaken adventure, but from a settled strategy, a military effort that has twenty years of uninterrupted momentum behind it.

---

ton ". . . apparently have told dinner parties hereabouts that there would be no elections in 1972 because the military were going to end all this 'turmoil' by taking over" (*I. F. Stone's Weekly*, September 22, 1969, p. 1). Now even the *Wall Street Journal* sees fit to report that the Rand Corporation "is studying the idea of cancelling the 1972 Presidential election if radicals threaten [*sic*] to disrupt it." It is hardly necessary to take such reports seriously however. The prospects for the year ahead are grave enough.

[38] Nixon, quoted by Richard Barnet, speech of May 20, 1970, to Business Executives Against the War, Washington.

34

The Leader of the "Free World"

JEAN DANIEL *

How did Nixon reach the decision to invade Cambodia? It is
rarely possible to achieve a quick yet accurate understanding
of the unfolding of events and actions preceding a war. Nevertheless, here is the story as we have just heard it from an American industrialist passing through Paris. This industrialist is a
member of Nixon's inner circle, and is very closely associated in
particular with Henry Kissinger, White House policy adviser on
international affairs.

For six months, through networks established at the Pentagon
and the CIA, the United States had been perfectly aware of the
strategic and logistical importance of the Vietnamese sanctuary
lodged in the part of Cambodia known as the Parrot's Beak.
Secretary of Defense Melvin Laird and Army Chief of Staff
General Westmoreland (former field commander in Vietnam)
had repeatedly drawn President Nixon's attention to the fact
that the Cambodian national army was powerless not only
against the 40,000 North and South Vietnamese who supplied
the NLF with men, provisions, and arms, but also against the
indigenous Khmer communist resistance. Several times, but to
no avail, Prince Sihanouk had called upon the Hanoi authorities
to safeguard Cambodian neutrality. He was aware of his weakness, his family was begging him to appeal to the Americans,
and he feared being caught up in an expansion of the war. In
February, 1970, according to the American interpretation, Sihanouk's relations with the Vietnamese revolutionaries were at
a very low ebb. It was then that he decided, *informing the
Americans of his intentions* [author's italics—eds.], to leave for
Moscow and Peking in order to induce the Soviet and Chinese
leaders to intervene on his behalf with Hanoi. These same

* From *Le Nouvel Observateur* (May 11, 1970), No. 287, pp. 20-1.
By permission. Translated by Kathy Brown and the editors. Jean Daniel,
a distinguished French journalist, is editor of *Le Nouvel Observateur*.

Americans declared that at that time it was not at all in their interest to let the CIA, or anyone else, overthrow Sihanouk. They were waiting for the outcome of his mission. On March 18, 1970, the Cambodian Parliament deposed Prince Sihanouk and General Lon Nol allowed himself to be persuaded by the Prince's mother to take power.

At the same time, the new fighting in Laos was convincing Washington that the Vietnamese were beginning to abandon the prospect of negotiations limited to the two Vietnams. For reasons still obscure, they were contemplating the enlargement of the war. The effects of this were felt at the Paris Conference: it was deadlocked over the same difficulties. And yet, still following the American interpretation, troop withdrawals were continuing, prisoners were being exchanged, and gestures of good will were being made on both sides. But Washington was uneasy. On March 21 or 22, for the first time, William Rogers was directed to inform the Soviet ambassador, Dobrynin, of the "decision" of the United States, namely that Nixon would *never* tolerate the non-neutrality of Laos and Cambodia, and that he would *never* accept capitulation in South Vietnam or an unconditional withdrawal of American troops. But he was prepared to withdraw gradually, allowing the Saigon Vietnamese to freely decide their future without any communist influence or pressure. At that time the Soviet ambassador seemed ill-informed about what was happening in Southeast Asia.

And a lot of things were happening; in particular, the celebrated conference of the Indochinese "left" was being held in China on March 24 and 25. It was during this conference that the French concept of a meeting between all states with an interest in Indochinese affairs, such as took place in Geneva in 1954 under the aegis of Mendès-France, was rejected. Chinese observers were present, but no Soviet ones. Washington surmised that the Moscow leaders were furious; previously the Vietnamese had contrived to maintain an equal balance between Moscow and Peking. But the Soviets had neither been invited to Canton nor informed of what was being planned there.

It was from this point on that action groups (Nixon's "brain trust") began to probe the possibility of an American initiative of some sort in Indochina. Henry Kissinger, a liberal by reputation, was persuaded to agree to such a plan, just as Arthur Schlesinger, President Kennedy's adviser, had allowed himself to become party to an action against Cuba. The international situation seemed favorable. Why? Thailand, the Philippines, Indonesia, and above all Japan, were plainly uneasy about future Chinese "expansionism." It was, of course, the governments of all these countries, and not the people, who expressed concern. But the anxiety was most urgently expressed. As for the West, Germany, Great Britain and even France needed the United States too much to resist it in any way.

Attorney General John Mitchell, one of those among the "hawks" who is closest to President Nixon, hit upon the solution: it was necessary to put an end to the Cambodian sanctuary in rapid and spectacular fashion. Failing this, the same thing would happen to General Lon Nol as had happened to King Hussein: Lon Nol would be outflanked by the Vietnamese the way the king had been by the Palestinians. Furthermore, the Vietnamese might think the Americans were prepared to see Cambodia and Laos fall to the communists. This would represent "the capitulation of the free world."

But what about the Soviets? The expert in the "brain trust" complacently painted a somber picture of what was going on in the USSR. The economic crisis there was reaching catastrophic proportions, and it was now being openly discussed in Moscow. Soviet leaders were very much at odds, while the people had no desire for any sort of military adventure. The army regretted having allowed itself to become bogged down in the Near East: it had nothing but contempt for the Arabs' lack of fighting spirit. Possibly the Soviets had reacted in Egypt because their honor was at stake there, but the Near Eastern situation was explosive in every way. Elsewhere, the USSR would react in an "ideological" manner, falling into line with Chinese and Vietnamese positions, temporarily taking a tough stance on the Vienna negotiations on nuclear arms limitation, and contenting themselves to wait.

The real obstacle being analyzed in the "brain trust" was the domestic one. The financial malaise was becoming worse and the number of unemployed was growing. The isolationist tendency of big businessmen was becoming pronounced; some of them had resigned themselves to abandoning Indochina to communism, convinced that they could do just as good business there as in Yugoslavia or Guinea. Nixon had been elected on the impetus provided by Johnson's "peace initiatives," and with the promise that his efforts would be devoted not to waving the American flag over far-off graveyards but to building a new American society. University strife was becoming alarmingly widespread. All this was serious. What was to be done?

Secretary of State William Rogers and Secretary of Defense Melvin Laird had grave doubts about the prospect of extending the war, but it was John Mitchell, with Kissinger's support, whose counsel was most persuasive. Mitchell spoke of the Chinese menace: Moscow, just as much as Washington, dreaded the time when Peking's missiles would become intercontinental in range. He revived John Foster Dulles' cold war rhetoric, speaking of the "free world;" if American businessmen fail to do their patriotic duty, then they'll have to be made to. Authority, even as it totters in the West, must be reasserted everywhere. Once the moment of shock and surprise is past, it will become a paying proposition.

"We will have the intellectuals and the 'highbrow' press against us for two or three weeks. But on our side we will have all those at home and abroad who still fear communism and in whose eyes the Reds are still the enemy to be destroyed. In fact, everything will depend on the rapidity and effectiveness of our intervention in Cambodia."

Now it was up to Nixon alone to decide. He was to deliberate for two nights and a day. All of a sudden, he turned back into the man he had been as Vice President under Eisenhower: impatient, sometimes ill-tempered, and above all exalted by the idea that he was to make the decision of the century in the name of the most powerful nation in history, seemingly against the public opinion of that nation. The hard-liners among his advisers had already made up their minds days ago. Nixon had always wanted to cultivate his image among the military. His speech re-echoed the vow he had pronounced before General Westmoreland: "This country will not suffer its first defeat while I am President." Even before he had given the go-ahead signal, all of the orders had been communicated to General Abrams in Saigon so that the expedition would be both a success and a surprise. General Abrams replied that he had been ready for a long time.

President Nixon gave the green light. He would destroy the Cambodian sanctuary. He would help the Phnompenh government hold off the communists until the monsoon season. Then, turning to the Vietnamese, he would tell them: nothing has changed, negotiations for a peace between the two Vietnams will continue. But now the neutrality of Laos and Cambodia could be guaranteed. And above all the Saigon government could more successfully repress an NLF, no longer supplied by the stores of the Parrot's Beak. The United States would force the North Vietnamese to limit the conflict by demonstrating to them that if they wanted to widen the war, as they had decided at Canton, the Americans were also capable of fighting on all fronts.

On April 29, American troops moved into the Parrot's Beak in the wake of devastating bombing raids. Everything was burned and razed. As the Americans had expected, they found tons and tons of provisions and ammunition buried in what were true subterranean cities, marvels of organization. The New York Stock Exchange fell; it had never been so low. On all sides the American press exploded: such vehement condemnation of the occupant of the White House by editorial writers ordinarily cool-headed—indeed, respectful—has rarely been seen. The Senate was alarmed; there was talk of the President's "madness," of his weakness in the face of the military men of the Pentagon, of the "crimes" of the CIA. The United States was swept by a wind of resistance. On May 1, one really had the impression that it was Nixon versus all of America, that the majority of the citizens of the United States were disgusted with their President. The most violent protests came from the universities. However, on May 4, the results of a poll were published: fifty-nine percent of Americans approved of the Cambodian expedition. But the poll had been taken prior to an event of considerable psychological significance: four students, all described by the *New York Times* as studious, peaceful, and patriotic, fell under the bullets of the National Guard on the campus of Kent State University in Ohio.

All over the world, public opinion was thunderstruck. Washington calmly awaited the reactions. From the West, little or nothing. The French government "deplored," but in the corridors of Parliament, majority deputies were heard to remark: "If the expedition is brought to a swift and successful conclusion, it will be a real coup. . . ." The visits of French officials to the United States embassy were more numerous than ever. The new Ambassador had arrived and everybody wanted to bid him welcome; Giscard d'Estaing, back from Washington, spoke in the Cabinet Council of his warm reception and of the wisdom of President Nixon's new economic measures. In London and Bonn, nothing was said: the hands of these "socialist" governments were tied. Kosygin held a "tough" press conference, no tougher than expected. The Soviets seemed preoccupied with extolling the fraternal ties between themselves and their new vassals, the Czechs. And for the first time there was talk of a *rapprochement* between Moscow and Peking.

The "brain trust" believed it had calculated well. So did the French who launched the war against Ho Chi Minh in 1946. So did those who bombed Sakiet during the Algerian War in 1958. So did the Americans who advised Kennedy on the first intervention in Vietnam. So did Johnson when he ordered the first B-52 bombings. Imperialism has a military logic all its own.

In Indonesia, South Korea, Formosa, the Philippines, Thailand, Franco's Spain and the Greece of the colonels, the regimes rejoiced: the "free world" had raised high its head. Since the carnage inflicted upon Cambodia, once again it had a leader.

35

The War Spreads

PAUL M. SWEEZY AND HARRY MAGDOFF *

Perhaps it is no more than a truism to say that wars either end or they spread: an endless war is a spreading war. But at least it is a truism which should not be ignored or forgotten. In his speech of November 3 Nixon talked about ending the war in Vietnam, but the policies he opted for were in fact designed to prolong it indefinitely. There should therefore be no surprise that now, just a few months later, the war is spreading and gives every evidence of continuing to spread.

Up until near the end of March the spreading process centered in northern Laos, which is sandwiched in between the bulk of North Vietnam on the east and Thailand on the west and south. Last year the pro-American Laotians, including a private mercenary army maintained by the CIA, captured the Plain of Jars, a strategically situated plateau more or less in the middle of northern Laos. This seemed to guarantee protection to the government centers of Luang Prabang and Vientiane and to constitute a buffer zone separating the North Vietnamese from northern Thailand, where guerrilla insurgency is under way but still largely isolated from outside support. All this changed quite suddenly in February, when an offensive by the revolutionary Pathet Lao troops (supported, according to the capitalist press, by North Vietnamese) routed the pro-American forces and recaptured the Plain of Jars. This offensive evoked a response from the Americans in the form of heavy bombings, involving a large proportion of the B-52's in the Southeast Asia

* From *Monthly Review: An Independent Socialist Magazine* [New York City], XXII May, 1970), pp. 1–10. By permission. The authors, who together edit *Monthly Review,* are economists. Sweezy has written *The Theory of Capitalist Development* (1942), *The Present as History* (1953) and other books. Magdoff's *The Age of Imperialism* (1969) is an important study of the economic roots of American foreign policy—eds.

area. It was this stepped-up bombing which called attention in the United States to the spreading of the war in Laos and had its repercussions in Washington, especially in the Senate.

As usual, the bombings did not prove militarily decisive. The Plain of Jars remains in "enemy" hands, and it seems to be generally agreed, or at least feared, that the Pathet Lao and its allies can now proceed to take over all of northern Laos and link up with the Thai dissidents any time they choose to. That this is a setback for the Americans, with potential long-run consequences of far-reaching importance, seems clear. But there was not much the Americans could do about it. A look at the map is enough to show the impracticality of introducing US ground forces into the area, which is 600 miles or so northwest of Saigon. Furthermore, an open escalation of the war at this time would ruin Nixon's carefully staged public relations campaign to convince the American people that he is seriously trying to end the war.

It follows that a countermove, to be effective, would have to be mounted elsewhere. And this may well be what accounts for at least the timing of the second stage of the spreading process—in Cambodia. The key move here was of course the overthrow of Prince Norodom Sihanouk as chief of state, which took place on March 18 while the prince was out of the country. Who wanted to get rid of Sihanouk and why? The prince himself provided the answer in a speech delivered at the University of Paris several years ago:

> The reason why we are opposing the United States is based on this fact: since 1955 the United States has tried various means, including the most treacherous and dangerous, to force us to join their side as a meek satellite. This is why we have carried on fierce resistance and spoken not very politely.[1]

Anyone familiar with CIA operations in such countries as Iran and Guatemala need be in no doubt about the nature of

---

[1] Quoted in Keith Buchanan, "Cambodia Between Peking and Paris," *Monthly Review*, XVI (December, 1964).

the means to which Sihanouk was referring: promotion of right wing politico-terrorist organizations (the *Khmer Serei* or Free Khmers), suborning of political and military leaders with bribes and offers of generous US aid, and so on. It was Sihanouk's great merit to have resisted all these efforts and thus to have spared his country and his people the twin horrors of war and American occupation. A dispatch to the *Washington Post* of March 14, four days before Sihanouk's overthrow, made the point with dramatic emphasis:

> "We could have had the billions of American dollars you see spent in Saigon, the skyscrapers and traffic jams of Bangkok, and the low-cost imported luxuries of Vientiane, if we had wished," said one government official recently. "But we also would have had, like those countries, American planes bombing our countryside, our cities filled with unemployed youths, a communist insurrection all around us, galloping inflation, and an enormous trade deficit." [2]

That these are precisely the blessings the new rulers of Cambodia are in the process of bringing down on their country hardly needs to be argued. According to the London *Economist* of March 21, the new rulers of Cambodia have had a long-standing quarrel with Sihanouk:

> Late last year they succeeded in launching a "new economic policy" opposed to Prince Sihanouk's system of state control. They clashed with him in December over a proposal to denationalize the banks. They believe that the economy has been doing badly ever since Prince Sihanouk rejected American aid in 1963. They will aim to secure new loans and a steady stream of foreign investment.

Here we have the tried-and-true formula for neocoloniza-

[2] Quoted in *I. F. Stone's Bi-Weekly*, March 23, 1970.

tion and satellization, and it makes utter nonsense of the new leaders' protestations that their foreign policy will continue to be directed at the neutralization of the country.

As for the Americans, it can of course be taken for granted that a prime objective of their policy is—and, as Sihanouk's statement quoted above indicates, long has been—to integrate Cambodia solidly into their Southeast Asian empire. But, as is usually the case, a policy and the timing of its implementation are different matters requiring different explanations. Why did the anti-Sihanouk coup take place at precisely this time?

One obvious reason is that the prince was out of the country. A head of state who has concentrated power in his own hands is much more vulnerable when he is away from the area where the power is exercised. This was illustrated in the overthrow of Kwame Nkrumah as President of Ghana, and it is confirmed by the coup in Cambodia. But absence from the country is not a sufficient explanation. After all, Sihanouk has made many trips abroad during his long years of rule, and up to now he has always managed to return unscathed. It seems likely that another factor was operating and that, given the domestic and international context, it played the decisive role. We refer to the urgent need of the Americans to escape from an increasingly untenable situation in Vietnam (and Laos).[3]

The nature of this untenable situation is of course well-known, though not much discussed, in the establishment media. In inheriting the Vietnam War from the Johnson administration, Nixon also inherited the danger of exactly the same kind

---

[3] In speaking of "the Americans" this way, we do not mean to imply a belief that the various agencies and individuals concerned with policy-making necessarily agree with each other or even know what some of the others are doing. The CIA, for example, undoubtedly enjoys a considerable degree of independence, and it may at times be able to create a *fait accompli* which forces the hands of those who are supposed to control it. But it is safe to assume that all those involved have pretty much the same conception of the national (i.e., ruling-class) interest, and that no course of action can be initiated and persisted in for long without the approval of the top policy-makers. We should therefore eschew "explanations" in terms of CIA-like plots and machinations, real though they are, and seek to identify the underlying interests involved in a given situation and the way the ruling class and its particular representatives and leaders at the time hope to benefit most (or lose least).

of political death which struck Johnson down: *get out of Vietnam or suffer the consequences.* But get out of Vietnam he could not. The US ruling class feels, with good reason, that defeat in Vietnam, which is exactly what withdrawal would be, would constitute a severe, and in the long run perhaps even fatal, blow to the whole structure of imperialist control over the Third World.[4] The ruling class is therefore not about to sanction, let alone encourage, a pullout from Vietnam. What it does in effect is therefore to jettison an administration which fails to solve the insoluble problem of how to end the war in Vietnam while still winning it, and turns the very same problem over to a new administration, always hoping for a miracle.

This was the situation which faced Nixon when he took office, and it must be said that during his first year he handled it with great political skill. By promising to "Vietnamize" the war and gradually withdraw US forces, revising the draft system, talking about going over to an all-volunteer army, etc., Nixon took the wind out of the anti-war movement's sails. But he accomplished this neat trick only by seeming to do what he was in fact not doing, i.e., moving toward a withdrawal of US forces from Vietnam. The respite was therefore in the nature of the case temporary, and the policy which produced it was certain to backfire as soon as its dupes woke up to what was really going on. In the meantime the poor fellow could only thrash around, vainly searching for a way out of the trap in which he was so firmly caught.

Under these circumstances it is hardly surprising that, in the words of a *Wall Street Journal* reporter, "the desire to 'do something' pervades top levels of government and may overpower other 'common sense' advice that insists the US ability to shape events is negligible." [5] Where the "do something" urge takes over, there is of course always ready a rationalization to

[4] For further discussion of this crucial point, see Paul M. Sweezy and Harry Magdoff, "Vietnam: Endless War," *Monthly Review* (April, 1969), [reprinted in Marvin E. Gettleman, ed., *Vietnam: History, Documents and Opinions* (2d ed., New York, 1970), Selection 76—eds.]

[5] Robert Keatley, under the headline "Nixon Feels Pressure to Expand Role of U.S. in the Fighting in Asia," *Wall Street Journal,* April 3, 1970.

explain why the contemplated action is the very acme of wisdom, the long-sought key to victory, etc., etc. We have seen this process in operation at every major turning point in Vietnam for nearly two decades now: the Cambodian escalation is merely the latest, and unfortunately probably not the last, in a long, long series.

The rationalization this time is nicely spelled out by the foreign affairs columnist of the *New York Times,* Cyrus Sulzberger. Here are excerpts from his column (under the heading "Has a Strategy Collapsed?") of March 27:

> The key to Hanoi's effort to communize South Vietnam has been the technique of sanctuary warfare seeking to outflank and infiltrate the main target area from protected bases and supply routes in theoretically neutral Laos and Cambodia.
>
> If the dramatic new situation in Cambodia can be made to stick, this strategy will come to a dead end. Cambodia, as terminus of the Ho Chi Minh Trail supply route across Laos, with its port of Sihanoukville for seaborne shipments to Hanoi's southern forces and as rehabilitation and reinforcement center for thousands of communist troops, is crucially important. That is why Hanoi, Peking, and Moscow are all happy to help Prince Sihanouk attempt a comeback.
>
> Sanctuaries are vital to modern revolutionary warfare. During the Greek civil conflict, Albania, Yugoslavia, and Bulgaria served as safe havens from which the rebels of General Markos were supplied and to which they could retreat. Only after Tito broke with Moscow, closed off his frontier with Greece, and isolated Albania, was Athens able to squash the insurrection . . . .
>
> Saigon could completely pacify the delta and reinsure the capital's safety if Cambodia becomes truly neutral and ceases to serve as a base for aggression by forces mustered, commanded, and supported by Hanoi . . . .

What is evident is that Hanoi's system of sanctuary warfare is threatened, and unless it can be forcibly reestablished, there is a chance that peace can eventually be arranged in South Vietnam as it was in Greece when the Albanian haven was cut off.

It is not necessary here to undertake to expose all the fallacies in this pipe dream of the military and its journalistic apologists—to show, for example, how basically different the Vietnamese situation today is from the Greek situation of the late 1940's. But it is necessary to point out that Sulzberger's basic assumption—that the war in Vietnam results from "Hanoi's effort to communize South Vietnam," and represents "aggression by forces mustered, commanded, and supported by Hanoi"—is US ruling class mythology which approaches no nearer to reality through repetition. The main "enemy" in Vietnam is the National Liberation Front, which is not going to go away or be pacified by the Saigon government no matter what happens in Cambodia. And as far as using Cambodia as a sanctuary is concerned, what reliable evidence we have suggests that it has not been anywhere near as important as US spokesmen and pundits have claimed, and that the Cambodian government even under Sihanouk did its best to keep the practice to a minimum. Writing in the *Far Eastern Economic Review* (February 26), a correspondent reported as follows:

> To get an idea of what the situation along the border was like, I travelled into Svay Rieng province [the region of Cambodia closest to Saigon], sometimes to within 500 meters of the frontier. Four things seem evident—at least as far as Svay Rieng province is concerned:
> • The Vietcong use Cambodian territory much less than the Americans in Saigon claim.
> • US aircraft violate Cambodian air space and bomb and strafe Cambodian territory in violation of the US guidelines, frequently with no cause at all, and much more often than the US admits.

- In fairness to all sides, it is obvious that the Americans, South Vietnamese, Viet Cong, and North Vietnamese are all making some degree of effort to keep the war out of Cambodia.
- The Cambodian effort to hold ground against all comers belies any reports that they have an "agreement" with the communists—or for that matter with the Americans.

The editorial writers of the *New York Times* showed themselves to be a great deal more sober and realistic than Sulzberger when they wrote a few days after the appearance of his column quoted above:

> The increased willingness of the Cambodian army under the new regime to permit allied cross-border raids against Vietnamese Communist sanctuaries undoubtedly strikes many South Vietnamese and American military men as a welcome opportunity. It opens the way to inflict more damage there on major Viet Cong and North Vietnamese units, supply dumps, and headquarters. But it is also an opportunity to get bogged down on a new front that is unlikely to prove any more decisive than the battlefields already engaged . . . .
>
> With 40,000 or more Vietnamese Communist troops in Cambodia, a huge allied military operation would have to be mounted if an effort were to be made to close down the sanctuary area. Even so, success undoubtedly would prove elusive . . . .
>
> If some bases on the Cambodian side of the border could be rendered unusable, the communist forces could move back a few miles to new bases. Or, if they felt seriously threatened in their sanctuary, they might be tempted to lend forces to Prince Sihanouk in an effort to restore him to power, a move that might bring an embarrassing request from Phnompenh for American military rescue. *Other possibilities can be imagined. They all*

> *lead not to ending the war but to widening it. . . .*[6]

This is certainly true as far as it goes. But it does not go far enough. What has to be understood now is that Sihanouk was the fulcrum in a precariously balanced equilibrium of forces. His removal has destroyed this equilibrium and released the forces which previously held each other in check. And the nature of these forces—the interests and objectives which energize them—is such that not only *may* they lead to a widening of the war, they *must* lead in that direction.

That the American and South Vietnamese military leaders want freedom to invade Cambodia is obvious. Hardly less obvious is the political interest of the Saigon government in sucking the Americans deeper into the Southeast Asian fighting. Perhaps not so obvious, at least as yet, is the fact that the new leaders in Cambodia have the same interest as the Saigon government in the deepest possible involvement of the Americans. As we saw above, they have deliberately chosen the role of US satellite, which implies, in Southeast Asia even more than anywhere else in the world, becoming a military ward of the United States. As to the NLF and Hanoi, now that the old equilibrium around Sihanouk has been destroyed, their interest clearly lies in doing whatever they can to strengthen and hasten the victory of the revolutionary forces in Cambodia, as in Laos and elsewhere in the region. That these forces exist in the form of the Khmer Rouge movement is well known, though little information seems to be available on their present numbers or fighting potential. Another unknown at this stage is the future role of Sihanouk. Reports from Cambodia all agree that he was very popular in the countryside. What is unclear is whether this popularity will survive his overthrow and, if it does, whether he has the will and the ability to play a revolutionary as distinct from a conciliatory role. Historical analogies suggest a negative answer on both counts.

But in any case, speculation, even if it were well informed, on the strength of the Khmer Rouge or the possible role of Sihanouk would not go to the heart of the matter. Cambodia

---

[6] The *New York Times,* editorial, March 31, 1970 (emphasis added).

has been relatively sheltered from the ravages of war up to now. This immunity is coming to an end, thanks to the initiative of the Americans and/or their friends in Phnompenh. As the war spreads, the Cambodian people will be dragged into it willy-nilly and forced to take sides: either for national independence and social revolution, or for satellization and counter-revolution. It may take considerable time and experience for these issues to become clear, but when they do there is little reason to doubt that the mass of Cambodian people will, like the mass of Vietnamese before them, opt for independence and revolution.

When that time comes, the Americans will no doubt fervently wish the old Sihanouk were back in power in Phnompenh. But by then it will be too late. As has happened so many times before, and doubtless will happen even more times in the future, the United States, by seeking to extend its direct control, will have raised up and taught the very forces which fight back to achieve real independence. Reporting on his famous 1965 interview with Mao Tse-tung, Edgar Snow wrote:

> During our conversation he repeatedly thanked foreign invaders for speeding up the Chinese revolution and for bestowing similar favors in Southeast Asia today . . . . He observed that the more American weapons and troops brought into Saigon, the faster the South Vietnamese liberation forces would become armed and educated to win victory.[7]

And now it is the turn of the Cambodians to receive American favors. May they make as good use of them as have their Chinese and Vietnamese brothers.

But these are the longer-term implications of the spread of the war into Cambodia. In the short run, in fact in the very near future, the most important consequence seems likely to be a major crisis in the United States itself. Nixon has kept the lid on by pretending to have a policy of getting out of Vietnam.

[7] The *New Republic*, February 27, 1965 [reprinted in Marcus G. Raskin and Bernard Fall, eds., *The Vietnam Reader* (Vintage Books, New York, 1965), pp. 213–16—eds.].

This illusion could perhaps be kept alive for quite a while by soothing talk and small withdrawals of US forces. But there is one proviso, that things should remain relatively quiet in Vietnam and the surrounding areas. With this proviso negated by the spread of the war, at first in Laos and now into Cambodia, the illusion itself must soon dissolve. And when the American people wake up to the reality that Nixon's policy, far from aiming at withdrawal from Vietnam, is to fight what Michael Klare aptly calls "the great South Asian war," [8] the US political scene could well be thrown into unprecedented turmoil.

In a speech in the Senate on April 2 [1970], Fulbright said that the communists "cannot drive us out of Indochina. But they can force on us the choice of either plunging in altogether or getting out altogether." Whether or not one agrees that it is "the communists" who are forcing this choice on us, there can be no doubt that Fulbright has accurately identified the real alternatives facing the United States in Southeast Asia. The first alternative is clearly unacceptable to the mass of Americans, the second to the US ruling class. Here are the makings of a crisis of world-shaking significance.

[8] Klare, "The Great South Asian War," *The Nation,* CCX (March 9, 1970).

36

Better Dead Cambodians Than Red

ANTHONY LEWIS *

LONDON, June 26—*"American forces have warned Cambodian rice field workers that they are in danger of being hit if they run for cover or 'look suspicious' when US helicopters fly over them, qualified sources said . . . ."*

—Reuter dispatch from Saigon

In the eight weeks since President Nixon sent troops into Cambodia, the debate about the wisdom of that action has tended to focus on its meaning for American involvement in Indochina. Would it enhance the prospects for our withdrawal or get us more deeply entangled? Would tactical gains in the field outweigh the divisive political effects at home? These have been the main questions argued.

EFFECT ON CAMBODIANS

It is not surprising that the impact of the Cambodian adventure on the United States should weigh most heavily with Americans critical of the Vietnam war, especially after the deaths at Kent State. But at this point there is reason to pay attention to another matter—the effect on the Cambodians.

We happen to have a remarkable first-hand description of what the incursion by American and South Vietnamese troops meant to some ordinary Cambodian peasants. That is the eloquent account by Richard Dudman, the *St. Louis Post-Dispatch* correspondent who was captured by the enemy forces May 7 and released June 15.

* From the *New York Times*, June 27, 1970. By permission. Anthony Lewis is head of the London Bureau of the *New York Times*.

Mr. Dudman is a notably level-headed man, with no sentimental illusions about communist regimes. In one of a series of dispatches on his time in captivity, he wrote of seeing hundreds of civilians fleeing westward together with guerrilla troops. He said:

> In this massive migration we felt that we were watching the terrorization of the peasants of Cambodia. We felt we were observing the welding together of the local population with the guerrillas. The peasants were turning to the fighters as their best friends. We felt that this held the most serious significance for American policy.

Other things Mr. Dudman experienced were a B-52 raid and an attack by helicopter gunships. His reports tell us graphically, if we needed to be told, how anyone in an area of such attacks may be hit—whatever his politics, whatever his status. In air assault there can be no fine distinctions.

PROBLEM FOR OUTSIDERS

Of course the communists and their supporters kill innocent people, too; they have much savagery on their record over twenty-five years of the Indochinese War. But the problem for us Americans, the political and moral problem, is that we are outsiders.

The alien character of our presence in Indochina is symbolized by our use of air power. For it is a means of killing at a distance, without involvement in the society we seek to order.

In the last week it has gradually emerged—as policies often do in that war—that the United States will go on bombing Cambodia after the promised withdrawal of American troops June 30. It is an open-ended policy. At first officials tried to draw a nice distinction between bombing "to interdict enemy supply lines" and bombing in support of ground operations, but

Secretary of State Rogers would not rule out the use of air power in close support of South Vietnamese or Cambodian ground forces.

We are apparently, then, going to repeat in Cambodia the mistake we made in Vietnam. Without any real political base, without the semblance of popular support, we are going to use the technology of modern warfare to try to defeat a guerrilla enemy. The result can only be to antagonize the people.

At a Pentagon press conference the other day, according to British newspapers, the Deputy Assistant Secretary of Defense for Public Affairs, Jerry W. Friedheim, was asked whether American bombing did not present a danger to the lives of Cambodian civilians. He reportedly replied that it would be "less than the danger of being overwhelmed by the Viet Cong."

In short, the American government has decided that Cambodians are better off dead than red. For sheer colonial arrogance, that rivals the best that Cecil Rhodes or Cortés could produce.

37

Only the Bums Can Save the Country Now

I. F. STONE *

The race is on between protest and disaster. Despite the first four martyr "bums" of Nixon-Agnewism at Kent State, the college shutdown their deaths precipitated, the outpouring of student and other protesters here last weekend, the campus lobbyists beginning to flood the halls of Congress, the Senate resolutions to limit or end Indochinese military operations, and the smoldering near-revolt within the Nixon Administration itself, we are still on the brink. We are in the first stages of a new and wider war from which withdrawal will be difficult. The military hold the reins and can precipitate new provocations and stage new alarms. The only hope is that the students can create such a plague for peace, swarming like locusts into the halls of Congress, that they stop all other business and make an end to the war the number one concern it ought to be. Washington must no longer be the privileged sanctuary of the warmakers. The slogan of the striking students ought to be: "Suspend Classes and Educate the Country." I see no other visible and adequate means to stop the slide into a conflict that may sweep very suddenly beyond the confines of Indochina if the man who gambled on Cambodia ends by gambling on the use of nuclear weapons.

THE UNWILLING LED BY THE UNQUALIFIED

In a dispatch from a landing zone in Cambodia, Jack Foisie of the *Washington Post* (May 8) described GIs jumping from

* From *I. F. Stone's Bi-Weekly* (May 18, 1970). By permission. A Washington journalist, I. F. Stone has been publishing his crusading newsletter, *I. F. Stone's Weekly*, since 1953. Among his books are *The Haunted Fifties* (New York, 1963) and *In Time of Torment* (New York, 1967)—eds.

helicopters under enemy fire with derisive denunciations of the war scrawled on their helmets. One of those he copied down sums up the situation of the whole country in this war. "We are the unwilling," it said, "led by the unqualified, doing the unnecessary, for the ungrateful." As usual the country is not being told the truth about why we went into Cambodia. In his war address of April 30, Nixon pictured the attack across the border as a preemptive exercise to hit an "enemy building up to launch massive attacks on our forces and those of South Vietnam." It was described as a swift preventive action from which we would soon withdraw and which was not part of any broader intervention in Cambodian affairs.

But thanks to the indiscretion of one Congressman, we now have the private—and more candid—version given members of Congress at special State Department briefings. This puts the origins and purpose of the Cambodian action in a very different light. The Congressman is Representative Hamilton Fish (Republican of New York), a right winger who has long questioned the logic of our heavy commitment in so peripheral an area as Southeast Asia. In a letter to constituents released May 13, Mr. Fish summarizes a private briefing by Undersecretary of State Richardson for selected members of Congress. Nixon said we moved across the border to nip enemy plans for an imminent attack. But from Richardson's briefing, Mr. Fish reports, "It was clear that the present military thrust into Cambodia hinged largely on the reportedly surprise overthrow of Prince Sihanouk." Nixon said in his April 30 speech that for five years "neither the US nor South Vietnam moved against those enemy sanctuaries because we did not wish to violate the territory of a neutral nation." [1] But Richardson gave the Congressmen a different story. He told them "US intelligence had known for years of those enclaves from which attacks on South Vietnam have been launched" but we had never attacked them before "because it was feared that Sihanouk would counter any invasion by allowing NVA [North Vietnamese Army] forces to enlarge their occupied areas."

Sihanouk was trying to maintain a precarious neutrality by playing one side against the other. Nixon was deceitful when

[1] See Selection 31, this volume—eds.

he said in the April 30 speech that our policy since the Geneva Conference of 1954 "has been to scrupulously respect the neutrality of the Cambodian people" and adding—as proof of our virtue—that since last August we have had a diplomatic mission in Phnompenh "of fewer than fifteen" and that for the previous four years "we did not have any diplomatic mission whatever." The truth is that Sihanouk ousted our mission and broke relations in 1965 because he claimed the CIA had been plotting against him for years and even tried twice to kill him. Sihanouk was especially resentful of the Khmer Serei (Free Khmer) mercenaries the CIA and our Special Forces had enlisted from among Cambodians living in South Vietnam and Thailand to act as an anti-Sihanouk commando force. The CIA gave it facilities to broadcast anti-Sihanouk propaganda from Saigon.

"For the past five years," Nixon said with bland hypocrisy, "we have provided no military assistance and no economic assistance whatever to Cambodia." He did not explain that Sihanouk threw out our military mission because he said it had been trying to turn his armed forces against him, and gave up economic aid, too, rather than have it used as a cover for US agents trying to overthrow him. This was not a figment of Sihanouk's imagination. As far back as 1958, in a police raid on the villa of one of his generals, Sihanouk found a letter from President Eisenhower pledging full support to a projected coup and to a reversal of Cambodian neutrality. This was part of a "Bangkok plan" worked out between the dictators of South Vietnam and Thailand (Diem and Marshal Sarit Thanarit) to dismember Cambodia and instigate civil war (see Wm. Worthy's account in the *York* [Pa.] *Gazette & Daily* of April 30). When Sihanouk resumed relations last August, in his desperate see-saw between the two sides, his condition was that the US mission be kept small. He didn't want too many CIA agents roaming around.

THE CIA'S TROJAN HORSE

That was poor Sihanouk's mistake. Cambodian neutrality was ended when the military we had long wooed finally overthrew Sihanouk on March 18. The most complete account yet published of the events leading up to the coup is to be found in *Le Monde Diplomatique* for April [1970]. It is by Daniel Roy, a Frenchman with fifteen years' experience in Indochina who was for a time press attaché to Prince Sihanouk.[2] He claims that funds for the coup were provided by a Cambodian adventurer turned banker in Bangkok who was associated in the enterprise with the notorious Son Ngoc Thanh, puppet President of Cambodia under the Japanese occupation. The latter fled to Thailand after the war and according to M. Roy is "today in the service of the CIA." M. Roy also charges that the coup was prepared by Khmer Serei forces who went over the border with their arms and wives and pretended that they were defecting to Sihanouk. They infiltrated the army and the police as a Trojan horse for the CIA.

Let us now return to Congressman Fish's account of the private state department briefing. "Following the fall of Sihanouk," the Congressmen were told, "the new anti-communist government cut all supply lines [of the North Vietnamese Army and Viet Cong] except the Ho Chi Minh Trail" which, of course, lies largely outside Cambodian territory. *"To re-secure their severed supply routes,"* the account in the private briefing continued, *"VC and NVA began moving out of the enclaves, thereby threatening the overthrow of the Cambodian government."* [3] It is "against this background," Rep. Fish's account of the briefing concludes, "that the American–South Vietnamese strikes into Cambodia were ordered."

The sequence is quite different from that given publicly by Mr. Nixon. Instead of preparing an attack on our forces in South Vietnam, the enemy was reacting to an attack on its supply lines. This upset the status quo, and risked a complete takeover of Cambodia by the other side. We intervened to save it from the consequences. Did our government give the new Lon Nol government of Cambodia assurances that we would defend it if its action in cutting all the supply routes precipitated an attack upon it?

[2] See Selection 26, this volume—eds.
[3] Author's Italics—eds.

WHAT IF SIHANOUK REGAINS POWER?

It is true that at the State Department briefing "it was stressed that the present attacks were not aimed at either the confrontation of the estimated 40 to 50,000 VC and NVA believed operating in Cambodia or the defense of the present government of Cambodia. The raids were described as strictly "spoiling actions," aimed at supply, bunker and communication network destruction" and to give the South Vietnamese army additional time while the enemy rebuilds its supplies. But you have to be pretty feebleminded to accept this at face value. What if Sihanouk, with NVA and Peking support, is restored to power, this time not as a precarious neutral but as an ally of the other side? What if we are then faced with the prospect, not just of restoring the old supply lines and bases but of Cambodia turning into one big enemy base? Who can believe that the Nixon administration will stand by and let this happen?

This is the wider war which lies ahead. The overthrow of Sihanouk was a grave political mistake. It gave the other side a new ally with legitimacy and mass support, basic necessities for the Indochinese people's war which has already been proclaimed against us. The situation inside Cambodia was succinctly summed up in an interview which the pro-Nixon and pro-war *U.S. News & World Report* for May 18 held by cable with its correspondent, James N. Wallace, in Phnompenh:

> Q. Have the allied attacks in Eastern Cambodia saved the rest of the country from a communist takeover?
>
> A. No. Unless the allied drive completely overwhelms the communists, Cambodia's position remains about the same . . . the short run result is even more chaos and confusion . . .
>
> Q. Did the Cambodians welcome the Allied move?
>
> A. Again, no. Cambodians do not like . . . the

idea of South Vietnamese troops' rolling across
Cambodia . . .

Q. What kind of reception would Sihanouk get?

A. Almost certainly he would receive more popular support than the Lon Nol government cares
to admit. Sihanouk still is popular among a great
many of Cambodia's 5.5 million peasants, who
respected his traditional status as a god-king and
liked his earthy personal relations with villagers.

EVEN IF NIXON WANTS TO WITHDRAW

The French journalist Max Clos, who has been covering
Indochina for years during both the French and US wars,
foresees (in *Le Figaro,* May 2–3 [1970]) a Cambodian resistance based on peasant support, doing in their country what
the Viet Cong have done in Vietnam and creating a "liberated
zone" from which in time they will be able to take over Phnompenh. "Mr. Nixon," M. Clos wrote, "hopes to withdraw his
troops from Cambodia in a month and a half. Even if he succeeds, it is safe to predict he will have to send them back
again."

The political folly of our latest move is not limited to Cambodia. The newly enlarged war must add to the shaky character
of the Thieu regime, which has had to close down all the
South Vietnamese schools in a rising student revolt much like
our own. The idea of South Vietnamese troops being used to
bolster a government which has been massacring Cambodian
citizens of Vietnamese origin must add to Thieu's unpopularity.
The bitterness between the Viets and the Khmers of Cambodia
is incomparably older and more bitter than the recent ani-
mosities of the Russo-American cold war. It is only two centuries since the Viets seized the Mekong delta from the Khmers.
Sihanouk, unlike his successors, never stirred up the mob
against the Vietnamese, and the VC and NVA intruders, unlike our forces, did not bomb and devastate Cambodian villages.
This new shift strengthens the forces opposing our puppets on
both sides.

YET ANOTHER OPERATION TOTAL VICTORY

This has been a political war from its very beginning against the French. We go on believing as they did that a political problem can be solved by military means. The annals of their war, like ours, is full of sensationally billed search-and-destroy operations which were finally going to cripple the rebels, like this latest "Operation Total Victory" across the Cambodian border. The Communists under Ho Chi Minh seized national leadership in the war against the French, as the adroit Sihanouk did in Cambodia. Now they both are allied against us. Sihanouk will now make it possible for the other side to implement the basic strategy of a people's war on a wider scale. The strategy is to force maximum dispersion upon the hated foreign invader to make him widen the area of his activity and stretch his lines of communication so that the guerrillas can pick and choose the most advantageous weak points for their concentrated attacks. We have picked up their treacherous gambit by invading Cambodia, and sooner or later, unless we get out of Indochina altogether, we must send ground troops into Laos and Cambodia, perhaps even into North Vietnam where a fresh army of 250,000 or more awaits our landing. Nowhere has air power, however overwhelming and unchallenged, been able to win a war.

What will happen when the country wakes up to find that instead of withdrawing troops we are going to send in fresh divisions? What happens to inflation, the budget and the stock market? To student and racial unrest? Nixon, in a mood of self-pity, complained in his April 30 address that past war Presidents did not have to face a nation "assailed by counsels of doubt and defeat from some of the most widely known opinion leaders of the nation." He seems to attribute this to some perversity. He takes it as personal. He does not stop to consider why this war has aroused so much more opposition than any past war, and done so in every class and every region and every age group, from Wall Street financiers to campus radicals. Even national guardsmen give the V sign to students, and soldiers go into battle with peace amulets around their necks. He seems to think there is something wrong with the critics. He will not face up to the possibility that there is something wrong with the war. Certainly this generation of Americans would prove no less patriotic and brave than any other if our country were really in danger.

COSVN MOVED TO VIETNAM IN APRIL

It is a measure of our stupid leadership that the Cambodian war was started on the phony pretext that just across the border was a kind of enemy Pentagon and that we could cripple the enemy by smashing it. One measure of the mendacity may be found in an intelligence briefing the *New York Times* reported April 4, two weeks after Sihanouk's overthrow. It said COSVN, the enemy headquarters, had been moved from Cambodian to South Vietnamese territory. The story even carried a map showing the old location at Mimot—which figures in recent accounts of the Cambodian operation—in the "fishhook," and the new location in a thick jungle area described as "virtually inaccessible to ground troops" and "probably not seriously vulnerable to air attacks." It is difficult to believe that Nixon and his aides are such idiots as not to be aware of this intelligence information.

The Eichmann trial taught the world the banality of evil. Nixon is teaching the world the evil of banality. The man so foolish as to talk to protesting students about football and surfing is the same man who (like Johnson) sees war in the puerile terms of "humiliation" and a challenge to his virility. He doesn't want us to be a "helpless giant" (which we are in Indochina) so he is plunging us into a wider quagmire where we will end up more helpless than ever.

The past week is the week in which the Nixon Administration began to come apart. Letters like Hickel's showed how isolated he is even from members of his own Cabinet where there seems to be a silent majority against him. The anti-war round robin signed by more than 200 employes of the State Department shows how deeply the Cambodian affair has stirred even the most timid, conformist and conventional section of the bureaucracy. Nothing Nixon says can be taken at face value. Even when he said on April 20, in his troop withdrawal announcement, that a "just peace" was at last in sight, he must have been planning this expansion of the war. Indeed General Westmoreland as Army Chief of Staff had already begun to lobby for a Cambodian invasion in off-the-record briefings.

There were two remarks of the deepest significance in the Nixon press conference of April 30. One was that if we withdraw from Vietnam "America is finished insofar as a peacekeeper in the Asian world is concerned." This revealed that he is still committed, despite that vague "low posture" talk on Guam, to a *pax Americana* in Asia. If we are to police Asia we are in for many years of war and internal disruption. The folly is as great as if China were to try and become the "Peacekeeper" of Latin America. The other remark was that unlike Johnson he would not escalate step by step but "move decisively." This is the Goldwater–LeMay thesis that we could have won the Vietnam war if we had smashed Hanoi and Haiphong in one great blow, perhaps with nuclear weapons. Hanoi, especially after the recent big bombing raids, expects something of the kind. Moscow and Peking are already trying to patch up their differences in expectation of it. If Nixon goes to nuclear weapons, the end result may well be World War III. Unless an army of students can fan out to the grass roots and make the country aware of these dangerous possibilities, terrible days may lie ahead.

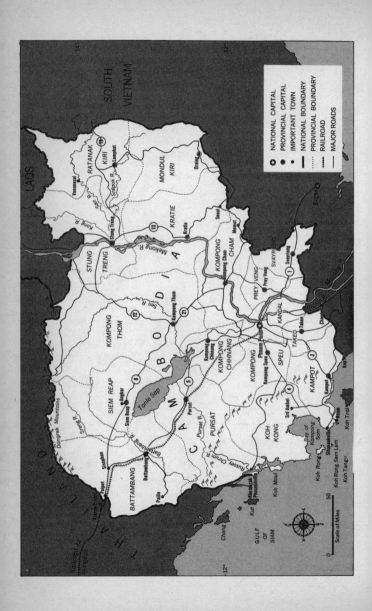

THE MILITARY SITUATION IN MAY, 1954

AREAS CONTROLLED BY THE VIETMINH

AREAS OF GUERRILLA ACTIVITY

Appendix

SELECT BIBLIOGRAPHY ON LAOS AND CAMBODIA*

Adams, Nina, and McCoy, Alfred, eds., *Laos: War and Revolution,* New York, Harper & Row, 1970. An essential collection of documents and analyses.

Ambekar, G. V., and Divekar, V. D., eds., *Documents on China's Relations with South and Southeast Asia: 1949–1962,* Bombay, Allied Publishers, 1964.

Armstrong, John P., *Sihanouk Speaks,* New York, Walker and Co., 1964. Mostly transcriptions of speeches.

Bernstein, Richard and Fredrick, Cynthia, *Laos and Cambodia: The Circle Widens,* Cambridge, Mass., Committee of Concerned Asian Scholars [1970]. A brief, well-informed pamphlet. Also see this committee's useful *Bulletin,* available from Bay Area Institute, 9 Sutter Street, San Francisco, California 94104. *Orville Schell, co-director*

Berval, René de, *Kingdom of Laos: The Land of the Million Elephants and of the White Parasol,* Saigon, France-Asie, 1959.

Briggs, Lawrence Palmer, *The Ancient Khmer Empire* (Transactions of the American Philosophical Society, New Series, Vol. 41, Part 1.) Philadelphia, The American Philosophical Society, 1951.

* We have made no attempt to list all of the books, articles and pamphlets cited in the footnotes in this volume. Nor have we, except for one or two instances, listed items that are reprinted or excerpted in the text—eds.

Briggs, Lawrence Palmer, "A Sketch of Cambodian History," *Far Eastern Quarterly,* Vol. V, August, 1946.

Buchanan, Keith, "Cambodian Royal Socialism," in *Revolution* Vol. I, March, 1964. See also Buchanan, "Cambodia Between Peking and Paris," in *Monthly Review,* Vol. XVI, December, 1964, and *The Southeast Asian World,* London, Bell, 1967, and New York, Doubleday, 1970.

Burchett, Wilfred G., *The Furtive War: The United States in Vietnam and Laos,* New York, International Publishers, 1963.

————, *Mekong Upstream,* Hanoi, Red River Publishing House, 1957. A unique work of eyewitness reportage. Burchett's *The Second Indochina War: Cambodia and Laos,* New York, International Publishers, 1970, is his latest book of reportage.

Cambodge, Royaume du, Ministère des Affaires Etrangérès, Livre Blanc des Agressions Americano-Sudvietnamiennes contre Le Cambodge, 1962–1969, Phnompenh, Imprimerie Sangkum Reastr Niyum, January 3, 1970. A graphic presentation of American and South Vietnamese incursions into Cambodia, sufficient to explode the myth that such events began in the spring of 1970. Once Sihanouk had been overthrown, this "White Paper" was quickly suppressed.

"Case Concerning the Temple of Preah Vihear (Cambodia v. Thailand), Merits, Judgment of 15 June 1962," *International Court of Justice Reports,* The Hague, 1962.

Chomsky, Noam, "Cambodia," in *The New York Review of Books,* Vol. XIV, June 4, 1970. An impassioned critique of the US invasion. See also Chomsky's eyewitness, "Destroying Laos," *ibid.,* Vol. XV, July 23, 1970.

Coedès, George, *Les Etats Hindouisés d'Indochine et d'Indonésie,* Paris, E. de Boccard, 1964.

Committee of Concerned Asian Scholars, *Indochina Handbook,* New York, Bantam Books, 1970. A handy, informative collection.

Devillers, Philippe, *Histoire du Viêtnam de 1940 à 1952*, Paris, Editions du Seuil, 1952. [See also Jean Lacouture]

Divekar, N. D., see Ambekar, G. V.

Dommen, Arthur J., *Conflict in Laos: The Politics of Neutralization*, New York/Washington/London, Praeger, 1964. Though written from a pro-US bias, this book is nevertheless, and almost inadvertently, useful.

Duffet, John, ed., *Against the Crime of Silence: Proceedings of the* [Bertrand] *Russell International War Crimes Tribunal*, New York and London, Bertrand Russell Peace Foundation, 1968. Contains evidence of US war crimes in Laos and Cambodia as well as Vietnam.

Eden, Anthony, *The Memoirs of Anthony Eden: Full Circle*, Boston, Houghton Mifflin, 1960, contains interesting data on the Geneva Conference of 1954.

Fall, Bernard B., "The Pathet Lao—A Liberation Party," in Scalapino, Robert, ed., *The Communist Revolution in Asia*, Englewood Cliffs, N.J., Prentice-Hall, 1965. An unsympathetic portrayal of the Laotian revolutionaries.

———, *Anatomy of a Crisis: The Laotian Crisis of 1960–1961*, Smith, Robert M., ed., Garden City, N.Y., Doubleday, 1969.

Fisher, Mary L., *Cambodia; An Annotated Bibliography of Its History Geography, Politics and Economy since 1954*, Cambridge, Mass., Center for International Studies, Massachusetts Institute of Technology, 1967.

Friedman, E., and Selden, Mark, eds., *America's Asia*, New York, Pantheon, 1970. A useful collection of radical essays.

Fredrick, Cynthia, see Bernstein, Richard.

Gettleman, Marvin E., ed., *Vietnam: History, Documents and Opinions*, 2nd ed., New York, New American Library, 1970. A comprehensive anthology with extensive bibliography which should be read as a complementary volume to this book.

Grant, Jonathan and others, eds., *Cambodia: The Widening War in Indochina,* New York, Simon and Schuster, 1970. An important, critical anthology.

Hall, D. G. E., *A History of Southeast Asia.* 2nd ed., London, Macmillan, 1964.

Halpern, Joel M., *Government, Politics, and Social Structure in Laos: A Study of Tradition and Innovation,* Southeast Asia Studies, Monograph Series, No. 4, New Haven, Yale University Press, 1964.

———, *The Lao Elite: A Study of Tradition and Innovation.* Santa Monica, The Rand Corporation (RM-2636-RC), November 15, 1960.

Hammer, Ellen. *The Struggle for Indochina,* Stanford, Stanford University Press, 1954.

Herz, Martin, *A Short History of Cambodia from the Days of Angkor to the Present,* New York, Praeger, 1958, An uncritically pro-US work.

Hubbell, John G., "President Nixon, Cambodia and New Chances for Peace," in *Reader's Digest* (July, 1970). A star-spangled defense of Nixon's policy in Cambodia based upon the kneejerk anti-communism that is endemic in America.

Kahin, George McT. *The Asian-African Conference, Bandung, Indonesia, April 1955,* Ithaca, Cornell University Press, 1956.

———, "Cambodia: The Administration's Version and the Historical Record," May 14, 1940 and "Consequences of the Invasion of Cambodia," May 15, 1970. Informed analyses prepared for a group of US Senators by the Director of Cornell University's Southeast Asia Program.

Katay, Thao. *Le Laos,* Bangkok, Editions Lao Issara, 1948.

Klare, Marshall, "The Great South Asian War," in *The Nation,* Vol. CCX, March 9, 1970.

Kolko, Gabriel, *The Roots of American Foreign Policy: An Analysis of Power and Purpose,* Boston, Beacon Press, 1969. A very important book.

Lacouture, Jean, and Devillers, Philippe, *The End of a War,* New York, Praeger, 1969, An essential book.

Lancaster, Donald, *The Emancipation of French Indochina,* London, Oxford University Press, 1961. The best book in English on all Indochina to 1955.

Langer, P. F., and Zasloff, J. J., *North Vietnam and the Pathet Lao: Partners in the Struggle for Laos,* Cambridge, Harvard University Press, 1970.

Leifer, Michael. *Cambodia; the Search for Security,* New York, Praeger, 1967. Liefer's "Rebellion or Subversion in Cambodia?" in *Current History,* February, 1969 is a balanced account of the rise of leftist opposition to Sihanouk, an opposition that has rallied to the prince's side after the March, 1970, coup.

McCoy, Alfred. See Adams, Nina.

Modelski, George A. *International Conference on the Settlement of the Laotian Question, 1961–62,* Canberra, Department of International Relations, Research School of Pacific Studies, Australian National University, 1962.

Neo Lao Hak Sat [Laotian Patriotic Front] *"Memorandum . . . des Bombardments par l'US Air Force de la Zone Sous Controle du Front Patriotique Lao . . . ,"* 1969.

———, *"Memorandum . . . Concernant l'extension et l'utilisation des "Forces Speciales" par les Imperialistes American pour impulser leur Guerre d'Aggression Contre Le Laos,"* 1969.

———, *La Revolution Lao à 20 Ans,* n.p., Editions du Neo Lao Hak Sat, 1965. An account of anti-imperialist struggles.

————, *"Sabotage of the Laotian Tripartite National Union Government by the US Imperialists and Henchmen and the Creation of the Present Vientiane Administration headed by Prince Souvana Phouma—an outgrowth of US Neo-Colonialism in Laos"* n.p., July, 1969.

Sihanouk, Norodom, "Le communisme au Cambodge," in *Réalités Cambodgiennes,* March 15 and 22, 1958.

————, *La monarchie cambodgienne et la croisade royale pour l'indépendance,* Phnompenh, Imprimerie Rasmey, 1961.

Osborne, Milton, *The French Presence in Cochinchina and Cambodia,* Ithaca, Cornell University Press, 1970.

————, "Beyond Charisma: Princely Politics and the Problem of Political Succession in Cambodia," *International Journal,* Vol. XXIV, Winter 1968–1969.

————, "Regional disunity in Cambodia," *Australian Outlook,* Vol. XXII, December, 1968.

Pavie, Auguste, *A la Conquête des Coeurs,* Paris, Presses Universitaires de France, 1947.

————, *Mission Pavie en Indochina, 1879–1895,* 10 vols., Paris, Leroux, 1898–1919.

Preschez, Philippe. *Essai sur la Démocratie du Cambodge,* Paris, Fondation Nationale des Sciences Politiques, Centre d'Etudes des Relations Internationales, 1961.

Pym, Christopher, *The Ancient Civilization of Angkhor,* New York, NAL/Mentor, 1968.

Reinach, Lucien de, *Le Laos,* 2 vols, Paris, A. Charles, 1901.

Schell, Orville, "Cambodian Civil War," in The *New Republic,* Vol. CLXII, June 6, 1970.

Schurmann, Franz, "Cambodia: Nixon's Trap," in The *Nation,* Vol. CCX, June 1, 1970.

Smith, Roger M., *Cambodia's Foreign Policy,* Ithaca, Cornell University Press, 1964. A sympathetic study of Sihanouk's efforts to maintain neutrality.

Stone, I. F., "Mack Sennett in Laos," "Where Communism was Really Contained" [Cambodia], from *In A Time of Torment,* New York, Random House, 1967.

Suyin, Han, "Why Cambodia Rejected Aid," in *Eastern Horizon,* Vol. III, February, 1964.

Thomson, R. Stanley, "Establishment of the French Protectorate over Cambodia," in *Far Eastern Quarterly,* Vol. IV, August, 1945.

Sweezy, Paul, and others, eds., *The Endless War in Asia,* New York, Monthly Review Press, 1970, Radical essays.

Toye, Hugh, *Laos: Buffer State or Battleground,* London, Oxford University Press, 1968. The best book in English on Laos.

Zasloff, J. J., See Langer, P. F.

INDEX

Index

About the Editors

MARVIN E. GETTLEMAN

Associate Professor of History, Polytechnic Institute of Brooklyn. Author of books and articles on American history and Southeast Asia. Professor Gettleman is currently at work on a study of early nineteenth-century American radicalism.

SUSAN GETTLEMAN

Staff psychotherapist at the Metropolitan Center for Mental Health, New York City, and Research Consultant to Project Headstart. Formerly psychiatric social worker at Jewish Board of Guardians and Bronx State Hospital.

LAWRENCE KAPLAN

Assistant Professor of History, City College of the City University of New York. Specializing in English history, Professor Kaplan is the author of a number of articles on the Puritan revolution and is at work on a study of comparative revolutions.

CAROL KAPLAN

A former graduate student in history at New York University, Mrs. Kaplan is now enrolled in the School of Social Work, Hunter College of the City University of New York.

VINTAGE POLITICAL SCIENCE
AND SOCIAL CRITICISM